FEMINIST INTERPRETATIONS OF MICHEL FOUCAULT

RE-READING THE CANON

NANCY TUANA, GENERAL EDITOR

This series consists of edited collections of essays, some original and some previously published, offering feminist reinterpretations of the writings of major figures in the Western philosophical tradition. Devoted to the work of a single philosopher, each volume contains essays covering the full range of the philosopher's thought and representing the diversity of approaches now being used by feminist critics.

Already published:

Nancy Tuana, ed., *Feminist Interpretations of Plato* (1994)

Margaret A. Simons, ed., *Feminist Interpretations of Simone de Beauvoir* (1995)

Bonnie Honig, ed., *Feminist Interpretations of Hannah Arendt* (1995)

Patricia Jagentowicz Mills, ed., *Feminist Interpretations of G. W. F. Hegel* (1996)

Maria J. Falco, ed., *Feminist Interpretations of Mary Wollstonecraft* (1996)

FEMINIST INTERPRETATIONS OF MICHEL FOUCAULT

EDITED BY SUSAN J. HEKMAN

THE PENNSYLVANIA STATE UNIVERSITY PRESS
UNIVERSITY PARK, PENNSYLVANIA

Library of Congress Cataloging-in-Publication Data

Feminist interpretations of Michel Foucault / edited by Susan Hekman.

     p.   cm. — (Re-reading the canon)
    Includes bibliographical references and index.
    ISBN 0-271-01584-5 (cloth : alk. paper)
    ISBN 0-271-01585-3 (pbk. : alk. paper)
    1. Feminist theory.   2. Sex role.   3. Power (Social sciences)
  4. Foucault, Michel.   I. Hekman, Susan J.   II. Series.
HQ1190.F4613   1996
305.42'01—dc20   95-47060
                                                    CIP

It is the policy of The Pennsylvania State University Press to use acid-free paper for the
first printing of all clothbound books. Publications on uncoated stock satisfy the
minimum requirements of American National Standard for Information Sciences—
Permanence of Paper for Printed Library Materials, ANSI Z39.48-1992.

Contents

Preface

Take into your hands any history of philosophy text. You will find compiled therein the "classics" of modern philosophy. Since these texts are often designed for use in undergraduate classes, the editor is likely to offer an introduction in which the reader is informed that these selections represent the perennial questions of philosophy. The student is to assume that she or he is about to explore the timeless wisdom of the greatest minds of Western philosophy. No one calls attention to the fact that the philosophers are all men.

Though women are omitted from the canons of philosophy, these texts inscribe the nature of woman. Sometimes the philosopher speaks directly about woman, delineating her proper role, her abilities and inabilities, her desires. Other times the message is indirect—a passing remark hinting at woman's emotionality, irrationality, unreliability.

This process of definition occurs in far more subtle ways when the central concepts of philosophy—reason and justice, those characteristics that are taken to define us as human—are associated with traits historically identified with masculinity. If the "man" of reason must learn to control or overcome traits identified as feminine—the body, the emotions, the passions—then the realm of rationality will be one reserved primarily for men,[1] with grudging entrance to those few women who are capable of transcending their femininity.

Feminist philosophers have begun to look critically at the canonized texts of philosophy and have concluded that the discourses of philosophy are not gender-neutral. Philosophical narratives do not offer a universal perspective, but rather privilege some experiences and beliefs over others. These experiences and beliefs permeate all philosophical theories whether they be aesthetic or epistemological, moral or metaphysical. Yet this fact has often been neglected by those studying the traditions of philosophy. Given the history of canon formation in Western philosophy, the perspective most likely to be privileged is that of upper-class, white males. Thus, to be fully aware of the impact of gender biases, it is imperative that we re-read the canon with attention to the ways in which philosophers' assumptions concerning gender are embedded within their theories.

This new series, *Re-Reading the Canon*, is designed to foster this process of reevaluation. Each volume will offer feminist analyses of the theories of a selected philosopher. Since feminist philosophy is not monolithic in method or content, the essays are also selected to illustrate the variety of perspectives within feminist criticism and highlight some of the controversies within feminist scholarship.

In this series, feminist lenses will be focused on the canonical texts of Western philosophy, both those authors who have been part of the traditional canon, as well as those philosophers whose writings have more recently gained attention within the philosophical community. A glance at the list of volumes in the series will reveal an immediate gender bias of the canon: Arendt, Aristotle, de Beauvoir, Derrida, Descartes, Foucault, Hegel, Hume, Kant, Locke, Marx, Mill, Nietzsche, Plato, Rousseau, Wittgenstein, Wollstonecraft. There are all too few women included, and those few who do appear have been added only recently. In creating this series, it is not my intention to reify the current canon of philosophical thought. What is and is not included within the canon during a particular historical period is a result of many factors. Although no canonization of texts will include all philosophers, no canonization of texts that exclude all but a few women can offer an accurate representation of the history of the discipline as women have been philosophers since the ancient period.[2]

I share with many feminist philosophers and other philosophers writing from the margins of philosophy the concern that the current canonization of philosophy be transformed. Although I do not accept the position that the current canon has been formed exclusively by power relations, I do believe that this canon represents only a selective history of the tradition. I share the view of Michael Bérubé that "canons are at once the location, the index, and the record of the struggle for cultural representation; like any other hegemonic formation, they must be continually reproduced anew and are continually contested."[3]

The process of canon transformation will require the recovery of "lost" texts and a careful examination of the reasons such voices have been silenced. Along with the process of uncovering women's philosophical history, we must also begin to analyze the impact of gender ideologies upon the process of canonization. This process of recovery and examination must occur in conjunction with careful attention to the concept of a canon of authorized texts. Are we to dispense with the notion of a tradition of excellence embodied in a canon of authorized texts? Or, rather than abandon the whole idea of a canon, do we instead encourage a reconstruction of a canon of those texts that inform a common culture?

This series is designed to contribute to this process of canon transformation by offering a re-reading of the current philosophical canon. Such a re-reading shifts our attention to the ways in which woman and the role of the feminine is constructed within the texts of philosophy. A question we must keep in front of us during this process of re-reading is whether a philosopher's socially inherited prejudices concerning woman's nature and role are independent of her or his larger philosophical framework. In asking this question attention must be paid to the ways in which the definitions of central philosophical concepts implicitly include or exclude gendered traits.

This type of reading strategy is not limited to the canon, but can be applied to all texts. It is my desire that this series reveal the importance of this type of critical reading. Paying attention to the workings of gender within the texts of philosophy will make visible the complexities of the inscription of gender ideologies.

Notes

1. More properly, it is a realm reserved for a group of privileged males, since the texts also inscribe race and class biases that thereby omit certain males from participation.

2. Mary Ellen Waithe's multivolume series, *A History of Women Philosophers* (Boston: M. Nijhoff, 1987), attests to this presence of women.

3. Michael Bérubé, *Marginal Forces/Cultural Centers: Tolson, Pynchon, and the Politics of the Canon* (Ithaca: Cornell University Press, 1992), 4–5.

Acknowledgments

Nancy Fraser, "Michel Foucault: A 'Young Conservative'?" is reprinted by permission of the publisher from *Ethics* 96, no. 1 (1985): 165–84. Copyright © 1985 by The University of Chicago.

Nancy Hartsock, "Postmodernism and Political Change: Issues for Feminist Theory," is reprinted by permission of the publisher from *Cultural Critique* 14 (Winter 1989–90): 15–33. Copyright © 1989 by Oxford University Press.

Monique Deveaux, "Feminism and Empowerment: A Critical Reading of Foucault," is reprinted from *Feminist Studies* 20, no. 2 (Summer 1994): 223–47, by permission of the publisher, Feminist Studies, Inc., c/o Women's Studies Program, University of Maryland, College Park, MD 20742.

Terry K. Aladjem, "The Philosopher's Prism: Foucault, Feminism, and Critique," is reprinted by permission of the publisher from *Political Theory* 19, no. 2 (May 1991): 277–91. Copyright © 1991 by Sage Publications.

Editor's Introduction

There is a certain irony in including Michel Foucault in a series devoted to transforming the canon of Western philosophical texts. Many contemporary philosophers, particularly those in the Anglo-American analytic tradition, argue that it is precisely the work of Foucault, and other theorists defined as "postmoderns," that threaten the tradition of Western philosophy. And this charge is certainly warranted. Foucault challenges the basic underpinnings of Western philosophy, particularly the modernist tradition that has held sway since the Enlightenment. He counters the definitions of truth, knowledge, power, and the subject that ground that tradition. His work transforms the tradition by questioning its fundamental goal: the will to truth.

It is precisely because of his canon-transforming potential that Foucault has been of particular interest to feminists.[1] Women, who have been excluded from the canon since its inception, have found common cause with Foucault in his challenge to the canon. Foucault's interest in the construction of sexuality has strengthened Beauvoir's claim that "woman is made, not born." His redefinitions of truth and subjectivity have fostered feminist explorations into the gendered connotations of these concepts. Despite these advantages, however, many feminists have been hesitant to embrace Foucault wholly in their transformative cause. Foucault is, despite his iconoclastic stance, yet one more androcentric European male theorist that feminists are exhorted to follow. Feminists have raised three related issues with regard to Foucault's work. First, does Foucault's location as a malestream theorist negate his usefulness for feminism? The feminist question, Can the master's tools dismantle the master's house? applies to Foucault as well as to the more orthodox authors of the canon. Second, despite Foucault's interest in sexuality he has little to say specifically about women and gender constructions. Feminists have used Foucault's methods to engage in gender analysis, but Foucault himself does not engage in such analysis. This omission is significant for feminism. Third, and perhaps most disturbingly, Foucault's work has raised profound questions about the viability of a feminist politics. Central to Foucault's approach is his deconstruction of a stable subject. Many feminists have argued that this deconstruction problematizes a feminist politics because "woman" disappears. How, they ask, can we seek the liberation of "woman" if, on Foucault's account, no such entity exists?

The essays in this collection reflect both the attraction of a Foucaul-dian feminism and the questions it poses. Some authors argue for the possibility of a Foucauldian feminism, others argue against it. Some apply a Foucauldian methodology to a particular topic while rejecting his substantive work on that same topic. The essays also reflect the breadth of feminist interest in Foucault. Each of the authors analyzes Foucault's work from a distinct perspective, reflecting the orientation of her or his particular discipline. Thus Nancy Fraser writes from the standpoint of Habermasian critical theory, holding Foucault up to the normative standards of that approach. Nancy Hartsock poses her ques-tions from the perspective of feminist standpoint theory, a position derived from the work of Marx. Jon Simons joins Foucault's work with the psychoanalytic approach of object-relations theory. Ellen McCallum applies a rhetorical perspective arising from recent trends in the theory of rhetoric. But it will become apparent that these and the other essays in the book represent more than an assessment of Foucault's work from a particular disciplinary perspective. In each of them the author's perspective is transformed by her or his feminist orientation. Although each comes out of a particular tradition, that tradition is redefined by the feminist purposes for which she or he writes.

The collection is divided into four parts. Part One, "A Foucauldian Feminism?" consists of two articles that set the stage for the feminist analysis of Foucault's work. Both Nancy Fraser and Nancy Hartsock pose the question of the feminist relevance of Foucault's work in the broadest terms, defining the issues that shape the debate over his work. Part Two deals with issues surrounding sex and the body. The issues have been at the forefront of feminist considerations of Foucault both because they are central to feminism and because Foucault is intimately concerned with these issues. One of the major innovations of Foucault's approach is his redefinition of the subject and, hence, identity. This redefinition has important implications for feminist theory that are discussed in Part Three. Finally, Foucault's approach raises questions concerning the definition or even possibility of a feminist politics; these questions are the topic of Part Four.

But although I have divided the collection into these parts, I should note that these divisions are, in one sense, misleading. The distinction between the identity politics discussed in Part Three and the politics of identity discussed in Part Four is, at best, arbitrary; issues of sexuality inform issues of identity and politics; the politics of the body fits into all the categories. I mention this not to excuse myself for sloppy categoriza-tion, but to argue for a particular interpretation of Foucault's work that focuses on method and epistemology. Questions concerning Foucault's applicability for feminism center on the possibility of a Foucauldian feminist politics. Critics contend that Foucault's approach precludes the possibility of a political program, feminist or otherwise. They assert that by deconstructing the concept of woman and denying the possibility of liberation, Foucault likewise deconstructs feminist politics.

The fluidity among the divisions in this collection is meant to suggest that Foucault offers not a theory or a politics but a method that defines a new epistemological space for both politics and the subject. Foucault's method represents a radical epistemological shift from previous ethical and political theories. Viewed from the perspective of modernist political theories, his work is deficient. It fails to define universal normative standards, the appeal to absolute values that characterizes modernist thought. It also radically redefines the autonomous subject of modernism, the subject that grounds modernist politics. Without such standards and such a subject, his critics contend, Foucault can only describe, not prescribe.

Against this I argue that in the epistemological space that Foucault inhabits there is no room for the modernist distinction between descrip-tion and prescription. My contention is that it is more useful to interpret Foucault as a chronicler of change than as its advocate and that in his role as a "historian of the present" he collapses the dichotomy between description and prescription. Foucault argues that we *do*, in fact, live in a different world from that theorized by the moderns, not that we *should* live in such a world or that we should do thus and so to achieve that world. Thus, for example, he argues that the conception of the subject that informs modernist thought is not adequate to describe the situation of subjects in our society, that there is no longer a universal standard that grounds our knowledge, that power is dispersed rather than concentrated. These situations dictate a very different role for the intellectual, the creator of theories of this world, and also a very different form of resistance. In other words, what Foucault discovers about the world he seeks to understand dictates the role he adopts as an intellectual, as well as the kind of politics he advocates. The line between description and prescription is necessarily and deliberately blurred. It is my contention that this approach is uniquely suited to the formation of a feminist politics.

The essays in this collection illustrate this thesis, that is, that Foucault breaks down modernist dichotomies and moves into a new epistemological space. The collection is organized according to a logic that is dictated by the necessities of feminist analysis: it begins with sex and ends with politics. That women *are* sex, that they represent the body side of the mind/body dualism, is one of the central tenets of the Western canon. Foucault's approach deconstructs this dualism, redefining sexuality and its truth. Feminists have used his redefinition to question the association of woman with the body and sex. Foucauldian-inspired feminists have not, however, tried to move "woman" to the other side of the dichotomy by claiming that women are just as rational as men. Rather, they have attempted to subvert the categories that define women's inferiority. Confusing the categories in this way has radical implications: it calls into question the identity of "woman" and the identity politics that it has produced. Destabilizing the identity of "woman" necessitates a new politics for feminism without a stable subject or universal normative goals. The significance of this challenge is acknowledged by all the contributors to this collection.

The collection begins with two articles by the well-known theorists Nancy Fraser and Nancy Hartsock, who offer broad assessments of the feminist potential of Foucault's work. I have set these two essays apart for a number of reasons. First, both look at Foucault's work as a whole rather than focusing on one particular aspect of his approach. Second, both raise key issues that have defined feminist assessments of Foucault and set the agenda for the discussion of his appropriateness for feminism. Third, both essays evince particularly clearly what I have defined as the transformative potential of Foucault's approach. Although both essays are critical of Foucault, each transforms the philosophical tradition out of which the authors speak.

Writing out of the tradition of Habermasian critical theory, Nancy Fraser argues that, because of his philosophical rejection of humanism, Foucault cannot justify any of his normative commitments. Fraser presents a persuasive argument for what has become a standard critique of Foucault. At the same time, however, she acknowledges that Foucault is moving us onto new epistemological terrain and, further, that a feminist appropriation of Foucault has transformative potential. Discussing the feminist critique of autonomy inspired by Foucault's work, she concludes: "The feminist interrogation of autonomy is the theoretical edge of a movement that is literally remaking the social identities and historical self-interpretations of large numbers of women and some men." For the tradition out of which Fraser writes, autonomy is the condition for moral action and the possibility of normative commitments. By questioning the concept of autonomy, feminists are in effect transforming moral theory itself and redefining the requirements for moral action.

Hartsock's article also advances a widely held critique of Foucault: that his thought cannot provide us with an emancipatory account of subjectivity. Hartsock contrasts Foucault's "postmodernism"[2] with the emancipatory subjectivity of feminist standpoint theory. Following Marx, Hartsock defines the feminist standpoint as the material location of women in social reality; that is, their position as oppressed and marginalized. Because of this location, she argues, women can discern the truth of that social reality and, hence, seek liberation. But if Hartsock's essay is read in light of her earlier work on feminist standpoint theory, a significant change can be detected. In *Money, Sex, and Power*[3] Hartsock argues for *the* feminist standpoint that defines the oppression of women. Here her perspective has shifted from *the* standpoint to "situated knowledges"—a plural conception of the truth and knowledge that allows for multiple realities. Her central claim against Foucault is that, in contrast to what she defines as Foucault's nihilism, her conception allows us to see "some things from somewhere." But in doing so she joins forces with Foucault in rejecting the possibility of seeing "everything from nowhere" and adopts a paradigm that is closer to the perspectivalism of Foucault than the universalism of modernism. Just as Fraser's Habermasian perspective was transformed by her feminist reading of Foucault, Hartsock's Marxist standpoint theory is similarly transformed.

Foucault's treatment of the body and sexuality has stimulated the most extensive feminist interest in his work. Judith Butler's feminist appropriation of Foucault has been at the forefront of these discussions.

In the essay reprinted here (Chapter 3) Butler argues that Foucault's claim in *The History of Sexuality* that we did not always have a sex amounts to a challenge to feminists who are necessarily concerned with the concept of sex. She explores the relationship between sex and death both in Foucault's work and in light of the AIDS epidemic. Her conclusions unsettle accepted understandings of all these issues. Following Foucault she argues that sexuality causes death, not vice versa. She also calls into question the necessity of positing a "true identity," arguing that such an identity is always mistaken. But perhaps her most significant insight is her analysis of an issue that Foucault's work only suggests: Can resistance to the diagnostic category of sex do anything but reduplicate the mechanism of the subjection constituted by sexual categories in our society? In her books, *Gender Trouble* and *Bodies That Matter*[4] Butler has explored this question in depth. She argues persuasively that opposition to the subjugating categories of sex, gender, and sexuality must involve more than doing the opposite of what these categories require. For example, with regard to homosexuality she argues that we must not just be queer, but "critically queer." By this she means that homosexuals should not passively accept the label queer but, rather, use the category as a site of resistance.

E. L. McCallum's essay (Chapter 4) further explores the relationship between sex, sexuality, and gender in light of Foucault's work. Modernist thought posits sex as the essence of gender, a relationship defined in terms of the relationship of nature to culture. Against this McCallum suggests that gender is the essence of sexuality, an essence that is not something sexual: "By not being sexual, gender enables sexuality to come into being as such." The key to this transformation, for McCallum, is Foucault's deconstruction of the relationship between truth and sexuality: "Foucault's displacement of truth as the essence of sex/uality enables us to understand how gender is the essence of sexuality." She concludes by arguing that the effectiveness of the strategy of gender is coming to an end, if that end has not already arrived.

Arguing that gender is the essence of sex does more than reverse the nature/culture dichotomy that informs it; it renders it meaningless. This is the radical import of Foucault's work on the concept of sex. He does not argue that gender is a social construct and, hence, that women can be liberated from its constraints to discover their essential sexuality. Rather, he argues that sex and sexuality are social constructs, that the nature/culture dichotomy itself has a discursive history that informs our concepts of sex and truth. The essays by Linda Martín Alcoff (Chapter 5) and Honi Fern Haber (Chapter 6) illustrate the radical results of applying Foucault's approach to topics relating to sexuality and the body. Alcoff's essay uses Foucault's method to fashion a new approach to sexual violence. Specifically rejecting Foucault's substantive reference to pedophilia, she develops a new articulation of this phenomenon that can counter the homophobic effect of its perceived tie to homosexuality and avoid a naturalistic account of pleasure. Her analysis challenges the definitions of "authentic desire" and "consent" that commonly frame discussions of pedophilia. Her personal narrative, furthermore, violates the accepted standards of philosophical analysis.

Haber's essay also violates accepted categories and standards. Her goal is to overthrow patriarchy at the level of women's bodies. She proposes a subversive image, the muscled woman, that confuses accepted gender categories. In the course of her analysis Haber neatly balances two key elements of Foucault's view of the subject: the subject as an act of self-creation and the subject as the product of discourses. Her work illustrates how Foucault's approach deconstructs a dichotomy that is central to modernist thought: the constituted versus the constituting subject. For modernism, unless a subject is the constitutor of meaning, it does not qualify *as* a subject; subjects who are constituted by social forces/discourses are not subjects at all, but "social dupes." Haber's description of the muscled woman displaces the neatness of this dichotomy. The muscled woman is both constituted by the discourse of bodybuilding and a violation of that discourse because she is a woman.

If, as Foucault-inspired feminist theorists have argued, we should articulate a new approach to the question of sexuality, it follows that we must also devise a new politics for feminism. Central to this new politics is a transformation of the identity of "woman," an identity that has informed feminist politics since its inception. The authors in the third part of the collection take up this challenge. Jana Sawicki (Chapter 7) questions whether, as many critics have claimed, there is a "problem" of identity in Foucault and feminism. Although she concedes that themes of resistance and political agency are underdeveloped in Foucault, she nevertheless asserts that Foucault's approach has been particularly useful in detailing how women are subjected through the body. She concludes that Foucault's position is especially appropriate to one of the major issues facing contemporary feminism: the global differences among women.

Jon Simons's essay (Chapter 8) expands on the theme of Butler's Foucauldian feminism: parodic performance. Butler argues that by parodying the role of "woman" in our society, we can subvert and transform that identity. Simons combines Butler's insight with object-relations theory, a psychoanalytic approach that posits that identity is constituted through relations with others in early childhood, particularly with the mother. Simons's appropriation of this theory through Butler, however, significantly transforms it. He argues that we need to define a subversive performance of motherhood that disrupts the coherence of the identity of "mother." Arguing that women's subject position as mothers is one of the central experiences of authority for women, Simons asks how this authority and the identity of motherhood can be used to subvert the rules. He develops a persuasive and innovative argument for a maternal politics that retains the empowerment of the maternal position while at the same time breaking the confinements of this subject position.

Monique Deveaux (Chapter 9) counters Simons's argument by asserting that Foucault's work is insufficient for the formation of identity politics. Deveaux expresses a feminist criticism of Foucault that was also articulated by Hartsock: that his paradigms of power and his treatment of the subject are inadequate for feminist projects. She asserts that Foucault erases women's specific experience of power and that his agonistic model of power, a model that defines power in exclusively oppositional terms, cannot account for the necessary empowerment of women. Yet despite, and, perhaps, because of its critical intent, Deveaux's essay illustrates the radical character of Foucault's politics very clearly. Deveaux understands all too well that Foucault's definition of bio-power—that is, his theory that power is inscripted on the bodies of those subjected by it (a definition that Butler, McCallum, and Haber find so useful)—alters the landscape of feminist politics. Foucault's concept destabilizes two central tenets of the modernist concept of power: that subjects are autonomous agents and that power emanates from a central source. Deveaux, like many feminists, finds this destabilization disturbing. She argues for retaining a modernist concept of the subject, particularly the feminine subject, that allows for the kind of agentic political action that informs modern feminism.

The issue that divides feminists who critique Foucault's politics is not politics itself, but, rather, his conception of the subject—once more illustrating my point that the categories of analysis collapse in Foucauldian critique. While Deveaux rejects Foucault's subject because it violates the modernist concept of agentic subjectivity, Moya Lloyd (Chapter 10) embraces it precisely because it deconstructs the modernist concept. Lloyd places her argument in the context of Lois McNay's recent critique of Foucault.[5] In an argument that impinges on many issues raised by the essays in this collection, McNay asserts that Foucault's position is consistent with a modernist conception of politics by positing a Foucauldian feminist politics of emancipation. Her strategy is to argue that Foucault's later work on the ethical subject is consistent with the modernist concept of emancipation and thus contradicts his earlier work on "docile bodies." Lloyd rejects this move, countering that Foucault's later work on the subject complements his earlier work. Lloyd acknowledges that Foucault's concept of the subject and, hence, politics pushes against the limits within which feminism has operated. But she embraces this "reconfigured relationship" as the strength of Foucault's approach. Implicit in her argument is the claim that if feminism itself is transformative, then a transformed politics is an appropriate strategy.

Amy Allen's (Chapter 11) assessment of a Foucauldian feminist politics stakes out a middle ground between the two extremes expressed by Deveaux and Lloyd. I suggest that Allen's approach in this essay provides a model for feminist critique of nonfeminist theorists. Allen interrogates Foucault by asking whether his theory of power is useful for feminism. She then goes on to define very clearly what a feminist theory of power requires and to hold Foucault to this standard. Allen's analysis reminds us that feminists are under no compulsion to accept the totality of any theorist's work. Rather, we can and should appropriate aspects of a particular body of work that suit feminist purposes. Applying this strategy leads Allen to the conclusion that Foucault's theory of power, although useful on the microlevel of analysis, is not useful for the kind of macro, structural analysis that feminism requires. Her critique raises an issue important to contemporary feminist theory. A number of feminist theorists are beginning to question the analytic possibilities of a postmodern approach, arguing that the proliferation of axes of analysis obviates effective critique.[6] Allen's exploration of this question indicates that formulating an answer is central to the feminist acceptance of a Foucauldian perspective.

Terry K. Aladjem's essay (Chapter 12) provides a fitting conclusion to the collection. Aladjem emphasizes that Foucault's work invites what he calls a "different set of trespass on the constitutive elements of the diffuse power that is the fabric of that 'freedom' itself." He argues that Foucault's work, while not rejecting liberal values, entails a "humble interrogation" of liberal themes. Foucault's work does not fit neatly into the liberal agenda; it trespasses its boundaries, destabilizes its categories. And, I would argue, so does feminism. The destabilization entailed by feminism is not identical to that suggested by Foucault. But Aladjem's essay suggests that, as radical critiques of modernism, feminism and Foucault can benefit from an intimate interaction.

Neither his detractors nor his defenders question that Foucault's perspective provides a challenge for feminism. The essays in this collection illustrate how feminist readings of Foucault transform the perspective out of which the author writes. But there is another aspect of transformation at work here. Foucault's approach transforms the basic concepts of modernist thought, and facilitates the transformative task of feminism. There are many ways of framing this transformation. Foucault suggests a radically new concept of the subject, politics, knowledge, and truth. In conclusion, however, I focus on one aspect of that transformation that is particularly relevant: the role of the intellectual. Foucault argues against what he calls the "universal intellectual." The age of the "universal intellectual," he claims, is passing.[7] This intellectual was "universal" in two senses: first, he [sic] relied on universal truths and principles to ground his arguments; second, he pronounced on the global order of things, the total picture. In opposition to this, Foucault describes what he calls the "specific intellectual," the intellectual who is concerned with local and immediate forms of power and oppression, who utilizes a "local" scientific truth to formulate arguments.[8] The task of the specific intellectual, Foucault argues, is "to struggle against the forms of power that transform him into its object and instrument in the sphere of 'knowledge,' 'truth,' 'consciousness,' and 'discourse.' "[9] Although Foucault uses the masculine pronoun in reference to the specific intellectual, I believe that this conception violates the masculine identification of the universal intellectual. As Foucault defines him, the specific intellectual is both a product of the changing configuration of the modern world—the diversity of subjects, the dispersal of power—and a commentator on those changes. The specific intellectual also embodies the possibility of resistance in such a world. If the struggle is directed against power, Foucault argues, then all those on whom power is exercised to their detriment can begin the struggle on their own terrain.[10] "The essential political problem for the intellectual is not to criticize the ideological content supposedly linked to science, or to ensure that his own scientific practice is accompanied by a correct ideology, but that of ascertaining the possibility of constituting a new politics of truth."[11]

The contemporary feminist movement was born in the era of the universal intellectual. In the early and mid-twentieth century feminists defined their project as revealing the oppression of women and arguing for women's liberation. Foucault's approach calls for different tactics. Our task, he argues, should be not to formulate global systemic theory but to analyze the specificity of mechanisms of power, to locate the connections and extensions, to build, little by little, a strategic knowledge.[12] He characterizes his method as the "freeing of difference." This requires "thought without contradiction, without dialectics, without negation, thought that accepts divergence; affirmative thought whose instrument is distinction; thought of the multiple—of the nomadic and dispersed multiplicity that is not limited or confined by the constraints of similarity."[13]

This Foucauldian view of politics as the freeing of difference is the basis for my claim that a Foucauldian politics is particularly appropriate to contemporary feminist politics. One of the major characteristics of feminism at the end of the twentieth century is the realization that the oppressions that women face are varied and multiple; they require specific (local) resistances designed for the particular situations that different women face. A unitary conception of "woman," an autonomous, constituting subject, a politics of identity and liberation fail to meet the needs of feminism in the late twentieth century. Foucault's work offers a means of transforming these concepts and defining a feminism that is transformative as well.

Notes

1. See Susan Hekman, *Gender and Knowledge: Elements of a Postmodern Feminism* (Boston: Northeastern University Press, 1990); and Irene Diamond and Lee Quinby, eds., *Feminism and Foucault: Reflections on Resistance* (Boston: Northeastern University Press, 1988).

2. I put "postmodernism" in quotes because Foucault rejected the label and because of the wide range of positions labeled "postmodern."

3. Nancy Hartsock, *Money, Sex, and Power: Toward a Feminist Historical Materialism* (New York: Longman, 1983).

4. Judith Butler, *Gender Trouble: Feminism and the Subversion of Identity* (New York: Routledge, 1990) and *Bodies That Matter: On the Discursive Limits of "Sex"* (New York: Routledge, 1992).

5. Lois McNay, *Foucault and Feminism: Power, Gender, and the Self* (Cambridge: Polity, 1992; Boston: Northeastern University Press, 1993).

6. See especially Susan Bordo, "Feminism, Postmodernism, and Gender-Skepticism," in *Feminism/Postmodernism*, ed. Linda Nicholson (New York: Routledge, 1990), 133–56.

7. Michel Foucault, *Power/Knowledge: Selected Interviews and Other Writings, 1972–1977*, ed. Colin Gordon, trans. Colin Gordon et al. (New York: Pantheon, 1980), 126.

8. Ibid., 128–29.

9. Michel Foucault, *Language, Counter-Memory, Practice*, trans. Donald Bouchard and Sherry Simon (Ithaca: Cornell University Press, 1977), 208.

10. Ibid., 216.

11. Foucault, *Power/Knowledge*, 133.

12. Ibid., 145.

13. Foucault, *Language, Counter-Memory, Practice*, 185.

Part One

A Foucauldian Feminism?

1

Michel Foucault:
A "Young Conservative"?

Nancy Fraser

In a 1981 discussion of postmodernism, Jürgen Habermas referred to Michel Foucault as a "Young Conservative."[1] This epithet was an allusion to the "conservative revolutionaries" of interwar Weimar Germany, a group of radical, antimodernist intellectuals whose numbers included Martin Heidegger, Ernst Jünger, Carl Schmitt, and Hans Freyer. To call Foucault a "Young Conservative," then, was to accuse him of elaborating what Habermas calls a "total critique of modernity." Such a critique, according to Habermas, is both theoretically paradoxical and politically suspect. It is theoretically paradoxical because it cannot but surreptitiously presuppose some of the very modern categories and attitudes it claims to have surpassed. And it is politically suspect because it aims less at a dialectical resolution of the problems of modern societies than at a radical rejection of modernity as such. In sum, it is Habermas's contention that although Foucault's critique of contemporary culture and society purports to be postmodern, it is at best modern and at worst antimodern.[2]

As Habermas sees it, then, the issue between him and Foucault concerns their respective stances vis-à-vis modernity. Habermas locates his own stance in the tradition of dialectical social criticism that runs from Marx to the Frankfurt school. This tradition analyzes modernization as a two-sided historical process and insists that although Enlightenment rationality dissolved premodern forms of domination and unfreedom, it gave rise to new and insidious forms of its own. The important thing about this tradition, from Habermas's point of view, and the thing that sets it apart from the rival tradition in which he locates Foucault, is that it does not reject *in toto* the modern ideals and aspirations whose two-sided actualization it criticizes. Instead, it seeks to preserve and extend both the "emancipatory impulse" behind the Enlightenment and that movement's real success in overcoming premodern forms of domina-tion—even while it criticizes the bad features of modern societies.

This, however, claims Habermas, is not the stance of Foucault. Foucault belongs rather to a tradition of rejectionist criticism of moder-nity, one that includes Nietzsche, Heidegger, and the French poststruct-uralists. These writers, unlike the dialecticians with whom Habermas identifies, aspire to a total break with the Enlightenment. In their zeal to be as radical as possible, they "totalize" critique so that it turns against itself. Not content to criticize the contradiction between modern norm and modern reality, they criticize even the constitutive norms of moder-nity, rejecting the very commitments to truth, rationality, and freedom that alone make critique possible.

What are we to make of this highly charged attack on the most political of the French poststructuralists by the leading exponent of German Critical Theory?

On the one hand, Habermas's criticism of Foucault directs our atten-tion to some very important questions: Where does Foucault stand vis-à-vis the political ideals of the Enlightenment? Does he reject the project of examining the background practices and institutions that structure the possibilities of social life in order to bring them under the conscious, collective control of human beings? Does he reject the conception of freedom as autonomy that that project appears to presuppose? Does he aspire to a total break with the long-standing Western tradition of emancipation via rational reflection?

But, on the other hand, even as Habermas's criticism directs our attention to such questions, it tends not to solicit the sort of inquiry that is needed to answer them. In fact, Habermas's formulation is too tendentious to permit a fair adjudication of the issues. It overlooks the possibility that the target of Foucault's critique may not be modernity *simpliciter* but, rather, only one particular component of it, namely, a system of practice and discourse that Foucault calls "humanism." Moreover, it begs an important question by assuming that one cannot reject humanism without also rejecting modernity. Finally, it jumps the gun with the alarmist supposition that if Foucault rejects a "universalistic" or foundationalistic metainterpretation of humanist concepts and values, then he must be rejecting these concepts and values entirely.

All told, then, Habermas raises the ante too precipitously and forecloses the possibility of posing to Foucault a more nuanced and analytically precise set of questions: Assuming that Foucault's target is indeed "humanism," then what exactly is it, and what is its relation to modernity more broadly conceived? Does Foucault really mean to reject humanism, and if so, then on what grounds? Does he reject it, for example, on strictly conceptual and philosophical grounds? Is the problem that the humanist vocabulary is still mired in a superseded Cartesian metaphysic? Or, rather, does Foucault reject humanism on strategic grounds? In other words, does he contend that though a humanist political stance may once have had emancipatory force when it was a matter of opposing the premodern forms of domination of the ancien régime, this is no longer the case? Does he thus think, strategically, that appeals to humanist values in the present conjuncture must fail to discourage—indeed, must promote—new, quintessentially modern forms of domination? Or, finally, does Foucault reject humanism on normative grounds? Does he hold that the humanist project is intrinsically undesirable? Is humanism, in his view, simply a formula for domination tout court?

If Habermas is to be faulted for failing to ask such questions, then Foucault must be faulted for failing to answer them. In fact, his position is highly ambiguous: on the one hand, he never directly pronounces in favor of rejectionism as an alternative to dialectical social criticism; on the other hand, his writings abound with rhetorical devices that convey rejectionist attitudes. Moreover, given his general reluctance to spell out the theoretical presuppositions informing his work, it is not surprising that Foucault fails to distinguish among the various sorts of rejectionism I've just outlined. On the contrary, he tends to conflate conceptual, strategic, and normative arguments against humanism.

These ambiguities have given rise to an interesting divergence among Foucault's interpreters, one that bears directly on the controversy sparked by Habermas. Because Foucault's texts contain stretches of philosophical, historical, and political reasoning that are susceptible to various rejectionist interpretations and because the conceptual, strategic, and normative dimensions of these are not adequately distinguished, interpreters have tended to seize on one or another of these elements as the key to the whole. David Hoy, for example, has interpreted Foucault as, in my terms, a merely conceptual or philosophical rejectionist of humanism; [3] other readers have taken or are likely to take him to be, again in my terms, a merely strategic rejectionist of humanism; and Hubert L. Dreyfus and Paul Rabinow have put the strongest construction of all on Foucault, reading him as, in my terms, a substantive, normative rejectionist of humanist values. [4] These, I believe, are the major, prototypical interpretations of Foucault now extant. Only by closely examining them can we hope to get to the bottom of the "Young Conservative" controversy.

In what follows, I shall consider each of these three interpretations of Foucault. I shall not be directly concerned, however, with the question, Who has got Foucault right? I believe that Foucault does not really have a single consistent position and that there is some textual evidence in favor of each reading; moreover, I do not wish here to debate where I think the balance of such evidence lies. My primary concern will be the substantive issues between Foucault and Habermas. I shall try to formulate these issues more precisely and persuasively than I think Habermas has done and to begin adjudicating them. My focus, then, will be the following problem: Which, if any, of the various sorts of rejectionism that can be attributed to Foucault are desirable and defensible alternatives to the sort of dialectical social criticism Habermas envisions?

One influential reading of Foucault is premised on the assumption that—pace Habermas—to reject a foundationalistic or universalistic metaphilosophical interpretation of the humanist ideals of modernity is not necessarily to reject modernity altogether. In this reading, a version of which has been expounded by David Hoy, Foucault is a merely philosophical rejectionist: he rejects only a certain philosophical framework, not necessarily the values and forms of life that that framework has served to underpin and legitimate.[5] Furthermore, this reading holds that such a position is defensible; Foucault is perfectly consistent in repudiating the Cartesian vocabulary in which humanist ideals have been articulated while retaining something like the substance of the ideals themselves.

Those who read Foucault in this way follow Dreyfus and Rabinow in seeing him as a Heideggerian of sorts, allegedly completing and concretizing Heidegger's program for the dismantling of Cartesianism.[6] Heidegger argued that the subject and object that modern philosophy (including political philosophy) took for necessary, universal, and ahistorical fundaments were actually contingent, historically situated products of the modern interpretation of the meaning of Being.[7] As such, they pertained only to one "epoch" in the "history of Being" (that is, Western civilization), an epoch that had exhausted its possibilities and was ending. That these Cartesian interpretations of Being were contingent and derivative was evident in view of their relativity to and dependence on a prior, enabling background that remained necessarily "unthought" by them. For a variety of logical, historical, and quasi-political reasons, Heidegger thought that this background could be evoked only indirectly and metaphorically via words like *Lichtung* (clearing).

Foucault is seen, accordingly, as continuing and concretizing Heidegger's delimitation of Cartesianism by spelling out what Heidegger might have or should have meant by the background, or *Lichtung*. The background is the historically specific system of norm-governed social practices (at first called the "episteme," later the "power/knowledge regime") that defines and produces each epoch's distinctive subjects and objects of knowledge and power. A new kind of historiography (first called "archaeology," later "genealogy") can chart the emergence and disappearance of such systems of practice and describe their specific functioning. Such historiography can illuminate the transitory character of any given episteme or power/knowledge regime, including, and especially, the modern humanist one. It can function as a kind of *Kulturkritik*, dereifying contemporary practices and objects, robbing them of their traditional ahistorical, foundationalistic legitimations, lending them an appearance of arbitrariness and even nastiness, and suggesting their potential openness to change. It can demonstrate, for example, that the

Cartesian concepts of subjectivity and objectivity that have served to legitimate humanist values are "fictions" and that these fictions and the values correlated with them have in turn served to legitimate practices that, denuded of their aura of legitimacy, take on an unsavory appearance.

In this reading, Foucault follows Heidegger in singling out a constellation both call "humanism" as a target for genealogical critique and delimitation. Heidegger argued that in the development of modern Western culture since Descartes, a complex and disastrous complicity has been elaborated between the subjectivity and the objectivity that humanism simplistically opposes to each other.[8] On the one hand, modern mathematical science and machine technology have objectified everything that is (the first taking as real only what can be fitted into a preestablished research ground plan; the second treating everything as "standing reserve," or resources to be mobilized within a technological grid). But on the other hand, and at the same time, the "age of anthropology" has created a realm of subjectivities; it has given rise to such entities as "representations," "values," "cultural expressions," "life objectivations," "aesthetic and religious experience," the mind that thinks the research plan and its objects, and the will that wills the mobilization of standing reserve. This objectification and this subjectification, says Heidegger, are two sides of the same coin. Humanists are at best naive and at worst complicit in thinking they can solve the problems of modern culture by asserting the dominance of the subject side over the object side. Ontologically, the two are exactly on the same (non-"primordial" and "forgetful") level; ethically—the very notion of ethics is part of the problem. But, says Heidegger, none of this is meant to sponsor the glorification of the inhumane; it is aimed, rather, at finding a higher sense of the dignity of "man" than that envisioned by humanism.[9]

Those who emphasize Heidegger's influence stress Foucault's account of the modern discursive formation of humanism. Humanism, claims Foucault, is a political and scientific praxis oriented to a distinctive object known as "Man."[10] Man came into existence only in the late eighteenth or early nineteenth century, with the emergence of a new power/knowledge regime. Within and by means of the social practices that regime comprises, Man was and is constituted as the epistemic object of the new "human sciences" and also instituted as the subject who is the target and instrument of a new kind of normalizing power.

Both as epistemic object and as subject of power, Man is a strange, unstable, two-sided entity, or "doublet." He consists in an impossible symbiosis of two opposing poles, one objective, the other subjective. Each of these poles seek to exclude the other but, in so doing, manages only to solicit and enhance it, since each in fact requires the other. Humanism, then, is the contradictory, ceaseless, self-defeating project of resolving this Man problem.

In *The Order of Things*, Foucault provides a grid for the varieties of modern humanism by identifying three forms of the Man doublet. First, there is the transcendental/empirical double, in which Man both constitutes the world of empirical objects and is constituted himself, an empirical object like any other in the world. Second, there is the cogito/unthought double, in which Man is both determined by forces unknown to him and aware that he is so determined; he is thus charged with the task of thinking his own unthought and thereby freeing himself. Finally, there is the return-and-retreat-of-the-origin double, in which Man is both the originary opening from which history unfolds and an object with a history that antedates him.

Each of these three doubles contains a subject pole that suggests the autonomy, rationality, and infinite value of Man. As the one who transcendentally constitutes the world, Man is a meaning-giver and lawmaker. As thinker of his own unthought, he becomes self-transparent, unalienated, and free. And as enabling horizon of history, he is its measure and destiny. But no sooner does this subject pole endow Man with this privilege and value than it defines the opposing object pole that denies them. As empirical object, Man is subject to prediction and control. Unknown to himself, he is determined by alien forces. And as a being with a history that antedates him, he is encumbered with a density not properly his own.

The humanist political project, then, is that of solving the Man problem. It is the project of making the subject pole triumph over the object pole, of achieving autonomy by mastering the other in history, in society, in oneself, of making substance into subject. Foucault's claim, both in *The Order of Things* and throughout his subsequent writings, is that this project, premised as it is on the "subjected sovereignty" of Man, is self-defeating, self-contradictory, and can lead in practice only to domination. Only a completely new configuration—a posthumanist one that no longer produces this bizarre Man doublet but, rather, some completely different object—offers a way out.

The reading of Foucault as a merely philosophical rejectionist takes the writings after *The Order of Things* as working out the social implications of the philosophical critique of humanism. *Discipline and Punish* is seen as chronicling the fabrication of the object side of Man; the first volume of *The History of Sexuality* and shorter pieces like "Truth and Subjectivity" chronicle the fabrication of the subject side.[11] Whereas a humanist might be expected to criticize the objectification of Man in the name of subjectivity, Foucault's work on sexuality putatively shows that subjectivity is every bit as problematic as objectivity. Indeed, the complicity and symmetry of the two poles is dramatically revealed in two other works, *Pierre Rivière* and *Herculine Barbin*.[12] In each of these books, Foucault juxtaposes the first-person subjective discourse of an individual (in the first, a nineteenth-century French parricide; in the second, a nineteenth-century French hermaphrodite) to the contemporary objective medical and legal discourses about him or her. Although he never explicitly clarified his intentions in these books, it seems safe to assume that Foucault's aim is not the humanist one of vindicating the subjective discourse over against the objective one. On the contrary, it must be the antihumanist aim of placing the two on a par, of showing that they depend on and require each other, that they are generated together within, and are illustrative of, the discursive formation of modern humanism.

When Foucault's works are read in this way, it is possible to treat his rejection of humanism as merely conceptual or philosophical. Just as Heidegger's delimitation of humanism was intended to enhance rather than to undermine human dignity, so Foucault's critique, *pace* Habermas, is not an attack on the notions of freedom and reason per se. It is rather a rejection of one contingent, superseded philosophical idiom or discursive formation in which those values have lately found their expression. What is novel and important in Foucault's social criticism, in this reading, is not its implied normative content—*that*, for all practical purposes, is "humanistic" in some looser sense. The novelty is rather the scrapping of the classical modern philosophical underpinnings of that content. Foucault has succeeded in producing a species of *Kulturkritik* that does not rely on—indeed, that explicitly repudiates—the subject-object framework in all of its familiar guises. He rejects the notion of progress—not only in its self-congratulatory Whiggish form but also in the more critical and sophisticated form in which it appears in Marxism and some versions of German Critical Theory. Thus, he produces genuine indictments of objectionable aspects of modern culture without presupposing a Hegelian teleology and a unitary subject of history. Similarly, he rejects the distinction between "real" and "administered" needs or interests, where the former are presumed to be grounded in something more than a contingent, historical power/knowledge regime or background of social practices. He is able, consequently, to condemn objectionable practices without presupposing the notion of autonomous subjectivity. Thus, David Hoy treats Foucault's explicitly political works—*Discipline and Punish* and the first volume of *The History of Sexuality*—as demonstrations of the dispensability of these anachronistic and questionable notions.[13] Foucault has shown that one does not need humanism in order to criticize prisons, social science, pseudoprograms for sexual liberation, and the like; that humanism is not the last word in critical social and historical writing; that there is life—and critique—after Cartesianism. One need not fear that in giving up the paradoxical and aporetic subject-object framework, one is giving up also and necessarily the possibility of engaged political reflection.

This reading of Foucault as a merely philosophical rejectionist is attractive. It suggests the possibility of combining something like Heidegger's and Foucault's postmodernism in philosophy with something like Habermas's modernism in politics. It thereby holds out the appealing promise that one can have one's cake and eat it, too. One gives up the foundationalistic meta-interpretation of humanist values: the view that such values are grounded in the nature of something (Man, the subject) independent of, and more enduring than, historically changing regimes of social practices. One gives up as well the idiom in which humanist values have had their classical modern expression; the terms "autonomy," "subjectivity," and "self-determination" lose their privilege. But one does not give up the substantial critical core of humanism. What Habermas would call its "emancipatory force" remains. One simply uses other rhetorical devices and strategies to do essentially the same critical work that the humanist tried to do, namely, to identify and condemn those forms of modern discourse and practice that, under the guise of promoting freedom, extend domination.

Aside from the question of the fidelity of this reading, is the project it attributes to Foucault a defensible and desirable one? I take it that a merely philosophical rejection of humanism is defensible and desirable in principle. It is very much on the current political-philosophical agenda, as can be seen from a wide variety of recent work: for example, analytic accounts of the concept of autonomy by John Rawls and Gerald Dworkin;[14] antifoundationalist reconstructions of liberalism by Richard Rorty and Michael Walzer;[15] antihumanist versions of Marxism inspired by Louis Althusser;[16] and deconstructive reconceptualizations of "the political" by French philosophers influenced by Derrida.[17] Even portions of Habermas's work can be seen as a (moderate) version of this project; his "communicative" reconstruction of Kantian ethics, for example, is an attempt to divest the humanist notion of autonomy of some of its Cartesian trappings (its "monologism" and its ahistorical formalism) while preserving its efficacy as an instrument of social criticism; his distinction between evolution and history is an attempt to disencumber humanism of the Hegelian presupposition of a metaconstitutive subject of history; and his "linguistic turn" is an attempt to detach humanism from the standpoint of the philosophy of consciousness.

But to endorse in principle the general program of de-Cartesianizing and de-Hegelianizing humanism is not yet to resolve a great many very important and difficult problems. It is only to begin to spell out the tasks and standards in terms of which a Foucauldian merely philosophical rejection of humanism is to be evaluated. Among these tasks and standards, I believe, is the adequacy of what Foucault has to say in response to the following sort of metaethical question: Supposing one abandons a foundationalist grounding of humanist values, then to what sort of nonfoundationalist justification can such values lay claim? This, however, is a question Foucault never squarely faced; rather, he tried to displace it by insinuating that values neither can have nor require any justification. And yet he never provided compelling reasons for embracing that extreme meta-ethical position.

This puts Foucault in the paradoxical position of being unable to account for or justify the sorts of normative political judgments he makes all the time—for example, that "discipline" is a bad thing. Moreover, it raises the question as to whether the values implicit in his unabashedly value-laden descriptions of social reality would, if rendered explicit, constitute a coherent and consistent first-order normative outlook. That question is especially pressing, since Foucault never, despite repeated insinuations, successfully argued that a coherent first-order normative outlook is dispensable in social criticism.

But the problems that arise when we read Foucault as propounding a merely philosophical rejection of humanism run still deeper. Even if we absolve him of the onus of producing an acceptable moral theory, we may still question whether he produced a satisfactory nonhumanist political rhetoric, one that does indeed do, and do better, the critical work that humanist rhetoric sought to do. We may question, for example, whether Foucault's rhetoric really does the job of distinguishing better from worse regimes of social practices; whether it really does the job of identifying forms of domination (or whether it overlooks some and/or misrecognizes others); whether it really does the job of distinguishing fruitful from unfruitful, acceptable from unacceptable forms of resistance to domination; and finally, whether it really does the job of suggesting not simply that change is possible but also what sort of change is desirable. These, I take it, are among the principal tasks of social criticism, and they are tasks with respect to which Foucault's social criticism might well be judged deficient.

It is worth recalling that the reading of Foucault as a merely philosophical rejectionist of humanism included the claim that he had succeeded in producing a species of *Kulturkritik* without relying on Cartesian underpinnings. But that claim now seems open to question. We should conclude, then, that however, laudable the general project, Foucault's version of merely philosophical rejectionism, or the version that has been attributed to him by readers like David Hoy, is incomplete and hence unsatisfactory. It tends, as a result, to invite the assumption that in Foucault's work one is dealing with a rejectionism of a stronger sort.

A second reading of Foucault holds that in addition to rejecting humanism on philosophical grounds, he also rejects it on strategic grounds. This reading offers a correspondent understanding of Foucault's position: it contends that he sees humanism as a political rhetoric and practice that developed at the beginning of the modern era in order to oppose what were essentially premodern forms of domination and oppression. Its targets were things like monarchical absolutism, the use of torture to extort confessions from criminals, and spectacular, cruel public executions. In opposition to such practices, humanism sought to limit assaults on people's bodies; it proclaimed a new respect for inwardness, personhood, humanity, and rights. However, the result was not the abolition of domination but, rather, the replacement of premodern forms of domination with new, quintessentially modern ones. The new concern for "humaneness" fed into the development of a powerful battery of social science technologies that massively transformed and vastly extended the scope and penetration of social control. The astonishing growth and near-ubiquitous spread of these techniques amounted to a revolution in the very nature of power in modern culture. The operation of power was so thoroughly transformed as to render humanism irrelevant and *dépassé*. The democratic safeguards forged in the struggle against premodern despotism have no force against the new modes of domination. Talk of rights and the inviolability of the person is of no use when the enemy is not the despot but the psychiatric social worker. Indeed, such talk and associated reform practice only make things worse. Humanism, then, must be rejected on strategic as well as philosophical grounds. In the current situation, it is devoid of emancipatory force.

This reading gives great weight to the argument of *Discipline and Punish*. There, Foucault chronicles the emergence of the "norm" and its replacement of the "law" as the primary instrument of modern social control. This change came about, he claims, as a result of the development of a new power/knowledge regime that produced a new subject and object of knowledge and a new target of power, namely, Man. Whereas an earlier regime had produced a knowledge of overt actions (crimes or sins) and a power whose target was bodies, the new regime sought to know and to discipline character, or the "soul." This new power/ knowledge object was a deeper one: it was the sensibility or personality that underlay overt actions, the self or set of dispositions that was the ground or cause of those actions. Its very temporality was different; it persisted well beyond the more ephemeral actions that were its mere outward expressions. Hence, the knowledge of this object had a fundamentally different structure, and the production of such knowledge employed fundamentally different techniques. Along with Man, the "human sciences" were born. These sciences investigated the laws governing the formation, perseverance, and alteration of sensibility. They produced character typologies and classifications of "souls." They constituted individuals as "cases" and treated their overt actions as manifest signs of latent realities. Such signs had to be deciphered so that the particular "nature" of the individual in question could be determined—then his or her acts could be explained by that nature. Furthermore, once the laws governing a particular nature were known, prescriptions for altering it could be devised. Selves could be reprogrammed, old habits dismantled, and new ones inculcated in their place. Moreover, individualizing knowledges were complemented by synoptical ones. Statistical methods for surveying and assessing masses of population were developed. Statistical norms were formulated that made it possible to locate individuals on a commensurating scale. From the standpoint of social control, the relevant categories ceased to be the old-fashioned juridical ones of guilt and innocence. Instead, they became the social-scientific ones of normalcy and deviancy. Henceforth, the world came to be populated less by malefactors than by "deviants," "perverts," and "delinquents."

Discipline and Punish thus describes the emergence and character of a new, distinctively modern form of power: normalizing-disciplinary power. It is the sort of power more appropriate to the bureaucratic welfare state than to the despotic regimes opposed by humanism. It is a power that operates quietly and unspectacularly but, for all that, continuously, penetratingly, and ubiquitously. It has no easily identifiable center but is "capillary," dispersed throughout the entire social body. Its characteristic agents are social scientists, expert witnesses, social workers, psychiatrists, teachers, progressive penologists, and the lay citizen who internalizes its categories and values. Above all, it is a power against which humanism is defenseless.

The reading of Foucault now under consideration takes him, then, to be rejecting humanism on strategic as well as on philosophical grounds. He is arguing, it is claimed, that the notions of subjectivity, autonomy, and selfhood to which the humanist appeals are in fact integral components of the disciplinary regime. Far from being genuinely critical, oppositional ideals with emancipatory force, they are actually the very norms and objects through which discipline operates. Selves and subjects in the proper sense came into existence only when the modern power/knowledge regime did. The humanist critic who appeals to them is thus not in a position to oppose that regime effectively. On the contrary, she or he is trapped in the doubling movement that defines the "age of Man."

Is this view defensible? The argument of *Discipline and Punish* consists in one extended historical example: the eighteenth-century European penal reform movement. This movement sought to end the ancien régime's practice of torturing bodies and to replace it with a penal practice aimed at the criminal's mind. It would reorder the offender's mental representations in order to provoke self-reflection and enlightenment, thus rehabilitating the malefactor as an agent and subject. But, claims Foucault, humanist reform never materialized; it was immediately transformed into a normalizing, disciplinary mode of punishment in which the criminal was made the object of a technology of causal reconditioning.

There are obvious logical reasons to doubt that this argument establishes that humanism should be rejected on strategic grounds. It extrapolates from one case, over a hundred years old, to the general conclusion that the humanist conception of freedom as autonomy is today without critical force with respect to disciplinary institutions.

Moreover, a closer look at this case reveals an important new wrinkle. Foucault's account implies that the humanist penal reform movement contained a significant ambiguity. It was unclear whether the new object of punishment, the criminal's "mind" or "humanity," meant the capacity to choose rationally and freely (roughly, the capacities attributed by Kant to the noumenal self) or the causally conditioned seat or container of representations (roughly, the self posited by associationist psychology with the properties attributed by Kant to the empirical self). The result was that it was unclear whether the project of restoring the juridical subject meant provoking a process of *self*-reflection whereby the criminal would undergo *self*-change, a project that would require adopting vis-à-vis the criminal what Habermas calls "the stance of communicative interaction" (or dialogic persuasion), or whether it meant redoing the association of ideas via cognitive conditioning, a project that would mean adopting what Habermas calls "the stance of strategic action" (or technological control). Foucault's account suggests that the penal reform movement conflated these two objects and their corresponding projects and action orientations and so, in effect, contained within itself the seeds of discipline. It posited, at least in embryo, objectified, predictable, and manipulable Man, thus effectively opening the door to the behavioral engineers and welfare technologists.

But if this is so, then what the argument of *Discipline and Punish* discredits is not a proper humanism at all but, rather, some hybrid form resembling utilitarianism. (Nor should this surprise, given that the archvillain of the book is Jeremy Bentham, inventor of the Panopticon.) Thus, it does not follow that a nonutilitarian, Kantian, or quasi-Kantian humanism lacks critical force against the psychological conditioning and mind manipulation that are the real targets of Foucault's critique of disciplinary power. Recall that Habermas has devised a version of Kantian humanism that goes at least some of the way toward meeting the philosophical objections considered in the previous section of this essay.[18] He has elaborated a pragmatic reinterpretation of Kant's ethics, one that divorces the autonomy-heteronomy contrast from the vestiges of the foundational subject-object ontology it retained in Kant and that pegs it instead to the pragmatic distinction between communicative interaction and strategic action. This moves strengthens the normative, critical force of the autonomy notion against discipline. It effectively condemns strategic action irrespective of whether the object of punishment be a body or a "soul" or a "self."

It seems plausible to me to follow this Habermasian line and still allow that Foucault is right to contend that in the context of punishment the outcome of Enlightenment penal reform was not merely contingent. It does indeed seem doubtful that the project of reaching agreement with a prisoner, of positing her or him as an autonomous subject of conversation, could ever in fact be anything other than manipulation and control of linguistic behavior, given that *ex hypothesi* it is to be carried out in the quintessentially non-"ideal speech situation" of involuntary incarceration. The same may also hold for women in the bourgeois patriarchal family, students in institutions of compulsory education, patients in mental asylums, soldiers in the military—indeed, for all situations where the power that structures discourse is hierarchical and asymmetrical and where some persons are prevented from pressing their claims either by overt or covert force or by such structural features as the lack of an appropriate vocabulary for interpreting their needs.

But the fact that the humanist ideal of autonomous subjectivity is unrealizable, even co-optable, in such "disciplinary" contexts need not be seen as an argument against that ideal. It may be seen, rather, as an argument against hierarchical, asymmetrical power. One need not conclude, with Foucault, that humanist ideals must be rejected on strategic grounds. One may conclude instead, with Habermas, that it is a precondition for the realization of those ideals that the "power" that structures discourse be symmetrical, nonhierarchical, and hence reciprocal. Indeed, one may reinterpret the notion of autonomy so as to incorporate this insight, as Habermas has done. For him, autonomy ceases to refer to a "monologic" process of will formation wherein an isolated individual excludes all empirical needs, desires, and motives and considers only what is required by pure formal reason. Autonomy refers rather to an ideal "dialogic" process wherein individuals with equal right and power to question prevailing norms seek consensus through conversation about which of their apparently individual empirical needs and interests are in fact generalizable. In this interpretation, the cases of disciplinary domination described by Foucault in *Discipline and Punish* are instances not of autonomy but of heteronomy precisely because they involve modes of discourse production that do not meet the procedural requirements specified by the "ideal speech situation."

Furthermore, it is worth noting that any strategic argument against humanism depends on complex empirical considerations. The antihumanist must demonstrate that the actual character of the contemporary world really is such as to render humanism irrelevant and *dépassé*. She or he must show, for example, that it really is the modern bureaucratic welfare state and not other forms of repression or oppression that constitutes the chief threat to freedom in our era. For even a "utilitarian-humanist" can argue that, with all of its problems, the "carceral" society described in *Discipline and Punish* is better than the dictatorship of the party-state, junta, or Imam; that, *pace* Foucault, the reformed prison is preferable to the gulag, the torture cell, the death camp, and the sex-slavery brothel; and that in *this* world—which is the real world—humanism still wields its share of critical, emancipatory punch.

Moreover, for nonutilitarian humanists like Habermas, the continuing strategic relevance of humanism is broader still. It is not confined to the critique of premodern forms of domination but applies equally to more modern "disciplinary" forms of power.

There is yet another way of reading Foucault that remains to be considered. This way takes him to be rejecting humanism not simply on conceptual and/or strategic grounds but, rather, on substantive normative grounds. It holds that Foucault believes that humanism is intrinsically undesirable, that the conception of freedom as autonomy is a formula for domination tout court. Furthermore, some exponents of this line of interpretation, such as Hubert L. Dreyfus and Paul Rabinow, claim that Foucault is right to reject humanism on normative grounds.[19]

This reading is or ought to be the real target of Habermas's attack, for it denies that his pragmatic, dialogic reconceptualization of autonomy meets Foucault's objections. Habermas's point would have weight, it is claimed, if Foucault were merely arguing that discipline is the use of social science in utilitarian programs aimed at normalizing deviancy in contexts of asymmetrical or hierarchical power and that humanism is inefficacious against it. In fact, however, he is arguing a much stronger thesis. Foucault is claiming that even a perfectly realized autonomous subjectivity would be a form of normalizing, disciplinary domination.

This reading depends heavily on Foucault's more recent work: the first volume of his *History of Sexuality* and the lecture "Truth and Subjectivity," which previews the direction pursued in the subsequent volumes of the *History*.[20] These texts are seen as doing for the subject side of the Man doublet what *Discipline and Punish* did for the object side. They provide a genealogical account of the fabrication of the hermeneutical subject, a subject that is not the empirical, causally conditioned container of representations but, rather, the putatively free, quasi-noumenal subject of communicative interaction. Foucault demonstrates, it is claimed, that far from providing a standpoint for emancipation, the fabrication of this subject only seals Man's domination. The subjectification of Man is in reality his subjection.

This reading correctly notes that Foucault's later work focuses on a host of subjectifying practices. Central among these are those quintessentially humanist forms of discourse that aim at liberation and self-mastery via the thematization and critique of previously unthematized, uncriticized contents of the self: unarticulated desires, thoughts, wishes, and needs. Foucault seeks the origins of the notion that by hermeneutical decipherment of the deep, hidden meaning of such contents, one can achieve lucidity about the other in oneself and thus master it and become free. He traces the career of this notion from its beginnings in Stoic self-examination and early Christian penance to its modern variants in psychoanalysis and the allegedly pseudoradical politics of sexual liberation. Foucault aims to show that "truth is not naturally free," that it took centuries of coercion and intimidation to "breed a confessing animal."[21]

Certainly, early forms of hermeneutical subjectification involved the sort of asymmetrical, hierarchical distribution of power in which a silent authority commanded, deciphered, judged, and eventually absolved the confessional discourse and its author. But the reading now under consideration holds that Foucault does not assume that asymmetry and hierarchy are of the essence of disciplinary power. Nor does he believe, it is claimed, that they are what is most objectionable about it. On the contrary, one can imagine a perfected disciplinary society in which normalizing power has become so omnipresent, so finely attuned, so penetrating, interiorized, and subjectified, and therefore so invisible, that there is no longer any need for confessors, psychoanalysts, wardens, and the like. In this fully "panopticized" society, hierarchical, asymmetrical domination of some persons by others would have become superfluous; all would surveil and police themselves. The disciplinary norms would have become so thoroughly internalized that they would not be experienced as coming from without. The members of the society would, therefore, be autonomous. They would have appropriated the other as their own and made substance subject. Class domination would have given way to the kingdom of ends. The ideal speech situation would have been realized. But, it is claimed, this would not be freedom.

This picture of total, triumphant panopticism is held to be significant not empirically—as a prediction about the future course of historical development—but, rather, conceptually—for the new light it casts on the humanist ideals of autonomy and reciprocity. It suggests that these cannot, after all, be seen as genuinely oppositional ideals but are, rather, the very goals of disciplinary power. Conversely, it suggests that hierarchy and asymmetry are not, as humanists suppose, essential to that power but, rather, that they are only imperfections to be eliminated through further refinement. It suggests, therefore, that even Habermas's version of humanist ideals is internal to the disciplinary regime and devoid of critical, emancipatory force with respect to it. Thus, such ideals must be rejected on normative grounds.

Is this position defensible? Consider how a sophisticated Habermasian humanist might reply to the line of reasoning just sketched. Suppose she were to claim that what Foucault envisions as the realization of autonomous subjectivity is not that at all but only pseudoautonomy in conditions of pseudosymmetry; that despite appearances, the subject side and the object side do not really coincide yet; that the internalized other is still other; that self-surveillance is surveillance nonetheless and implies the hierarchical domination of one force by another; that the fact that everyone does it to herself or himself equally does not make it genuinely symmetrical self-rule of autonomous subjects.

I take it that a Habermasian humanist would be hard-pressed to make good such claims. By hypothesis, the members of the fully panopticized society are in an ideal speech situation, so that notion will have no critical force here. It will be necessary to invoke some other criterion to distinguish between "real" and "pseudo" autonomy, and it is not clear what such a criterion could possible be.

Suppose, though, that the Habermasian humanist takes a different tack and grants Foucault his assumption of "real" autonomy and symmetry. Suppose that she simply digs in and says, "If that's discipline, I'm for it." This would be to concede that these humanist notions have no critical force with respect to the fully panopticized society. But it would also be to claim that this is no objection to them, since there is no good reason to oppose such a society. Such a society seems objectionable only because Foucault has described it in a way that invites the genetic fallacy, that is, because he has made it the outcome of a historical process of hierarchical, asymmetrical coercion wherein people have been, in Nietzschean parlance, "bred" to autonomy. But this is a highly tendentious description. Why not describe it instead as a form of life developed on the basis of new, emergent communicative competences, competences that, though perhaps not built into the very logic of evolution, nonetheless permit for the first time in history the socialization of individuals oriented to dialogic political practice? Why not describe it as a form of life that is desirable since it no longer takes human needs and desires as brute, given facts to be either satisfied or repressed but takes them, rather, as accessible to intersubjective linguistic reinterpretation and transformation? Such access, after all, would widen the sphere of practical-political deliberation and narrow that of instrumental-technical control and manipulation.

This response shifts the burden of argument back onto Foucault. By claiming that panoptical autonomy is not the horror show Foucault took it to be, the Habermasian humanist challenges him to state, in terms independent of the vocabulary of humanism, exactly what is wrong with this hypothetical society and why it ought to be resisted. Moreover, it would not suffice for this purpose for Foucault merely to invoke such terms as "subjection" and "normalization." To say that such a society is objectionable because it is normalizing is to say that it is conformist or represents the rule of *das Man*: this, in effect, would be to appeal to something like authenticity, which (as Derrida and perhaps even the later Heidegger himself understood) is simply another version of autonomy, albeit a detranscendentalized one.

Ultimately, then, a normative rejection of humanism will require appeal to some alternative, posthumanist, ethical paradigm capable of identifying objectionable features of a fully realized autonomous society. It will require, in other words, nothing less than a new paradigm of human freedom. Only from the standpont of such a paradigm can Foucault or his interpreters make the case for a normative rejection of humanism.

Foucault, however, does not offer an alternative, posthumanist ethical paradigm. He does occasionally suggest that protest urged in the name of the pleasures of our bodies may have greater emancipatory potential than that made in the name of the ideal of autonomy. But he neither justifies nor elaborates this suggestion. Nor does he give us convincing reasons to believe that claims couched in some new "body language" would be any less subject to mystification and abuse than humanist claims have been.

It looks, therefore, as though the reading of Foucault as a normative rejectionist of humanism pushes us to choose between a known ethical paradigm and an unknown x. As long as we keep the discussion on this moral-philosophical plane, we are justified in siding with Habermas; we must balk at rejecting the idea of autonomy, at least until the Foucauldians fill in their x. But I suspect it will be more fruitful to hold off that conclusion for a while and to shift the debate onto a more hermeneutical and sociological plane. Let me rather recast the issue as a choice between two sets of fears or conceptions of danger.

Recall Foucault's nightmare of the fully panopticized society. Now consider that Habermas, too, describes a possible "brave new world" scenario for the future—but his version is the diametrical opposite of Foucault's. Habermas fears "the end of the individual," a form of life in which people are no longer socialized to demand rational, normative legitimations of social authority.[22] In this dystopian vision, they just cynically go along out of privatized strategic considerations, and the stance of communicative interaction in effect dies out.

Instead of asking which of these "brave new worlds" is the good one and which is the bad, we might ask which best captures our worst fears about contemporary social trends. But the question is too complex to be settled by exclusively moral-philosophical means. It is in part a question about empirical tendencies within contemporary Western societies and in part a question about the fears, and thus about the social identities and historical self-interpretations, of member of such societies. Hence, it is a question with an irreducible hermeneutical dimension: it demands that we weigh alternative ways of situating ourselves with respect to our past history and that we conceive ourselves in relation to possible futures, for example, as political agents and potential participants in oppositional social movements. To pose the issue in this way is to acknowledge the need for a *major* interdisciplinary, hermeneutical effort—an effort that brings to bear all the tools of historical, sociological, literary, philosophical, political, and moral deliberation in order to assess both the viability of our very strained and multivalent traditions and the possibilities of oppositional social movements. But once this is acknowledged, there is no assurance that such an effort can be contained within the terms of a choice between Habermas and Foucault.

This last point becomes especially salient when we consider that just such an interdisciplinary reassessment of humanism is now being undertaken by a social and intellectual movement without strong links to either Habermas or Foucault. I refer to the interdisciplinary community of feminist scholars and activists who are interrogating the concept of autonomy as a central value of male-dominated modern Western culture. Within this movement, a number of different perspectives on autonomy are being debated. At one end of the spectrum are those, like Simone de Beauvoir, who understand women's liberation precisely as securing our autonomy in the classical humanist sense.[23] At the other end are those, like Alison M. Jaggar, who reject autonomy on the grounds that it is an intrinsically masculinist value, premised on a mind-body, intellect-affect, will-nature dualism, linked to an invidious male-female dichotomy and positing woman (nature, affect, body) as the other to be mastered and suppressed.[24] In between are several mediating positions. There are those, like Carol Gould, who argue that autonomy is only one-half of a fully human conception of freedom and the good life and that it must be supplemented with the "feminine" values of care and relatedness that humanist ideology has denigrated and repressed.[25] These are those, influenced by Carol Gilligan, who claim that we need to acknowledge that there are now in operation two (currently gender-associated) moralities with two different concepts of autonomy correlated with public life and private life, respectively.[26] And there are those, like Iris Young, who insist that the task is, rather, to overcome the split between those moralities and to sublate the opposition between autonomy and "femininity" or humanism and antihumanism.[27]

We cannot at present anticipate the outcome of these debates, but we can recognize their capacity to resituate, if not altogether to displace, the normative dimension of the Habermas-Foucault dispute. For the feminist interrogation of autonomy is the theoretical edge of a movement that is literally remaking the social identities and historical self-interpretations of large numbers of women and of some men. Insofar as the normative dispute between Habermas and Foucault is ultimately a hermeneutical question about such identities and interpretations, it cannot but be affected, perhaps even transformed, by these developments.

Has Foucault, then, given us good reasons to reject humanism on normative grounds? Strictly speaking, no. But with respect to the larger question of the viability of humanism as a normative ideal, the results are not yet in; not all quarters have been heard from.

Was Michel Foucault a "Young Conservative"? Did he demonstrate the superiority of a rejectionist critique of modernity over a dialectical one? The scorecard, on balance, looks roughly like this.

First, when Foucault is read as rejecting humanism exclusively on conceptual and philosophical grounds, Habermas's charge misses the mark. Foucault was not necessarily aspiring to a total break with modern values and forms of life just because he rejected a foundationalistic meta-interpretation of them. Indeed, the project of de-Cartesianizing humanism is in principle a laudable one. But, on the other hand, it is understandable that Habermas should take the line that he has, since Foucault did not do the conceptual work required to elaborate and complete a merely philosophical rejection of humanism.

Second, when Foucault is read as rejecting humanism on strategic grounds, Habermas's charge is on target. Foucault failed to establish that a pragmatic, de-Cartesianized humanism lacks critical force in the contemporary world. On the contrary, there are grounds for believing that such humanism is still efficacious, indeed doubly so. On the one hand, it tells against still-extant forms of premodern domination; on the other hand, it tells against the forms of administratively rationalized domination described in Discipline and Punish. Foucault did not, then, make the case for strategic rejectionism.

Finally, when Foucault is read as rejecting humanism on normative grounds, moral-philosophical considerations support Habermas's position. Without a nonhumanist ethical paradigm, Foucault could not make good his normative case against humanism. He could not answer the question, Why should we oppose a fully panopticized, autonomous society? And yet, it may turn out that there will be grounds for rejecting, or at least modifying and resituating, the ideal of autonomy. If feminists succeed in reinterpreting our history so as to link that ideal to the subordination of women, then Habermas's own normative paradigm will not survive unscathed. The broader question about the normative viability of humanism is still open.

All told, then, Michel Foucault was not a "Young Conservative." But neither did he succeed in demonstrating the superiority of rejectionist over dialectical criticism of modern societies.

Notes

1. Jürgen Habermas, "Modernity versus Postmodernity," New German Critique 22 (Winter 1981): 3–14. The present essay was originally published in 1985. I reprint it here unrevised except where references to then-current events required updating.

2. Habermas, "Modernity versus Postmodernity," and "The Entwinement of Myth and Enlightenment: Rereading *Dialectic of Enlightenment*," *New German Critique* 26 (Spring-Summer 1982): 13–30.

3. David C. Hoy, "Power, Repression, Progress: Foucault, Lukes, and the Frankfurt School," *Triquarterly* 52 (Fall 1981): 43–63, and "The Unthought and How to Think It" (American Philosophical Association, Western Division, 1982).

4. Hubert L. Dreyfus and Paul Rabinow, *Michel Foucault: Beyond Structuralism and Hermeneutics*, with an afterword by Michel Foucault (Chicago: University of Chicago Press, 1982).

5. Hoy, "Power, Repression, Progress," and "The Unthought and How to Think It."

6. Dreyfus and Rabinow, *Michel Foucault*.

7. Martin Heidegger, "Overcoming Metaphysics," in *The End of Philosophy*, trans. Joan Stambaugh (New York: Harper and Row, 1973), 84–110, and "The Age of the World Picture," in *"The Question Concerning Technology" and Other Essays*, trans. and with an introduction by William Lovitt (New York: Garland, 1977), 115–24.

8. Heidegger, "Overcoming Metaphysics"; "The Age of the World Picture"; "The Question Concerning Technology," in *"The Question Concerning Technology" and Other Essays*, 3–35; and "The Letter on Humanism," trans. Frank A. Capuzzi, in *Basic Writings*, ed. David Farrell Krell (New York: Harper and Row, 1977), 189–242.

9. Heidegger, "The Letter on Humanism."

10. Michel Foucault, *The Order of Things: An Archaeology of the Human Sciences*, translated by the publisher (New York: Vintage, 1973), and *Discipline and Punish: The Birth of the Prison*, trans. Alan Sheridan (New York: Pantheon Books, 1979).

11. Foucault, *The History of Sexuality*, vol. 1, *An Introduction*, trans. Robert Hurley (New York: Pantheon Books, 1978), and "Truth and Subjectivity," Howison Lectures, University of California, Berkeley, 20–21 October 1980.

12. Foucault, *I, Pierre Rivière, Having Slaughtered My Mother, My Sister, and My Brother . . . : A Case of Parricide in the Nineteenth Century*, trans. Frank Jellinek (New York: Pantheon Books, 1975), and *Herculine Barbin: Being the Recently Discovered Memoirs of a Nineteenth-Century French Hermaphrodite*, trans. Richard McDougall (New York: Pantheon Books, 1980).

13. Hoy, "Power, Repression, Progress," and "The Unthought and How to Think It."

14. John Rawls, *A Theory of Justice* (Cambridge: Belknap Press of Harvard University Press, 1971), and "Kantian Constructivism in Moral Theory," *Journal of Philosophy* 77, no. 9 (September 1980): 505–72; and Gerald Dworkin, "The Nature and Value of Autonomy," unpublished transcript, 1983.

15. Richard Rorty, "Postmodern Bourgeois Liberalism," *Journal of Philosophy* 80 (October 1983): 583–89, and "Solidarity or Objectivity?" in *Post-Analytic Philosophy*, ed. John Rajchman and Cornel West (New York: Columbia University Press, 1985), 3–19; and Michel Walzer, *Spheres of Justice: A Defense of Pluralism and Equality* (New York: Basic Books, 1983).

16. Louis Althusser, *For Marx*, trans. Ben Brewster (New York: Pantheon Books, 1970).

17. See, for example, essays by Philippe Lacoue-Labarthe and Jean-Luc Nancy in *Rejouer le politique* (Paris, 1982).

18. Habermas, *Legitimation Crisis*, trans. Thomas McCarthy (Boston, 1975).

19. Dreyfus and Rabinow, *Michel Foucault*.

20. Foucault, *The History of Sexuality*, vol. 1: "Truth and Subjectivity"; *The History of Sexuality*, vol. 2, *The Use of Pleasure*, trans. Robert Hurley (New York: Pantheon Books, 1983); and *The History of Sexuality*, vol. 3, *The Care of the Self*, trans. Robert Hurley (New York: Pantheon Books, 1986).

21. Foucault, "Nietzsche, Genealogy, History," in *Language, Counter-Memory, Practice: Selected Essays and Interviews*, ed. and with an introduction by Donald F. Bouchard, trans. Donald F. Bouchard and Sherry Simon (Ithaca: Cornell University Press, 1977).

22. Habermas, *Legitimation Crisis*.

23. Simone de Beauvoir, *The Second Sex*, trans. and ed. H. M. Parshley (New York: Bantam Books, 1961).

24. Alison M. Jaggar, *Feminist Politics and Human Nature* (Totowa, N.J.: Rowman and Allanheld, 1983).

25. Carol C. Gould, "Private Rights and Public Virtues: Women, the Family, and Democracy," in *Beyond Domination: New Perspectives on Women and Philosophy*, ed. Carol C. Gould (Totowa, N.J.: Rowman and Allanheld, 1983).

26. Carol Gilligan, *In A Different Voice: Psychological Theory and Women's Development* (Cambridge: Harvard University Press, 1982).

27. Iris Young, "Humanism, Gynocentrism, and Feminist Politics," *Hypatia: A Journal of Feminist Philosophy* 3, special issue of *Women's Studies International Forum* 8, no. 3 (1985): 173–85.

2

Postmodernism and Political Change: Issues for Feminist Theory

Nancy C. M. Hartsock

Throughout the eighties, white North American feminist theorists have been responding to arguments originating from radical women of color that feminist theory must take more account of diversity among women.* Too much feminist theory was written from a perspective in which white middle-class women were seen as the norm and women of color were

*This article builds on and may be read in conjunction with "Rethinking Modernism: Minority vs. Majority Theories," *Cultural Critique*, no. 7 (Fall 1987): 187–206, and "Foucault on Power: A Theory for Women?" in *The Gender of Power*, ed. Monique Leyanaar et al. (Leiden, The Netherlands: Vakgroep Vrouwenstudies, 1987), reprinted in *Feminism/ Postmodernism*, ed Linda J. Nicholson (New York: Routledge, 1990), 157–75. I also thank those who responded to the paper at the conference "Marxism Today" in December 1989 and groups at York University, the University of Chicago, and the Univeristy of California, Los Angeles. The problems that remain are, of course, my own.

excluded and devalued. This exclusion had important effects on the theories white feminists developed. To give just one example, white feminist theory often assumed a split between the private world of the family, on the one hand, and public life on the other. Yet black feminists have pointed out that in the black community there is no private sphere protected from state intervention. Social workers, police, courts, and other state agencies all intervene on a scale that does not allow for a private familial world insulated from the state.[1] Feminist theory must take account of these structurally different situations. Note, too, that given this example, it is not a matter of simply adding women of color and their situations to the list of things feminist theory is concerned about. The inclusion of many different women will and must affect the concepts and theories themselves.

I believe that it was in response to these arguments that a number of feminist theorists found postmodernist theories attractive. Here were arguments about incommensurability, multiplicity, and the lack of definitive answers. These writings, many of them by radical intellectuals, ranged from literary criticism to the social sciences. The writers— Foucault, Derrida, Rorty, Lyotard, and others—argued against the faith in universal reason we inherited from European Enlightenment philosophy. They rejected stories that claimed to encompass all of human history. In its place they proposed a social criticism that was ad hoc contextual, plural, and limited.

Although feminist theorists have noted that postmodernist theories may contribute to the development of less totalizing theories, they have also recognized that postmodernism develops only an "anemic" politics and therefore that postmodernist approaches need to be supplemented with feminist politics.[2] My own view, however, is that postmodernist theories suffer from a number of epistemological difficulties that cannot be fully remedied by the addition of a dose of feminist politics.

The Enlightenment Tradition

Postmodernism is reacting against a particular body of thought that postmodernists argue is characterized several important features. Most frequently, this body of thought is termed "the Enlightenment." This specifically modernist and Western tradition of political thought, which emerged in western Europe over the last several hundred years, is characterized by several distinctive epistemological features. First, the "god-trick" was pervasive, and the tradition depended on the assumption that one can see everything from nowhere, that disembodied reason can produce accurate and "objective" accounts of the world.[3] Second, and related, the Enlightenment was marked by a faith in the neutrality of reasoned judgment, in scientific objectivity, in the progressive logic of reason in general and of science in particular. Third, it claimed to assume human universality and homogeneity, based on the common capacity to reason. Differences were held to be fundamentally epiphe-nomenal. Thus, one could speak of human nature, truth, and other imperial universalities. Fourth, all this had the effect of allowing for transcendence through the omnipotence of reason. Through reason, the philosopher could escape the limits of body, time, and space and could therefore contemplate the eternal problems related to man as knower. Finally, Enlightenment political thought was characterized by a denial of the importance of power to knowledge and concomitantly by a denial of the centrality of systematic domination in human societies. The subject/individual and power were held to be distinct.[4]

It is worth remembering that these fundamentally optimistic philoso-phies both grew out of and expressed the social relations of the expanding market/capitalist societies of Europe.[5] At the same time, many of the philosophers who were central to Western political thought also contributed to the development of ideologies that supported colonialism, the slave trade, the expansion of Western patriarchal relations, and so forth. One can recall J. S. Mill's statements about despotism being a proper government for savages or Montesquieu's views about the effects of climate on human nature—to the detriment of those who lived in the tropics—and his use of women in the harem as symbols of human de-pravity.

Thus, despite a stated adherence to universal principles, the epistemo-logical and political thought of the Enlightenment depended on the dualistic construction of a different world, a world onto which was projected an image of everything that ruling-class, male Europeans wanted to believe they were not. Edward W. Said names the fundamental dynamic of the process clearly when he states that the creation of the Orient (and one might add, the creation of various other racial, gender, and even class categories) was an outgrowth of the will to power. "Orientalism," he said, is "a Western style for dominating, restructuring, and having authority over the Orient."[6]

It must be remembered that this Eurocentric, masculinist, and capitalist world was constructed not only in theory but also in fact through such practices as the Atlantic slave trade, the development of plantation agriculture in the New World, the introduction of markets and private property in Africa, the colonization of large parts of Asia, Latin America, and Africa, and the introduction of European forms of patriarchal and masculinist power. These were the means by which the duality and the domination of Europe, and later North America—the "rich North Atlantic democracies" as Richard Rorty has termed them—were institutionalized in fact as well as in thought. Duality, inequality, and domination were established in the name of universality and progress; ironically, power relations were institutionalized in and through a mode of thinking that denied any connections between knowledge and power or between the construction of subjectivity and power. The philosophical and historical creation of devalued Others was the necessary precondition, then, for the creation of the transcendent, rational subject who can persuade himself that he exists outside time and space and power relations. The subject is the speaker in Enlightenment philosophy.

The social relations that both express and form the material base for the theoretical construction of this Enlightenment subjectivity have been rejected on a world scale over the last several decades.[7] Decolonization struggles, movements of young people, women's movements, and racial liberation movements all represent the diverse and disorderly Others beginning to take political power, to demand participation in the "public realm," and to chip away at the social and political power of the "individual."

I believe that, as a result of these social and political changes, some European intellectuals are beginning to reject many of the totalizing and universalizing theories of the Enlightenment. In efforts to develop alternatives to the imperialist universalities of the Enlightenment, a number of authors have argued that postmodernist theories can provide helpful guidance. For example, Chantal Mouffe argues that the postmodern critique comes into its own when one attempts to take account of the variety of democratic struggles in the contemporary world. As she puts it, "[T]o be capable of thinking politics today, and understanding the nature of these new struggles and the diversity of social relations that the democratic revolution has yet to encompass, it is indispensable to develop a theory of the subject as a decentered, detotalized agent." In these circumstances, identity is never definitively established.[8]

My own view is that postmodernist theorists remain imprisoned on the terrain of Enlightenment thought and fail to provide the ground for alternative and more emancipatory accounts of subjectivity. Moreover, despite the theorists' own desires to avoid universal claims and their stated opposition to these claims, some imperial and universalist assumptions creep back into their work. For those of us who have been marginalized and subjugated in various ways and who need to understand the world systematically in order to change it, postmodernist theories at their best fail to provide an alternative to the Enlightenment.

The Failures of Postmodernism

Let us return to the several issues broached at the outset of this argument—the several characteristic assumptions of Enlightenment thought as characterized by postmodernist thinkers. Rather than simply argue against a generalized postmodernism, I shall discuss the ways in which issues of concern appear in the work of two quite different theorists, Richard Rorty and Michel Foucault.[9] Because they emerge from quite different intellectual traditions and have divergent political views, together they can stand for a substantial range of postmodernist thought. Both Rorty and Foucault reject (in different ways) each of the several Enlightenment assumptions I listed at the beginning of this paper. Yet despite profound differences in their stated projects and, indeed, in their work, both projects ultimately inhabit the terrain defined by the Enlightenment. At best these postmodernist theories criticize Enlightenment assumptions without putting anything in their place. And at worst they recapitulate the effects of Enlightenment theories that deny the dominated the right to participate in defining the terms of interaction.

First, both Rorty and Foucault claim to have rejected the "god-trick," or the view of everything from nowhere. Rorty has done so in the name of rejecting "Epistemology." It must be noted that his choice of terminology implies that the epistemology of the West constitutes the only possible theory of knowledge. Without *that* theory, we must give up claims to knowledge. Because of their different styles and intellectual ancestors, it may be surprising to suggest that Foucault makes a very similar move. But Foucault's arguments—that truth must be seen as simply legitimized errors, that what we have called reason is born from chance, and that the essence of things must be understood to have been fabricated "in piecemeal fashion from alien forms"[10]—represent a similar rejection of Enlightenment assumptions. He, like Rorty, has come to the conclusion that if one cannot see everything from nowhere, one cannot really see anything at all. Thus, both argue for taking parodic and satiric positions, for taking the position that one is not in a position to take a position, and their analyses indicate that they take the position that if one cannot engage in the god-trick, there is no such thing as knowledges.[11]

It should be recognized that Foucault's attack is far more systematic and thorough than Rorty's. Not only does he reject the gaze from nowhere, but he is clear that the attack must also include the subject who claims to engage in disembodied knowledge gathering. Thus, unlike Rorty, Foucault argues that the question of the subject must be attended to by "creating a history of the different modes by which, in our culture, human beings are made subject," or, as I would put it, are made objects or "objectified subjects."[12]

Second, both Rorty and Foucault reject the neutrality of reason. Rorty simply suggests abandoning claims to rationality, objectivity, and certain knowledge: one should give up the process of constructing theoretical schemes and be reactive and peripheral instead. Foucault, too, attacks the notions of reason, of the solemnity of history, and argues for a reverence for irreverence. One must reject, he states, the "great stories of continuity."[13] Thus, once reason has been exposed as biased rather than neutral, the very possibility of knowledge must be abandoned. Once again, the assumptions underlying this form of argument point to the implicit conclusion that if the objective knowledge claimed (falsely) by Enlightenment thought is not available, then one must abandon the search for any knowledge at all.

Third, both Rorty and Foucault argue in their different ways that we must give up on human universals. Rorty proposes that instead we should accept the notion of incommensurable discourses and abandon the search for commensurability. Foucault's argument takes a different form to reach similar conclusions: one must unmask the demagogy cloaked by universals such as truth and laws of essences.[14] One must be suspicious not only of claims to universal truths, but even of claims to reject these truths. Indeed, at least one commentator has argued that Foucault "doesn't take a stand on whether or not there is a human nature. Rather, he changes the subject."[15]

Fourth, both Foucault and Rorty reject the search for transcendence and omnipotence. But they put forward alternatives that lead in the direction of passivity and immobility. Rorty tells use we must abandon the search for truth in favor of joining in edifying conversation. Because the great certainties available to omnipotent and eternal reason no longer obtain, one must settle for conversations rather than search for knowledge. Nor do there appear to be urgent issues of social change or justice that need to be addressed by means other than a conversation.

Foucault's political commitments appear to be quite different, yet his counsels lead in very similar directions. He feels that we should at least unmask and criticize political violence.[16] But at the same time his rejection of the hope of transcendence leads him to conclude that the only possibilities open to us involve the tracing of the ways humans have been subjugated. Marshall Berman has eloquently summed up the conclusion to which Foucault presses us:

> Do we use our minds to unmask oppression—as Foucault appears to be trying to do? Forget it, because all forms of inquiry into the human condition "merely refer individuals from one disciplinary authority to another," and hence only add to the triumphant "discourse of power." There is no point in trying to resist the oppressions and injustices of modern life, since even our dreams of freedom only add more links to our chains; however, once we grasp the total futility of it all, at least we can relax.[17]

Finally, their quite different relationships to power both reject and depend on Enlightenment assumptions; Rorty recapitulates one of these assumptions by simply ignoring power relations. Moreover, his defense of the values of the Enlightenment amounts to an acknowledgment of his status as the inheritor of its values, and thus, the epistemology that supports them. It is implicitly a statement about the need to ignore power relations in order to adhere to these values.

On this point, as elsewhere, Foucault's case is more complex. He explicitly rejects the values of the Enlightenment and recognizes that a stance of ignoring power relations implicitly endorses domination. This he refuses, yet despite his efforts, these values creep back in, not with any explicit endorsement, but rather through his reliance on his reader's adherence to these values to give his project force. Moreover, his arguments that efforts at transformation are too dangerous, and that even attempting to imagine alternatives implicates us in the system, suggest that we should not change the power relations of our culture, which extend everywhere around us. Finally, insisting on metaphors of web and net, rather than structures of domination, we are led to conclude merely that each of us both dominates and is dominated. We are all responsible, and so in a sense no one is responsible. Thus, the question of how to analyze structures of domination is obscured.

But if these two postmodernist theorists present less an alternative to the overconfident theories of the Enlightenment than a parasitic continuation of its preoccupations, positions associated with dominated and marginalized groups can offer quite different ways of looking at the world, ways that can not only situate these knowledges but can also reveal both Enlightenment and postmodernist theories to be the situated knowledges of a particular group—Euro-American, masculine, and racially as well as economically privileged.[18] Postmodernist theories should be understood as a situated knowledge that reveals itself as "the felt absence of the will or the ability to change things as they are . . . the voice of epistemological despair."[19] Indeed, these moves represent the transcendent and omnipotent voice of Enlightenment subjectivity attempting to come to grips with the social and historical changes of the middle to late twentieth century. But there are alternatives to adopting the position of either an omnipotent god or an impotent critic.

Alternative understandings of knowledge are possible, and feminist theory faces tasks that require moving to a new terrain. Most important, I believe that the task facing all progressive theorists is that of trying to expose and clarify the theoretical bases for political alliance and solidarity. Such analyses are, of course, no substitute for collective action and coalition building but a necessary adjunct to it. What can be the bases of solidarity among those who have been defined as the Native, the Woman, the Oriental, the negative and enigmatic others who have experienced the powerful distortions, inversions, and erasures of oppression?[20] While these groups share the experience of being marginalized and devalued, the primary lived experience itself takes a variety of disparate forms. The question I address is, What sorts of subjectivities—in this case, oppositional consciousnesses—can grow out of these

experiences? Put differently, what are the epistemological features characteristic of marked as opposed to fictionally unmarked subjectivities?

Epistemologies of Marked Subjectivities

But what do these alternatives look like? First, it must be remembered
that these epistemologies grow out of an experience of domination. And
it must be recognized that the historical creation and maintenance of
the dominance of Euro-American masculinist culture requires a series of
renamings and redefinings. For example, Eduardo Galeano, writing of
the situation in Latin America, states that " 'Freedom' in my country is
the name of a jail for political prisoners, and 'democracy' forms part of
the title of various regimes of terror; the word 'love' defines the relationship of a man with his automobile, and 'revolution' is understood to
describe what a new detergent can do in your kitchen." He adds that
perhaps one should recognize Latin America's "inspired contributions"
to methods of torture and techniques of assassination.[21] Or consider the
fact that the massacres carried out in Central America and elsewhere in
recent years by the "forces of order" or "peacekeeping forces" are referred
to as "normalization." Driving people from their homes and destroying
their crops are the actions of "freedom fighters." The U.S. State
Department has decreed that instead of "murder" one must refer to
"illegal or arbitrary deprivation of life." And of course the CIA has long
since ceased to kill people: it "neutralizes" them.[22] Condemning poor
women in the United States to death from back-room abortions because
no state funding is available is termed "pro-life." These are not merely
verbal sleights of hand, but are conditions of life made real through the
power of the ruling group.

The problem posed for the oppressed and marginalized is clearly stated
in Gabriel Garcia Márquez's Nobel prize address: "[O]ur crucial problem
has been a lack of conventional means to render our lives believable.
This, my friends, is the crux of our solitude. . . . The interpretation of
our reality through patterns not our own serves only to make us ever
more unknown, ever less free, ever more solitary."[23] The result is that
the dominated and marginalized are forced to inhabit multiple worlds.
W. E. B. DuBois has described this situation well: "It is particular
sensation, this double consciousness, this sense of always looking at

one's self through the eyes of others, of measuring one's soul by the tape
of a world that looks on in amused contempt and pity."[24]

This situation leads to a number of epistemological results and to an
elaboration of knowledges of the world that grow out of and express the
specific forms of oppression and exploitation experienced by each group.
While the content of these knowledges is specific to the group in
question, the similarities some scholars have pointed to between Afro-
centric and feminist epistemologies mark one instance that supports my
contention that material conditions of existence may differ profoundly
but still generate some uniformity in the epistemologies of subordinate
groups.[25] In addition, one must recognize that not all members of a
group will uniformly share an epistemology. Thus, Patricia Hill Collins
argues, despite the presence of a black women's standpoint, the material
conditions structured by social class will have effects on the perspective.[26]

As Fredric Jameson has put it: "the presupposition is that owing to its
structural situation in the social order and to the specific forms of
oppression and exploitation unique to that situation, each group lives
the world in a phenomenologically specific way that allows it to see, or
better still, that makes it unavoidable for that group to see and to know,
features of the world that remain obscure, invisible, or merely occasional
and secondary for other groups."[27]One must also recognize that these
situated knowledges are at once available to members of oppressed groups
and at the same time represent an achievement in the face of dominant
ideologies. There is a role for intellectuals in making these knowledges
clear, in explaining a group to itself, in articulating taken-for-granted
understandings. As one author put it, intellectuals can be historically
useful if they can help others become aware of who they are and can
help to reveal collective identity.[28]

The significance of experiences of marginalization and subordination
for developing knowledge and subjectivity has been described in a
number of ways. I have argued elsewhere that for Western (white)
women, the experience of life under patriarchy allows for the possibility
of developing an understanding both of the falseness and partiality of
the dominant view and a vision of reality that is deeper and more
complex than that view.[29] Several others have put forward similar
accounts of the nature of the knowledge available to the subjugated.
Thus, Sangari writes that for Third World people, the difficulty of
arriving at fact through the "historical and political distortions that so

powerfully shape and mediate it" leads them not to destroy the status of fact (as she argues postmodernist theories do), but rather to assert a different level of factuality, "a plane on which the notion of knowledge as provisional and of truth as historically circumscribed is not only necessary for understanding but can in turn be made to work from positions of engagement within the local and contemporary." Her conclusions about Márquez's marvelous realism as one response to this situation are similar to my own quite different arguments about the possibilities made available by the experiences of patriarchy in women's lives. She argues that marvelous realism operates because "if the real is historically structured to make invisible the foreign locus of power, if the real may thus be other than what is generally visible, . . . then marvelous realism tackles the problem of truth at a level that reinvents a more comprehensive mode of referentiality."[30]

Gloria Anzaldúa, writing out of the experience of a Chicana living on the Mexico-Texas border, describes a similar phenomenon in terms reminiscent of Sangari's discussion. She points not only to the experience of living in two realities and thus being forced to exist in the interface, but also to "la facultad," the capacity to see in surface phenomena the meanings of deeper realities, to see the "deep structure below the surface." And she argues, "Those who are pounced on the most have it the strongest—the females, the homosexuals of all races, the dark-skinned, the outcast, the persecuted, the marginalized, the foreign." It is a survival tactic unknowingly cultivated by those caught between the worlds, but, she adds, "it is latent in all of us."[31]

Sylvia Wynter, self described as a dark-skinned, middle-aged Caribbean woman, has made another similar argument about out shared identity as a "set of negative Ontological Others." (She includes women and minorities in opposition to "man-as-a-natural-organism.") From our systemic role, she argues, we can make potentially innovative contributions based on our liminal status as defined by our location in the social structure. As liminal subjects who experience to varying degrees the injustices of the social structures that define us, we can disenchant our fellow systemic subjects. The status of liminality gives us a "cognitive edge."[32]

The knowledges available to these multiple subjectivities have different qualities than that of the disembodied and singular subject of Western political thought. Moreover, despite the specificity of each view from below, several fundamental aspects are shared. While I cannot discuss these qualities in detail here, I will describe some of their general outlines.[33]

Most fundamentally, these are situated knowledges; that is, they are located in a particular time and space. They are therefore partial. They do not see everything from nowhere but they do see some things from somewhere. They are the knowledges of specific cultures and peoples. As an aspect of being situated, these knowledges represent a response to and an expression of a specific embodiment. The bodies of the dominated have been made to function as the marks of their oppression: we are not allowed to pretend they do not exist.

Because situated, these knowledges cannot be other than social and collective. Those of us that Euro-American masculinist thought marked as Other cannot but experience the world collectively since our stigmatized identities are formed as members of groups. As Albert Memmi so powerfully noted, we carry the "mark of the plural."[34] This profoundly affects the possibilities of perception and makes it far more difficult (though certainly not impossible) to imagine ourselves as isolated and abstract individuals.

One can describe the shape of these knowledges in still more detail by attending to the features of the social location occupied by dominated groups. These knowledges express multiple and often contradictory realities; they are not fixed but change with the changing shape of the historical conjuncture and the balance of forces. They are both critical of and vulnerable to the dominant culture, and are separated off and opposed to it, yet also contained within it. Gloria Anzaldúa's poem expresses and enacts these characteristics:

> To live in the Borderlands means
> you are at home, a stranger wherever you are
> the border disputes have been settled
> the volley of shots have shattered the truce
> you are wounded, lost in action
> fighting back, a survivor.[35]

All these characteristics mark the fact that these knowledges represent a series of achievements: they result from and express a series of ongoing efforts to keep from being made invisible, to keep from being destroyed by the dominant culture. The struggle has very high stakes—survival

itself. As Audre Lorde has put it: "we were never meant to survive; Not as human beings."[36]

In addition, the knowledge of marked subjectivities opens possibilities that may or may not be realized. To the extent that these knowledges are self-conscious about their aspects and assumptions, they make available new epistemological options. The struggles they represent and express, if made self-conscious, can go beyond efforts at survival to recognize the centrality of systematic power relations; they can become knowledges that are both accountable and engaged. As the knowledges of the dominated, they are "savvy to modes of denial" including repression, forgetting, disappearing.[37] Thus, while they recognize themselves as never fixed or fully achieved, they can claim to present a truer or more adequate account of reality. As the knowledges that recognize themselves as those of the dominated and marginalized, these self-consciously situated knowledges must focus on changing contemporary power relations and thus point beyond the present.

I must insert a caveat here. I do not contend that white Western women share the situation of either Western women or men of color or of colonized peoples. In any effort at alliance, close attention must be given to the specific situations of each group as defined by axes of gender, race, class, and sexuality. I hope to avoid the "we are all sisters in struggle" move in which the feminist subject is unmarked and therefore implicitly Western.[38] It is important to locate white feminst theory in terms both of victimhood and complicity.[39] It is certainly true that white feminist theory has made a number of moves that failed to include the situations of many women of color. These included such things as assumptions that the family is by definition patriarchal and an advocacy of female separatism.[40] Attention to the specifics of each group's situation can allow for recognition of the fact that the subordination of different groups is often obtained and maintained by different mechanisms. Aida Hurtado has pointed to the differing strategies of rejection and seduction in subordinating women of color as opposed to white women. And she points out that when white middle-class women rebel they are likely to end up in mental hospitals, as opposed to people of color, who are more likely to go to prison.[41] Lorde has made the point very clearly: "Some problems we share as women, some we do not. You fear your children will grow up to join the patriarchy and testify against you. We fear our children will be dragged from a car and shot down in the street and you will turn your backs upon the reasons they are dying."[42] As a result of these differences, one must expect the feminisms of different groups to emphasize the political issues that are most salient in that particular social location: white feminists' efforts to bring the concerns of the private sphere into public life, black feminists' emphasis on economic issues, and Chicana feminists' attention to issues of language and family illustrate the ways in which certain issues become unavoidable for some groups while they remain less salient for others.

My argument here, however, is that at the level of epistemology there are a number of similarities that can provide the basis for differing groups to understand each other and form alliances. In addition, attention to the epistemologies of situated knowledges can allow for the construction of important alternatives to the dead-end oppositions set up by postmodernism's rejection of the Enlightenment. Rather than attempt the god-trick or reject the possibility of knowledge altogether, these alternatives to Enlightenment thought recognize themselves, as well as Enlightenment and postmodernist theories, as views from somewhere. They recognize that the knowledge we claim is conditioned by the locations we occupy.

Second, rather than insist on the false dichotomy of the neutrality of reason as opposed to bias, these views from below recognize the multiple and contradictory nature of their reality. Lack of neutrality need not mean lack of knowledge; indeed, when self-conscious, these knowledges can help us recognize how doctrines of the neutrality of reason have been used to distort, deny, and erase realities other than that of the dominant group.

Third, the oppressed have experienced the murderous effects of the exclusive universalities promulgated by the West, which are predicated on the disembodied status of reason. The situated knowledges of the oppressed make no claim to the disembodied universality of reason. Because of their embodied, social, and collective nature, they can also avoid the opposite problem of a descent into a particularistic relativism.

Fourth, rather than accept the false choice of omnipotence or impotence, these knowledges can be recognized as limited and changing, as ongoing achievements of continuing struggles. Finally, as engaged knowledges, born of struggle and survival against the odds, they must give close attention to issues of power. Fear, vulnerability, struggles to survive, and thus issues of power and empowerment are at the heart of these knowledges.

Therefore, to develop an alternative account of the world requires both the changing of power relations and the development of subjectivities grounded in the experience of the dominated and marginalized. Those of us who have been constituted as sets of negative qualities need to engage in the historical, political, and theoretical process of constituting ourselves as subjects as well as objects of history, subjects who inhabit multiple, superimposed, and opposed realities. We must recognize ourselves as both makers of history and the objects and victims of those who have made history. Our nonbeing was the condition of being of the One, the center, of the taken-for-granted ability of one small segment of the population to speak for all. Our various efforts to constitute ourselves as subjects (through struggles for colonial independence, racial and sexual liberation struggles, and so forth) were fundamental to creating the preconditions for the current questioning of claims to universality.

Attention to the epistemologies contained in our various subjugated knowledges can allow us to shift the theoretical terrain in fundamental ways and to exit from the false dichotomies that define and limit both oEnlightenment thought and postmodernist efforts to reject it.

Notes

1. Aida Hurtado, "Relating to Privilege: Seduction and Rejection in the Subordination of White Women and Women of Color," Signs 14, no. 4 (Summer 1989): 833–55.

2. See, for example, Nancy Fraser and Linda Nicholson, "Social Criticism Without Philosophy," in Feminism/Postmodernism, ed. Linda J. Nicholson (New York: Routledge, 1990), 19–38.

3. I owe the phrase "god-trick" to Donna Haraway, "Situated Knowledges: The Science Question in Feminism and the Privilege of Partial Perspective," Feminist Studies 14, no. 3 (Fall 1988): 575–99.

4. This is a case made about Enlightenment epistemology. Clearly there were other worldviews extant, but this is the one that seems to have come down to us as the dominant one and the one against which postmodernists argue.

5. See Chantal Mouffe, "Radical Democracy: Modern or Postmodern," trans. Paul Holdenraber, in Universal Abandon: The Politics of Postmodernism, ed. Andrew Ross (Minneapolis: University of Minnesota Press, 1988), 31–45. See also my critique of the ways assumptions express the epistemology of the commodity in chap. 5 of my Money, Sex, and Power: Toward a Feminist Historical Materialism (New York: Longman, 1983; Boston: Northeastern University Press, 1984), 95–114.

6. Edward W. Said, Orientalism (New York: Vintage, 1978), 3.

7. I use the term "subjectivity" rather than "identity" to mark what I see as the achievement of developing a political worldview. Thus one can speak of Euro-American men of the ruling class, but to speak of subjectivity is to speak of the epistemology and account of the world that grew from this identity.

8. Mouffe, "Radical Democracy," 35.

9. I have analyzed their work on more detail in *Postmodernism and Political Change* (forthcoming) and simply summarize my conclusions here.

10. Michel Foucault, *Language, Counter-Memory, Practice: Selected Essays and Interviews*, trans. Donald Bouchard and Sherry Simon (Ithaca: Cornell University Press, 1977), 142–43.

11. In "Situated Knowledges" Donna Haraway has argued that relativism itself is another form of the god-trick.

12. Michel Foucault, "The Subject and Power," afterword to Hubert L. Dreyfus and Paul Rabinow, *Michel Foucault: Beyond Structuralism and Hermeneutics*, 2d ed., including an interview with Michel Foucault (Chicago: University of Chicago Press, 1983), 208.

13. Foucault, *Language, Counter-Memory, Practice*, 140–63.

14. Ibid., 158.

15. Paul Rabinow, ed., *The Foucault Reader* (New York: Pantheon, 1984), 4.

16. Ibid., 5. Note that he argues that one should not fight for justice since it is a notion too tied to power.

17. Marshall Berman, *All That Is Solid Melts into Air: The Experience of Modernity* (New York: Simon and Schuster, 1982), 34.

18. The phrase "situated knowledge" comes form Haraway's essay "Situated Knowledges." My analysis here is indebted to this piece. The fact that a situated knowledge represents and expresses the experience of a particular group does not rule out the possibility that other groups may choose to subscribe to it. Indeed, the dominant group actively constrains others to accept their views.

19. Kum Kum Sangari, "The Politics of the Possible," *Cultural Critique*, no. 7 (Fall 1987): 161. She makes a case similar to my own when she argues that the tenuousness of knowledge in the West is but a symptom and critique of the contemporary social and economic situation of the West (185).

20. The use of the singular is important: it indicates that there are no individual differences among members of these groups.

21. Eduardo Galeano, "In Defense of the Word: Leaving Buenos Aires, June, 1976," in *The Graywolf Annual Five: Multicultural Literacy*, ed. Rick Simonson and Scott Walker (Saint Paul, Minn.: Graywolf, 1988), 124, 114.

22. See Eduardo Galeano, *Century of the Wind* (New York: Pantheon, 1988), 14, 270.

23. Ibid., 262. Márquez's work makes similar points about incommensurable realities. He argues that ordinary people who have read *One Hundred Years of Solitude* have found no surprises, because "I'm telling them nothing that hasn't happened in their own lives" (*The Fragrance of Guava*, trans. Ann Wright [London: Verso, 1982], 36, and cited in Sangari, "The Politics of the Possible," 164). The links between female, the powerless and colonized, chastity—the unknown to be conquered—are all explored in his fiction (Sangari, "The Politics of the Possible," 169).

24. *The Souls of Black Folk* (New York: Fawcett World Library, n. d.), 16, cited in Joyce Ladner, *Tomorrow's Tomorrow* (New York: Anchor Books, 1971), 273–74.

25. See Sandra Harding, *The Science Question in Feminism* (Ithaca: Cornell University Press, 1986); and Patricia Hill Collins, "The Social Construction of Black Feminist Thought," *Signs* 14, no. 4 (Summer 1989): 745–73.

26. Collins, "Social Construction of Black Feminist Thought," 758.

27. Fredric Jameson, "History and Class Consciousness as an 'Unfinished Project,' " *Rethinking Marxism* 1, no. 1 (Spring 1988): 65.

28. Galeano, "In Defense of the Word," 116. See also Collins, "Social Construction of Black Feminist Thought," 750.

29. See my argument in chap. 10 of *Money, Sex, and Power*. I add the parenthetic "white"

in the text because that was the focus of my analysis. Collins has produced a much more nuanced account of a feminist standpoint in the context of black women's experience that shows the utility of the concept for other groups; see her "Social Construction of Black Feminist Thought."

30. Sangari, "The Politics of the Possible," 161, 163.

31. Gloria Anzaldúa, *Borderlands: The New Mestiza = La Frontera* (San Francisco: Spinsters Ink/Aunt Lute, 1987), 37–39.

32. Sylvia Wynter, "On Disenchanting Discourse: 'Minority' Literary Criticism and Beyond," *Cultural Critique*, no 7 (Fall 1987): 235–37. I should note that she argues not for the development of totalistic narratives or any narratives at all but, rather, that minority discourse must call into question the grounding premises of all the systems of the West.

33. I acknowledge my debts to several theorists. Most important is Donna Haraway, whose term "situated knowledges" I have appropriated, although I use it in slightly different ways than she has. I also found Kum Kum Sangari's article "The Politics of the Possible" most instructive. Finally, I have drawn on Fredric Jameson's essay commenting inter alia on my work: "History and Class Consciousness as an 'Unfinished Project.' " Where possible I have noted specific debts to them.

34. Albert Memmi, *The Colonizer and the Colonized* (Boston: Beacon, 1967), 85.

35. Anzaldúa, *Borderlands*, 14.

36. Audre Lorde, *Sister Outsider: Essays and Speeches* (New York: Spinsters Ink, 1982), 42.

37. See Haraway, "Situated Knowledges," on this point.

38. See Chandra Talpade Mohanty, "Under Western Eyes," *Boundary 2* 12, no. 3 and 13, no. 1 (Spring–Fall 1984): 333–58.

39. It may begin to sound as though I am replicating Foucault's move of locating oneself in a web of power relations. But I am arguing not so much for examining the "capillary " actions of power as for giving attention to location in systematic structures of domination.

40. See Deborah King, "Multiple Jeopardy, Multiple Consciousness: The Context of a Black Feminist Ideology," *Signs* 14, no. 1 (Fall 1988): 58.

41. Hurtado, "Relating to Privilege," 849.

42. Lorde, *Sister Outsider*, 131–32, and quoted in Hurtado, "Relating to Privilege," 851.

Part Two

Sex/Body

3

Sexual Inversions

Judith Butler

In honor and memory of Linda Singer

Some might say that the scandal of the first volume of Foucault's *History of Sexuality* consists in the claim that we did not always have a sex. What can such a notion mean? Foucault proposes that there was a decisive historical break between a sociopolitical regime in which sex existed as an attribute, an activity, a dimension of human life, and a more recent regime in which sex became established as an identity. This particularly modern scandal suggests that for the first time sex is not a contingent or arbitrary feature of identity but, rather, that there can be no identity without sex and that it is precisely through being sexed that we become intelligible as humans. So it is not exactly right to claim we did not always *have* a sex. Perhaps the historical scandal is that we *were* not always our sex, that sex did not always have the power to characterize and constitute identity with such thoroughgoing power. (Later there will be occasion to ask after the exclusions that condition and sustain the Foucauldian "we," but for now we will try on this "we," if only to see where it does not fit.) As Foucault points out, sex has come to characterize and unify not only biological functions and anatomical traits but sexual activities as well as a kind of psychic core that give clues to an essential, or final meaning to, identity. Not only is one one's sex, but one has sex and, in the having, is supposed to show the sex one "is" even as the sex one "is" is psychically deeper and more unfathomable than the "I" who lives it can ever know. Hence the "sex" requires and secures a set of sciences that can mediate endlessly on that pervasive indecipherability.

What conditioned the introduction into history of this notion of sex that totalizes identity? Foucault argues that during the course of the eighteenth century in Europe famines and epidemics start to disappear and that power, which had previously been governed by the need to ward off death, now becomes occupied with the production, maintenance, and regulation of life. It is in the course of this regulatory cultivation of life that the category of sex is established. Naturalized as heterosexual, it is designed to regulate and secure the reproduction of life. Having a true sex with a biological destiny and natural heterosexuality thus becomes essential to the aim of power, now understood as the disciplinary reproduction of life. Foucault characterizes early modern Europe as governed by *juridical* power. As juridical, power operates negatively to impose limits, restrictions, and prohibitions; power reacts defensively, as it were, to preserve life and social harmony over and against the threat of violence or natural death. Once the threat of death is ameliorated, as he claims it is in the eighteenth century, those juridical laws are transformed into instances of *productive* power, in which power effectively generates objects to control, in which power elaborates all sorts of objects and identities that guarantee the augmentation of regulatory scientific regimes.[1] The category of "sex" is constructed as an "object" of study and control, which assists in the elaboration and justification of productive power regimes. It is as if once the threat of death is overcome, power turns its idle attention to the construction of objects to control. Or, rather, power exerts and articulates its control through the formation and proliferation of objects that concern the continuation of life. (Later I shall briefly examine the way in which the term "power" operates in Foucault's text, its susceptibility to personification and the interrelations of the juridical and productive modalities.)

I raise two kinds of questions in this essay, one concerning the problematic history Foucault tries to tell, and why it cannot work in light of the challenge of the recent emergence of the epidemic of AIDS; and a second, subordinate here, concerning the category of sex and its suppression of sexual difference. To be sure, Foucault could not have known in 1976 when he published the first volume of *The History of Sexuality* that an epidemic would emerge within the very terms of late modern power that would call the terms of his analysis into question. "Sex" is constructed not only in the service of life or reproduction but, what might turn out to be a logical corollary, in the service of the regulation and apportionment of death. In some recent medico-juridical discursive efforts to produce sex, death is installed as a formative and essential feature of that sex. In some recent discourse, the male homosexual is figured time and again as one whose desire is somehow structured by death, either as the desire to die or as one whose desire is inherently punishable by death (Mapplethorpe); paradoxically and painfully, this has also been the case in the postmortem figuration of Foucault himself. Within the medico-juridical discourse that has emerged to manage and reproduce the epidemic of AIDS, the juridical and productive forms of power converge to effect a production of the homosexual subject as a bearer of death. This is a matrix of discursive and institutional power that adjudicates matters of life and death through the construction of homosexuality as a category of sex. Within this matrix, homosexual sex in "inverted" into death, and a death-bound desire becomes the figure for the sexual invert. One might ask here whether lesbian sexuality even qualifies as sex within hegemonic public discourse. "What is it that they do?" might be read as "Can we be sure they do anything at all?"

For the most part, I shall concentrate on the question of how Foucault's historical account of the shift in power calls now to be rewritten in light of the power/discourse regime that regulates AIDS. For Foucault, the category of "sex" emerges only on the condition that epidemics are over. So how are we now, via Foucault, to understand the elaboration of the category of sex within the very matrix of this epidemic?

Along the way, I shall ask about the adequacy of this notion of "sex" in the singular. Is it true that "sex" as a historical category can be understood apart from the sexes or a notion of sexual difference? Are notions of "male" and "female" similarly subjected to a monolithic notion of sex, or is there here an erasure of difference that precludes a Foucauldian understanding of "the sex which is not one."[2]

Life, Death, and Power

In the final section of the first volume, the "Right of Death and Power over Life," Foucault describes a cataclysmic "event" that he attributes to the eighteenth century: "nothing less than the entry of life into history."[3] What he means, it seems, is that the study and regulation of life becomes an object of historical concern; that is, that life becomes the site for the elaboration of power. Before this unprecedented "entry" of life into history, it seems that history and, more important, power were concerned with combatting death. Foucault writes:

> the pressure exerted by the biological on the historical had remained very strong for thousands of years; epidemics and famine were the two great dramatic forms of this relationship that was always dominated by the menace of death. *But through a circular process*, the economic—and primarily agricultural—development of the 19th century, and an increase in productivity and resources even more rapid than the demographic growth it encouraged, allowed a measure of relief from those profound threats: despite some renewed outbreaks, the period of great ravages from starvation and plague had come to a close before the *French Revolution*; death was ceasing to torment life so directly. But at the same time, the development of the different fields of knowledge concerned with life in general, the improvement of agricultural techniques, and the observations and measures relative to man's life and survival contributed to this relaxation: a relative control over life averted some of the imminent risks of death. (142)

There are of course several reasons to be suspicious of this kind of epoch-making narrativizing. It appears that Foucault wants to make a historical shift from a notion of politics and history that is always threatened by death, and guided by the aim of negotiating that threat, to a politics that can to some extent presume the continuation of life and, hence, direct its attention to the regulation, control, and cultivation of life. Foucault notes the Eurocentrism in his account, but it alters nothing. He writes: "it is not that life has been totally integrated into techniques that govern and administer it; it constantly escapes them. Outside the Western world, famine exists, on a greater scale than ever; and the biological risks confronting the species are perhaps greater, and certainly more serious, than before the birth of microbiology" (143). Foucault's historical account can perhaps be read only as a wishful construction: death is effectively expelled from Western modernity, cast behind it as a historical possibility, surpassed or cast outside it as a non-Western phenomenon. Can these exclusions hold? To what extent does his characterization of later modernity require and institute an exclusion of the threat of death? It seems clear that Foucault must tell a phantasmatic history in order to keep modernity and productive power free of death and full of sex. Insofar as the category of sex is elaborated within the context of productive power, a story is being told in which sex, it seems, surpasses and displaces death.

If we accept the historically problematic character of this narration, can we accept it on logical grounds? Can one even defend against death without also promoting a certain version of life? Does juridical power in this way entail productive power as its logical correlate? "Death," whether figured as prior to modernity (as that which is warded off and left behind) or as a threat within premodern nations elsewhere, must always be the death, the end, of a specific way of life; and the life to be safeguarded is always already a normatively construed way of life, not life and death pure and simple. Does it make sense, then, to reject the notion that life entered into history as death took its exit from history? On the one hand, neither one ever entered or departed, since the one can only appear as the immanent possibility of the other; on the other hand, life and death might be construed as the incessant entering and departing that characterizes any field of power. Perhaps we are referring neither to a historical shift nor to a logical shift in the formation of power. Even when power is in the business of warding off death, that can only be in the name of some specific form of life and through the insistence on the right to produce and reproduce that way of life. At this point, the distinction between juridical and productive power appears to collapse.

And yet this shift must make sense for Foucault to argue convincingly that "sex" enters history in later modernity and becomes an object that productive power formulates, regulates, and produces. When sex becomes a site of power, it becomes an object of legal and regulatory discourses; it becomes that which power in its various discourses and institutions cultivates in the image of its own normative construction. There is no "sex" to which a supervening law attends; in attending to sex, in monitoring sex, the law constructs sex, producing it as that which calls to be monitored and *is* inherently regulatable. There is a normative development to sex, laws that inhere in sex itself, and the inquiry that attends to that lawlike development postures as if it merely discovers in sex the very laws that it has itself installed at the site of sex. In this sense, the regulation of "sex" finds no sex there, external to its own regulation; regulation produces the object it comes to regulate; regulation has regulated in advance what it will only disingenuously attend to as the object of regulation. In order to exercise and elaborate its own power, a regulatory regime will generate the very object it seeks to control.

And here is the crucial point: it is not as if a regulatory regime first controls its object and then produces it or first produces it in order then to control it; there is no temporary lag between the production and the regulation of sex; they occur at once, for regulation is always generative, producing the object it claims merely to discover or to find in the social field in which it operates. Concretely, this means that we are not, as it were, (merely) discriminated against on the basis of our sex. Power is more insidious than that: either discrimination is built into the very formulation of our sex, or enfranchisement is precisely the formative and generative principle of someone else's sex. And this is why, for Foucault, sex can never be liberated from power: the formation of sex is an enactment of power. In a sense, power works on sex more deeply than we can know, not only as an external constraint or repression but as the formative principle of its intelligibility.

Here we can locate a shift or inversion at the center of power, in the very structure of power: what appears at first to be a law that imposes itself upon "sex" as a ready-made object, a juridical view of power as constraint or external control, turns out to be—all along—performing a fully different ruse of power; silently, it is already productive power, forming the very object that will be suitable for control and then, in an act that effectively disavows that production, claiming to discover that "sex" outside of power. Hence the category of "sex" will be precisely what power produces in order to have an object of control.

What this suggests, of course, is that there is no historical shift from juridical to productive power but that juridical power is a kind of dissimulated or concealed productive power from the start and that the shift, the inversion, is within power, not between two historically or logically distinct forms of power.

The category of "sex," which Foucault claims is understandable only as the result of a historical shift, is actually, as it were, produced in the midst of this shift, this very shiftiness of power that produces in advance that which it will come to subordinate. This is not a shift from a version of power as constraint or restriction to a version of power as productive but a production that is at the same time constraint, a constraining in advance of what will and will not qualify as a properly sexed being. This constraining production works through linking the category of sex with that of identity; there will be two sexes, discrete and uniform, and they will be expressed and evidenced in gender and sexuality, so that any social displays of nonidentity, discontinuity, or sexual incoherence will be punished, controlled, ostracized, reformed. Hence, by producing sex as a category of identity, that is, by defining sex as one sex or another, the discursive regulation of sex begins to take place. It is only after this procedure of definition and production has taken place that power comes to posture as that which is external to the object—"sex"—that it finds. In effect, it has already installed control in the object by defining the object as a self-identical object; its self-identity, presumed to be imma-nent to sex itself, is precisely the trace of this installation of power, a trace that is simultaneously erased, covered over, by the posturing of power as that which is external to its object.

What propels power? It cannot be human subjects, precisely because they are one of the occasions, enactments, and effects of power. It seems, for Foucault, that power seeks to augment itself within modernity just as life sought to augment itself prior to modernity. Power acts as life's proxy, as it were, taking over its function, reproducing itself always in excess of any need, luxuriating in a kind of self-elaboration that is no longer hindered by the immanent threat of death. Power thus becomes the locus of a certain displaced vitalism in Foucault; power, conceived as productive, is the form life takes when it no longer needs to guard itself against death.

Sex and Sexuality

How does this inversion from early to late modern power affect Foucault's discussion of yet another inversion, that between sex and sexuality? Within ordinary language we sometimes speak, for instance, of being a given sex, and having a certain sexuality, and we even presume for the most part that our sexuality in some way issues from that sex, is perhaps an expression of that sex, or is even partially or fully caused by that sex. Sexuality is understood to come from sex, which is to say that the biological locus of "sex" in and on the body is somehow conjured as the originating source of a sexuality that, as it were, flows out from that locus, remains inhibited within that locus, or somehow takes its bearings with respect to that locus. In any case, "sex" is understood logically and temporally to precede sexuality and to function, if not as its primary cause, then at least as its necessary precondition.

However, Foucault performs an inversion of this relation and claims that this inversion is correlated with the shift from early to late modern power. For Foucault, "it is apparent that the deployment of sexuality, with its different strategies, was what established this notion of 'sex' " (154). Sexuality is here viewed as a discursively constructed and highly regulated network of pleasures and bodily exchanges, produced through prohibitions and sanctions that quite literally give form and directionality to pleasure and sensation. As such a network or regime, sexuality does not emerge from bodies as their prior cause; sexuality takes bodies as its instrument and its object, the site at which it consolidates, networks, and extends its power. As a regulatory regime, sexuality operates primarily by investing bodies with the category of sex, that is, making bodies into the bearers of a principle of identity. To claim that bodies are one sex or the other appears at first to be a purely descriptive claim. For Foucault, however, this claim is itself a legislation and a production of bodies, a discursive demand, as it were, that bodies become produced according to principles of heterosexualizing coherence and integrity, unproblematically as either female or male. Where sex is taken as a principle of identity, it is always positioned within a field of two mutually exclusive and fully exhaustive identities; one is either male or female, never both at once, and never neither one of them. Foucault writes:

> the notion of sex brought about a fundamental reversal; it made it possible to invert the representation of the relationships of

power to sexuality, causing the latter to appear, not in its essential and positive relation to power, but as being rooted in a specific and irreducible urgency which power tries as best it can to dominate; thus the idea of "sex" made it possible to evade what gives "power" its power; it enables one to conceive power solely as law and taboo. (155)

For Foucault, sex, whether male or female, operates as a principle of identity that imposes a fiction of coherence and unity on an otherwise random or unrelated set of biological functions, sensations, pleasures. Under the regime of sex, every pleasure becomes symptomatic of "sex," and "sex" itself functions not merely as the biological ground of cause of pleasure but as that which determines its directionality, a principle of teleology or destiny, and as that repressed, psychical core that furnishes clues to the interpretation of its ultimate meaning. As a fictional imposition of uniformity, sex is "an imaginary point" and an "artificial unity," but as fictional and as artificial, the category wields enormous power.[4] Although Foucault does not quite claim it, the science of reproduction produces intelligible "sex" by imposing a compulsory heterosexuality on the description of bodies. One might claim that sex is here produced according to a heterosexual morphology.

The category of "sex" thus establishes a principle of intelligibility for human beings, which is to say that no human being can be taken to be human, can be recognized as human, unless that human being is fully and coherently marked by sex. And yet it would not capture Foucault's meaning merely to claim that there are humans who are marked by sex and thereby become intelligible. The point is stronger: to qualify as legitimately human, one must be coherently sexed. The incoherence of sex is precisely what marks off the abject and the dehumanized from the recognizably human.

Luce Irigaray would clearly take this point further and turn it against Foucault. She would, I think, argue that the only sex that qualifies as a sex is a masculine one, which is not marked as masculine but parades as the universal and thereby silently extends its dominion. To refer to a sex that is not one is to refer to a sex that cannot be designated univocally as sex but is outside identity from the start. Are we not right to ask, which sex is it that renders the figure of the human intelligible, and within such an economy, is it not the case that the feminine functions as a figure for unintelligibility? When one speaks of the "one" in language—as I do now—one makes reference to a neuter term, a purely human term. And though Foucault and Irigaray would agree that sex is a necessary precondition for human intelligibility, Foucault appears to think that any sanctioned sex will do, whereas Irigaray would argue that the only sanctioned sex is the masculine one; that is, the masculine that is reworked as a "one," a neuter, a universal. If the coherent subject is always sexed as masculine, then it is constructed through the abjection and erasure of the feminine. For Irigaray, masculine and feminine sexes are not similarly constructed as sexes or as principles of intelligible identity; in fact, she argues that the masculine sex is constructed as the only "one," and that it figures the feminine other as a reflection only of itself; within that model, then, both masculine and feminine reduce to the masculine, and the feminine, left outside this male autoerotic economy, is not even designatable within its terms or is, rather, designatable as a radically disfigured masculine projection, which is yet a different kind of erasure.[5]

This hypothetical critique from an Irigarayan perspective suggests something problematic about Foucault's constructivism. Within the terms of productive power, regulation and control work through the discursive articulation of identities. But those discursive articulations effect certain exclusions and erasures; oppression works not merely through the mechanism of regulation and production but by foreclosing the very possibility of articulation. If Foucault claims that regulation and control operate as the formative principles of identity, Irigaray in a somewhat more Derridean vein would argue that oppression works through other means as well, through the *exclusion* and *erasure* effected by any discursive formation, and that here the feminine is precisely what is erased and excluded in order for intelligible identities to be produced.[6]

Contemporary Identity in the Age of Epidemic

This is a limitation of Foucault's analysis. And yet he offers a counter-warning, I think, to those who might be tempted to treat femaleness or the feminine as an identity to be liberated. To attempt that would be to repeat the gesture of the regulatory regime, taking some aspect of "sex" and making it stand synecdochally for the entirety of the body and its psychic manifestations. Similarly, Foucault did not embrace an identity politics that might in the name of homosexuality combat the regulatory effort to produce the symptomatic homosexual or to erase the homosexual from the domain of intelligible subjects. To take identity as a rallying point for liberation would be to subject oneself at the very moment that one calls for a release from subjection. For the point is not to claim, "yes, I am fully totalized by the category of homosexuality, just as you say, but only that the meaning of that totalization will be different from the one that you attribute to me." If identity imposes a fictive coherence and consistency on the body or, better, if identity is a regulatory principle that produces bodies in conformity with that principle, then it is no more liberatory to embrace an unproblematized gay identity than it is to embrace the diagnostic category of homosexuality devised by medicojuridical regimes. The political challenge Foucault poses here is whether a resistance to the diagnostic category can be effected that does not reduplicate the very mechanism of that subjection, this time— painfully, paradoxically—under the sign of liberation. The task for Foucault is to refuse the totalizing category under either guise, which is why Foucault will not confess or "come out" in the *History of Sexuality* as a homosexual or privilege homosexuality as a site of heightened regulation. But perhaps Foucault remains significantly and politically linked to the problematic of homosexuality all the same.

Is Foucault's strategic inversion of identity perhaps a redeployment of the medicalized category of the invert? The diagnostic category "invert" presumes that someone with a given sex somehow acquired a set of sexual dispositions and desires that do not travel in the appropriate directions; sexual desire is "inverted" when it misses its aim and object and travels wrongheadedly to its opposite or when it takes itself as the object of its desire and then projects and recovers that "self" in a homosexual object. Clearly, Foucault gives us a way to laugh at this construction of the proper relation between "sex" and "sexuality," to appreciate its contingency, and to question the causal and expressive lines that are said to run from sex to sexuality. Ironically, or perhaps tactically, Foucault engages a certain activity of "inversion" here but reworks that term from a noun to a verb. His theoretical practice is, in a sense, marked by a series of inversions: in the shift to modern power, an inversion is performed; in the relation of sex and sexuality, another inversion is performed. And with respect to the category of the "invert," yet another inversion is performed, one that might be understood to stand as a strategy of refiguration according to which the various other inversions of the text can be read.[7]

The traditional invert gets its name because the aim of its desire has run off the rails of heterosexuality. According to the construction of homosexuality as narcissism, the aim has turned back against itself or exchanged its position of identification for the position of the object desired, an exchange that constitutes a kind of psychic mistake. But to locate inversion as an exchange between psychic disposition and aim, or between an identification and an object, or as a return of an aim upon itself is still to operate within the heterosexualizing norm and its teleological explanations. Foucault calls this kind of explanation into question, however, through an explanatory inversion that establishes sexuality as a regulatory regime that dissimulates itself by setting up the category of "sex" as a quasi-naturalistic fictive unity. Exposed as a fiction, the body becomes a site for unregulated pleasures, sensations, practices, convergences, and refigurations of masculine and feminine such that the naturalizing status of those terms is called radically into question.

Hence the task for Foucault is not to claim the category of invert or of homosexual and to rework that term to signify something less pathological, mistaken, or deviant. The task is to call into question the explanatory gesture that requires a true identity and, hence, mistaken one as well. If diagnostic discourse would make of Foucault an "invert," then he will invert the very logic that makes something like "inversion" possible. And he will do this by inverting the relation between sex and sexuality. This is an intensification and redoubling of inversion, one that is perhaps mobilized by the diagnosis but that has as its effect the disruption of the very vocabulary of diagnosis and cure, true and mistaken identity. This is as if to say: "Yes, an invert, but I will show you what inversion can do; I can invert and subvert the categories of identity such that you will no longer be able to call me that and know what it is you mean."

The pathologization of homosexuality was to have a future that Foucault could not have foreseen in 1976. If homosexuality is pathological from the start, then any disease that homosexuals may sometimes contract will be uneasily conflated with the disease that they already are. Foucault's effort to delineate a modern epoch and to claim a break between the era of epidemics and that of recent modernity must now become subject to an inversion, which he himself did not perform but which in a sense he taught us how to perform. Foucault claims that the epidemic is over, and yet he may well have been one of its hosts at the time he made that claim, a silent carrier who could not know the historical future that arrived to defeat his claim. Death is the limit to power, he argued, but there is something that he missed here, namely, that in the maintenance of death and of the dying, power is still at work and that death is and has its own discursive industry.

When Foucault gives his grand narrative of epidemiology, he can only be mistaken: to believe that technological advance forecloses the possibility of an age of epidemic, as Linda Singer has called the contemporary sexual regime,[8] is finally evidence of a phantasmatic projection and a vainly utopian faith. It not only presumes that technology will ward off death, or already has, but that it will preserve life (a highly questionable presumption). And it fails to account for the way in which technology is differentially deployed to save some lives and to condemn others. When we consider which technology receives federal funding, and we note that recent AIDS appropriations bills have been drastically cut, it becomes clear that inasmuch as AIDS is understood to afflict marginalized communities and is itself taken as a further token of their marginalization, technology can be precisely what is withheld from a life-preserving deployment.

On the Senate floor one hears quite specific references to AIDS as that which is somehow *casued* by gay sexual practices. Here homosexuality is itself made into a death-bearing practice, but this is hardly new. Jeff Nunokawa argues that a long-standing discursive tradition figures the male homosexual as always already dying, as one whose desire is a kind of incipient and protracted dying.[9] The discourse that attributes AIDS to homosexuality is an intensification and reconsolidation of that same tradition.

On Sunday, 21 October 1990, the *New York Times*[10] ran a memorial story on Leonard Bernstein who had recently died from lung disease. Although this appears not to be a death from AIDS or from AIDS-related complications, a journalistic effort is nevertheless made to link his death with his homosexuality and to figure his homosexuality as a death drive. The essay tacitly constructs the scene of his death as the logical consequence of a life that, even in the romantic music he liked, seemed to know that "death was always standing in the wings." It is usually friends, admirers, lovers who stand in the wings when a conductor performs, but here it is somehow death who is uneasily collapsed into the homosexual phantasm. Immediately following this statement comes another: "his compulsive smoking and other personal excesses certainly could be interpreted in classic death-wish terms. In the romantically committed mind, for every plus there must be a minus, for every blessing of love, a compensating curse." Here death is understood as a necessary compensation for homosexual desire, as the telos of male homosexuality, its genesis and its demise, the principle of its intelligibility.

In 1976 Foucault sought to disjoin the category of sex from the struggle against death; in this way he sought, it seems, to make of sex a life-affirming and perpetuating activity. Even as an effect of power, "sex" is precisely that which is said to reproduce itself, augment and intensify itself, and pervade mundane life. Foucault sought to separate sex from death by announcing the end of the era in which death reigns. But what kind of radical hopefulness would consign the constitutive power of death to an irrecoverable historical past? What promise did Foucault see in sex, and in sexuality, to overcome death, such that sex is precisely what marks the overcoming of death, the end to the struggling against it? He did not consider that the regulatory discourse on sex could itself produce death, pronounce death, even proliferate it, and that, insofar as "sex" as a category was supposed to secure reproduction and life, those instances of "sex" that are not directly reproductive might then take on the valence of death.

He warned us, wisely, that "we must not think that by saying yes to sex, one says no to power; on the contrary, one tracks along the course laid out by the general deployment of sexuality. It is the agency of sex that we must break away from."[11] And that is right, for sex does not cause AIDS. There are discursive and institutional regimes that regulate and punish sexuality, laying down tracks that will not save us, indeed, that may lead rather quickly to our demise.

One ought not to think that by saying yes to power, one says no to death, for death can be not the limit of power but its very aim.

Foucault clearly saw that death could become an aim of politics; he argued that war itself had become sublimated into politics: "the force relationships that for a long time had found expression in war, in every form of warfare, gradually became invested in the order of political power" (102). He writes in The History of Sexuality: "One might say that the ancient right to *take* life or *let* live was replaced by a power to *foster* life or *disallow* it to the point of death" (138).

When he claims that "sex is worth dying for," he means that preserving the regime of "sex" is worth dying for and that political wars are waged so that populations and their reproduction can be secured. "Wars are no longer waged in the name of sovereign who must be defended; they are waged on behalf of the existence of everyone; entire populations are mobilized for the purpose of wholesale slaughter in the name of life necessity: massacres have become vital" (137). He then adds:

> the principle underlying the tactics of battle—that one has to be capable of killing in order to go on living—has become the principle that defines the strategy of the states. But the existence in question is no longer the juridical existence of sovereignty; at stake is the biological existence of a population. If genocide is indeed the dream of modern powers, this is not because of a recent return of the ancient right to kill; it is because power is situated and exercised at the level of life, the species, the race, and the large-scale phenomena of population. (137)

It is not only that modern states have the capacity to destroy one another through nuclear arsenals but that "populations" have become the objects of war, and it is in the name of whole "populations" that ostensibly defensive wars are waged.

In a sense, Foucault knew full well that death had not ceased to be the goal of "modern" states but only that the aim of annihilation is achieved through more subtle means. In the political decisions that administer the scientific, technological, and social resources to respond to the epidemic of AIDS, the parameters of that crisis are insidiously circumscribed; the lives to be saved are insidiously demarcated from those who will be left to die; "innocent" victims are separated from those who "deserve it." But this demarcation is, of course, largely implicit; modern power "administers" life in part through the silent withdrawal of its resources. In this way politics can achieve the goal of death, can target its own population, under the very sign of the administration of life. This "inversion" of power performs the work of death under the signs of life, scientific progress, technological advance;

that is, under the signs that ostensibly promise the preservation of life. And because this kind of dissimulated killing takes place through the public, discursive production of a scientific community in competition to find a cure, working under difficult conditions, victims of economic scarcity, the question of how little is allocated and how poorly it is directed can hardly be heard. The technological aim to preserve life, then, becomes the silent sanction by which this dissimulated killing silently proceeds. We must not think that by saying yes to technology, we say no to death; there is always the question of how and for what aim that technology is produced. The deeper offense is surely to be found in the claim that it is the failure neither the government nor of science but of "sex" itself that continues this unfathomable procession of death.

Notes

1. See Michel Foucault, *The History of Sexuality*, vol. 1, *An Introduction*, trans. Robert Hurley (New York: Pantheon, 1978), 85–91. The text was originally published as: *La Volonté de Savoir* (Paris: Editions Gallimard, 1976).

2. See Luce Irigaray, *This Sex Which Is Not One*, trans. Catherine Porter with Carolyn Burke (Ithaca: Cornell University Press, 1985).

3. *History of Sexuality*, 141.

4. Foucault writes: "It is through sex—in fact an imaginary point determined by the deployment of sexuality—that each individual has to pass in order to have access to his own intelligibility (seeing that it is both the hidden aspect and the generative principle of meaning), to the whole of his body (since it is a real and threatened part of it, while symbolically constituting the whole), to his identity (since it joins the force of a drive to the singularity of a history)." Ibid., 155–56.

5. In this sense, the category of sex constitutes and regulates what will and will not be an intelligible and recognizable human existence, what will and will not be a citizen capable of rights or speech, an individual protected by law against violence or injury.

The political question for Foucault, and for those of us who read him now, is *not* whether "improperly sexed" beings should or should not be treated fairly or with justice or with tolerance. The question is whether, if improperly sexed, such a being can even be a being, a human being, a subject, one whom the law can condone or condemn. Foucault has outlined a region that is, as it were, outside of the purview of the law, one that excludes certain kinds of improperly sexed beings from the very category of the human subject. The journals of Herculine Barbin, the hermaphrodite, demonstrate the violence of the law that would legislate identity on a body that resists it; see *Herculine Barbin: Being the Recently Discovered Memoirs of a Nineteenth-Century Hermaphrodite*, ed. Michel Foucault, trans. Richard McDougall (New York: Pantheon, 1980). But Herculine is to some extent a *figure* for a sexual ambiguity or inconsistency that emerges at the site of bodies and that contests the category of subject and its univocal or self-identical "sex."

6. This gives some clues to what a deconstructive critique of Foucault might look like.

7. If sexuality takes sex as its instrument and object, then sexuality is by definition more diffuse and less uniform than the category of sex; through the category of sex, sexuality

performs a kind of self-reduction. Sexuality will always exceed sex, even as sex sets itself up as a category that accounts for sexuality *in toto* by posturing as its primary cause. In order to claim that one is a given sex, a certain radical reduction must take place; "sex" functions to describe not only certain relatively stable biological or anatomical traits but also an activity, what one does, and a state of mind or psychic disposition. The ambiguities of the term are temporarily overcome when "sex" is understood as the biological basis for a psychic disposition, which then manifests itself in a set of acts. In this sense, the category of "sex" functions to establish a fictive causality among these dimensions of bodily existence, so that to be female is to be disposed sexually in a certain way, namely, heterosexually, and to be positioned within sexual exchange such that the biological and psychic dimensions of "sex" are consummated, integrated, and demonstrated. On the one hand, the category of "sex" works to blur the distinctions among biology, psychic reality, and sexual practice, for sex is all of these things, even as it proceeds through a certain force of teleology to relate each of these terms. But once the teleology is disrupted, shown to be disruptible, then the very discreteness of terms like *biology* and *psyche* becomes contestable. For if sex proves no longer to be so encompassing as it seems, then what in biology is "sex," and what contests the univocity of that term, and where, if at all, is sex to be found in the psyche, if sex can no longer be placed within that heterosexualizing teleology? These terms become disjointed and internally destablized when a biological female is perhaps psychically disposed in nonheterosexual ways or is positioned in sexual exchanges in ways that the categories of heterosexuality cannot quite describe. Then what Foucault has called "the fictive unity of sex" is no longer secure. This disunity or disaggregation of "sex" suggests that the category only works to the extent that it describes a hyperbolic heterosexuality, a normative heterosexuality, one that, in its idealized coherence, is uninhabitable by practicing heterosexuals and as such is bound to oppress in its status as an impossible idealization. This is an idealization before which everyone is bound to fail and which of course is a failure, for clear political reasons, to be savored and safeguarded.

8. See her "Bodies—Powers—Pleasures," *differences* 1 (1989): 45–66; see also her *Erotic Welfare: Sexual Theory and Politics in the Age of Epidemic* (New York: Routledge, 1990).

9. Jeff Nunokawa, "In Memoriam and the Extinction of the Homosexual," *English Literary History*.

10. Donal Henahan, sect. H, pp. 1, 25. Later Henahan remarks that "it struck some who knew him as contradictory that the conductor who struggled to reveal himself in every performance, faithful to the great romantic tradition, nevertheless kept his private life out of the public eye. His homosexuality, never a secret in musical circles, became more overt after the death of his wife, but, perhaps, out of his concern for his carefully cultivated image, he was not eager to disillusion the straight-arrow public that had adopted him as the all-American boy of music." Here the romantic tradition of self-disclosure would appear to demand that he disclose his homosexuality, which suggests that his homosexuality is at the heart of his romanticism and, hence, his commitment to being cursed by love. The use of "straight-arrow" for straight imports the sense of "straight as an arrow," a phrase used to connote honesty. The association here suggests that to be straight is to be honest, and to be gay is to be dishonest. This links back to the question of disclosure, suggesting that the author takes Bernstein's insistence on privacy to be an act of deceit and, at the same time, that homosexuality itself, that is, the content of what is concealed, is a kind of necessary deceitfulness. This completes the moralistic circle of the story, which now constructs the homosexual as one who, by virtue of his essential deceitfulness, is cursed by his own love to death.

11. *History of Sexuality*, 157.

4

Technologies of Truth and the Function of Gender in Foucault

E. L. McCallum

The relation of Foucault's work to feminism—whether it is useful for feminists or not—goes to the heart of categories and debates central to feminist theory, particularly the category of "woman" or "women" and the issue of essentialism. Feminism has done much to change the conditions of possibility for women by making claims on behalf of "women"; in deploying this category, however, it has constituted the notions of "woman" and "women" in often problematic ways. This has been particularly evident in the debates over essentialism in the late 1970s and early 1980s, and the thinking that has emerged from reconsidering these debates in the late 1980s through the early 1990s.[1] Neither politics nor biology, neither power nor bodies, provides a simple ground for the differences encompassed under the term *gender* to be worked through; that is, elaborated, equalized, complicated.

What has emerged from the essentialism debates is a need to challenge "women" as the grounds or condition of possibility for feminism, even as we recognize—as Diana Fuss has shown[2]—the importance of this category for a political movement that has yet to achieve fully its goal of transforming gender-based relations of domination. From the essentialism debates we have learned how to talk about gender, and whether to distinguish it from sexuality. Yet while these lessons have been instructive, they are not timeless. The interpretations we have of gender and sexuality must be more than formulaic if they are to be profitable. To turn this profit, we must recognize the ways in which fundamental terms of feminist analysis are hammered out within specific cultural and historical contexts, and liable to change as other elements in those contexts change. Just as it is important to use feminist frameworks to illuminate the shortcomings and blindspots of key writers outside feminism, it is equally important to question how the historical constitution of feminism's basic categories can circumscribe our ability to draw useful conclusions from such writers. Reading Foucault provides a particularly auspicious opportunity to challenge our ways of thinking about the constitution of the fundamental concepts of gender and sexuality; his work offers a radically different paradigm for understanding sexed relations.

In many ways, Foucault's work provides a practical model for feminist studies: his interdisciplinary approach, his historical perspective, and his thematic emphasis on power relations and the contingency of our institutions echoes strategies and themes that feminists have found valuable in their work. Certainly feminists cannot ignore such an influential thinker—nor have they, as the number of feminists influenced by Foucault attests. Yet the marginality of women's concerns to Foucault's studies suggests to many that even though the forms may be similar, the content is not feminist. Indeed, the problem of the relation of Foucault and feminism echoes the question haunting feminists of earlier generations concerning the relation of Freud and feminism. Each male thinker touched on key issues for feminism, spawning a good deal of feminist thinking in response, both for and against drawing upon his ideas.

While it may seem that the issue of Foucault's relation to feminism is not any different than the long-standing question of the extent to which feminists should rely on the male masters, it is precisely the similarity of

Foucault's work to feminist work—not only in terms of form, but also content, particularly in his studies of sexuality and madness—that makes this relation particularly vexing. Like Freud, Foucault's work has provided paradigms for thinking and opened up new paths of questioning that feminists have found valuable. And as in the case of Freud, the central question bearing upon the relation of Foucault and feminism is not so much whether or not to draw upon his theory, but how. To begin to work through this relation, let us examine the text that has been most roundly criticized for failing to tackle the issues of sexual difference brought to the fore by feminism: the first volume (titled *An Introduction*) of his *History of Sexuality*.[3]

Toward the end of the first volume of *The History of Sexuality* Foucault makes an interesting move; he reverses the terms of the debate from "sex" as the real, foundational, or unconstructed category and "sexuality" as the constructed, dependent category produced by sex, to posit "sexuality" as the basic category, the "real historical formation . . . [that] gave rise to the notion of sex" (157), and "sex" as the imaginary ideal this effect seeks to evoke or express. Foucault's history of sexuality, at least in the introductory volume, becomes a map of the technology of sex, the interconnected network of its transformations, rather than a chart of the discrete series of static moments. This reversal is striking in its counterintuitiveness, challenging the very grounds of the problem of sexuality. Yet Foucault, through recourse to the formulation "technology of sex," aligns this theme of sexuality with his previous studies of power relations and their effects as networks that structure the conditions of possibility. This context deflects the counterintuitiveness of the reversal, making it seem productive rather than paradoxical. Both the counterintuitive challenge to conventional understandings of sex and sexuality and the emphasis on these categories as the rubrics used to distribute power suggest that Foucault's work would be a natural ally for feminist theory.

However, there is another important effect of Foucault's reversal: the separation of "sex" and "sexuality" from "gender." By refocusing the foundation of the debate around the reversal of the order of sex and sexuality, Foucault seems to place an inordinately narrow emphasis upon the relation of these two terms at the expense of considering any others—most notably "gender." This myopia perhaps results from the fact that Foucault is easily read, following in the mainstream of the philosophical tradition, as perceiving ontological difference to come before sexual difference, thus allowing a neutral theoretical space to emerge in which we can speak about such things as power and social formations before they are gendered. This ground of neutrality has come under interrogation by feminist thinkers who charge that such a conceptual structure marginalizes women and femininity while privileging men and masculinity under the very guise of neutrality. Foucault's history is likewise open to the charge of attempting to neuter or neutralize sex/uality insofar as it does not foreground or even bring into play differences of gender. As Naomi Schor points out in her discussion of this text, "the question of gender cannot be said to inform Foucault's project. In the *Will to Power* [sic] we are introduced to a History of Sexuality wherein the notion that through history of sexuality might be different if written by women is never entertained; a single universal history is presumed to cover both sexes, as though the History, and, more important, the Historian of sexuality himself had no sex."[4] Thus, this distinction that Foucault makes, between sex and sexuality, seems already to be limited by its failure to account for the third term, gender. Is it possible that Foucault has willfully described a sex/uality that is blind to the structure imposed by the category of gender, which feminists have so persuasively argued must be interrogated? Is it true that in this introduction Foucault is silent on the issue of gender?

Schor argues, apparently flying in the face of the prevailing feminist understanding of Foucault, that gender does matter—indeed, is central—to Foucault's history of sexuality: that is, at least, in the *second* volume. The first, as we see in the quote above, erroneously referred to as the *Will to Power* instead of the *Will to Knowledge*, cannot be saved.[5] Other feminists have not let this omission of gender stop them from finding uses for Foucault's theory. Teresa de Lauretis, for example, notes Foucault's lack of attention to gender, but she capitalizes on this lack to develop her argument through Foucault's theory.[6] In the opening of "The Technology of Gender" de Lauretis demarcates her position as parallel to Foucault's—only, where he says "sexuality" she says "gender": "A starting point may be to think of gender along the lines of Michel Foucault's theory of sexuality as a 'technology of sex'" (2). This shift, however, is more than just moving from one term to another. Agreeing with Schor, de Lauretis writes that "Foucault's theory, in fact, excludes, though it does not preclude, the consideration of gender" (3). Yet as she goes on to explore the question of gender in terms of ideology, persuasively arguing that indeed gender functions as ideology, as a representational relation among individuals and institutions, she arrives at the striking formulation that women are both within and outside of gender, and effortlessly adds, "at once within and without representation" (10).

Juxtaposing Schor and de Lauretis prompts us to ask: If a woman were to write the history of sexuality, would she not be poised on this paradoxical boundary of representation? Is the liminal position that women occupy precisely why none has opted to take on such a project in the way that Foucault does? Raising this question as we turn back to Foucault must serve not to excuse women, but rather to problematize the sexuality of the Historian of sexuality. Is it possible that he could, as it were, write "like a woman"; that is, to likewise position or find himself on this boundary? Can his *History of Sexuality*, which seems to have excluded women in the pursuit of truth (supposing, contra Nietzsche, truth were not a woman), truly be written outside of gender? These questions point to the difficulty of being either purely outside (in some neutral, agendered space) or purely inside gender (inhabiting only one side of the distinct ideal of a "man" or a "woman"), and this difficulty suggests that gender may indeed haunt Foucault's *Introduction*, albeit perhaps not in a commonly recognized form.

As de Lauretis points out, in Foucault and elsewhere, "sexuality is perceived as an attribute or property of the male," regardless of whether the male or female embodies it (14). In this sense, sexuality is indeed gendered; it occupies a specific position on one side of a binary gender matrix: male/female or masculine/feminine. A history of sexuality that fails to account for the differential relations men and women have to sexuality under a binary gender matrix would not only be incomplete; quite possibly it would sustain the problematic privilege "men" have in relation to "women." Hence, de Lauretis takes up the reconfiguration Foucault offers of sex-sexuality and turns it back upon his thought: if you want to talk about sexuality as a juncture of knowledge-power practices, you have to acknowledge explicitly the differences of gender and the way they function ideologically to structure sexualities. Revealing the contingent foundation of sexualities, as Foucault's move does, renders them much more complex than the "difference" of sexual difference, precisely because they now extend beyond the "hetero"sexual binarism that, by naturalizing and essentializing them, kept these differences in place.

I bring up de Lauretis's move at the beginning of my own attempt to work through Foucault's thinking on sexuality because hers is clearly an effort to confront the chimera of neutrality, to deal with this nonexistent gap between sexual and ontological difference without recourse to an absolutist essentialism. This nonexistent gap provides an unreal, abstractly neutralized space, without which it seems we cannot theorize, even though we can never in truth think within it. This paradox echoes the liminal position of woman de Lauretis describes in her chapter; being both within and without representation is not only the case of women, it is the case of the neutral as well. It is therefore as important to acknowledge the strategic function of the neutral as it is to recognize the strategic function of essentialism, to know that neither offers a safe refuge from paradox or contradiction.

Where de Lauretis's reading of Foucault emphasizes the risk of neutrality, Schor's foregrounds the problem of perspective. Her remark that "a single universal history is presumed to cover both sexes" indicates that Foucault's history falls short in adopting an omniscient position that fails to locate "the Historian of sexuality himself" in the text as a gendered subject. Her criticism of Foucault's gender blindness suggests that in fact a history of sexuality would be different if written by a woman, that the presumption of a universal perspective is precisely what obstructs a more complete view, one that would include women. Such a charge raises the question of the essence of sexuality; that is, what, exactly, women are and what their inclusion or exclusion means. We must know what a woman is in order to know what is the precise or essential difference that a history of sexuality written by a woman would make to a history of sexuality. How significant is that difference in light of the heterogeneity of the category of "women"?

The risk of essentialism is only part of a political strategy, but that risk remains within a binarism of women's *difference from* men. It is thus a conservative risk that does not challenge our deeper assumptions or the grounds for defining sexual difference in heterosexuality. De Lauretis, however, wants to negotiate the heterogeneity of homosexuality, as does Foucault: this desire already places her understanding of the category of "women" at odds with the traditional constructions offered by the heterosexual binary law. The desire to move outside the boundaries of the law is shared by Foucault: it is his motivating force for writing this history. Foucault's notion of sexuality is widely understood as articulating a positive or generative (rather than negative and destructive) view of power that thereby demonstrates how even the apparently constraining limits imposed upon subjects actually work to construct rather than restrict or destroy sex/uality. His notion that the bourgeoisie's seemingly repressive sexuality served in fact as a consolidation of their class position provides a good example of this view. Yet this understanding of power and its link to sexuality is only the beginning of the interpretation he provides to us.

To understand that and how Foucault brings gender into play in his theory means we must move beyond accepting his reading of sex/uality as a productive power/knowledge formation. To be sure, the hypothesis that the apparent repression of sexuality in our society is in fact a means to further produce and control it promotes a dramatic turn in our thinking about sexuality. However, if we limit ourselves to viewing the repressive hypothesis as the fulcrum of his argument, what emerges is Foucault's apparent inability or unwillingness to confront the influential structuring of gender in its historical and discursive power—exactly that fault which leaves his work unsatisfactorily incomplete for many feminists. This dissatisfaction is due to the difficulty of following Foucault to the limits of his thinking, exploring the full consequences of his theory. Indeed, the more fundamental movement of his thesis, the more politically radical and theoretically challenging aspect to this thought, is the critique of unity that permeates this introductory volume.

One manifestation of this limit is the move I opened with, the inversion of sex and sexuality that Foucault makes at the culmination of *Introduction*. There he is already trying to work from a position much like that de Lauretis ascribes to women, one both within and beyond this production-configuration of sex/sexuality/gender to demarcate the bounds and conditions under which sexuality is deployed. Because he works from such a paradoxical position, gender as we generally understand it appears to fall by the wayside. But in fact, gender is very much contained by and constructed through the deployment of sex/uality and thus is inscribed in Foucault's analysis. The juxtaposition of these feminist readings of Foucault foregrounds the ontological and rhetorical status of gender as one of the central problems in the relation of feminism and Foucault. More important, I suggest that there is a deeply challenging and provocative use of gender that Foucault puts to work, both on the level of theory and of rhetoric.

Indeed—and again this is a point de Lauretis herself raises, though she does not apply it to reading Foucault—the very being of gender is already problematized in the languages used to describe it (4). While English allows a semantic slippage (which, although a recent development, has become more and more common of late) in the term "gender" so that it may apply equally to classify grammar and people, in other languages—notably Romance—gender lacks a human sexual connotation. Whereas in English, and in the American academy, gender and sex have been not only linked but explicitly explored in that link (especially in feminist work), in French language and theory "genre" is notably separate from people or subjects while "sexe" is doubled, ambiguously referring to categories or genitals. This disparity, which is elided in translation, suggests that reading Foucault's "sex" as "gender" may not be a gross misinterpretation.

Reading this thematic confrontation between de Lauretis and Foucault, then, leads me to pose the following question: Is gender the essence of sexuality? (and would sex would be the "property" of sexuality?) It seems useful to try to think through the possibility that the essence of sexuality is not something sexual. But in what framework, following what model, could we make such a proposition? In asking about "essence"—a risky proposition indeed, as the virulence of the feminist debates around essentialism have demonstrated—I mean to provide a different ground from which to think through the relation of sex, sexuality, and gender in Foucault's work. At the same time, I use this apparently more philosophical perspective of inquiring into the "essence" of sexuality to call into question, explore, or warp the understanding of "essence"—especially as it relates to another philosophical standby, truth. This latter term becomes key in Foucault's own understanding of his work.

Without focusing at length on this term "essence," I maintain that my introduction and use of "essence" in this instance derives from Heidegger's move in "The Question Concerning Technology" where he argues that the essence of technology is that which is not technological: it is, rather, the "Gestell," the contextual framework of resources, forces, and powers (such as human agency) that enables technology to produce its effects.[7] The term is translated into English as "enframing," but a translation from Heideggerian into Foucauldian terms might render the "Gestell" as "the conditions of possibility." The essence of technology is thus what enables technology to happen—the needs it serves and the means it employs. It seems that the notion of gender likewise necessarily governs the networks of power and their effects that Foucault labels "sexuality" and "sex," even if Foucault seems to choose not to foreground this. This analogy is further reinforced through emergence of technology as a key term in both Foucault's and de Lauretis's texts: as a technology of gender in hers, as technology of sex in his. In both cases, the term "technology" serves more to demarcate a particular power/knowledge network, a framework of possible deployments, than to describe the machinations of applied science that Heidegger more likely means by technology. "Technology" has thus in these later texts become its own metaphor, a replacement that catachrestically describes what Heidegger wants to designate as the essence of technology.

This reading provides a useful model to map gender as the essence of sex/uality. In "life" or "reality," gender provides a point of identification, a cathexis for the deployment of power within and throughout the sexual sphere; it functions, then, as its own mechanism, as itself a technology in the nonenframing sense. Gender is thus doubled, but not in the way we may have first understood it as a binary division. Gender-as-technology demarcates difference, but in so doing it also organizes the very possibilities of difference, as well as the attribution of sexuality, as de Lauretis rightly points out. Thus this inextricable relation gender bears to sexuality, without itself *being* sexuality, suggests that an essential relation, if not an essence, is at stake here. By not being sexual, gender enables sexuality to come into being as such. Gender provides the "Gestell" of sexuality, the essence in the sense of providing the very conditions that make sexuality possible. If this is so, then one must conclude that any investigation into sexuality that ignores gender fails to be a persuasive or accurate one. At the same time, the possibility of performing an investigation into sexuality that ignores gender becomes significantly less likely.

Rather than agree that Foucault completely ignores gender as he seems on the surface to have done, then, we should consider that he has formulated a theory for seeing the limits of gender and opened the way to think through a response to Jacques Derrida's call for thinking a "sexual otherwise."[8] This reformulation would necessarily rattle many of our most tacitly accepted categories of thinking. In developing a reading of a different kind of gender formation in Foucault, however, one confronts the possibility that it is neither gender nor sex/uality that is Foucault's main concern in *The History of Sexuality*. As he points out in a later interview, his goal in focusing his investigation upon sexuality is a matter of writing "the political history of the production of 'truth.' "[9] "I want to follow a much finer thread: the one which has linked in our societies for so many centuries sex and the search for truth."[10] Of course, this shift from sex/uality to truth does not introduce clearer or simpler terminology or a less complicated and troublesome level of analysis. What's more, this shift seems to lead us further away from the apparent elision of gender in the text; "truth" evokes a whole philosophical discourse with pretensions to neutrality. What, then, is the significance of truth's substitution for sex/uality in Foucault? And how does it relate to gender?

At first glance, the move from sex/uality to truth provides merely another way for what Schor characterizes as "the discourse of sexual indifference/pure difference" to exercise its oppressive and phallogocentric power through neutralization.[11] Yet if we shift our attention to *what* this term "truth" means, and explore instead *how* it means, we can see this move as more than illusory neutralization. At the beginning of the interview "The End of the Monarchy of Sex," Foucault is asked by his interviewer to clarify what he means by "sex and the search for truth," the two categories whose link he claims is the focus of *The History of Sexuality*. The way Foucault frames the term truth, one might well wonder whether this truth is indeed truth at all, but rather a veiled assertion of an investigation into the question of essence, in the traditional philosophical understanding of a core of being, opposed to accident. Foucault asks:

> How is it that sexuality has been considered the privileged place where our deepest "truth" is read and expressed? For this is the essential fact: that since Christianity, Western civilization has not stopped saying, "To know who you are, know what your sexuality is about." Sex has always been the center where our "truth" of the human subject has been tied up along with the development of our species.[12]

No sooner are the terms "sexuality" and "truth" introduced in the interview than Foucault begins immediately to distance himself from them. At the same time, this "truth" seems to be configured as some sort of center or core—both by Foucault and by the traditions and discourses he is examining, albeit differently. He accepts this assumption of a "core" as the catalyst or justification for his focus on sex/uality even as he may claim to challenge how this truth has been understood or constructed in his concern for the "politics of truth" (147). Around this fulcrum of truth—Foucault never says essence in the philosophical sense, but arguably this is what is at stake in the way that truth is here construed—a different semiotic instability plays itself out through the terms that have been displaced from the center: sex and sexuality.

In this passage from the interview Foucault shifts unproblematically from "sexuality" to "sex" as if the two terms were synonymous: one is the "privileged place" for "our deepest 'truth' " and the other is "the center where our 'truth' of the human subject has been." Each of these terms is explicitly centered around truth, but again a certain reading of truth, as a (perhaps catachrestic) name for a particular kind of center of being. Foucault signals this catachresis by putting the term in scare quotes, marking its difficulty in signifying while distancing himself from it. Yet he does not refuse its invitation to situate the core of his investigation around the question of truth and sex/uality, however he might contain or note the instability of these terms. The slippage here from sexuality to sex is easily overlooked in the emphasis on truth or "truth"; it is striking nonetheless given the carefulness and attention that Foucault paid to their distinction at the close of his *Introduction*—to say nothing of the importance of their reversal for his argument. Furthermore, Foucault displaces the terms that had appeared to be the center of his project—sex and sexuality—with this other difficult and strikingly un-Foucauldian term, truth, thereby suggesting that to have read him as speaking of sex/uality was to have misread him. Such a suggestion significantly changes the stakes for our understanding of sex/uality and indeed gender in this work. I shall return to this problem after following the remarkable thread of truth in this interview.

Though Foucault claims that his goal in writing *The History of Sexuality* is the focus on truth, nonetheless this category falls further and further out of sight in the course of the interview, becoming more and more problematic. From being unproblematically asserted in Foucault's first response to the interviewer's challenge that he justify his project's scope—where truth is not even highlighted by quotes—to being captured in quotes in the citation above, to being (dis)placed at the end of the phrase "political history of the production of 'truth' " on the following page, it becomes more and more difficult for Foucault to say simply truth. Finally, there is an extended burst of discussion of "truth" on page 139 before the term recedes from the vocabulary, reemerging only when Foucault begins to reiterate points he has already staked out in this opening foray. In light of this uneven use of the term, it is all the more striking that Foucault insists that his project or problem all along has been, fundamentally, about truth (139, 147).

In two paragraphs on page 139 where "truth" peppers the page,

Foucault appears to be honing his use of the term "truth" and providing a way for us to get a handle on it. In the same stroke, he is justifying the importance of this term in both his text(s) and context. This is the one place in the interview where he comes close to explaining directly what he means or could mean by truth. Glossing the shifts in history's object, from "kings and institutions," to the economy, to behaviors and feelings, leads Foucault to announce:

> Soon they'll understand that the history of the West cannot be dissociated from the way in which "truth" is produced and inscribes its effects.
>
> We live in a society which is marching to a great extent "towards truth"—I mean a society which produces and circulates discourse which has truth as its function, passing itself off as such as thus obtaining specific powers. The establishment of "true" discourses (which are, however, incessantly changing) is one of the fundamental problems of the West. The history of "truth"—of the power proper to discourses accepted as true—has yet to be written. (139)

In this passage one can easily see how difficult it has become for Foucault to speak of truth; not only are quote marks used throughout, but he consistently pauses to clarify immediately after he invokes the term. Here too the more recognizably Foucauldian vocabulary emerges: notably, discourse ("which has truth as its function") and power. This vocabulary is linked up with "truth" as if to contain its semiosis. Each of these is configured as producing truth, and it becomes clear that without either discourse or power truth would not exist. Of course, both power and discourse, as well as their relation to each other, are central to Foucault's articulation of sexuality. Yet does this mapping of the interrelation of sexuality, power, and discourse truly clarify what's at stake in this notion of truth? Does it merely provide two options—either truth or sexuality—that are produced by power and discourse? By linking truth to discourse and power, Foucault has not brought us to a better understanding of what he has been saying all along; rather, he has produced a displacement of meaning within the term "truth." This truth is not the same as the one from a page before. At the outset of the interview "truth" was figured as being at the heart of sex/uality, the product of sex's practices of confession, prohibition, and knowledge-seeking, an object whose study is made possible by the positive analysis of sex/uality's deployment. With such an understanding of the notion of truth, Foucault can assert that he wants to write "the political history of the production of 'truth'" (139). Yet now within the space of a page, Foucault transforms "truth" into an orientation rather than an object, a function rather than a product.

Does this new permutation of truth work against how Foucault has just described his project? Not necessarily. The concern for truth that Foucault claims undergirds his project is by no means clearly either subordinated or dominant; "truth" is not revealed to be behind "sexuality" all along, as the more important or more fundamental term. Indeed the relationship between truth and sexuality in this project seems to be already intricately deconstructed rather than maintained in a static hierarchy with one term privileged over the other. We can see this in what is perhaps the most striking feature of this passage: that the word "truth" can be replaced by the word "sexuality" without much change in the meaning, as far as it describes Foucault's particular project:

> Soon they'll understand that the history of the West cannot be dissociated from the way in which "sexuality" is produced and inscribes its effects.
>
> We live in a society which is marching to a great extent "towards sexuality"—I mean a society which produces and circulates discourse which has sexuality as its function, passing itself off as such as thus obtaining specific powers. The establishment of "sexual" discourses (which are, however, incessantly changing) is one of the fundamental problems of the West. The history of "sexuality"—of the power proper to discourses accepted as sexual—has yet to be written. (139)

This ease with which the two terms can be interchanged underscores the link between sex/uality and truth as Foucault sees them, emphasizing their fundamental tie in Western thought. Foucault's project here emerges not as the writing of the history of either truth or sexuality, but more as the path-breaking means by which we can begin to think through or write the future of truth or sexuality differently. Thus, the transformation Foucault makes in the sense of "truth" in this passage parallels the transformation in *The History of Sexuality* of the sense of "sex" from gritty reality to imaginary ideal.

This imbrication of sex and truth is evident not only in the interview I have been following here, but also toward the end of *An Introduction*. At first, the description of sex seems contrary to any notion of truth: Foucault asserts that sex is what "makes it possible to evade what gives 'power' its power; it enables one to conceive power solely as law and taboo" (155). Yet it is precisely this possibility of evasion that connects "sex" to "truth" in Foucault's analysis. In the imaginary space opened up by sex, power can be distinguished from truth; it is power that conceals its traces and implementations, not truth or sex. Sex is the ideal point through which we must come to know ourselves, what enables each of us "to have access to his own intelligibility . . . to the whole of his body . . . to his identity" (155–56).

As he brings *An Introduction* to a close, Foucault looks back at the present from the future:

> Perhaps one day people will wonder at this. They will not be able to understand how a civilization so intent on developing enormous instruments of production and destruction found the time and the infinite patience to inquire so anxiously concerning the actual state of sex; people will smile perhaps when they recall that here were men—meaning ourselves—who believed that therein resided a truth every bit as precious as the one they had already demanded from the earth, the stars, and the pure forms of their thought. (158)

Clearly in Foucault's view, our understanding of sex—if not of sexuality—is bound up with profound truth. Yet Foucault's strategic move to displace "sex" with "sexuality" requires a new formulation or construction of that truth, or of the place of truth. And what holds this truth together with sex/uality? I believe that a reading of this passage brings the answer to light. The gendered way that Foucault formulates our societies' insistence on truth's intrication with sex is hardly accidental. The play of gender between the characters in this sentence is richly telling: "people will smile perhaps when they recall that here were men—meaning ourselves." By calling those of the present "men," and adding insult to injury by underscoring that that term is to be read inclusively as "meaning ourselves," Foucault may appear to be sustaining philosophy's blind spot toward women and sexual difference. In fact, however, this choice juxtaposed against the ungendered and more explicitly inclusive term "people" can be read to suggest a contrast in perspectives. The thinking that links essential truth to sex/uality is that which inhabits the binary gender framework in which men are the privileged category; this is the structure of our thought within the deployment of sexuality, and those who articulate this discourse are "men," whatever their biological gender. Outside of this deployment, insofar as one can begin to imagine what could be beyond the boundaries of sexuality and a different gender matrix, would be "people" who, living under a different power-knowledge configuration, would be able to perceive the limits of ours. Foucault's call for "bodies and pleasures" in *The History of Sexuality* to provide the "rallying point for the counterattack against the deployment of sexuality" suggests a desire to move us out of this particular relation of truth and sex/uality and into a differently-ordered power-knowledge schema, inhabited by "people" we can only begin to imagine (157).

Foucault, then, only appears not to be dealing with gender; when it crops up, as in the aforementioned passage, it does so as part of a specific strategy to move beyond or open the way for a different power and/or gender configuration. Foucault's displacement of the notion of truth as the essence of sex/uality enables us to understand how gender is the essence of sex/uality. Foucault can no more write a history of sexuality without any reference to gender than he can without reference to truth. But as we see, his history remolds our conception of truth, pushing us to read differently to detect how "truth" may operate rhetorically in the interests of power. So too, does his evacuation of the category of gender enable us to see more clearly how contingent our binary ideal constructions of gender are, how they operate rhetorically, and how these genders could be interpreted differently or multiply, as means rather than ends.

One example for understanding such a different construction of gender is Foucault's strategic but curious use of "center" in focusing his discussion of sexuality as a juncture of subject relations ordered by power-knowledge. Given the Foucauldian perspective of sex as the conjunction of power and desire in a network of relations among subjects, the notion of "centers" illuminates how a more complex or expanded notion of gender might function within Foucault's cybernetic configuration of sexuality. By focusing on a positive notion of power, rather than on a biological understanding of difference, Foucault warps gender into an interface, a liminal confrontation with power differential that may be dynamic and unstable. Thus, gender is not an identity in the static, absolute sense, but an interactive process of identification.[13] On page 98 of his *Introduction*, Foucault marks as a starting point for analysis the " 'local centers' of power-knowledge: for example the relations that obtain between penitents and confessors, to the faithful and their directors of conscience." Clearly these "centers" are not centers in a pre-structural sense: they are in fact boundaries demarcating differential power relations between subjects. The example Foucault chooses here is perhaps striking; ecclesiastical "centers" are not what we might ordinarily recognize as gendered or sexual differences, but rather purely a power difference. Yet this exemplary choice is strategic for a radical reformulation of what "gender" means once we understand the degree to which power, desire, and knowledge are thoroughly intertwined and deployed along the lines of our most intimate relations.

This notion of center is described in the next chapter as "an especially dense transfer point for relations of power: between men and women, young people and old people, parents and offspring, teachers and students, priests and laity, and administration and population" (103). This series of examples is perhaps less surprising than the previous one, but the inclusion of the ecclesiastical pair in a series of pairs more widely recognized as being at least potentially sexually charged underscores the point that a "center" is not purely a power relation, but also a gender relation, a point where the processes of truth and sex converge. Such an interpretation makes our understanding of gender much more complex— and fruitful. Foucault has arranged around this notion of "local center" a variety of different "genders," all of which maintain a binarism and a differential relation of power within a sexual context, but which are not necessarily tied to an overarching male/female structure. It is across such thresholds—"genders" in a radically different sense—that sexuality is deployed, according to Foucault's analysis.

Foucault sketches out how this threshold works within larger themes: for example, in the Victorian age, when concern over childhood sexuality emerged, the surveillance of the child became one such "local center," ringed by anxiety over class purity. Differences in the sexuality of working-class and middle- or upper-class women in the same epoch, where class status inflected biological gender to determine sexual accessibility, demonstrates the inadequacy of a binary gender division and suggests the potential complexities of a "local center" if, for instance, it should happen to focus around the Victorian home. Foucault does not rely on orthodox categories of gender (as a binary structure construed as man/woman, male/female, or masculine/feminine) to discuss the truth of/in sex because such binarisms fail to describe adequately the limits of this truth. Instead, he develops his analysis around the positive reading of power and resistance, of which arguably gender is merely one particular manifestation. This positive reading of power pushes us to see not just the binary relation of power-resistance but, more important, the triad of power, knowledge, and desire. Neither power nor resistance, however, offers refuge from plurality in the form of a reassuring binarism. Reading through his description of resistances, which follows close on the heels of his persuasive articulation about the nature of power, one begins to see how inadequately the categories of gender—as we know them in their rigid binary form—provide a path to a new understanding of power and the truth in sex/uality. Resistance, the flip side of power, its "irreducible opposite," is equally imbricated in a pluralized network of differences:

> Are there no great radical ruptures, no massive binary divisions then? Occasionally, yes. But more often one is dealing with mobile and transitory points of resistance, producing cleavages in society that shift about, fracturing unities and effecting regroupings, furrowing across individuals themselves, cutting them up and remolding them, marking off irreducible regions in them in their bodies and minds. (96)

Although Foucault is describing here the micro-mechanisms of power and resistance in an effort to complicate our assumptions about liberatory politics, this passage could just as easily describe how sexual difference functions in our society, insinuating itself not only through a singular binarism of gender but inflected by how race, class, occupation, religion, and sexual orientation differentially cut across this supposedly monolithic category. Analyzing this operation of sexual difference is at the heart of feminist theory's liberatory project in particular. Yet while feminist work as it is now constructed often relies, if only strategically, upon essentialist categories (and their breakdown), the effectiveness of this essentialism versus its risk have only recently begun to be interrogated. Gender under the rubric of identity is too limited and inadequate a category to enable us to consider fully the relation of truth and sex/uality; it restricts rather than enhances our view. Once we grasp the radical implications of Foucault's thinking, it makes perfect sense that Foucault would not bring gender as we know it into consideration as he pursues his "political history of truth." In contrast to gender, this truth fails to operate categorically, but rather exercises itself across local points of power differences.

Foucault's point in examining this imbrication of truth and sex as it is generated in our understanding of sexuality is to examine the power relations that organize sexuality and to challenge their ordering. Indeed, Foucault's extended analysis of what he calls "juridical power" in section 4, "The Deployment of Sexuality," culminates in a call for a different kind of power. Thus, no point of the power-knowledge-desire triangle is left untouched, untransformed by his analysis. "We must construct an analytics of power that no longer takes the law as a model and a code" (90). He adds, "we must at the same time conceive of sex without the law, and power without the king" (91). These perhaps paradoxical revisions follow on what feminists have been developing on their own: an analysis of local, immanent relations of power that is fully attentive to the contingencies of the context. Thus, while he situates these "local centers" of inter-individual power relations as a starting point for coming to understand the strategies within "relationships of force," Foucault is careful to point out that the larger framework of possibility—a geography of possible tactics, as it were—envelops and conditions these strategies (97). "[O]ne must conceive of the double conditioning of a strategy by the specificity of possible tactics, and of tactics by the strategic envelope that makes them work "(100). Between these two scales of interaction, we find not a rigidly microcosmic-macrocosmic relation, but one more fluidly multiple and complex.

The "local centers" provide the model for an analysis that attends to both situation and context, and that pushes our thinking about sex and sexual difference out of a binary or biological mold. They are only a manifestation of power, however, not power itself. In this same section on "Method" where he discusses "local centers," Foucault describes power as "the multiplicity of force relations immanent in the sphere in which they operate and which constitute their own organization" (92). Whereas "local centers" are a space-based metaphor for the functioning of power within a network, Foucault offers the idea of "force relationships" as not only a temporal but diachronic model for power's manifestations. According to Foucault, force relationships inherently carry with them change and multiplicity. Is this notion of "force relationships" at the core of Foucault's effort to write this history of truth? Is this "force relationship" the same as, or rather a broader version of, gender? Certainly this new relation is crucial to Foucault's attempt to demarcate the limit of juridically structured power relations and move into envisioning strategic ones. It is the touchstone of the new perspective on sex/uality and its truth, as he explains in the close of his section on "Method." Force relations are the point through which we can reconceive power relations, just as sex is the ideal through which we reinterpret desire and sexuality, and truth the catalyst through which we reinvent our relation to knowledge. Yet strikingly, Foucault finds the motivation for this shift to derive from historical momentum—not to rewrite the historical configuration of our sexual or potent circumstances, but rather to catch up with what has already inscribed. The change Foucault seems to be advocating has indeed already begun to take place. The preeminent example of this change, Foucault finds, is the shift from warfare as the site of the expression of force relationships to "the order of political power" (105).

However, this celebration of positive power, this boiling down of sex/uality to its raw truth of force relations is not entirely unproblematic. Critics—especially feminist ones—will be quick to notice a certain blindness in this formulation. If what Foucault calls force relationships are the skeletal framework for sexual relationships in our society, this interpretation significantly elides the difficult but no less very real historical struggle by and for women's participation, desire, or formulation of sexual relationships outside of force. Furthermore, there is a long and problematic history—deeply rooted in both myth and fact—behind the conceptualization of sexual relationships as force relationships; the problem of rape serves as one example to indicate how risky the call for a strategic configuration of sexual boundaries would be for those on the short end of the power stick. Foucault's call for strategic choices and tactical efficacy has a darker side to its happy polyversity: the question remains, *whose* efficacy, *whose* strategy is served? The danger is that these strategies and tactics will not go far enough, and will be co-opted by the hegemonic power structure and developed into another deployment of juridical power. The role of consent in a relationship of force remains a serious difficulty to be worked out, partly because of its problematic relation to the law. The very reason Foucault privileges the notion of relationships of force—that force remains outside the law—is the same reason feminists have to be skeptical of this privileging.

Despite the dark overtones that resonate immediately to any feminist, Foucault's metaphor of "relations of force" calls us to confront that which two decades of feminist challenges to patriarchy have worked hard to efface or change: sexuality is deeply and ineradicably rooted within differential relations of power. This includes gender as its "Gestell" or essence, without which we could not imagine sexuality. The feminist dream of equality, of equal power relations between sexes and sexual partners, is seriously challenged in this truth as Foucault writes it. How to reconstruct this dream of getting beyond or outside of an oppressive power relation without simply overturning the forces of oppression? How do we learn to accept and work with this differential power relation rather than expunge it? How to formulate a conception of liberation that will not further oppress us? These are the serious, essential, and highly productive questions that Foucault's work poses for feminists. The political problem is no longer a question of changing relations through opposition; we are past the point where categorical changes are effective. Foucault's work demonstrates that the context or framing of sex/gender relations is itself entirely bound up in power/resistance dynamics as well as the production of knowledge, discourse, and truth. The answer, it seems, is not to eliminate, but to produce more, to multiply and mutate powers and resistances.

There is no neutral, because there is no outside to relationships of force. All truth is bound up with these relationships of force, which are expressions of power and the resistance to that power. This play of power and resistance creates a boundary that is either maintained or mutated. Foucault's well-known call for "bodies and pleasures" is a strategic awareness of the way these boundaries are constituted and de-constituted within a seemingly unified field that is fundamentally divided and liminal. The traditional discourses for examining gender and truth, feminist theory and philosophy, respectively, have proffered their central terms as unary and unitary. Such coherence serves as tactical fictions that mask the deployment of power more often than it serves to reveal and disrupt that deployment. If Foucault speaks of truth—even as he effaces it—more than he speaks of gender, it may be because the latter is still too strategically effective as a unity for certain purposes. Our skepticism of the claims made possible through gender has not even begun to reach the extent of our skepticism of the claims made possible through truth; we still believe that gender is an effective political and rhetorical category, even if we have given up hope that the truth will set us free. Yet this effectiveness is limited by the same constraints that problematize liberation strategies; at bottom one remains within the same philosophical categories and (hetero)sexual matrix, rather than transforming the conditions of possibility and moving us beyond that horizon. The time for the effectiveness of the strategy of gender is coming to an end—if that end has not already arrived. The more we discern how sex/gender is enframed within the triangulation of desire-power-knowledge, the more effectively we can develop strategies to transform not only the conditions of our existence, but the possibilities for our imagination.

Notes

1. The second issue of the journal *differences* (Summer 1989), called "Another Look at Essentialism," exemplifies this return to the question.

2. Diana Fuss, *Essentially Speaking: Feminism, Nature, and Difference* (New York: Routledge, 1989).

3. Michel Foucault, *The History of Sexuality*, vol. 1, *Introduction*, trans. Robert Hurley (New York: Vintage, 1990).

4. Naomi Schor, "Dreaming Dissymmetry: Barthes, Foucault, and Sexual Difference," in *Coming to Terms: Feminism, Theory, Politics*, ed. Elizabeth Weed (New York: Routledge, 1989), 55.

5. The first volume of *The History of Sexuality* appeared in French as *La Volonté du Savoir*, or *The Will to Knowledge*.

6. Teresa de Lauretis, "The Technology of Gender," in her *Technologies of Gender: Essays on Theory, Film, and Fiction* (Bloomington: Indiana University Press, 1987).

7. Martin Heidegger, "The Question Concerning Technology," in *The Question Concerning Technology and Other Essays*, trans. William Lovitt (New York: Garland, 1977).

8. Jacques Derrida, "Choreographies. Interview with Christie V. McDonald," *Diacritics* 12 (1982): 76.

9. Michel Foucault, "The End of the Monarchy of Sex," trans. Dudley M. Marchi, in *Foucault Live: Interviews, 1966–84*, ed. Sylvère Lotringer (New York: Semiotext[e], 1989), 139.

10. Ibid., 137.

11. Schor, "Dreaming Dissymmetry," 57.

12. Foucault, "The End of the Monarchy of Sex," 137–38.

13. Judith Butler's work in both *Gender Trouble: Feminism and the Subversion of Identity* (New York: Routledge, 1990) and *Bodies That Matter: On the Discursive Limits of "Sex"* (New York: Routledge, 1993) explores some of the consequences of this line of thinking. Combining both Nietzschean and Foucauldian threads, for example, she writes in the introduction to *Bodies* that "the matrix of gender relations is prior to the emergence of the 'human' "; just as there is no "I" before grammar, there is no "I" that comes before or after the process of gendering (7). This position reformulates identity as a process not a product—indeed, even materiality (and in particular the body), which may seem to be the best guarantor of a fixed point of reference, is shown to be a process that stabilizes rather than a static given.

5

Dangerous Pleasures: Foucault and the Politics of Pedophilia

Linda Martín Alcoff

> The use of the word ["sexuality"] was established in connection with other phenomena: the development of diverse fields of knowledge . . . ; the establishment of a set of rules and norms . . . ; and changes in the way individuals were led to assign meaning and value to their conduct, their duties, their pleasures, their feelings and sensations, their dreams.
>
> —Foucault, *Use of Pleasure*

In a post-Foucauldian academic world, most of the traditional theoretical grounds for evaluating sexual practices are no longer viable. If we accept Foucault's account of the discursive constitution of sexuality, his counterargument to the thesis that "sex constitutes our innermost truth," and his reconfiguration of the relationship between domination and discourse, then we are forced to question many standard theoretical and methodological approaches to the study and evaluation of the politics of sexual practices.[1] Foucault argues compellingly against the assumption that bringing sexual activity into discourse and studying it "scientifically" will stay the hand of prejudice and liberate sexual desire. He argues against any general presumption about the liberatory nature of discourse and the law, or the belief that theoretical and legal discourses will reveal injustice and champion the needs of victims. Given his critique of the way even liberatory discourses impose order through constructing norms of identity and practice, one may wonder whether Foucault would reject *any* project to develop a normative account of sexual practices.

For theorists who work on issues of sexual violence, Foucault's arguments challenge us to reassess our previous framing of sexual issues, including sexual violence. The notion that the sexual aggressor is pathological or has a personality disorder hearkens back to a pre-Foucauldian reliance on a discourse of essential identity. And on the basis of the view quoted from Foucault above—that the meaning of sexual experience is discursively constructed—theorists such as Gayle Rubin have argued that in our culture, "sexual acts are burdened with an excess of significance."[2] Following this logic, we might wonder whether the labeling of some acts as sexual violence or sexual abuse is produced by just such an "excess of significance."

Now on the one hand, it may seem that Foucault could not countenance such a concept as "excess of significance"; it implies that there exists a norm of significance that has been exceeded. And his work consistently declines to prescribe or vindicate, preferring instead to suggest new questions rather than answer old ones. On the other hand, there are places in which Foucault would seem to agree with Rubin. For example, although Foucault never sanctioned coercive acts against children, he rejected the view that sexual relations between adults and children are always harmful for the children involved. He argued against legal interventions in such relations, and against the consensus position held by psychiatric institutions that such relations, in whatever form they take, inevitably produce trauma for children and indicate pathological problems in the adult. In one passage in volume 1 (*An Introduction*) of his *History of Sexuality*, Foucault relates an incident in nineteenth-century France in which a farmhand sexually molested a small child and was brought before the legal and medical experts for analysis. For Foucault, the principal significance of this event was:

> The pettiness of it all; the fact that this everyday occurrence in the life of village sexuality, these inconsequential bucolic pleasures, could become, from a certain time, the object not only of a collective intolerance but of a judicial action, a medical intervention, a careful clinical examination, and an entire theo-

retical elaboration. . . . So it was that our society . . . assembled around these timeless gestures, these barely furtive pleasures between simple-minded adults and alert children, a whole machinery for speechifying, analyzing, and investigating.[3]

For many of his feminist readers, Foucault's insightful work in uncovering new mechanisms of domination appears painfully at odds with his stated positions on sexual relations between adults and children, in which he renders such relations "inconsequential" and "petty," and presents the children involved as simply "alert" or "precocious." How can we make sense of such positions given his general work? Is there a conflict between his critique of domination and his analysis of sexuality? What are the implications of his declaration that "sexuality" does not exist for an account of sexual violence? *Has* our culture attributed an excessive significance to sex with children?

In this essay I shall explore Foucault's position on sexual relations between adults and children and try to make sense of it in the context of his other relevant theoretical work. While agreeing with a significant part of Foucault's account of sexuality in its relationship to discourse and the law, I shall also challenge Foucault's position on pedophilia but seek a post-Foucauldian or Foucauldian-informed manner in which to analyze sexual relations between adults and children. The goal of this essay, therefore, is not simply to charge Foucault with an incorrect, politically dangerous position on adult-child sex, but to explain the connection between his position on pedophilia with his larger account of sexuality and to attempt to use Foucault's own insights about the relationships between discourse, power, and pleasure to advance our theoretical analysis and evaluation of these sexual practices.

Foucault on Pedophilia

Every morality, in the broad sense, comprises codes of behavior and
forms of subjectivation.
—Foucault, *Use of Pleasure*

We have two principal sources through which to hear Foucault's views on this topic. One is the striking (but ignored) passage already cited, the "village simpleton" story. The other is a transcript from an interview conducted on the topic with Foucault, Guy Hocquenghem, and Jean Danet, broadcast by France-Culture in 1978. In this section I shall analyze both these texts and explore how the positions they articulate could emerge out of Foucault's work. In the next section, I shall consider an essay by Gayle Rubin that represents, I believe, her version of an "applied Foucault"; that is, an application of Foucault's views toward the development of a radical politics of sexual diversity.

The interview with Foucault, Hocquenghem, and Danet has been published under the title "La Loi de la Pudeur" and also as "Sexual Morality and the Law."[4] The topic of the interview was the question of legal jurisdiction over sexual practices between adults and children or youths, and the panelists' support of a petition campaign in France against several specific laws that criminalized acts between adults and children "below the age of fifteen" (Guy Hocquenghem, *PPC*, 273). Since all three panel participants were in major accord on this issue, I shall discuss the text in full rather than only Foucault's contributions to it, though I will indicate the specific author of each passage quoted.

Foucault's interest and concern with this issue resulted from his critique of the relationship between the institutions of psychiatry and psychology on the one hand and the law on the other. The former institutions, acting in their capacity as expert discourses, have been implicated in the negotiation of relations of power between the state, the law, and the individual, usually (or in his view, perhaps always) with the effect of increasing and consolidating structures of domination. One of the principal examples of this is the construction of criminal identities, in which juridical procedures take as their object of evaluation not the crime but the criminal. The goal becomes to understand, categorize, and, where possible, reform the "criminal mind." It is Foucault's argument that highly contentious species of subjectivity are theoretically and in some cases experientially constituted in this way. Foucault's concern is thus with the unchallenged and increasing hegemony of both psychological discourses and practices and the law via their mutual association on the topic of pedophilia.

Foucault is very much troubled by the view that sexuality is "the business of the law" (*PPC*, 271) for two reasons. The first is that the law has instituted outrageous repressive maneuvers against homosexuality and something it calls "sodomy" through a contrived association with pedophilia and through its presumption to judge and intervene in the sexual practices of its citizens, as well as through a widespread and officially sanctioned heterosexism and homophobia. Second, Foucault is concerned about the fact that the law presumes to make judgments, not of practices or acts, but of individuals, based on so-called objective facts about how individuals can and should be categorized. Foucault uses the Jouy case to suggest that the designation "pedophile" was historically the paradigm category of "dangerous individuals." Pedophilia has thus played a key role in justifying the view that sexuality is the "business of the law." Moreover, Foucault argues that children have their own sexuality over which historically the law has imposed an absolute repression. And finally, Foucault finds incredible the psychiatric establishment's claim to "know" the "nature" of childhood sexuality. He therefore suggests that we reject their assertion that childhood sexuality "is a territory with its own geography that the adult must not enter" or that "the child must be protected from his own desires, even when his desires orientate him towards an adult" (PPC, 276).

The general position of the panelists is, then, to call into question the paternalism adopted by the law and psychiatry over children's sexuality. A key aspect of this paternalism involves the refusal to accept the possibility that a child may authentically consent to sex with adults. The panelists point to the fact that children may not have the ability to articulate what they are feeling or wanting, and when they are unable to formulate their own desires the courts unfailingly presume to speak for them. Foucault characterizes this as the imposition of hegemonic discourses on the subjugated discourse of the child. Demanding that the child be able to articulate her or his consent involves bringing sex "into discourse," which will entail bringing it into the dominant discourse and subjecting it to the dominant discourse's codes of normality. The concept of consent itself implies that sex is a contractual relationship, a view that the panelists find absurd. Children cannot always articulate their desires in a form that can be represented as legal consent, and even when they can the authorities interpret their consent as an inauthentic or otherwise unreliable expression. In contrast to this form of discursive paternalism and control, the panelists accept the authenticity of children's stated consent, and they advocate listening to the children themselves without assuming that we can know their "true" desires. But the panelists also express reservations about the use of consent as a criterion of judgment in these cases because it may be difficult for a child to articulate his or her own desire and because the consensual/contractual model is unsuitable for sexual relations.

The members of the panel were careful to distinguish their views on this topic from the issue of (adult) rape, although they bemoan the fact that feminists' agitation around rape has reinforced the power of the state over sexuality. Foucault expressed the concern that "sexuality will become a threat in all social relations" (PPC, 281); that is, that sex will always be seen as a potential danger, which will then authorize the state to constitute "dangerous individuals" and "vulnerable populations" and to enforce massive policies of oversight and intervention. The result will be, in Foucault's words, "a new regime for the supervision of sexuality" (PPC, 281), or a new totalitarianism. In order to avert this result, sexual practices, in whatever form they take, should not be within the punitive jurisdiction of the state. As Hocquenghem warned, "The constitution of this type of criminal [the "pedophile"], the constitution of this individual perverse enough to do a thing that hitherto had always been done without anybody thinking it right to stick his nose into it, is an extremely grave step from a political point of view."[5]

In the above I reconstituted in summary form the panel's general argument in its most persuasive light. But there are some other passages in the interview that, perhaps, reveal more about the panelists' views (and desires) than the above thematic synopsis, though the last statement quoted suggests that their primary motivation may not be the protection of children from unfair discursive and sexual subordination. For example, an important recurring theme is the deflation of adult-child sex itself as an event of any significance. In the panelists' view, dominant society has inflated these acts far beyond their true significance (as is suggested by Hocquenghem's point that these are things that "had always been done"), but now adult-child sex is being sensationalized by authoritative institutions for their own opportunistic reasons. At another point in the discussion Hocquenghem derided the emphasis put on child pornography as a priority for political action over other issues such as racist violence, clearly rejecting the view that such issues have equal importance. Danet also takes issue with the current hierarchy of heinous crimes: "A lawyer will be quite happy to defend someone accused of murdering ten old ladies. That doesn't bother him in the least. But to defend someone who has touched some kid's cock for a second, that's a real problem" (PPC, 279). Danet's point is that it is very difficult to get good legal defense for those accused of pedophilia, but his ironic phrasing and his reference to "some kid" indicates the almost laughable insignificance he accords to sex acts between adults and children.

Foucault's use of terms such as "petty," "inconsequential," and "everyday," in reference to the farmhand incident demonstrates a similar desire to deflate the importance of these acts. In their view, sexual acts of any type between adults and children or youths have been invested with inordinate meaning and "fabricated" as a crime, when in reality it "is quite simply the erotic or sensual relationship between a child and an adult" (Hocquenghem, *PPC*, 277). Thus sometimes, though not always, such sexual relations have nothing criminal or harmful about them, and those accused of pedophilia have been unfairly hounded and vilified by vigilante mobs as well as state functionaries in a manner disproportionate to their crimes, if indeed any crime occurred at all.

Despite the problems they have with applying the notion of consent to sexual practices, the panelists rely on just such a notion in their argument that not all sexual relations between adults and children are violent or exploitative. Foucault says that we must "listen to children" and that "the child may be trusted to say whether or not he was subjected to violence" (*PPC*, 284). The way Hocquenghem puts it is more ambiguous:

> When we say that children are "consenting" in these cases, all we intend to say is this: in any case, there was no violence, or organized manipulation in order to gain affective or erotic relations. . . . The public affirmation of consents to such acts is extremely difficult, as we know. Everybody—judges, doctors, the defendant—knows that the child was consenting, but nobody says anything, because, apart from anything else, there's no way it can be introduced. It's not the effect of the prohibition by law: it's really impossible to express a very complete relationship between a child and an adult—a relation that is progressive, long, goes through all kinds of stages, which are not all exclusively sexual, through all kinds of affective contacts. To express this in terms of legal consent is an absurdity. In any case, if one listens to what a child says and if he says "I didn't mind," that doesn't have the legal value of a consent. (*PPC*, 285)

This passage is telling on a number of counts. Hocquenghem evidently holds the position that a "very complete" relationship between a child and an adult will include sexual relations. On the one hand, he points out rightly that consent should indicate the absence not only of violence but also of organized manipulation, but on the other hand, his articulation of the "authentic" consent is not at all reassuring. When does one use the phrase "I didn't mind"? When someone is *doing something to me*, without my participation. This hardly sounds like an expression of spontaneous desire on the child's part, or the description of a reciprocal relationship. It sounds much more like the child is willing to put up with something the adult wants to do.

We can next turn to take a closer look at the passage in *An Introduction* in which Foucault introduces a case of what would now be commonly called child molesting as an illustration of his thesis about the connection between discourse and sexuality. Contra the repressive hypothesis, which holds that sexuality has been repressed in Victorian discourse, Foucault argues, convincingly, that in the last two centuries sexuality has been less repressed than produced and managed, and that the primary mechanism for this has been precisely bringing sexual practices into the realm of discourse. Behaviors that had heretofore received scant attention came to be extracted orally in the confessional, analyzed in detail, painstakingly related in autobiographical form, and articulated into "expert discourses" in the human sciences. And the sexuality of children came into view as a "problem" of increasing importance within a context organized around the control of populations and the production of docile bodies. Children's masturbation was subjected to parental, religious, and scientific observation and monitoring, and a host of discourses were developed to analyze, explain, and provide "solutions" to the problem.

It was in connection to this development that sexual relations between adults and children, Foucault intimates, became the subject of scrutiny as well as punitive judgments. The change was clearly evident by 1867, where a "simple-minded" farmhand was turned in to the authorities after having

> obtained a few caresses from a little girl, just as he had done before and seen done by the village urchins round about him; for, at the edge of the wood, or in the ditch by the road leading to Saint-Nicolas, they would play the familiar game called "curdled milk." . . . [and] this village half-wit . . . would give a few pennies to the little girls for favors the older ones refused him.[6]

But this time, Foucault relates, the familiar, ordinary incident in the life of the village, the "everyday occurrence [of] inconsequential bucolic pleasures" became the subject of judicial and medical intervention. The farm hand was subjected to detailed, invasive questioning about his "thoughts, inclinations, habits, sensations, and opinions" (31). The "experts" inspected his anatomy to the point of studying his "facial bone structure" and measuring his "brainpan" for signs of "degenerescence" (31). In the end, he was shut away at a hospital.

Foucault's object in discussing this case is to mark that moment in the history of sexuality in which sex is brought under the jurisdiction of expert discourses in the human sciences. But his goal is not merely to develop a more accurate history of the West: he wants to defamiliarize his readers to this alignment between sexual practices and the will to truth. Thus his use of this particular case is intended to suggest that the medical and legal responses were odd and inappropriate; that is, that they exceeded the significance of the event. Given the disparate juxtaposition between the insignificance of the event itself and the portentous response it received from the authorities, what he refers to as the overlay of an "everyday bit of theatre with their solemn discourse" (32), Foucault's implication is that the responses were involved in discursive structures of domination. This argumentative strategy is also evident in the full passage that was partly quoted earlier:

> So it was that our society—and it was doubtless the first in history to take such measures—assembled around these timeless gestures, these barely furtive pleasures between simple-minded adults and alert children, a whole machinery for speechifying, analyzing, and investigating. (32)

Foucault relates with irony the fact that the farmhand's name was Jouy, a word that resonates in French with the verb "jouir" meaning to enjoy, delight in, and to have an orgasm. This suggests the fact that, for Foucault, before the intervention of the authorities the principal meaning of this event was pleasure.

Foucault clearly wants to disrupt any easy assurance that we "know" the true meaning of this event or the quality of its felt experience for the participants. Yet his construction of this narrative paradoxically works to replicate without critical reflection most of our own culture's presumptions (in his term, its "historical a priori") about such sexual practices. Foucault's narrative encourages the view that they are primarily committed by adults whom he unfeelingly characterizes as "half-wits," and thus that adults who engage in these acts are motivated by sexual needs, being incapable of achieving sexual satisfaction with their peers. And by characterizing the children who participate in these acts as especially "alert" and "precocious," Foucault reinforces the common view that these children take an active and willing role, uncoerced, and may even be seductive.[7] It hardly need be said that Foucault lacked sufficient evidence to warrant his claims about the girl's participation in or feelings about the event. His quickness to assume such knowledge manifests unfortunately typical male and adult patterns of epistemic arrogance. If such relations were reciprocally desired and pleasurable for both parties, why did there need to be an exchange of a "few pennies" to ensure the girl's participation? Whose point of view is silently assumed when one determines that the prostituting of small girls is a petty and trivial event? For whom are such "bucolic" pleasures inconsequential? Thus, here we have an apparent contradiction: Foucault seeks to problematize and de-essentialize sexuality and sexual experience; yet the rhetorical strategy he uses to subvert standard assumptions simply invokes an alternative set, arguably more patriarchal than the first.

The point of view Foucault adopts in the Jouy example is one curiously at odds with his principal thesis in An Introduction. It is a picture in which pleasure stands on one side, in almost pure form, innocent and harmless, and on the other side stands discourse, power, and domination. On the basis of such a picture we are led through the analysis to posit pleasure as antithetical to power, even as exempt from its discursive constitutions and machinations. But in other places in this book Foucault takes pains to reveal precisely the way in which power effects its domination not simply or primarily through the repression of pleasures or through negation, but through productive maneuvers (which include the production of pleasure itself). This is what prompts Judith Butler to say in her commentary on this book that for Foucault, "If the repressive law constitutes the desire it is meant to control, then it makes no sense to appeal to that constituted desire as the emancipatory opposite of repression."[8] Yet clearly he is doing so in this passage.

This apparent inconsistency begins to recede once we realize that, for Foucault, pleasure is a force that can be taken up, used, incited, fomented, and manipulated, but is not itself discursively constituted.

Foucault's concern is with the relationship among pleasure, discourse, and power, and the way in which pleasures can get used and taken up by institutional discourses and aligned with power/knowledges. Thus, he is concerned about the way in which various sexual pleasures get categorized and correlated to specified personality profiles and identities that can then be managed and disciplined. And he is also concerned with the way in which institutional discourses and disciplinary regimes are proliferated, disseminated, and consolidated through their complicated relationships with pleasure. The model of opportunism I alluded to earlier is strictly speaking inaccurate, as Foucault attributes no conscious strategy of self-maximization to discourses; still, the streams of circulating discourse are made wider and stronger to the extent they can merge with streams of pleasure. The intersection between knowledges and pleasures occurs through such codifications as "the pedophile." To the extent that the pedophile can be characterized as an ever-present threat, a "dangerous individual," detectable only through the expert analysis of "signs" by recognized authorities, the discursive focus on the pleasures of the pedophile serve to enlarge the scope of institutional discourses.

There are also ways in which such discourses not only take up preexisting pleasures, but create the structural arrangements necessary for new pleasures to be formed, such as the pleasure the priest or therapist enjoys through the process of extracting a confession that details some sexual practice, or the pleasure the general public can now enjoy in reading about sexuality, whether in "objective" studies, autobiographical narratives, or "how-to" manuals. But in all of these analyses pleasure itself remains, in an important sense, untouched. Foucault does not engage in, and in fact argues against, the practice of doing a political and/or moral evaluation of various forms of pleasure. He never condemns the priest, for example, for achieving pleasure through a practice that involves the humiliation and shaming of the penitent, but simply shows the role that voyeuristic sadism plays in the construction of various discursive arrangements and distributions of power. Like Marx, for whom everything was included in the realm of the dialectical movement of history except for the "natural" heterosexual relations regarding childbirth and childcare, Foucault demonstrates a similar blindspot by exempting his own favored entity from his theory of discursive constitution and flux: pleasure. Pleasures are vulnerable to social shifts in the sense that different discourses and different societies allow for differing arrangements between bodies, or what he refers to in

An Introduction as "a different economy of bodies and pleasures" (159). But the variability in the distributions of bodies and pleasures is not the same as their constitution by a discourse. Intriguingly, then, *The History of Sexuality* ends up naturalizing pleasure, as outside the domain of the discursively constituted ontological realm and as an inappropriate subject for social and political evaluation as well as sanction by the state or any legislative body. It is for this reason that Foucault can end the book declaring that "the rallying point for the counterattack against the deployment of sexuality ought not to be sex-desire, but bodies and pleasures" (157).

Butler grapples with this problem in Foucault as well in relationship to his account of discourse and desire. She initially reads him as holding that there is no desire outside of discourse, which is the apparent theme of this volume. But she also finds a moment of contradiction in his account. Foucault posits, according to Butler, a more fundamental form of desire that exists below discourse, prior to history, and reminiscent of the basic life-affirming energy found in both Hegel's mythology of the lord and bondsman and in Nietzsche's positive variation on Schopenhauer's will-to-power. This "productive desire seems less an historically *determined* than a historically *occasioned* desire which, in its origins, is an ontological invariant of human life."[9] This would seem to solve our puzzle, if it allows for a level of desire/pleasure free from discursive construction that can then indeed stand as the innocent other to power. But can it allow for this? I would say it cannot if Butler is right (as I think she is) that for Foucault all desire is historically occasioned. Desires and pleasures are not identical, but they are connected, and if there is no desire that is not historically occasioned, then there can be no pleasure innocent of history, where history especially for Foucault is the very site of the movements and developments of discursive regimes. But if this is the case, then how can any pleasure, such as the pleasure of Jouy, exist on the other side of power/knowledge, apart from or prior to the structured relations between discourses and power? And how can Foucault end with a rallying cry for bodies and pleasures presented as if in contrast to the discursive deployment of desire?

My argument is, then, that, despite appearances to the contrary, Foucault in fact does not hold that pleasure is ontologically constituted by discourse and exists in intrinsic and not only extrinsic relationship to structures such as patriarchy. Such a view would have allowed him to consider the ways in which certain pleasures are not merely redistributed but produced, such as the pleasure of violating, the pleasure of harming, and the pleasure in vastly unequal and nonreciprocal sexual relations. And most important, it would also work against the possibility that pleasure, in all its various forms, could serve as the haven or bulwark against the mechanisms of dominant power/knowledges. If pleasure is itself the product of discursive constitution, it cannot play the role of innocent outsider. It is because Foucault sees pleasure as playing this latter role that he repudiates the view that pleasures can and should be open to political and moral evaluation and assessment. Foucault argues that this would simply increase the hegemony of dominant discourses to intervene in minute practices of everyday life, which in his view is the principal feature of contemporary domination.

But here we have a true note of discord between conflicting tendencies in his own work: on the one hand, the uncovering of the machinations of power at work in the multiple sites of "personal life"; on the other, the fear of striking a judgmental pose with respect to individual practice in any form. Despite the significant dangers of the latter, given that we live in a period of more efficient social discipline than perhaps the West has ever experienced, I would argue that a feminist Foucauldian cannot afford to repeat Foucault's own disenabling ambivalence. If we are persuaded by his (and others') account of domination in "everyday life," we must risk putting forward our judgments about when and where it occurs. It is a mistake to think that putting forward such judgments will necessarily result in an overall increase in repression: the repression of adult-child sex may effect a decrease in the constraints by which children's own sexual energies are policed, managed, and deflected.

There is no necessary contradiction between a view that takes seriously the connection among discourse, power, and sexuality, and a politics of sexuality that repudiates various sexual pleasures. Why does Foucault presume such a conflict? Most likely because he has seen such a discourse of repudiation itself integrated within the currently dominant discourses of power/knowledge. Certainly, too, his concern with the strategies by which homosexual practices have been condemned is evident here, though the connection between homosexuality and pedophilia is again discursively constituted rather than "natural." A further reason, as I have suggested, is that pleasure figures too innocently in Foucault's own discourse, connected to power only in what might be called extrinsic rather than intrinsic ways. Thus, my reading of Foucault suggests that his position on pedophilia results from his conflict about evaluative judgments, his overriding concern with the persecutions inflicted by the currently dominant discourses of sexuality, and from his assumption that, when disinvested of its relation to discourse, pleasure is necessarily resistant to domination. This account of pleasure as an intrinsic good is what drives the sexual politics developed by Gayle Rubin.

Rubin's "Applied" Foucault

Like communists and homosexuals of the 1950's, boy-lovers are so stigmatized that it is difficult to find defenders of their civil liberties, let alone for their erotic orientation. . . . In twenty years or so, it will be much easier to show that these men have been the victims of a savage and undeserved witchhunt.

—Gayle Rubin, "Thinking Sex"

In her powerful and influential essay, "Thinking Sex: Notes for a Radical Theory of the Politics of Sexuality," Rubin develops and extends Foucault's insights about the disciplining of erotic life to develop a new politics of sexual practices. Rubin's interpretation of Foucault is not above contention, but her use of Foucault to develop a "descriptive and conceptual framework for thinking about sex and its politics" is suggestive of the kind of practical, applicable politics on contemporary issues that at least one influential reading of Foucault can engender (275).

Rubin uses Foucault's analyses of the nonessentialist status of sexuality, the fictional character of sexual identities, and the role sexuality has played both discursively and nondiscursively in the consolidation of dominating structures, to advance what she calls a "radical thought about sex" (274). She starts by giving an overview of the contemporary crusade against sexual diversity and shows how this "anti-sex backlash" is connected to a hierarchical categorization of sexual acts and sexual identities (which themselves imply essentialist understandings of sexuality) and to a Christian-inspired assumption that sex is "negative"; that is, guilty until proved innocent.[10] She details the chilling degree of persecution inflicted on what she calls "erotic minorities" and makes an analogy between such "systems of sexual judgement" (282) and racism and anti-Semitism. She convincingly argues that the acceptance of an excessively narrow, officially sanctioned form of sexual activity and the condemnation of all other possible variations "rationalize[s] the well-being of the sexually privileged and the adversity of the sexual rabble" and manifests one of the major forms of unacknowledged oppression existent in our society (280).

Her counterargument is more problematic. She argues for a "pluralistic sexual ethics" that borrows the concept of "benign variation" from evolutionary biology. But for evolutionary biology, of course, variation is not only neutral, it is necessary. Thus in Rubin's view variation is inherently morally positive (as implied in the very term "benign"). Moreover, in her evocation of evolutionary arguments to theorize the diversity of sexual practices, Rubin resuscitates a naturalistic account of sexuality once again, repeating Foucault's own tendencies (283). The implication of the argument is that evaluative analyses and moral hierarchies are no more appropriate for sexual practices than for plant diversity. The only appropriate value system is the one she borrows again from evolutionary biology, in which more and different is inherently better, and freedom equals variety and proliferation. Her account succeeds in effacing the role of power in constructing and proliferating all social relations including sexual practices; thus she ends by endorsing a form of moral relativism, or perhaps moral equivalency, in which power disappears from the frame.

Such a position would be obviously implausible when applied to sexual violence, but Rubin stipulates that her account does not apply to "sexual coercion, sexual assault, or rape" though it does apply to "the 'status' offenses such as statutory rape" as well as to what she calls consensual adult-child sex (288). Thus, her benign variations are meant to exclude acts of coercion and violence. And though she neglects to theorize such acts, her proposal for a "democratic morality" evidences a concern for them: "A democratic morality should judge sexual acts by the way partners treat one another, the level of mutual consideration, the presence or absence of coercion, and the quantity and quality of the pleasures they provide" (283).

I find this last proposal very promising, and I also agree that most sexual variation is benign and that many sexual practices are inappropriately categorized in a hierarchy of value. But there are at least three major problems with Rubin's formulation of a radical sexual politics, and each of these problems bear crucially on the issue of adult-child sexual relations.

In her category of benign sexual variations that face unfair repression

Rubin includes "fetishism, sadism, masochism, transsexuality, transvestism, exhibitionism, voyeurism and pedophilia" as well as promiscuous
homosexuality and commercial sex (280, 281, 283). She lumps together
all these activities into one monolithic unity, and assumes they can be
adequately analyzed in a single account. But adult-child sex and, for
example, transvestism involve extremely different moral as well as
political issues, and cannot be usefully placed in the same category for
the purpose of political or moral analysis. Rubin not only lumps them
together, but maintains that the persecution of transvestites is no more
outrageous than the persecution of pedophiles, both of whom suffer
from a "prejudice" inflicted against them that she likens to "racism,
ethnocentrism, and religious chauvinism" (280).

   Second, it is a grave error for Rubin to believe, along with Foucault,
Danet, and Hocquenghem as discussed above, that the issue of sexual
violence can be excluded from any theory of the politics of sexuality.
This is an error not simply because of the importance of understanding
sexual violence, but because the way in which we identify sexual
violence will affect the way in which we will come to understand and
analyze all other sexual practices (and vice versa). For example, I think
it can be shown that there is an intrinsic relationship between the
persecution of "sodomy" and the acceptance of the violation of young
children. Both of these are connected to an institution of patriarchy
that has legitimated itself through a macho heterosexuality founded in
part on the ownership and control of children. The particular version of
macho heterosexuality found in Christianity justifies the absolute power
and authoritarianism of elite men, which includes their right to determine the treatment of all subordinates, on the basis of each being the
father of a heterosexual family unit, and thus a provider and progenitor
of the species. This schema pits both homosexuality and the rights of
children in direct conflict with the legitimation of patriarchal power,
which is here defined as a form of heterosexual paternalism.[11] Therefore,
to understand both the persecution of homosexuality as well as the
violation of children, we need to understand these phenomena in the
complex details of their interrelationship.

   Moreover, where Rubin tosses off the categories of "sexual coercion,
sexual assault and rape" as if these are unambiguously defined, in actual
fact their scope of application is constantly being contested and their
definition is nowhere clear or unchallenged. In nineteenth-century U.S.

culture, sex between a white woman and an African-American man was defined as a violation whether or not she consented. Within heterosexual marriage, rape has usually been considered impossible, by virtue of the terms of the marriage contract. And there are further arguments today about how to construe "date rape" and statutory rape. Thus, the line of demarcation between the practices that are considered violent and those thought to be harmless is not at all clear and is being incessantly redrawn. Rubin's own account of "benign" sexual practices will have a direct effect on where that line can be located within her own theory, whether or not she acknowledges this fact. No account of sexuality can present itself as inapplicable or irrelevant to sexual violence because each account will influence the way in which sexual violence is conceptualized and identified.

Finally, Rubin's specific discussion of adult-child sex is itself extremely problematic. Her very use of the term "cross-generational sex" lumps together such disparate issues as the social disapproval of relations between older women and younger men with the relations between adults and children. The term "cross-generational sex" is becoming more and more widely used in discourses of sexual libertarianism, even though the specific analyses usually center around sex between adults and children or youths. For example, the average age of membership of England's Pedophile Information Exchange is 37, and they describe themselves as "chiefly interested" in males between the ages of 14 and 19. Pedophilic interest in girls is focused primarily on the ages from 8 to 10.[12] The René Guyon Society advocates sex without intercourse with girls up to the age of 12, and then "initiation" at the age of 13.[13] When the statistics focus on incest and exclude incidents with strangers or acquaintances, the *average* age of the child drops to 7. The all-inclusive notion of "cross-generational sex" to discuss these events together with relations between differently aged adults tends toward obscuring the specificity of the issues involved in sexual relations between fully matured adults and dependent children.

Rubin has nothing but sympathy for the "men [who] have been the victims of a savage and undeserved witchhunt" ("Thinking Sex," 273). She likens pedophiles to African-Americans and to Jews in suffering unjust persecution (298). She sympathizes with their vulnerability to exposure and points out that "having to maintain such absolute secrecy is a considerable burden" (292). Nowhere in the article does she mention or cite references to victims of child sexual abuse, or their own accounts of these events in their lives and the impact it has had on their adult sexuality.

Rubin also asserts that "cross-generational" sex is the "lowliest category on the hierarchy of sex" (279). This is hardly the case. Cross-generational relations between old men and young women are the subject of so many approving cultural representations that they may seem to typify one of the normative scenarios for "romance." It is only sex with children that receives a pretension of condemnation, but even here the facts concerning prosecution belie this stated concern. Rubin is mistaken to claim that children are "ferociously" protected from adult sexuality when the reality is that actions are generally only taken when more than the violation of children is at stake: to justify the persecution of homosexuals, to enable a criticism of "working mothers," or to extend and legitimate the paternalistic power of the repressive apparatus of the state.

Rubin's "applied Foucault," while it follows his valorization of pleasure as an intrinsic good, misses the better parts of Foucault's analysis, which insists on the constitutive relationship among desire, discourse, and power. I find it remarkable, for example, that Rubin refuses to interrogate the desire of a thirty-seven-year-old man for a fourteen-year-old boy, or the systematic preferences of some adults for children who are physically much weaker and emotionally and intellectually much less articulate (and more flexible and responsive to adult influence than a peer would be). This critical absence seems to follow from an unacknowledged premise that where there is desire, pleasure, and any semblance of consent, there is a good that deserves to be defended. In Rubin's "sex-positive" view, all sexual practices should be considered innocent until proven guilty. This type of "pro" attitude toward sexual pleasure may be correlated with what Eric Presland calls the "want/have syndrome" (if I want it then I automatically have a right to it), endemic to both masculinist ideology and consumer capitalism.[14] If Rubin had consulted the growing literature written by survivors of childhood abuse and assault, she might have changed her view about the innocent status of pedophilia. In the next section I shall try to develop a new articulation of pedophilia that can avert the homophobic effect of its perceived tie to homosexuality, avoid a naturalistic account of pleasure, and retain a "metaphysics of suspicion" with respect not only to puritan condemnations but likewise to adult assurances that the children "don't mind."

A "Countersentence"

A demand rather than a method, a morality more than a theory.
　　　　　　　　　　　　　　　—Georges Canguilhem

Both children and youths, or young teenagers, have been discussed throughout this analysis. Putting age limits on these categories is obviously arbitrary, since children reach puberty and attain maturity at very different ages due to sex and glandular differences or other idiosyncratic variables. Dissimilar cultures can also significantly affect empowerment by imposing diverse social expectations and practices. The concept of childhood is culturally and historically variable, and currently dependent on controversial developmental theories. The concept of the teenager is even more recent. For all of these reasons it is impossible to devise a categorization by age that will be applicable across sexual identity, culture, historical period, and the individual differences. Clearly the best approach would be as local as possible, and thus specific to a group of children or youths who have most of these variables in common.

There is no resolution to the inherent complexity involved in establishing age demarcations for such categories as children and youth. Still, we might be able to identify the critical determinants by which such categories would be developed, such as basic motor skills for running away; language skills for articulating questions, desires, and commands; the onset of puberty; and economic independence. The most common distinction used to separate children and youths is puberty, although puberty itself is an elastic concept. But even after puberty most youths in Western societies are economically dependent and emotionally vulnerable to adult manipulation and coercion. In the following analysis I am relying on literature and data from Western countries; based on this, I shall assume that at least one broad analysis of pedophilia can be made in regard to all children and youths under the age of sixteen, though there will be obvious differences that need to be taken into account within this grouping in relation to specific issues and practices. The virtue of a general account is not that it can deal with every single case, but that it can shed light on general features of a class of cases.

Perhaps the most crucial distinction besides age that needs to be made is that between homosexual and heterosexual practices. Pedophilic practices vary enormously; some prefer only girls, some have sex with boys while married or otherwise sexually engaged with adult women, and some focus on boys alone. Florence Rush claims that no such distinction is relevant: that the impulse to engage with children sexually transcends any distinction of sexual orientation.[15] This view seems shortsighted, however. Given the enormous difference in social attitudes toward homosexual and heterosexual practices, and given the real differences between these respective sexual communities, surely one must avoid generalizations that would subsume these practices into a single account.

On the one hand, plausible arguments can be made that in a homophobic context, same-sex relations between youths of the same age are structurally impractical, and older men or women can play a useful role in making it possible to express homosexual desire. As Foucault suggests, sexual pleasures and sensations can be assigned different meanings and values with different affective components, from which it surely follows that it is unwise to make inferences from a heterosexual context to a homosexual one or vice versa. However, it is not necessarily useless to theorize pedophilia (as the adult desire for children) and pederasty (as the desire of men for adolescent boys) in the same account.[16] Across the significant differences lies at least one important similarity: unequal, nonreciprocal relations of power and desire. Tom Reeves, founder of the North American Man/Boy Love Association (NAMBLA), stresses that he has no interest in children or in molestation, but he also says that it is the boys' intermediate status as not-yet-adults that holds his attraction. He likes their freedom and rebelliousness, their mixture of "rough yet innocent," and admits that he likes to be in charge of things, even though he repudiates the notion that in relationships with boys he always is.[17] I am certain that he is correct to say that he is not always in control, but in his affairs with boys from the ages of thirteen to eighteen I doubt the power is ever equal. Reeves's argument is that it is the repressive laws against such relationships that create the furtive situations that produce prostitution and the unethical and manipulative treatment of boys by men. The law may well exacerbate some problems well beyond what they would be otherwise. But it is not the law alone that is responsible for the inequalities of independence, emotional and psychic development, and susceptibility to manipulation between boys and men.

Pat Califia defends relations between adults and children or youth on similar libertarian grounds. She argues that "there is nothing wrong with a more privileged adult offering a young person money, privacy, freedom of movement, new ideas and sexual pleasure."[18] The "and" in this list suggests that the first four are tied to the last, turning what may appear to be a beneficent relationship into a form of opportunist manipulation where an adult procures sex by providing important benefits the child or youth wants or needs. But this is precisely the common scenario of pedophilia, in which there is seduction and manipulation rather than overt violence, and in which the young person is taught to use sex to get her other needs met, and so learns to offer sex for attention, for companionship, for money, and so on. When sex is exchanged for an adult's "goods" that the young person or child wants or needs, how can this indicate an authentic consent to the sex itself much less a desire?

In preparation for writing this essay I have been reading two very disparate sets of literature, one set concerned with the crisis of childhood sexual abuse and a second set focused on the increasing problems of homophobia and rightist sexual repression. No one seems to be able to share a concern with both of these issues as equal priorities, or to attempt an account of the relationship between them.[19] Sexual libertarians always make a point of condemning abuse and coercion, but never explore the reasons for the epidemic proportions and prevalence of these sexual events. Advocates for child victims usually espouse a condemnation of homophobia and often distance themselves from statist, legalistic solutions, but their analyses rarely employ social criticisms of the role of law in discourse, such as Foucault offers. Both sides thus perceive the other as guilty of bad faith. Child advocates wonder if the libertarians are really concerned about child abuse or if they believe that the statistics (and even the trauma) are produced by a moralistic climate of discourse. Libertarians wonder if every child advocate harbors an anti-sex authoritarian attitude and a tendency to invest in sexual acts "an excess of significance," perhaps ultimately motivated by their participation in the profitable self-help institutions.

What is needed, it seems to me, is an account that can bring together these disparate concerns in full equality. This is not to deny that in local contexts certain elements may pose a greater danger, and merit more extensive attention and intervention. A perfectly evenhanded approach in all situations would achieve only an abstract, superficial justice, and would likely result in many all too concrete injustices. What is needed, rather, is an approach that puts all of these considerations into play—that is, concern with sexual violence, abuse, patriarchy, homophobia, disciplinary forms of domination (though not always in equal measure)—

while remaining attentive to the fallibility and indeterminateness of any account of sexual life. The following account attempts to enact this charge insofar as it can apply to a general analysis of pedophilia.

Let us assume for the sake of argument that the position articulated by Foucault, Hocquenghem, Danet, and Rubin is grounded in a genuine concern to transform the conditions of sexual oppression in which children live. In the context of the United States where a brilliant surgeon general can be fired merely for mentioning masturbation and sex education in the same sentence, we should all share this concern. The question then becomes, What is the best way to enact this transformation?

In their view, the liberation of children's sexuality must necessarily include an end to the repression of consensual sexual relations between adults and children. This assumes that we can demarcate sexual relations based on physical violence and overt manipulation from sexual relations that are in some sense consented to by the children themselves. But this assumption is difficult to maintain. Verbal consent can be easily produced by background structural conditions such as economic and emotional dependence. When children are involved there is also a significant possibility of real confusion about how to describe the experience. Many adult survivors from childhood assaults recall that in the beginning they were not clear on what was happening to them or what the other person was doing; this further complicates consent. One man relates, "He showered me with gifts and attention. And he knew how to get both of us going. . . . I fought him at first. But he excited me. And soon I was hooked."[20] When such a seduction is practiced not on an adult but on a child, the effect is a manipulation that takes advantage of the child's susceptibility and confusion.

Consent can be produced in a variety of ways, from seductive manipulation to coercion. A woman writes:

> Then one afternoon when I was just waking up from a nap, he sat next to me on the side of the bed. He put his big heavy fingers in my pants and began rubbing my clitoris. I had no idea what he was trying to do. He asked, yet sort of told me, "It feels good, doesn't it?" All I knew was I couldn't say no. I felt powerless to move. I said Yes. . . . He told me never to tell anyone. But I already knew I wouldn't say a word. My mother adored him,

idealized him, and I felt I needed to protect our image of our great Daddy.[21]

Consent alone can never serve as a sufficient means to ensure that the child or young person is safe.

I would agree with Foucault that a consensual/contractual model makes little sense when applied to sexual relations, no more than applied to love. This is not because desire does not admit of a yes or no expression, but because the nature of sexual expression is not an exchange or a trade, but (ideally) a mutual engagement. Desire is enacted and enhanced in the performance of sexual practices, and not simply lying there inert beforehand ready to be exchanged. The concept of consent is a sometimes useful abstraction that can help to clarify what happened and to articulate the presence or absence of coercion, but it has only a limited ability to capture the nature of sexual experience.

Furthermore, from a position of moral concern over the well-being of the participants in a sexual encounter, what one needs to know is not whether there was stated consent, but whether the actions performed represented the authentic desires of each participant. I fully acknowledge how problematic the concept of authenticity is, given the fact that neither desires nor selves are ontologically independent in the way the concept has historically implied, and yet it is the authenticity of the children's desires that is at stake here. A concern with the presence or absence of consent is derivative on this more basic consideration. If a child does express consent, we must still ask whether or not it is an "authentic" expression.

The concept of authenticity may imply that there is an essential sexual desire (or lack of desire), intrinsic to an individual prior to social interactions or cultural influence. Such an implication is highly dubious, but it is not a necessary part of any and all accounts of authenticity. The criticism of old accounts of authenticity is that they presume an essential self with essential desires and needs prior to the cultural, social, and discursive insertion of the individual; but this criticism is directed at concepts of essentialism, not authenticity. For example, a distinction between authentic and inauthentic forms of consent might be based not on a concept of the essential or the natural but on the particular configuration of the existent relationship among power, desire, and discourse in a given situation. Such a configuration as typically exists in a psychiatric relationship, for example, suggests to many of us that the desire of the patient for her therapist (or vice versa) is in some sense problematic. The concept of authenticity captures this sense, by suggesting that without that configuration of power and discourse, the desire would not be the same. This argument presumes no essentialism.

Foucault's analysis suggests that desire must be analyzed in terms of its location with respect to power and discourse, and he implies, even on a critical reading, that there is no desire that is not "historically occasioned," to use Butler's words. The problem with the desire of the patient for her therapist is not that it is historically occasioned, but the kind of occasion that prompted it. Given this, the question we must ask is, What are the kinds of historical occasions that prompt desires between adults and children? This question calls for an exploration of the interconnections between adult-child sexual practices, discourse and power, or a genealogy of particular occasions of pedophilia.

It is obvious that children are disempowered relative to adults in both discursive and extradiscursive ways. Their discourse is subordinate and subjugated, and their actions are constrained within systems of possibility set out beforehand without their participation. This is not to say that they cannot resist or articulate new positions discordant with dominant regimes, but that they are positioned differently than adults and subject to more strenuous and invasive techniques of domination.

In every culture that exists children are dependent on adults for their very survival, though this dependence can vary in degree and form. Children are usually most dependent on the adults in their family or the adults who care for them but they are also dependent on the adults in their community generally. Their position vis-à-vis adults can therefore be characterized by its dependency, vulnerability, and relative powerlessness. This results not simply from the fact that children are usually smaller and physically weaker but because they are economically dependent on adults for their livelihood, and for a thousand other things like the quality of their education, the adjudication of their fights with other children, their sense of security and well-being, their hygiene, and their health. The very range of actions within which they may maneuver is set out for them, though children continually contest this range, sometimes successfully. Their relationship with adults is not reciprocal, mutually interdependent, or equal: children have a vastly reduced ability to get away or fight back, to talk or argue back, and to maintain their sense of self against adult mediation. Most children are not complete victims of adult power, but neither is their power equal to ours, either individually or collectively. As one survivor wrote, "a victim doesn't know he has a choice. That's the problem. If nobody else knows what's going on, then we don't know what to do."[22]

Some have argued that all of the above is correct but remediable. For example, Jamie Gough uses a Marxist analysis of oppression to suggest that children's subordination is socially constructed, and therefore the solution should be empowerment rather than paternalism.[23] It is true that the position of children is analogous in important respects to the position of slaves, insofar as both are disempowered, vulnerable, and dependent with respect to the adult or master. Would Rubin or Foucault countenance a view that masters can have sex with their slaves when the slaves "truly" desire it? Does the notion of a slave's authentic desire for sex with her master make any sense or have any credibility? If we are against sexual relations coerced through manipulation, the structural features of a master-slave relationship calls into question any assertion of desire for the master on the part of the slave, since such an expression may be too easily overdetermined by her position of dependence, either economic or psychological dependence or both in combination. Gough is certainly right that the solution to this situation is to eradicate the position of the slave through eradicating slavery, but here is where slavery and childhood are disanalogous. The institution of childhood can be radically altered, and children can become significantly more empowered than at present, but the vulnerability, dependency, and relative powerlessness of children vis-à-vis adults cannot ever be completely eradicated.[24]

Despite this, the analogy Gough suggests between children and other oppressed groups remains instructive. For example, the laws and social structures designed (purportedly) to protect women from violation have resulted in an increase in women's vulnerability. Those women who were "protected" from the dangerous public sphere of waged work were left more vulnerable to male violence in the home, without an effective escape route. Such "protections" of children have often had similar results. The lesson here is that children's rights must be extended, not curtailed, and they must have access to power outside the scope of their family or immediate caregivers.

The issue of power is precisely, though oddly, what Foucault leaves out of his analysis. When he speaks of "precocious little girls" he is blind to the way in which young girls who are often subject to multiple forms of domination based on their class, race, and gender have very few avenues by which to get their basic needs met. Sexual behavior is a common avenue that the dominant structures which favor adult men provide for girls and sometimes for boys as well. The "seductive," coy, or coquettish behavior of young girls must be analyzed in the context of a system of differential power relations and domination. When we leave the constitutive role of power aside we end up with the version of liberal or libertarian pluralism Rubin adopts, where sexual practices are treated under a descriptive model like a natural variety of plant species.

Power, as Foucault helped us to see, is not only often linked to discourse; it is constitutive of discourse. When adults interpret children's behavior, verbal or otherwise, as expressions of desire to have sex with them, the adults are assimilating that behavior within an economy of meaning to which it may very well not conform. They are interpreting the children within an economy based on sameness, incorporating the child's expressions within a system of meaning based on the adult's. Grubman-Black puts this point as follows:

> We were children whose rights and needs were denied. We were required to meet someone else's definition of us and of him. We were unable to escape the dream that was not of our making or choice. Whatever we sought, for whatever reason, we were met with one fixated response. I needed to be held and hugged, not fondled or aroused. We needed companionship and guidance, not sexual initiation. For many of us, there was emptiness in our lives. The offender chose to fill his own emptiness, his own needs, leaving us to feel even more barren.[25]

Grubman-Black describes a scenario too many of us can remember and identify with: a situation in which a child's entreaty is met with a kind of misresponse from an adult. The child wants and needs one thing, perhaps affection, attention, closeness, warmth, love, companionship, guidance, or affirmation, and the adult responds with his or her own agenda involving genital stimulation and erotic desire. Such missed communications may of course result from willful ignorance and manipulation on the adult's part, but they are also exacerbated by the disparate economies of meaning between the discursive and gestural practices of children and adults.

My claim is not that the world of children and the world of adults is absolutely incommensurable. It is not necessary to claim that children and adults can never communicate with each other in order to argue that every communicative interaction between them is mediated by the vulnerability, dependence, and relative powerlessness of children. My point is that the adult interpretation of children's behavior and expressions will always be structured by this ubiquitous inequality, and given the intrinsic connections among meaning, power, and truth, the discourse of children will always be distinct in significant ways from the discourse of adults, structured as it is around a different set of relationships.

Linguistic styles and practices emerge out of lived realities, which are themselves structured and filtered through language. But significantly different lived realities will correspond to significant differences in the metaphysics and epistemologies embedded in language; that is, the ontological assumptions and patterns of discursive authorization operative in a language. Who gets to speak, who will be accorded authority or at least presumption in their favor, what it is possible to express and what ontological objects (such as "desire") it is possible to entertain will all vary between such linguistic practices as exist among, say, Western scientists, gay Latinos, or lower-class children. These group demarcations can be drawn in multiple ways, as discrete, as overlapping, through the criss-crossing grids that can exist within the complexity of group exchange and relations in multivocal and multilayered societies. But substantive epistemic and semantic demarcations persist among adults, youth, and children. Adults who interpret children's behavior and linguistic practices as "consent" are imposing their own usage of "consent" across a linguistic border over which meanings can change drastically. Children certainly have the ability to consent to any number of things, but the meaning of that consent may shift in important respects when it is transported from an adult's to a child's context. We can use Foucault's expanded conception of a discourse, as embodying both meanings and ontological commitments as well as practices to identify the existence of a different discourse between adults and children, not incommensurable discourses but organized around a different set of strategic rules. Once we follow Foucault in acknowledging the relationship between power and discourse, we must also acknowledge that a significant difference in one's positioning with respect to dominant structures of power will result in a significant difference in the strategic rules by which discursive moves can be made.

When we incorporate the discourse of children with our own, and translate their desires within an economy of adult sexuality characterized by genital, orgasmic sex, we are exerting our force once again to eradicate any possible difference that may be there. The only way to avoid this is to leave children alone sexually, and thus allow the development and maintenance of their own sexual differences, either with themselves or with each other.

The possibility remains that children sometimes authentically consent to sex with adults, and this possibility is real, not merely logical or technical. Indeed, the male survivor literature often includes some accounts of pleasure. In my own experience of support groups, I remember one woman who said that she enjoyed her sexual relationship with her older brother. The simple infrequency of such narratives should not cause us to deny their validity and might in fact be the result of the current discursive prohibition against such statements. There are also victims of childhood sexual abuse that appear to be asymptomatic of traumatic aftereffects. This apparent absence of trauma is a difficult issue for those of us who are symptomatic survivors to face.

The existence of asymptomatic victims (whose status as "victims" is obviously problematic here) is insufficient to establish that adult-child sex is nonharming. There might be any number of alternative explanations before we confirm this hasty conclusion. For example, we need to look carefully at the widely variable context of sexual abuse, from sustained activity with a family member to a brief incident with a stranger. The type and degree of sexual interaction is relevant, as are the relations between those involved, the child's prior state of self-esteem, the general context of her security and well-being, her ability to be heard and believed about the incident soon afterward, her age, and so forth. In some cases negative aftereffects are immediate but responded to so effectively that they quickly diminish. Or the child herself is strong and secure enough to incorporate the event without being traumatized by it. Sexual experiences that children have with adults are so variable that the existence of some asymptomatic adult survivors in and of itself does not disconfirm the general harm of adult-child sex unless we were to find out more information about the patterns and contexts of symptomatic responses.

The issue of stated consent or felt pleasure needs to be assessed separately. There are several different ways one might understand such reports: (1) on the Freudian model, that the child is enacting an authentic desire of its own for a parent or parent figure; (2) that such stories indicate the possibility that adult-child sex is innocuous, and it is only the feminist or psychological literature that influences adults to reconstruct their experiences as damaging, painful, and coercive (in which case the narratives I have drawn from will be held invalid); (3) that no analytic model can account for all cases, and these are the exceptions to the rule; (4) that such accounts represent a kind of false consciousness where the survivor is still participating in the common tendency among children to protect the adult and rationalize his or her behavior. Taking (1), (2), or (4) as the full story strikes me as too simplistic, each assuming a monolithic analysis. The problem with (3) is that, while not assuming a monolithic analysis, it offers no explanation of the variability. And none of these options address the issue that desire and pleasure can be structurally and discursively constituted.

An alternative option would be one that allowed for variability in lived experience, but that also maintained that pleasure and damage can coexist in a single event. Children often "authentically" ask for things which would harm them if they got them. A desire for x does not make it harmless. This is not to say that the question of children's authentic desires is no longer relevant, but that it must be supplemented by an exploration of the issue of harm. In the narratives contained in Broken Boys/Mending Men, for example, the instances where pleasure and desire on the part of the boy are reported present seem to in no way mitigate against the trauma and harm that resulted. "It felt good," and yet the negative aftereffects make a long list: fear of trusting anyone, feeling like everyone who expresses concern ultimately wants only sex, self-destructiveness, self-loathing, shame, humiliation, fear of abandonment, and a host of pathological emotional and psychic disorders.[26]

Foucault argued that codes of morality comprise forms of subjectivation; I would argue the same for sexual practices. Sexual practices are self-constituting; that is, they affect the constitution of psychic life, the imaginary construction of one's self, and the structure of internal experience. A child's sexual practices with an adult will have an effect on that child's psychic structuring and subjectivity. All such constituting effects occur within specific discursive contexts, and for this reason some might claim that the harm of adult-child sex results from a disapproving social context rather than the event itself. But this claim is implausible if only because of the phenomenology of sex itself, which involves uniquely sensitive, vulnerable, and psychically important areas of the body, a fact that persists across cultural differences. Thus sexual experiences have the capacity to impart crucial meanings concerning one's body and, therefore, one's self. This capacity does not establish that sexual acts have uniform meanings, but that they have in any case significant subject-constituting meanings rather than an absence of meaning. It is not social context alone that makes sexual acts significant, but social context in relation to the phenomenology of embodiment.

Moreover, sexual practices are profoundly intersubjective and relational, and impart meanings also about the limits and possibilities of one's relationship to others. (Given the role of fantasy in masturbation, even it can be seen as intersubjective, though of course one cannot harm others in an act of private masturbation.) NAMBLA argues (similarly to Rubin) that the state is motivated to repress sexuality because sex represents the ultimate individualism, and thus a kind of inherent resistance to state control.[27] But this argument betrays NAMBLA's own belief that sexual practices are fundamentally a sphere of the individual rather than the social. I believe the truth is exactly the reverse: the fact that sexual practices are intersubjective rather than individual suggests that the intersubjective and relational aspects of sexual practices can never by set aside in one's analysis.

In my own case a relatively brief series of assaults at a young age led to fairly fundamental alterations in my sense of self, my construction of intersubjective relations, and my experience of embodiment. I had many of the negative feelings discussed above, including a deep sense of shame (despite the fact that, in my case, there was no semblance of consent). It was terrifying to be dragged about against my will, to have my body poked and prodded and used for purposes I only dimly perceived, to have my screams and pleas ignored, and to have all this done to me with impunity. This gave me a profound message about my status as a social subject in the community. If I could be harmed to this degree with no one seeming to care, I thought it must be because I deserved it. Thus I came away from this experience with a self-image of worthlessness that I have struggled with ever since.

Such a narrative as I just gave is, of course, a reconstruction. At the time of the events, I remember clearly feeling only terror, pain, confusion, and a kind of shock. My grades went from A's to D's, I became withdrawn, and I cried so incessantly that my parents thought I had started puberty (at nine!). My current understanding of both the events and their full effect on me was produced through therapy, feminist consciousness, talking with others who had had similar experiences, and a number of other experiences and readings. Such processes of reconstructing and reassessing events is an inevitable part of any child-hood traumatic experience (indeed, of any childhood). One alters one's understanding of events on the basis of the enlarged discursive domain one develops and on the basis of a constantly changing self. The point is not to suspect all such reconstructions as fictional overlays, nor to posit a pre-discursive, pre-theoretical experience that can be simply discovered once and for all when one is an adult. Experience is always reconstructed in memory, and memories are not pure representations, but we can make evaluative distinctions between better and worse reconstructions.

What I resist is the notion that it is possible to "interpret away" sexual trauma. Psychic harm is not a spiritual substance that can remain locked away as if in Descartes's pineal gland. If it exists, it makes itself manifest, though of course the "signs" of such manifestation will themselves require interpretation, admittedly a fallible and difficult enterprise. One man writes, "It took me years before I realized that I had been lied to, manipulated, and taken advantage of. . . . I avoided most people, had no friends, and I was a mess."[28] Such phenomenological descriptions belie the claim that trauma is produced after the fact. It is certainly possible for reconstructed narratives to be adversely influenced by dubita-ble theories or even political motivations. But we cannot reduce this possibility by denying that reconstructions are an inevitable part of all childhood memories. A better approach would be to explore the ties between institutional discourses of knowledge and power, using Fou-cault's critique as a starting place.

For all the reasons given above, I believe that the dangers of adult-child sex are significant enough to warrant a general prohibition. I realize that my position might be seen to validate an undesirable maternalism (or paternalism, but I will use the feminine form since there seems to be no neutral equivalent) that would reinforce the powerlessness of children. The concern here is that, if we do not allow for children's authentic consent to sex with adults, and always interpret children as not "truly" or "authentically" desiring to have sex with adults, perhaps we are silencing them once again, and restricting their desires. But we must disentangle a repudiation of sex between adults and children with a repudiation of children's sexuality. These have usually been linked. "Unnatural" sexual relations between children have often been theorized as the result of sexual relations with adults, and therefore the former were condemned as deviations caused by adult violation. Although this may be the case some of the time, it is clearly not the case that all sexual relations between children (even genital ones) are a deviation brought on by adults. Separating these issues will help to avoid an unnecessarily restrictive maternalism that would police and repress all sexual practices by children. I would argue that the latter would not be a true maternalism but rather, as Foucault suggests, a domination of children aligned with pleasure—the pleasure of observing their sexual actions and forcing their confessions—and the regulation of children as a population of docile, manipulable bodies. The intervention into children's own sexual behavior should be restricted to violent or coercive behavior or sexual relations between children from disparate ages, in which case a power differential exists analogous to the one between adults and children.

M(p)aternalism is a relationship between unequals, and so is often rejected by feminists and anticolonialists on the grounds that maternalistic support can never bring about or instantiate relations of equality or freedom. I agree with that analysis. But relations between adults and children can never achieve complete equality and freedom, and children require care from adults in order to survive and flourish. It is a self-serving illusion for adults to believe that we can completely avoid maternalistic relations toward children or renounce the responsibility that all adults have toward all children.

It might be objected that if we dismiss our ability to interpret accurately the linguistic utterances of children we will restrict their ability to have any input into our behavior toward them. I would agree that such a result is highly undesirable, and despite the arguments I made above, I would disagree with the view that our languages are so different that any communication is unreliable. And yet when the risks are exceedingly high, as in the case of sexual abuse given the depth and longevity of its traumatic aftereffects, and when the possible gains are almost inversely low, surely the best course of action is to hedge our bets and prevent the possibility of such aftereffects from occurring.

The problem of adult sexual relations with children is not a problem of the "violation of innocence." This is one of the most prevalent traditional reasons given, and it is linked to the notion that the rape of a virgin is somehow worse than the rape of women who are not virgins, so that the rape of prostitutes and of married women by their husbands is not accorded the seriousness of the rape of "innocents." Historically, the concern with sexual "innocents" was a result of the commodification of virgins: once raped, they stood to lose substantial market value as marriageable property. The rape of women already deflowered was therefore of less importance because it would not alter their market value.

The argument that adult-child sexual relations are wrong because children are "innocent" is also mistaken for at least two reasons. First, it puts a presumption of value on the absence of sexual experience over its presence, such that "innocence" should be maintained as long as possible because it is inherently desirable. Such a presumption is surely false, and makes sense only when one has a negative orientation toward sexual experience generally, as for example, in Christian dogma. Moreover, the argument assumes, and mandates, that children are properly asexual. This is again patently false, and in that sense children are not innocent. Children have a variety of sexual feelings and some act on them in various ways. Therefore, the reason for opposing adult-child sex should not be the innocence of children. It is that logic which leads to the practice of asking rape victims about their sexual past, of taking the rape of sexually active persons less seriously, and of judging sexually active or knowledgeable children as "bad" and therefore necessarily complicit in their violation.

But to the extent that the concern with "innocence" includes a concern with those who are especially vulnerable, there is a kernel of truth here. Children are not innocent of sexuality, though their sexuality may significantly diverge from adult manifestations. But children are more vulnerable, whether or not they have acted out sexual feelings and desires. Children are still in the process of forming their sense of themselves, of sexuality, and of embodied relations with others. This process never stops completely, but it is more significant and dramatic during childhood, with more long-lasting effects. Because children have less experience, they are more flexible and suggestive to mediations that would construct their subjectivities. It is easier to "season" a young girl and turn her into a prostitute than an older woman. Therefore, when children are raped and violated, it is likely that such an experience will more deeply and profoundly affect their sense of their self, their worth, their future possibilities, their relations with others, and their sexuality. This has nothing to do with their innocence of sexuality; it results from the fact that they are more actively and intensely engaged in self-creation and world-interpretation than adults, and that their developing account of themselves and their world is more open, fluid, and flexible, since it has enjoyed fewer repetitions and developed less into a practiced habit of belief.

Some might object to the line of reasoning presented here on the grounds that, if this argument stands that power differentials adversely affect the possibility of "authentic" consent, then a lot of adult-adult sex should not be engaged in either, such as student-teacher, husband-housewife, employer-employee, and so on. I would agree: all such sex is extremely dangerous, though we can note that in adult-adult situations in many cases, the subordinate adult will still have more options to fight back and get away than a child would.

Michael Alhonte has written an interesting essay, as an eighteen-year-old "boy" in a man-boy relationship who began his involvement with men at the age of thirteen, defending his legal right to man-boy love.[29] He argues instructively against an ageism that stereotypes both boys and men and works against perceiving individual differences. But his article spends most of its time criticizing problems in man-boy relationships. He talks about the problems of inequality, the "unpleasant unbalance" caused by finances, and says that boys in such relationships come to feel embarrassed and irritated by their own maturation processes, which diminish the source of their attractiveness to men. He points out that in most of these relationships the boy is expected to play a submissive role. And he offers a rather negative portrait of "the problem of objectification":

> Too many men adore boys as abstract sexual beings, but refuse (or are unable) to deal with them as people. If they *do* pretend to show interest in what a boy has to say after sex, it is usually in a patronizing, superior manner; often it is punctuated with degrading estimations of the boy's sexual value—as if this were the only level on which a boy can be valuable—perhaps intended as sincere compliments but more likely to be the only statements the man can honestly make, since he is not bothered in the slightest to get to know something about the boy. (158)

He also argues that a desire based solely on youth is damaging:

> one must never allow the desire for youthfulness to obstruct the avenues for growth and self-expression in a relationship. To

identify the factor that enchants a man with a boy as merely the boy's youth is to ageistically negate the whole range of positive traits that the boy has. (159)

He says that the result of such attractions based solely on youth is to keep the relationship from evolving as the boy matures and even to stagnate the boy's metamorphosis into an adult in order to retain the basis of desire. In the cases Alhonte discusses, the youth in the relationship is not a child and is hardly powerless. Such cases might seem to be best-case scenarios, least likely to inflict psychic damage on the youths involved. Perhaps the damage is small in some instances, but Alhonte's descriptions actually support many of my concerns.

I have tried to show that the problem with the "excess of significance" view is that it assumes a more primordial sexual experience below the discursive overlay of power/knowledges, and it assumes that at this deeper level sex is light, inconsequential, relatively trivial. But sexual practices, like codes of morality, comprise forms of subjectivation: that is, they are self-constituting. A normative account of sexual practices such as pedophilia could begin here, not with an attempt, like Rubin's, to disinvest pleasure from power (a hopeless project), but with an analysis of the modes of subjectivation produced by various configurations of pleasure, power, and discourse.

In the first blush of the second wave of feminism, there was a period in which it was very important to begin to envision the contours of a future nonsexist society, to create a new imaginary possibility for women. During this period, feminist theorists such as Andrea Dworkin, Shulamith Firestone, and Kate Millett envisioned a future utopia in which children would be empowered enough to choose who they lived with, what kind of lives they would lead, and to engage in sexual relations with each other as well as with adults and family members. These works were written from an impulse toward envisioning a better future for children. But it is not transformative to posit a future where children have sex with adults: this is our uninterrupted past and present. A truly transformative future would be one in which children could be, for the first time, free from the economy of adult sexual desire and adult sexual demands. Only this future will be truly new and unknown, and the sexuality of children that emerges from it, and that we indeed have no way to predict, will be determined then and only then by children themselves.

Notes

1. I thank Raja Halwani, Joy Rouse, Margaret Himley, Robert Praeger, Steven Seidman, Tom Wartenburg, Linda Nicholson, Laura Gray, and Ingeborg Majer O'Sickey for their helpful criticisms and comments on this paper.

2. Gayle Rubin, "Thinking Sex: Notes for a Radical Theory of the Politics of Sexuality," in *Pleasure and Danger: Exploring Female Sexuality*, ed. Carole S. Vance (Boston: Routledge and Kegan Paul, 1984), 279.

3. Foucault, *The History of Sexuality*, vol. 1, *An Introduction*, trans. Robert Hurley (New York: Pantheon, 1978), 31–32.

4. The first title appeared in *Recherches* 37 (April 1979): 69–82; the second, in *Michel Foucault: Politics, Philosophy, Culture: Interviews and Other Writings, 1977–1984*, ed. Lawrence D. Kritzman, trans. Alan Sheridan et al. (New York: Routledge, 1988), 271–85. Subsequent references will be to the second text, cited as *PPC*.

5. *PPC*, 278. Perhaps one of the working assumptions here is that discourses of sexuality must always or necessarily end up constituting figures of identity: for example, the "pedophile," the "homosexual." But consider the efforts of (some of the) safer-sex discourses to resist such identity-talk in favor of practices-talk: for example, "anal sex" rather than "the gay male."

6. Foucault, *An Introduction*, 31–32.

7. Foucault refers to "precocious little girls" on page 40.

8. Judith P. Butler, *Subjects of Desire: Hegelian Reflections in Twentieth-Century France* (New York: Columbia University Press, 1987), 218.

9. Ibid., 228 (emphases in original).

10. Here is an issue where I find her reading of Foucault implausible: she interprets the right-wing crusade as simply anti-sex, whereas Foucault would surely say, at the very least, that a more complicated relationship between desire and rightist discourses exists than one characterized by a flat negation.

11. See, for example the justifications of patriarchy used by Rousseau in Linda Bell, *Visions of Women* (Clifton, N.J.: Humana, 1983), esp. 196. Here he tells us, "the husband ought to be able to superintend his wife's conduct, because it is of importance to him to be assured that the children, whom he is obliged to acknowledge and maintain, belong to no one but himself."

12. Jeffrey Weeks, *Sexuality and Its Discontents: Meanings, Myths, and Modern Sexualities* (New York: Routledge, 1985), 228.

13. Ellen Bass and Louise Thornton, eds., *I Never Told Anyone: Writings by Women Survivors of Child Sexual Abuse* (New York: Harper and Row, 1983), 30–31.

14. Eric Presland, "Whose Power? Whose Consent?" in *The Age Taboo: Gay Male Sexuality, Power, and Consent*, ed. Daniel Tsang (London and Boston: Gay Men's Press and Alyson Publications, 1981), 75.

15. Florence Rush, *The Best-Kept Secret: Sexual Abuse of Children* (New York: McGraw-Hill, 1980), 173.

16. Do adult women practice pedophilia and pederasty? Yes, certainly. To the same degree as adult men? It is doubtful. Jamie Gough suggests that the general denial of women's sexuality accounts for the fact that women are rarely considered capable of pedophilia. It could also be that women's sexuality is different or has developed differently from men's; it certainly has been treated differently by societies. See Gough, "Childhood Sexuality and Pedophilia," in *The Age Taboo: Gay Male Sexuality, Power, and Consent*, ed. Daniel Tsang (London and Boston: Gay Men's Press and Alyson Publications, 1981), 67.

17. See Tom Reeves, "Loving Boys," in *The Age Taboo: Gay Male Sexuality, Power, and Consent*, 25–37.

18. Pat Califia, "Man/Boy Love and the Lesbian/Gay Movement," in *The Age Taboo: Gay Male Sexuality, Power, and Consent*, 138.

19. An impressive exception is Steven Seidman's *Embattled Eros: Sexual Politics and Ethics in Contemporary America* (New York: Routledge, 1992).

20. Stephen D. Grubman-Black, *Broken Boys/Mending Men: Recovery from Childhood Sexual Abuse* (Blue Ridge Summit, Pa.: Tab Books, 1990), 25.

21. Bass and Thornton, *I Never Told Anyone*, 180–81.

22. Grubman-Black, *Broken Boys/Mending Men*, 92.

23. Gough, "Childhood Sexuality and Pedophilia," 65–71.

24. I make this case for classes, not for every individual. Consider the child of a slaveowning plantation master vis-à-vis an adult slave. Even though power in this case may reside more with the child, she or he is still developmentally unequal.

25. Grubman-Black, *Broken Boys/Mending Men*, 15–16.

26. See Grubman-Black, *Broken Boys/Mending Men*.

27. NAMBLA, "The Case for Abolishing the Age of Consent Laws," in *The Age Taboo: Gay Male Sexuality, Power, and Consent*, esp. 95.

28. Grubman-Black, *Broken Boys/Mending Men*, 90.

29. Michael Alhonte, "Confronting Ageism," in *The Age Taboo: Gay Male Sexuality, Power, and Consent*, 156–60.

6

Foucault Pumped: Body Politics and the Muscled Woman

Honi Fern Haber

A woman without a body, dumb, blind, cannot possibly be a good fighter.

—Hélène Cixous

One is not radical because one pronounces a few words;
no, the essence of being radical is physical.

—Michel Foucault

Embodied Resistance

This essay is part of a larger project whose goal is to contribute to the overthrow of patriarchy and the hegemony of phallocentric desire. The battle will have to be fought at many points; here I am fighting at the level of the body, specifically at the level of women's bodies.[1]

Not everyone starts here. Barbara Brandon, a black feminist and nationally syndicated cartoonist (the only black woman to have that distinction), fights patriarchy by erasing female bodies. Her characters are pictured as talking heads. She says of this technique: "Where I'm coming from uses only heads so that we can get away from tits and ass, and instead of focusing only on bodies, will focus on character instead."[2]

The problem I see with Brandon's approach is that real women have "tits and ass," and it is precisely because they are read *as* tits and ass that their character is deformed or ignored. Effective feminist strategies cannot ignore the body.

Within patriarchal culture the body of woman has been constructed as a sign establishing and reestablishing the values of that culture and the hegemony of phallocentric desire. The male gaze replaces a woman's character with flesh; however a woman may see herself (and I shall argue that this seeing too is informed by the male gaze), when she enters a public space and is whistled at, mauled, molested, ignored, or approved, she is put in her place, a place not of her own making.[3] Since at present, woman is first and foremost read as body, it is with her body that she must fight. Fundamental change will occur only when we can see a woman's body and not be blinded to her character, when we can pan back from the head (a body part also judged from the standpoint of male desire) and not read her as tits and ass. We need to explore the ways in which women can take back public space and their own identities, can reshape possibilities and re-vision culture. I locate this project on the body of women.

Body Aesthetics/Body Politics:
The Foucauldian Background

Foucault's writings on power have given feminists a useful theoretical framework for understanding the body as a site of political struggle. In "Nietzsche, Genealogy, History," *Discipline and Punish*, volume 1 of *The History of Sexuality*, and elsewhere, Foucault describes the body as a surface upon which the rules, hierarchies, and metaphysical commitments of a culture are inscribed and reinforced. Foucault teaches us that bodies are literally shaped by power, and with the aid of genealogical analysis, he also shows us how power can be read off from the surface of bodies. A quick example of embodied power differences can be found in our everyday surroundings if we pay attention to the political implications of how men and women take up space. Men are trained to open their bodies up to the world; encouraged to rush out to meet it, they learn to view their bodies as extensions of *their* world. Women, on the other hand, are taught to shrink away from the world; their bodies, both in mass and motion, are trained to take up as little space as possible.[4] Something as mundane as the fact that men sit with their legs spread wide apart, while a woman is trained to cross her legs and sit tucked into herself, can, with the aid of Foucauldian analysis, be read as shaping the meaning of male and female subjectivities (and also the different meanings of male and female sexuality) both culturally and phenomenologically.

But if in Western cultures the meaning of a woman's body has been constructed by phallocentric desire as Other to that desire, and women wish to refuse this role, then Foucault's writings on the body and power challenge us to fight back with our bodies, to find new ways of meaning our bodies, and hence new ways of understanding ourselves and shaping our culture. For feminists concerned with body politics the challenge becomes, How can women take control of embodied signification, of the way she is read and the way she reads herself? One possibility of resignifying women's bodies is to confuse, or perhaps refuse, traditional gender distinctions, to problematize phallocentric seeings and readings of women's bodies. One way of embodying this possibility, I suggest here, is to do it with muscle.

The value of the strategy I am proposing—namely, that we need to problematize seeing in order to achieve the revaluation of values, of desire, of knowledge and politics—gets its sense from the Foucauldian premise that power, politics, and aesthetics are all three always found together in mutually supportive roles. Aesthetics and politics are complicitous in strategies of power. Because power is *repressive* it takes the form of political strategies, and because it is also, and simultaneously, *constitutive*, power operates and is reproduced—both passively and actively—through aesthetic strategies. Power would be weak if it only functioned on a repressive level through modes of censorship, exclusion, blockage, and oppression. When power is strong, it is strong because it also operates on an aesthetic level, on the level of pleasure and desire. Power shapes what we come to recognize as individuals. As Foucault says, "it is already one of the prime effects of power that certain bodies, certain gestures, certain discourses, certain desires, come to be identified and constituted as individuals."[5] And through the process of normalization, we learn to categorize bodies and desires, and to shape our own bodies and pleasures, into those that are beautiful (good) and ugly (bad), pleasurable (to be sought) and distasteful (to be shunned). So when we attach aesthetic/normative importance to types of bodies and desires, we are in turn carrying on the process of power: "The individual is an effect of power, and at the same time, or precisely to the extent to which it is that effect, it is the element of its articulation. The individual which power has constituted is at the same time its effect."[6]

Foucauldian analysis is instructive for understanding the oppression of women, both as it appears from the outside, to create the individual as an "effect" of power, and as it comes from within, making the individual the articulation and the vehicle of her own oppression. In order to produce desire, power perpetually reinscribes its relations in forms of unspoken aesthetic ideologies: reinscribes it in gender and social relations, in language, in fashion, on canvas, stage, and screen, in the architectural form of social space, and in bodies themselves—especially, and most literally, in the bodies of women. Women are made and make themselves objects for the male gaze, or are limited and limit themselves to a prescribed range of possibilities (wife, mother, vamp, virgin, dyke), and learn their place through linguistic exclusions ("one small step for man, one giant step for mankind"). Our desires are constructed and become our truth; they delimit our possibilities and our world.

But when power works its way into knowledge, truth, and desire, it is not just something forced on us; power is also something we internalize and are complicitous in producing. We come to desire the very same things that limit our life choices. This is power's constitutive dimension. We choose to have ribs removed, eyeliner tattooed on our eyes, to appear childlike, submissive, scintillating, stupid. And it is at this point that the Foucauldian model becomes worrisome. Foucault makes it quite clear that there is no outside of power: "It seems to me that power is 'always already there,' that one is never 'outside' of it, that there are no 'margins' for those who break with the system to gambol in."[7] But if power is everywhere, and if we cannot get outside it, and if indeed, individuals are created as its effect and articulation, how can it be resisted? Can we resist, even while we speak, both literally, and in our material or bodily constructions, with the tongue of patriarchal power?[8]

These questions are urgent and troublesome for women considering alternatives while also operating within the parameters of patriarchal culture. Women's bodily constructions take place within a network of ideological power relations so complicated and subtle, it is difficult, if not impossible, to escape indoctrination. Not only popular culture, but also high culture, and not just disciplines relegated to the so-called subjective sphere of taste, but also the disciplines of medicine, economics, and legality, serve to put woman in her proper place, making her subject to the male gaze, to male desires and purposes. And women are not just subjected to these desires; they also constitute themselves as subjects defined by such desires.

Women act in collusion with patriarchal power because they are constituted within discourses that give "woman" meaning as subjects of the male gaze. In the major classical genres, the female body *is* sexuality, providing the exotic object for the male spectator; I am speaking not only of the fine art and literary traditions, but also of the philosophic tradition of moral aesthetics handed to us by Hume, Burke, and Kant. Witness, for example, a typical passage from Burke's *Philosophical Enquiry*, the treatise that is meant to argue the justification for a standard of taste when it is based in universal, natural sentiments. In section 15, entitled "Gradual Variation," which establishes the criteria of perfectly beautiful bodies, Burke's gaze fixes on the submissive body of woman:

> Observe that part of a beautiful woman where she is perhaps the most beautiful, about the neck and breasts; the smoothness, the softness; the easy and insensible swell; . . . the deceitful maze, through which the unsteady eye slides giddily, without knowing where to fix or whither it is carried. Is not this a demonstration of that change of surface continual and yet hardly perceptual at any point which forms one of the great constituents of beauty?[9]

Of such theories are skin lotions, blushes, surgery implants, reductions, tucks, and women's bodily insecurities made. This is the tradition in which women have been constituted and within which they have also constituted themselves, thereby serving to further their subjection to the male gaze and to maintain their own economic and social marginalization.

Within such a framework, body aesthetics takes on urgent proportions and subversive possibilities: to escape the domination of the male gaze, to take control of the signification of their bodies, to refuse to be constructed as sexuality, is not merely an aesthetic battle over imagery; it is also a political battle. To succeed in formulating empowering subversive images of women would be to revolutionize the dominant power regime, to re-vision culture.

A Foucauldian analysis of the ubiquity of power forces us to wonder whether these possibilities be actualized. Can women re-vision them-

selves as subversive and empowered bodies? Can women re-vision themselves along lines of resistance that would restructure aesthetic pleasures
and desires and in so doing, revamp the existing gender order?

The Muscled Woman

I focus now on the body of the female bodybuilder: in confusing accepted
gender dichotomies, the body of the muscled woman problematizes
seeing in a way that calls attention to the cultural presuppositions
oppressing both men and women on an unconscious or ideological level.
The muscled woman makes visible the artificiality of the norms of
masculinity and femininity, and the artificiality of the distinction that
one is *either* male *or* female. In making us aware of the artificiality of
such distinctions, the body of the muscled woman is a subversive tool
because it motivates questions about the taken for granted, questions,
for example, about desire, sexuality, and domination. The construction
worker who had his lips pursed to whistle at the woman walking past has
to think about what he is desiring when the woman turns out to have
bulging muscles. It also forces him to stop and think about what he is
doing, for the image of the muscled woman is not a passive image. At
the very least it calls the inevitability of sexual domination into question
by evoking the response "Hey, wait a minute! How do I read this? What
do I do now?"

Adapting Foucault, I would emphasize that the meaning of what it is
to be a woman, her oppression, and her inferior status, has been
inscribed and continues to be inscribed on her body. For that reason I
am looking for a bodily protest, a protest that problematizes seeing. I
think it is important, especially for women, to locate the re-visioning of
culture in alternative images that are immediately and obviously—even
shockingly—present.

I am looking for alternatives that are inscribed on the surface of the
body, because it is the everyday male readings of the visible body (and
whether the subject is actually male or female is irrelevant here since
the woman also, to a large extent, reads with the male gaze) that have
played a large part in restricting her possibilities to those that serve, or
at least to those that do not too radically challenge the interests,
economic and otherwise, of patriarchal power. And this is why the

woman bodybuilder is suited to my project in a way that other women athletes are not.[10] The body of a woman runner or tennis player, for example, may in fact be strong, and may make her feel empowered, but such internal feelings do not problematize seeing, and the need for such problematizing is my thesis, the achievement of such, my goal.

But the female bodybuilder is not the only immediately readable and shocking body alternative. The anorexic is an example of a body image that is also immediately and obviously shocking. But the anorexic fails to meets my criteria of a body protest for two reasons. First, because despite what the anorexic may claim (Amy Liu's confessional book *Solitaire* provides a valuable source for how anorexics read themselves), her body is not empowering. I mean nothing complicated by this: the anorexic, if not cured, will die. The body of the female bodybuilder is not a correspondingly "sick" image (the steroid controversy and pre-competition starvation notwithstanding; both are only necessary to professional bodybuilding, the institution of which has many problems for women as I detail below). Second, and perhaps more problematic, I am trying to find a way of re-visioning the body that is not complicitous with patriarchal domination and the process of normalization. Paradoxically, and often tragically, many of the candidates for empowering female body protests, like that of the anorexic, function as if in collusion with the cultural conditions that produce them. Even if female bodybuilders allow themselves to be used to package new forms of erotics, the image *itself* does not function in collusion with the dominant ideology; I shall argue, it is that image that makes it finally, a revolting body.

The movement beyond oppression requires new eyes for the oppressed as well as the oppressor, and also new images, for new eyes come about when faced with images that problematize seeing and assimilation. Images that problematize *seeing* are those that will most readily move us beyond oppression. But can the female body be radically re-visioned? Can those aesthetic codes that ground our cultural understanding and identity be radically altered?[11]

There are both reasons to be hopeful that such revisionings are possible, and reasons to be concerned that they are not. I shall briefly outline the philosophical background that gives hope to the possibility of success for the muscled woman as an empowering subversive image, and I shall offer as well some philosophical arguments that worry the possibility of an aesthetic revolution fought at the level of the body. To ground my discussion of woman bodybuilders philosophically, I sketch the Nietzschean/Foucauldian injunction to create oneself as a work of art.

An Aesthetics of Existence: Its Promises and Problems

If the Nietzschean doctrine of perspectivism were applicable to women, women's bodies could be constructed as sites of empowered revolt; to paraphrase Nietzsche, women would know that they create the world that possesses values. Knowing this, women would know too that reverence for truth is already the consequence of an illusion and that one should value more than truth the force that forms, simplifies, shapes, invents. Women would know that "everything is false; everything is permitted!"

This liberation speaks from Nietzsche's perspectivist thesis, which denies that the world possesses any feature that is prior to interpretation. Interpretations introduce all the meaning there is; there is nothing preexisting for interpretations to conform to (except, of course, other interpretations). This means that in itself the world has no features that can be either correctly or incorrectly understood. Reality is nothing more than the totality of interpretations; the truth there is is created and not discovered.

This truth, the truth that there is no truth, that all is a matter of interpretation, is the creative challenge embraced by the "noble spirits" of the *Gay Science* and the "immoralists" of *Beyond Good and Evil*; it is this truth of humans as essentially creative authors that informs the consciousness and gives strength and power to the Übermensch (Super-person) heralded throughout the *Will to Power*.

Foucault is explicit about his intellectual debt to Nietzsche, and even claims a "fundamental Nietzscheanism."[12] He too is taken with the search for what he calls "styles of existence." In his last works Foucault writes about the moralities of antiquity as a search for an aesthetics of existence. He describes these moralities as attempts to give a style to one's life, an "elaboration of one's one life as a personal work of art."[13] In Foucault's reading, Christianity overrode this search for personal style in its insistence on obeying rules, but he believes that the Christian ethic is disappearing and that what is taking its place is once again the search for an aesthetics of existence.

Like Nietzsche, Foucault does not just write about this evolution from the standpoint of a disengaged chronicler of historical events; rather, he sees himself as showing us how to search for an aesthetics of existence. Genealogical knowledge is the key tool in this search. What genealogical accounts of the body, sexuality, and discipline do, is show how social mechanisms have been able to operate, and how the forms of repression and constraint have acted. And once armed with this knowledge, he believes people are free to "choose their own existence."[14]

The doctrine of perspectivism and the search for an aesthetics of existence, are exciting to the aesthetic revolutionary, for it would seem to open the way not just for the Superman but also for the Superwoman. All essentialisms are false, all truths have a history. Armed with this knowledge, the Superwoman turns deaf ears to the patriarchal tradition for which Burke is an eloquent spokesman; she refuses to be lumped together with ideas of beauty and elegance among animals. She refuses to be a member of Burke's audience when he smugly asserts the feminine virtue of weakness and delicacy: "I need here say little of the fair sex, where I believe the point will be easily allowed me. The beauty of women is considerable owing to their weakness, or delicacy, and is even enhanced by their timidity, a quality of mind analogous to it."[15]

The muscled Superwoman makes her body resistant to readings of timidity, weakness, and inferiority by creating her body as her own interpretation. Her reshaped body forces the revelation that the idea that women are by nature destined to be weak and delicate is an invention—an invention that doesn't suit her purposes. The Superwoman is not constrained by gender roles; she eschews the idea of an essence, a nature to which she must conform. She denies the existence of a naturally proper way of feminine bodily comportment, just as she denies the existence of a set of natural feminine virtues and duties, or a naturally determined ideal of beauty. In fact, she might argue, both the idea of femininity and masculinity, and their binary opposition are inventions, are ideas invented by the dominant ideological forces to suit the purposes of phallocentric desire. The Superwoman re-creates her image, and in doing so, forces cultural reinterpretations. The thesis of perspectivism, and the possibility of choosing one's existence, is thus empowering because to those who are able to look their truth straight on, they offer the possibility of self-creation.

This possibility of self-creation is the empowering aspect of Nietzsche's perspectivism, and an empowering moment in Foucault's theory of the self. But Nietzsche and Foucault would both argue the impossibility of a pre-social or asocial self, and this opens up a whole host of problems for the prospect of radical self-creation.

For Nietzsche, imaginative interpretations are confined to the normalizing limits of language: "We cease to think," says Nietzsche, "when we refuse to do so under the constraint of language."[16] And this brings Nietzsche up short. We can never get behind language and language is always leveling. Language is meant to be understood, but because it is meant to be understood it must of necessity operate on the basis of a common denominator.[17] As Nietzsche sadly notes:

> consciousness does not really belong to man's individual existence but rather to his social or herd nature. . . . [Consciousness] has developed subtly only insofar as this is required by social or herd utility. Consequently, given the best will in the world to understand ourselves as individually as possible, "to know ourselves," each of us will always succeed in becoming conscious only of what is not individual but "average." Our thoughts themselves are continually governed by the character of consciousness . . . and translated back into the perspective of the herd.[18]

And for Foucault, there can be no autonomous subject behind the mechanisms of power. There is no possibility of a subject's being able to stand back and study a situation and make choices from some unaffected standpoint; the subject is still that individual who is the effect, and vehicle, of power.[19]

This embeddedness effects the injunction to create oneself as a work of art, for it sets limits on the nature of creation: How radical can a work of art be and still be understood? Isn't it the case that the self doing the creating is already created, already a self not of the self's own making? And if this is true then the imaginative possibilities of the artist, of the muscled Superwoman, are already limited. And this problematizes not only how we read ourselves, but how we are read by others. Self-creations have to be read, and those readings are filtered through the leveling effect of language, or the normalizing effect of power. As soon as one acts, that act is no longer one's own but is out there in the public realm, at the mercy of readings (and subject to misreadings) and available for power stratagems. So the question becomes, Can one successfully write a radically new text for the female body, given that resistance is never the property of an autonomous subject?

Pushing Desire

The re-visioning of the female body along with its broad cultural and social repercussions is, then, the goal. But, as I have already said, the reading of the female is not only undertaken by men; it is undertaken by women as well: power/knowledge/desire work hand-in-hand to both repress and constitute the self. This being the case, it becomes important to consider the implications of re-visioning the female body for the well-being of women constituted within the domain of phallocentric desire.[20] What image can women create that would call attention to the fact that she is not just what society made her, while at the same time not create a psychological, economic, and sexual ostracism within that very society in which she must compete, form relationships, and find happiness? The image of the muscled women is subversive, but will she find it empowering?[21]

The male gaze is internalized to a greater or lesser extent by all women who are themselves always already social (linguistic) subjects (think, for example, of how difficult it is for even the most liberated woman to escape the feeling of disgust at seeing her legs unshaved). The sense of oneself as a distinct and valuable individual is tied to the sense of how one is perceived, and it would be irresponsible to deny the degree to which most women to a large extent, and all women to some extent, depend on the look of men for their own sense of self-worth—a worth that sometimes includes the need to feel desired. Hence, ironically enough, feminism, especially a feminism that questions the patriarchal construction of the female body, is potentially threatening to women; many women will resist the abandonment of an aesthetic that defines what they take to be beautiful. Women may feel that the demand by some feminists to reconceptualize desire pushes them too far. I think it is important for Sandra Lee Bartky to have pointed out to feminist theorists that having

> a body felt to be feminine—a body socially constructed through appropriate practice—is in most cases crucial to a woman's sense

of herself as female and, since persons currently can be only male or female, to her sense of herself as a sexually desiring and desirable subject. Hence any political project that aims to dismantle the machinery that turns a female body into a feminine one may well be apprehended by women as something that threatens her with desexualization, if not outright annihilation. (78)[22]

Feminist theory will have to negotiate the role present configurations of desire have in women's conception of their well-being in its attempt to move us beyond the oppression that results from those limited configurations.

In *Discipline and Punish* Foucault writes,

Our society is not one of spectacle, but of surveillance; under the surface of images, one invests bodies in depth; behind the great abstraction of exchange, there continues the meticulous, concrete training of useful forces; the circuits of communication are the supports of an accumulation and a centralization of knowledge; the play of signs defines the anchorages of power; it is not that the beautiful totality of the individual is amputated, repressed by our social order, it is rather that the individual is carefully fabricated in it, according to a whole technique of forces and bodies.[23]

As we shall see in the next section, when bodies resist and threaten to becomes disruptive, there is a whole host of forces that work to resignify the "new look," to resignify the subversive body into one more tactic of power/knowledge. And especially, if we agree with Foucault that power is not just repressive but also constitutive, and responsible for the very formation of bodies and individuals along with their desires, discourses, and pleasures, then it becomes very difficult to imagine where a chosen, and phenomenologically empowering, self-conscious resistance would come from, or why it would occur. To imagine this kind of tactical rearticulation within the domain of constitutive power becomes a provocative and frustrating challenge for those of us concerned with gender politics.

The Co-option of the Professional Female Bodybuilder

As has been suggested, there may well be a tension between the demand for an image that is both subversive *and* empowering. Many women, even those who may seem to be the embodiment of radical possibilities, do not want to be liberated from phallocentric desire. This may explain why most professional women bodybuilders have allowed their potentially subversive bodies to be re-eroticized, have themselves become once again submissive to the male gaze, and have also contributed to the formation of a new way of oppressing women through their bodies.

In professional bodybuilding the image of the muscled woman is only successful to the extent to which she allows her image to be used for the purposes of male desire. It is not strength and power that is emphasized, but that the muscled look is sexy, desirable, and "still feminine." So Cory Everson, six-time winner of the Ms. Olympia contest, promotes muscles as enhancing sex appeal. She appears on the cover of a calendar pulling at the crotch of her silver snakeskin G-string next to the caption "Body Heat," and is used by *Muscular Development*, a magazine for male and female bodybuilders, to instruct women bodybuilders (and titillate the male ones) on how to achieve a "sexy waist" in ten easy steps. Sandy Riddel hosts a column in that same magazine called "Lifestyles of the Fit and Feminine" and advertises posters of herself as a leather-clad domina-trix. Laura Creavalle's personality is headlined alongside her photograph and seems to consist mainly of having a "romantic nature,"[24] and Penny Price is pictured in a gym smiling at two male bodybuilders who are evaluating her with serious and lustful expressions. This photograph is used to illustrate the article "Welcome to the Erogenous Zone," an article written in the authoritative voice of male desire. Male desire speaks, the woman's identity is obliterated, and she is again a sexual body valuable because she is approved by a male gaze:

> She moved between the equipment with poise and confidence, displaying a sense of self-control and a sensuality that turned numerous heads. . . . this was a woman through and through. . . . As she started slowly pumping out triceps kickbacks, I admired her (at moments unabashedly, at others surreptitiously). As her arm worked rearward contracting the triceps, (no jiggling underarm wattles here), yet subtle enough so as not to betray her

femaleness. The back had just the right kind of architecture and thickness to connote strength without bellowing machaness; the mild sweep of her thighs was provocative and inviting, and her glutes were, well, since this is a family magazine, let us say her glutes were heavenly.[25]

And it just gets worse.

In *Discipline and Punish*, Foucault illustrates how modern disciplinary regimes use the science of individuals and the process of normalization as effective procedures for the individual and collective coercion of bodies. What happens to professional women bodybuilders and their readership bears this out. What is particularly interesting (troubling) in the example given above is how the dominant ideology subverts radical imagery. The message becomes, real men like muscled women; the fact that they can find her body lustworthy and are not threatened is a test of their own manliness. And there are lessons here for women as well; the newly expanded male desire works to burden her with yet one more product she must buy into in order to see herself as, and to be, desirable. The woman reading this article is made to be horrified at the possibility of "jiggling underarm wattles" and so is supposed to rush to take up or take more seriously bodybuilding and all the bodybuilding paraphernalia the magazines would have its readers believe are necessary. Women, then, are directed to take up bodybuilding not in order to create a subversive image, or to become empowered, but in search of approval from the male gaze. And successful professional women bodybuilders are allowing themselves to be so directed. Can the image of the female bodybuilder only survive at the cost of complicity in male desire? Or is this only necessary where she hopes to make her living from her imaged body? Is the muscled woman faced with only two possibilities: acceptance of her image as another outlet for male desire (in which case she is complicitous with her own oppression), or nonacceptance (in which case she is ostracized by society and hence disempowered)? Is there a third alternative, or a redescription of the two I have presented?

Revolting Bodies

I argue that the phenomena described above speak less to an unwillingness or inability to rethink desire, than to the economics that forces professional women bodybuilders to comply with the wishes of an industry owned and operated by men. Given the economic reality of the profession, I would argue that it would be a mistake to generalize from the failure of *professional* women bodybuilders to the intrinsic inability of the muscled woman to re-vision herself and her culture. The image itself is still fraught with possibility.

If the success of the professional woman bodybuilder is tied to her ability to sell her image to a society whose desires are already informed by the male gaze, and she is forced to act in collusion with patriarchal desires in a way that the nonprofessional bodybuilder is not, then perhaps only the nonprofessional bodybuilder can act as vanguard of the aesthetic revolution. And even the nonprofessional bodybuilder may feel conflicted about challenging phallocentric configurations of desire. There is no denying that it is difficult and frightening to move from what we know to what has not yet existed.

But while being sensitive to the fact that a feminism that attacks present constructions of desire may well be threatening to the well-being of many women, we must not minimize the threat that present desire poses to the lives of all women. The point I make in defense of the reconceptualizing of desire is that the majority of women are ambivalent about locating their happiness in phallocentric desire. If they have sided so far with traditional roles it is because patriarchal ideology has been successful in limiting the images available to serve as role models.

The image of the muscled woman does offer a challenge to traditional images: if happiness and male/female natures are not natural but conventional, if they are a matter of interpretation, then offering new images at least opens up the field for possible redescriptions. And I suggest that it is not so easy for hugely muscled women to be co-opted by phallocentric desire. Despite what I have said about professional women bodybuilders, there are also women who are now being featured in mainstream bodybuilding magazines, who do not seem to be allowing themselves to be made into larger versions of Barbie dolls. The images of these women are frightening, thrilling, difficult to read, *and* their images are available.

But even if images that problematize desire may come to be seen as empowering, there are still problems to be addressed regarding the subversive impact of these images. New images may be available, but are new readings available? Let us consider the consequences of the thesis that signs signify in a social context. The text of the muscled woman has no choice but to recombine images that already carry social meanings. If, as Nietzsche feared, language always speaks the herd, then we are faced with the thesis that subversive texts are normalized in the process of being read.

The pessimistic worry is that the image of the muscled woman will not remain a subversive image for very long because the choices for reading such an image are already delimited by cultural norms. All too often the reading of the muscled woman falls back on the binary division insisted upon by our culture: (1) she is seen as too masculine, in which case the culture is able to deny her image serious contemplation—she's sick, abnormal (lesbian!)—or (2) the notion of femininity is expanded to include the image of a muscled woman. And as I have argued, far from being subversive, such an expansion disempowers the woman: it defuses the radical import of the image by making it one more possibility for that which arouses phallocentric desire. The image of the muscled woman becomes one more line of products that the woman must buy if she is to be desirable or even healthy.

In addition, one has to note that the "new look" the female body-builder is creating is not a wholly new creation. In problematizing the injunction to create oneself as a work of art I have said that the self-creating artist must use the materials already available to her. In the case of the female bodybuilder the woman is muscling in on an image that has served as the text of the macho warrior. The macho message of muscles, while on the one hand, signifying power, strength, dominance, self-sufficiency, and so forth, may at the same time also be associated with values or ways of life at odds with certain feminist utopian visions. And this puts us in a quandary. Women have been denied power, strength, self-sufficiency. In a culture that places a premium on these characteristics, the denial or feminization of these character traits assures her status as second-class citizen. So it would seem that the very things she needs are the same things that harm her. The message of muscles offers the woman traditionally defined as weak and delicate empower-ment at the same time as it perpetuates ideals that carry on those very values that are the lifeblood of patriarchal ideology. If the only way a woman can become empowered is to be "like a man," the aesthetic revolution is lost.

We do not need to buy into this pessimism: we do not have to buy into the reading that the muscled woman has to be "like a man." When muscles are inscribed on the body of a woman we have the possibility to create some third category beyond the choice masculine/feminine. If we grant that women do, in fact, have sensibilities different from men (and how to understand whether this "fact" is a function of nature or convention is not being argued here), then there is reason to believe that bulging muscles on the body of women will change the meaning of muscles, of power, of strength, making strength soft, power gentle—and also gentleness powerful, softness strong. Of course there are no assurances. We shall have to watch out for attempts to take the significance of our images away from us, to make our protests complicitous with those very things we are trying to change. Power is always lurking on the other side of resistance.

But while it is true that the muscled woman does not speak her body in a private language, she is nevertheless speaking her body in a way that challenges traditional hierarchies. Her body combines two ready-made images that are not supposed to go together: muscles, which connote masculinity; and the physiological female body, which is supposed to connote femininity. The fact that these images do not usually go together is what gives her image subversive potential. While we know how to read the two images—the muscled body and the female body— separately, we do not know how to read their combination. Placing them side by side will expand our language, will present us with new metaphors, that like all good metaphors, will reshape our ways of seeing. Indeed, Nietzsche's worry about the leveling nature of language is misleading. Language can be leveling, but it can also be made to speak new worlds, and the best catalysts of change are those that put together familiar images in unfamiliar ways. They are responsible for expanding our language, and hence for expanding the way we view the world and our possibilities. In a culture, and within a power network that has insisted on, and benefited from, keeping the domains of the masculine and the feminine separate, the unexpected and shocking body of the muscled woman does indeed present a subversive image ripe with the possibilities of empowerment and revaluation.

Foucault is notorious for insisting that resistance is the other side of power, without ever really explaining what this resistance can be if there is no outside of power. But with the body of the muscled woman we have a form of resistance that does not need to step outside of power; rather, she recombines already given images and resignifies them in the process. This is how we might engage in an aesthetics of existence.

Such recombinations are effective in the same way genealogical analysis is. Genealogy is supposed to show us how the past worked so that we might understand how social mechanisms operated, how forms of repression and constraint worked so that we might then become conscious of those unconscious forces that have shaped our lives, and with this knowledge choose our truths, our existence. Recombining body images in the way the muscled woman does has a similar effect. Each kind of body, the muscled body and the female body, has been inscribed with meaning. As long as these bodies stay in their proper place, their ideological dimension goes unnoticed. But when they are recombined in unexpected ways, we have to learn to read them all over again. This forces us to articulate their "normal" meanings and to invent or choose new meanings for their new combination, to invent or choose new ways of understanding ourselves and each other.

In Foucault's last interview he gives primacy to the "ethics of the intellectual," suggesting that the best way to alter one's own and others' thoughts is through the intellectual analysis of ideas.[26] But I am suggesting that we must also engage in a politics of embodiment, where we "disturb people's mental habits," and especially the habits of oppression occurring at the level of bodies, by forcing the re-reading of bodies through a redesigning of our bodies. And the image of the muscled woman is not the only image to be used in this re-valuation. Tattooed bodies, bodies practicing homosexual or lesbian revolts, flagrantly sexual bodies, flagrantly ambiguous bodies, wrinkled bodies, bodies that take up space, bodies that refuse to wear prostheses, surgically constructed bodies . . . many kinds of bodies will be needed for the aesthetic revolution.

But a woman without a body, dumb, blind, cannot possibly be a good fighter. Right now women need to fight. Now is not the time to erase our bodies, to hide behind veils, or habits, or replace our flesh with bones.

Notes

1. An earlier, not so explicitly Foucauldian, version of this paper will be appearing in *Exercising Power: the Making and the Remaking of the Body*, ed. Cheryl L. Cole and Michael Mezner (Albany: State University of New York Press, forthcoming).

2. From an interview on National Public Radio, 2 November 1991. I am indebted to Sandra Bartky, who offered helpful comments on an early draft of this essay.

3. When I talk in this paper about women being oppressed by means of their bodies I am assuming that the analysis extends to all women regardless of race, class, or economics. While I would like to avoid treating "woman" as a universal category, part of the problem is that

women have been constructed as if they were all essentially the same, created for the same purposes (sex, childbirth, diversion, and so forth). While there are certainly different ways in which women of various races, ethnicities, classes, or ages have been constructed by the male gaze, I am assuming that the value of women has been inscribed on their bodies no matter who they are or what their differences are. It is the general fact of this inscription rather the particular form it takes that I am addressing in this essay.

4. For a wonderful discussion of the political and phenomenological importance of how bodies are trained to take up space in the world see Iris Young, "Throwing Like a Girl," in her *Throwing Like a Girl and Other Essays in Feminist Philosophy and Social Theory* (Bloomington: Indiana University Press, 1990).

5. Michel Foucault, "Two Lectures," in *Power/Knowledge: Selected Interviews and Other Writings, 1972–1977*, ed. Colin Gordon, trans. Colin Gordon et al. (New York: Pantheon, 1980), 98.

6. Ibid.

7. Foucault, "Power and Strategies," in *Power/Knowledge*, 141.

8. The difficulty with women speaking (and hence even thinking) their resistance has been forcibly developed by French feminists. If our thoughts are constructed with the tools of language, then since language speaks the phallus, in speaking language women have already internalized the ideology of patriarchy. Hence Irigaray's claim that language always speaks the male. As Annette Kolodny and others have pointed out, the problem extends to reading (desire) as well; the female gaze would be informed by the male gaze. These charges must be addressed because unless they can be met the reality of woman disappears. A counterargument to the view that women can have no voice is attempted by Judith Butler in her book *Gender Trouble: Feminism and the Subversion of Identity* (New York: Routledge, 1990). Her argument follows from her distinction that being constructed by discourse and being determined by discourse is not the same thing: the former is true, the latter is not (see, for example, 143ff.).

9. Burke, *A Philosophical Enquiry into the Origin of the Sublime and the Beautiful* (Oxford: Oxford University Press, 1990), 105.

10. I am indebted to Jay Coakley for calling to my attention the need for an explanation of why women athletes in general do not serve as subversive images.

11. In both cases what I mean by "radically" is, Can it be altered or re-visioned in such a way as to escape being co-opted by normalizing discourse and phallocentric desire? I talk about this more below. The worry is that there is always the danger that the image of the muscled woman will be used as one more sexual commodity, one more thing the woman must have if she is to be beautiful and desirable. If this happens we run the risk that while the aesthetic codes might be expanded to include new forms of domination, the essential structure of desire is left in place.

12. Michel Foucault, "The Return to Morality," in *Michel Foucault: Politics, Philosophy, Culture: Interviews and Other Writings, 1977–1984*, ed. Lawrence D. Kritzman (New York: Routledge, 1988), 251.

13. Michel Foucault, "An Aesthetics of Existence," in *Politics, Philosophy, Culture*, 49.

14. Ibid., 50.

15. Burke, *Philosophical Enquiry*, 106.

16. Nietzsche, *Will to Power* (New York: Random House, 1968), 522.

17. For a different perspective on language see Richard Rorty, *Contingency, Irony, and Solidarity* (Cambridge: Cambridge University Press, 1989). There he argues that the poets, those who invent new metaphors, are the vanguards of society. He takes himself to be a follower of Nietzsche but I do not think he adequately addresses the leveling problem of language that so bothered Nietzsche.

18. Friedrich Nietzsche, *The Gay Science*, translated by Walter Kaufmann (New York: Vintage, 1974), sect. 354.

19. See however "The Concern for Truth," *Politics, Philosophy, Culture*, 263: "What can the ethics of an intellectual be . . . if not this: to make oneself permanently capable of detaching oneself from oneself?"

20. On this point as on many others I am indebted to Sandra Lee Bartky's article "Foucault, Femininity, and the Modernization of Patriarchal Power" found in the excellent collection of essays edited by Irene Diamond and Lee Quinby, *Feminism and Foucault: Reflections on Resistance* (Boston: Northeastern University Press, 1988).

21. There has been a great deal written on women's dependence for their sense of self-worth on the aesthetic acceptability of their breasts. If this is the case, then what happens to the self-esteem of the female bodybuilder whose breasts' size shrinks significantly when she loses body fat, or whose breasts develop stretch marks from doing flies? One can point out that she shouldn't care, that her attachment to a certain image as the acceptable breast aesthetic is a social construction meant to keep her down. But what if she does mind, and minds so much that she comes to hate herself (her body)? In such an instance even if her body is subversive, it will not be liberating. While we hope that some day women will be freed from defining their self-worth by body ideals, at the moment we may have to negotiate present forms of desire with radicalized ones. At the very least, a woman who chooses bodybuilding as a body protest should be made aware of the effects it will have so that if her sense of self-worth would be unacceptably altered were her breasts to change (whatever the political correctness of such an emotion may be) she can choose another bodily protest. While the shrinkage of breast size is frequently obvious (despite the number of woman who have implants to assure their place in the bodybuilding magazines), other effects like stretch marks are air-brushed out. For more on women's relationship to their breasts see Daphna Ayalah and Isaac Weinstock, *Breasts: Women Speak About Their Breasts and Their Lives* (New York: Simon and Schuster, 1979); Audre Lord, *The Cancer Journals* (Spinsters Ink/Aunt Lute Press, 1980); and Iris Marion Young, "Breasted Experience" in her *Throwing Like a Girl and Other Essays in Feminist Philosophy And Social Theory* (Bloomington: Indiana University Press, 1990).

22. It is interesting to speculate on how successful lesbian desire is able to escape dependence on male gaze. When lesbian pornography recalls imagery of women found in mainstream pornography it is re-creating traditional forms of desire or constructing something new? When Monique Wittig constructs the lesbian body through a deconstruction of body parts and uses imagery reminiscent of rape and domination, is she radicalizing desire or speaking from a position (wittingly or not) of internalized phallocentricism?

23. Michel Foucault, *Discipline and Punish: The Birth of the Prison*, trans. Alan Sheridan, (New York: Random House, 1979), 217.

24. *Muscle and Fitness* (May 1990): 155.

25. Jerry Kindela in *Muscle and Fitness* (May 1990): 79.

26. Foucault, "The Concern for Truth," *Politics, Philosophy, Culture*, 265.

Part Three

Identity/Subject

7

Feminism, Foucault, and "Subjects" of Power and Freedom

Jana Sawicki

Since the early 1980s Foucault's work has been especially influential among North American feminists.[1] Why? Among the many influential French critical theorists Foucault was distinct insofar as his aim was to intervene in specific struggles of disenfranchised and socially suspect groups such as prisoners, mental patients, and homosexuals. Insofar as Foucault's discourse appeared to be more activist and less narrowly academic than those of some of his poststructuralist counterparts, it compelled activist feminist theorists to take a serious look at his work, even if they were predisposed to dismiss other intellectual trends emanating from Paris. Moreover, during the early 1980s a particularly impassioned and embittered set of feminist debates known as the "sex wars" took place. Promising as it did to radically alter the terrain of sexual theory, Foucault's *History of Sexuality* emerged as one of several key texts proffered by pro-sex feminists who were challenging feminist orthodoxies concerning gender and its relationship to issues of sexual freedom. Finally, during the same period women of color openly criticized "second wave" feminists' exclusionary practices. Some antiracist feminists argued that Foucault's analysis of power and his genealogical critiques of the exclusionary functions of universalism and essentialism could be used to understand such tendencies within white, middle-class feminism.

In addition, the following convergences of feminism and Foucault were especially striking: Foucault's analyses of the dimensions of disciplinary powers exercised outside the confines of the political realm of the modern liberal state overlapped with those of feminists already engaged in the project of exploring the micropolitics of "private" life. His analytic of power/knowledge could be used to further feminist explorations into the dynamics of patriarchal power at the most intimate levels of experience in the institutions of marriage, motherhood, and compulsory heterosexuality and in the everyday rituals and regimens that govern women's relationships to themselves and their bodies. In particular, his emphasis on the sexual body as a target and vehicle of "bio-power" promised to open up new possibilities for understanding the "controlled insertion of bodies into the machinery" not only of production, but also of reproduction and sexuality. The history of modern feminist struggles for reproductive freedom might be understood as central to the history of bio-power.

In addition to his analysis of micropower and his emphasis on the body as a site of power, Foucault's critique of Enlightenment humanism and its appeals to a universal a priori subject of knowledge and history also echoed radical challenges that feminists posed to fundamental epistemological and political assumptions in modern Western philosophical thought. His critical genealogies of "subjectification" and his skepticism regarding universalism and essentialism in modern emancipatory theories coincided with feminists' ambivalence about core concepts of liberalism and Marxism (that is, the presocial individual, the subject of history, authenticity, autonomy, false consciousness, and so forth) for feminist politics. Finally, both feminists and Foucault identified the "crucial role of discourse in its capacity to produce and sustain hegemonic power and emphasized the challenges contained within marginalized and/or unrecognized discourses."[2]

It would be surprising if the emergence of Foucauldian feminist discourses had not produced a counterdiscourse. Indeed, the relationship between Foucault and feminism has not been entirely happy. Criticisms have been launched from both sympathetic and more hostile camps. Most feminists point to Foucault's androcentric gender blindness; some do not regard it as a fatal flaw; others believe it contaminates the entire enterprise.

In what follows, I address a central issue in debates among feminists about the value of Foucault (and other poststructuralists) for feminism, namely, the question of the subject and the possibility of resistance. I begin by presenting the most trenchant feminist criticisms of Foucault. Then, I briefly outline two basic trends in feminist appropriations of Foucault: those that use his analyses of disciplinary power to isolate disciplinary technologies that subjugate women as both objects and subjects; and those that acknowledge domination, but center on cultures and strategies of resistance to hegemonic regimes of power. The former face the problem of agency. The latter attempt to develop the possibilities of a posthumanist politics opened up by genealogical critique. Finally, I construct my own response to feminist critics drawn from the later volumes on the history of sexuality and selected interviews from the early 1980s.[3]

Feminism and Foucault: Critique, Convergence, and Possibility

It is by now commonplace to point to a fundamental tension in Foucault's work on disciplinary power. In *Discipline and Punish* and *The History of Sexuality* (vol. 1), whenever Foucault spoke of the subject he referred principally to the subject as "subjected"—as the product of dominating mechanisms of disciplinary power. Foucault sometimes seemed to be describing forms of power that insinuate themselves so deeply within the subject that it is difficult to imagine how change might be possible. At the same time he claimed that wherever there is power, there is resistance. Presumably, what makes disciplinary power so effective is its ability to grasp the individual at the level of its self-understanding—of its very identity and the norms that govern its practices of self-constitution. As "subjected," the individual is either bound to others by dependency or control, or to categories, practices, and possibilities of self-understanding that emerge from medico-scientific discourses associated with the "normalizing" panoptic disciplines (medicine, criminology, psychoanalysis, sexology, and so forth) that Foucault describes in his genealogical writings. Thus, in his portraits of disciplinary society even modes of self-governance seem to emerge as perniciously disciplinary.

In one of the most impressive critical analyses of Foucault's middle writings to date, Nancy Fraser characterizes the scenario of the perfected Panopticon as one in which "disciplinary norms have become so thoroughly internalized that they . . . [are] not experienced as coming from without."[4] In others words, the difference between autonomy and internalized domination is erased. Fraser argues that Foucault's lack of explicit normative foundations makes it impossible for him to make such a distinction at all. If this is the case, then his assertions that resistance to power is everywhere appear at best gratuitous, and at worst incoherent. In short, his notion of resistance would appear to require some grounding in a theory of an autonomous subject.

Despite her significant reservations about feminist appropriations of Foucault, Fraser has consistently made use of genealogical critique and discourse analysis in her own compelling critiques of the welfare state.[5] This has not been true of Nancy Hartsock, a leading feminist critic of poststructuralism, who argues that Foucault's "wholesale" rejection of modernity and its emancipatory theories, his refusal to envision alternative orders, and his emphasis on resistance and destabilization over transformation rob feminism of elements (in particular, the effort to establish epistemological and moral foundations for its enterprise) that are indispensable to its emancipatory goals. Hartsock claims: [S]ystematically unequal power relations ultimately vanish from [Foucault's] work."[6] Moreover, like feminist literary critic Barbara Christian, Hartsock is suspicious of Foucault's alleged moves to reject a constitutive subject and universal theories of history at a time when many marginal groups are finally breaking silence, rejecting their object status within dominant discourses, and constructing oppositional political subjectivities, theories, and progressive visions of their own.[7]

Ultimately, Hartsock claims that Foucault's analytic of power fails feminism because it is not a theory developed *for* women. It is the theory of a colonizer who rejects and resists the colonizers, but who, because he does not think from the perspective of the colonized, "fails to provide an epistemology which is usable for the task of revolutionizing, creating and constructing."[8] She regards his vision of struggle as a "war of all against all" as dystopian and unacceptable.

In a more sympathetic reading of Foucault's contributions to critical theory, Joan Cocks echoes Hartsock when she comments upon Foucault's "anarchistic" tendencies:

> [W]e must be clear on his two great weaknesses, both constitutional weaknesses of anarchism. These are the inability to support any movement that through its massiveness and disciplined unity would be popular and yet powerful enough to undermine an entrenched legal-political regime; and the inability to stand on the side of any positive new cultural-political order at all, such an order's always being at once a new system of imposed prohibitions and permissions, with respect to which opposition properly can respond only negatively. Both inabilities are symptoms of a basic failure of nerve before the whole question of order—which, after all, every tolerable as well as intolerable mode of social life must and will have, and which any serious countermovement at some juncture will have to develop as well.[9]

What does Hartsock propose instead? It is noteworthy that Hartsock links the inadequacy of Foucault's account of power and knowledge to his social location as a privileged white male; for the logic of her standpoint epistemology commits her to the view that certain situations are more likely to produce distortions and partial visions than others. Employing a feminist revision of Marxian standpoint epistemology, she argues for the epistemic privilege of the feminist standpoint. Among the features that she identifies as essential to this revised theory are the following:

> First, rather than getting rid of subjectivity or notions of the subject, as Foucault does, and substituting his notion of the individual as an effect of power relations, we need to engage in the historical, political, and theoretical process of constituting ourselves as subjects as well as objects of history. . . . Second . . . if we are to construct a new society, we need to be assured that some systematic knowledge about our world and ourselves is possible. . . . Third . . . we need a theory of power that recognizes that our practical daily activity contains an understanding of the

> world . . . a "standpoint" epistemology . . . [based upon] the claim that material life . . . not only structures but sets limits on the understanding of social relations, and that, in systems of domination, the vision available to the rulers will be both partial *and will reverse the real order of things.*[10] (my emphasis)

Hartsock finds Foucault's analysis of power deficient insofar as it presumably rejects subjectivity (and the possibility of transformative agency), systematic knowledge, and epistemological foundationalism.

Hence the most trenchant criticisms of Foucault by feminists identify two major defects in his work: his rejection of modern foundationalist epistemologies (and their humanistic philosophies of the subject), and the related question of the adequacy of his politics of resistance. (Who resists power? Toward what ends should resistance aim? Can Foucault envision possibilities of collective resistance?) These feminist critiques of Foucault overlap significantly with those from the nonfeminist quarters of social and political theory.[11] Thus, they point to the dangers of relativism, nihilism, and pessimism often associated with his work.

To be sure, despite such criticisms, many feminists have used Foucault's analysis of disciplinary power effectively to address the micropolitics of gender. For example, in her analyses of the fashion/beauty complex in contemporary America, Sandra Bartky gives compelling descriptions of disciplinary technologies that produce specifically feminine forms of embodiment. Bartky suggests that many women have resisted or ignored feminist critiques of prevailing standards of fashion and beauty because abandoning them threatens women with de-skilling and challenges their very sense of identity. Thus, this form of patriarchal power operates by attaching women to certain norms of feminine identity.

Bartky's use of Foucault corrects a deficiency that most feminists find in his writings: its androcentrism. Yet, she also reproduces a problematic dimension of the Foucauldian account of modern disciplinary practices to which I have already alluded. She, too, portrays forms of power that insinuate themselves within subjects so profoundly that it is difficult to imagine how we might alter them.

Despite his rejection of totalizing theory and teleological narratives of closure, Foucault's holistic rhetoric and sometimes shrill condemnations of the carceral society in *Discipline and Punish* lent credence to those who claimed that in this book Foucault was describing a wholly disciplined society. As we have seen, critics claimed that he provided no convincing account of how resistance to power is possible.

Elsewhere, I have argued that despite its occasional holistic rhetoric, *Discipline and Punish* was not intended as a portrait of the whole of modern society, but rather, a genealogy of the emergence of the ideal of a perfectly administered one. Bentham's Panopticon is not a symbol of modern society, but a theoretical model that should be analyzed in terms of its impact. Foucault's view of power is neither deterministic, nor systemic in any closed sense. He is not describing modern society tout court, but particular practices—that is, practices of subjection—found within it.

In her own defense—one that might also be enlisted in support of Foucault, who, after all, referred to himself as a "hyperactive pessimist"—Bartky writes: "Theoretical work done in the service of political ends may exhibit a 'pessimism of the intellect,' but the point of doing such work at all is the 'optimism of the will' without which any serious political work is impossible."[12] Moreover, as Deborah Cook has suggested, Foucault and Bartky are not alone. Much of left-wing political theory in the twentieth century (Horkheimer, Adorno, Sartre, Merleau-Ponty) has expressed despair about the efficacy of traditional emancipatory theory. Even Habermas has suggested that our chances for emancipation today "are not very good."[13] Cook claims that Foucault opens a space for the resistance of "those who have yet to be defined within the traditional political spectrum": women, homosexuals, lesbians, queers, mental patients, the imprisoned, postcolonial subjects, and so forth.[14] Indeed, as I shall suggest below, despite his skepticism about our capacity to control history (a ruse of certain versions of universal humanism) and his belief that total emancipation—"the realisation of a society where the individual is entirely free to define him or herself"—is not possible, he did identify areas he believed were vulnerable to criticism, forms of subjection that might be effectively resisted.[15] While he was skeptical about the prospects of total emancipation, he believed it was possible to alter particular normalizing practices and thereby make particular lives more tolerable.

Furthermore, Bartky and Foucault maintain that there is a value in negative criticism, criticism that does not point to specific remedies or alternatives. John Rajchman's fitting description of Foucault's critical task provides another defense for this view:

> One task for "critical thought" is thus to expose [the costs of our self-constitution] . . . , to analyze what we did not realize we had

to say and do to ourselves in order to be who we are. . . . The experience of critical thought would start in the experience of such costs. Thus, before asking, or at least when asking, what we must do to behave rationally, this kind of thinking would ask: What are "the forms of rationality" that secure our identity and delimit our possibilities? It would ask what is "intolerable" about such forms of reason.[16]

Through genealogical analysis, description and criticism of existing power/knowledge regimes, Foucault (and Bartky) hoped to open the space necessary for resistance by freeing us from uncritical adherence to particular disciplines and identities, or, using his later terminology, particular "technologies of the self."

Other feminist engagements with Foucault (as well as Lacan and Derrida) have produced exciting and provocative efforts to open up new possibilities for thinking about political agency. In a brilliant and imaginative, if problematic, effort to revise modern conceptions of emancipatory politics and identity, Judith Butler argues that feminist politics without a feminist subject is possible and desirable. In Butler's framework "feminist subject" refers to a fixed, stable, and essentialist identity (whether natural or socially constructed) constituting the ground and reference point of feminist theory and practice. What Butler objects to about identity politics is their tendency to appeal to a prediscursive "I" as their ground and support—their tendency "to assume that an identity must first be in place in order for political interests to be elaborated and, subsequently, political action to be taken."[17]

Butler contends that critics of Foucault and other poststructuralists are wrong to conclude that discursive constructionism entails historical determinism. To the contrary, she states, "Construction is not opposed to agency; it is the necessary scene of agency" (Gender Trouble 147). Butler describes identities as self-representations; that is, "fictions" that are neither fixed nor stable. Hence the subject is not a thing, a substantive entity, but rather a process of signification within an open system of discursive possibilities. The gendered self is a regulated, but not determined, set of practices. Butler states: "[An ontology of gender] is, thus, not a foundation, but a normative injunction that operates insidiously by installing itself into political discourse as its necessary ground" (148).

Of course, to claim that the subject and its identifications are merely effects of practices of signification is not to deny that these effects are real or that identity is artificial and arbitrary. Discursive practices are rule-governed structures of intelligibility that both constrain and enable identity formation. Neither wholly determined nor wholly arbitrary, the view of identity promulgated here is one that attempts to move beyond the dichotomy of free will versus determinism and to recognize the possibilities for critical and transformative agency that do not require us to establish an absolute and uncontestable ground of knowledge and experience beyond relations of power. Drawing on Lacanian psychoanalytic theory, Butler locates agency within domains of cultural possibility and intelligibility produced by the very failures of dominant gender norms to contain the multiplicity of gender expressions that exceed and defy the norm by which they are generated.

In effect, Butler endorses Foucauldian critical genealogies of the mechanisms that have produced dominant understandings and possibilities of gender identity as a strategy for bringing liminal identities into play: that is, such liminal types as the "assertive female," the "effeminate man," the "macho gay," the "lipstick lesbian," and so forth. She concludes:

> If identities were no longer fixed as the premises of a political syllogism, and politics no longer understood as a set of practices derived from the alleged interests that belong to a set of ready-made subjects, a new configuration of politics would surely emerge from the ruins of the old. (149)

What I find particularly illuminating in Butler's position is its articulation of the poststructuralist argument against the subject. It is the foundationalist subject that is challenged, not the practices of assuming subject positions and representing oneself. Indeed, the latter are inevitable. Nor is agency denied; it is simply reformulated as enactments of variation within regulated, normative, and habitual processes of signification. Poststructuralists like Foucault do not deny that we can or should "constitute ourselves as subjects" as Hartsock alleges, for this is unavoidable. It is the epistemological move to ground our politics in a foundational subject that is challenged and bypassed. Foucault and Butler shift the focus of political analysis from the epistemological project of grounding political and social theories to analyzing the production of certain forms of subjectivity in terms of their costs. Both conclude that the costs associated with many modern practices of identity formation have been too high. Finally, both seem to be suggesting that we develop a form of politics that is relatively independent of modern foundational epistemological projects.

Another alternative to identity politics based on some naturalized or essentialized subject may be found in the writings of Donna Haraway. Haraway has introduced the notion of a politics based on "affinities" or political kinship. She recommends that we draw upon the writings of women of color to learn how to construct political unities "without relying on a logic of appropriation, incorporation, and taxonomic classification."[18] What distinguishes these modes of identity formation is their self-consciously political character. What they attempt to avoid is the reduction of politics to projects of self-discovery and personal transformation, or to the formation of narrowly defined countercultural communities.[19]

The new political identity offered by Haraway is crystallized in the image of the "cyborg." Created by the very forces that we oppose in postindustrial capitalist patriarchal societies, the cyborg is neither wholly human, machine, nor animal. It defies categorization and takes pleasure in the fusion of boundaries (human-animal, human-machine, nature-culture), but also takes responsibility for their construction. It is an identity stripped of innocent origins and yet opposed to domination. Although many may find her optimism ungrounded, Haraway describes the cyborg's perspective as one of hopeful possibility:

> Feminisms and Marxisms have run aground on Western epistemo-logical imperatives to construct a revolutionary subject from the perspective of a hierarchy of oppressions and/or a latent position of moral superiority, innocence, and greater closeness to nature. With no available original dream of a common language or original symbiosis promising protection . . . to recognize "one-self" as fully implicated in the world, frees us of the need to root politics in identification, vanguard parties, purity, and moth-ering.[20]

In effect, Haraway's cyborg politics retrieves and subversively repeats elements of identity politics. It is, in Butler's terms, an identity politics with a difference. It involves a continuation of the practice of writing narratives of marginalized subjects. Partially rooted as it is in the experiences of women of color, Haraway's cyborg politics emphasizes the significance of personal storytelling as a strategy of resistance. The power to signify, to enter the struggle over meanings is crucial to any feminist politics. However, these stories do not rely on the origins myths of essentialist feminisms and humanism; instead they explore the theme of identity on the margins of hegemonic groups and thereby attempt to deconstruct the authority and legitimacy of dominant humanist narratives by exposing their partiality. Nor do the storytellers appeal to a seamless identity. As partial and mixed, such identities remain open to establishing connections with others despite many differences.

Thus, narratives of oppressed groups are important insofar as they empower these groups by giving them a voice in the struggle over interpretations without claiming to be epistemically privileged or incontestable. They are not denied the "authority" of experience if, by "authority," one means the power to introduce that experience as a basis for analysis, and thereby to create new self-understandings. What is denied is the authority of unanalyzed experience. Rather than "construct defenses of . . . experience," to use Edward Said's phrase, they promote knowledge of it.[21] Here "knowledge" is understood as potentially linked to relations of power and not as a completely autonomous domain of inquiry.

Thus far, I have suggested that it is not evident that under Foucault's influence, feminism is deprived of elements absolutely indispensable to its liberatory aims as long as one is willing to jettison the utopian humanist notion of total emancipation. Foucault was in fact pessimistic about this hope. Nonetheless, he had no monopoly on this characteristic. And he believed that particular intolerable relations of power could be resisted.

In addition, to assume, as Hartsock does, that emancipatory politics requires a foundationalist subject of history is to beg the questions that Foucault and others have raised about the degree to which Enlightenment humanisms have either masked forms of disciplinary power that operate by producing forms of modern individuality or participated in extending domination. Moreover, Foucault does not deprive feminists of developing a systematic knowledge of society; instead, he warns us of the normalizing impact of certain forms of such knowledge. Finally, while Foucault and feminists who appeal to him do repudiate Cartesian or transcendental subjectivities, this does not leave us without relatively autonomous subjects capable of resisting the particular forms of subjection that Foucault has identified in modern society.

In what follows, I turn to Foucault's last writings to develop the outlines of a more complete response to those critics troubled by Foucault's positions on the humanist subject and the possibilities of social transformation.

The Late Foucault on Subjectivity, Power, and Freedom

Foucault himself offered another set of possibilities for thinking about subjectivity, freedom, and resistance in his last writings on the Enlightenment and ancient Greek ethics.[22] His references to Kant and to ancient ethics were partly inspired by his desire to develop the outlines of a more positive account of freedom and a clarification of his relationship to Enlightenment humanism.

In the early 1980s Foucault entered into dialogue with critics who demanded criteria for distinguishing malevolent, benign, or beneficial forms of power. Moreover, as I have suggested, this coincided with a softening of his critique of the Enlightenment. Whereas in his middle writings he sometimes implied that traditional emancipatory theories were inherently totalizing, hence dominating, in his later works he suggested that theory, along with everything else, is simply "dangerous": "My point is not that everything is bad, but that everything is dangerous."[23] As if in response to the progressive and liberal critics (Habermas, Rorty, Fraser) who challenged his model of power and resistance for its lack of normative guidance, Foucault clarified the distinction between domination and power. Whereas "domination" refers to a situation in which the subject is unable to overturn or reverse the domination relation—a situation where resistance is impossible—"power" refers to relations that are flexible, mutable, fluid, and even reversible. Foucault remarks:

> the important question . . . is not whether a culture without restraints is possible or even desirable but whether the system of constraints in which a society functions leaves individuals the liberty to transform the system. Obviously constraints of any

kind are going to be intolerable to certain segments of society. But a system of constraint becomes truly intolerable when the individuals who are affected by it don't have the means of modifying it.[24]

Insofar as Foucault distinguishes domination from power, he denies that all forms of power or order are pernicious. Hence, he distances himself from anarchism.

Furthermore, Foucault also distinguishes among forms of power such as exploitation, racial or ethnic hegemony, and "subjection." He endorses efforts by colonized peoples to liberate themselves from totalitarian domination. Thus, Hartsock is mistaken when she claims that Foucault does not acknowledge systematically unequal power relations. Yet, in his own work rather than focus on top-down forms of totalitarian domination, he attempted to provide tools for those struggling against the latter form of power, namely, subjection. Thus, he states: "[N]owadays, the struggle against the forms of subjection—against the submission of subjectivity—is becoming more and more important, even though the struggles against forms of domination and exploitation have not disappeared."[25] Indeed, what Foucault found problematic about the theme of "liberation" is the fact that not only can it sometimes be a ruse of power (as in the case of those versions of sexual liberation that rely on the repressive hypothesis) but it often does not go far enough. Reversing power positions without altering relations of power is rarely liberating. Neither is it a sufficient condition of liberation to throw off the yoke of domination; a liberated people is still left with the problem of deciding upon acceptable forms of political society for themselves. Ultimately, for Foucault, liberty or freedom is not a state of being or an institutional structure but a practice: "[Liberty] is never assured by the institutions and laws that are intended to guarantee them. This is why almost all of these laws and institutions are quite capable of being turned around. Not because they are ambiguous, but simply because 'liberty' is what must be exercised."[26] For example, although Foucault supported homosexual rights, he more often cautioned rights activists about the limits of liberal reform and stressed the importance of establishing "practices of freedom"; that is, new attitudes and patterns of behavior, new cultural forms that give such legal reforms their force.

Unlike Kant, Foucault preferred to emphasize the importance of expanding our sense of possibility in the present rather than imagining alternative social orders. Yet he did not jettison appeals to Enlightenment values such as reason, autonomy, and human dignity. In a lecture on Kant's essay "What is Enlightenment?" published the year of his death, Foucault situates his own work within a philosophical tradition devoted to philosophical and historical reflection on the significance of the present for self-understanding. He identifies with a version of Kantian critical reflection and thus locates himself squarely within the Enlightenment tradition of critical theory. Foucault comments:

> one [does not have] to be "for" or "against" the Enlightenment . . . one has to refuse everything that might present itself in the form of a simplistic and authoritarian alternative: you either accept the Enlightenment and remain within the tradition of its rationalism . . . or else you criticize the Enlightenment and then try to escape from its principles of rationality.[27]

In the same essay he elaborates:

> there is the problem raised by Habermas: if one abandons the work of Kant . . . one runs the risk of lapsing into irrationality. I am completely in agreement with this, but at the same time our question is quite different. . . . What is this Reason that we use? What are its historical effects? What are its limits and its dangers? How can we exist as rational beings, fortunately committed to practicing a rationality that is unfortunately crisscrossed by intrinsic danger? . . . If it is extremely dangerous to say that Reason is the enemy that should be eliminated, it is just as dangerous to say that any critical questioning of this rationality risks sending us into irrationality.

In other words, while Foucault believed that a constant critique of the historical instantiations of political rationality is necessary, he refused to capitulate to what he referred to as the "blackmail of the Enlightenment." He continued to operate with (Kantian) liberal humanist values such as liberty, dignity, and autonomy—even rights and obligations. He also refused to choose between rationality and its critique; he used reason to critique itself. What he wanted to preserve of our Enlightenment heritage was not "faithfulness to doctrinal elements," but rather the attitude of critique and inquiry into the limits of possibility in the present.[28]

Foucault regarded Enlightenment as a complex historical process. In contrast, "humanism" is a theme, a set of characterizations of the human, that represents a variety of points of view. Consider his following remarks about humanism:

> What we call humanism has been used by marxists, liberals, Nazis, Catholics. This does not mean that we have to get rid of what we call human rights, but that we can't say that freedom or human rights has to be limited to certain frontiers. . . . What I am afraid of about humanism is that it presents a certain form of our ethics as a universal model for any kind of freedom. I think that there are more secrets, more possible freedoms, and more inventions in our future than we can imagine in humanism as it is dogmatically represented on every side of the political rainbow.[29]

In effect, Foucault finds humanism unreliable because as a theme in history it has meant so many different things, been enlisted in so many different causes. But this is not its only problem. It also "presents a certain form of ethics as a universal model for any kind of freedom." In particular, he objected to forms of humanism that began with an a priori theory of the subject and proceed to define the universal and necessary conditions for the possibility of ethical action and thought. Thus, even Kantian humanism with its relatively abstract noumenal subject delineates necessary criteria of autonomous moral action for any subject such as intention and duty. What Foucault objects to is the tendency to supply innate structures of autonomous subjectivity—the tendency to reify and render necessary contingent structures of being. As one commentator aptly characterizes the situation:

> Foucault resists the subject of Kantian humanism for fear of the mistaken claims of necessity, the optional and "loaded" meta-phors and concerns that Kant transcendentalizes in his depiction of the free subject. Although Foucault is committed to freedom, he is reluctant to theorize that freedom in terms of the subject. Instead, Foucault seems to opt for a minimalist theory of freedom: a theory which says only as much as it needs to make an ethical

commitment to freedom intelligible without hypostatizing innate structures of the autonomous subject.[30]

Foucault's turn to ancient Greek ethics can be understood as his effort to establish a normative basis for practices of self-formation and invention ("practices of liberty") that avoid the universalism of the Kantian "science of morals" and its inquiry into the necessary structures of morality, and which, insofar as they operate at the practical and not the theoretical level, might provide us with a practice aimed at the concrete realization of our ideals.

What did Foucault admire about Greek ethics? Why did he spend the last years of his life writing about them? Foucault denied that his studies of the ancients represented a radical shift in direction: "My objective [over the past twenty years] . . . has been to create a history of the different modes by which, in our culture, human beings are made subjects."[31] Whereas his earlier genealogies focused on anonymous processes through which individuals are constituted heteronomously, in his later genealogies of the self he focused on modes of self-constitution, historical processes through which individuals develop particular relationships to themselves. Foucault's preoccupation with the Greeks was also inspired by his desire to develop the outlines of a more positive account of freedom. Rather than define freedom principally in terms of resistance to normalization, to "rebelling against the ways in which we are categorized and classified"—a strategy more reactive than affirmative—Foucault turned to art as a way of facing the question of order that he so often avoided in his earlier writings. His aim was to suggest the outlines of criteria for distinguishing between better and worse expressions of freedom without capitulating to a traditional liberal micropolitics of subjection. He was fascinated by the fact that the Greeks had developed a plurality of ethical schools devoted to providing disciplinary models (technologies of self) for self-mastery and self-formation, that is, for an art of life. In effect, they enacted a *rapport à soi* (a relation to self) in which ethical comportment was dissociated from both ethico-religious imperatives and scientific determination.

Foucault identifies an important similarity between modernity and antiquity. He remarks:

> I wonder if our problem nowadays is not, in a way, similar to [the Greeks], since most of us no longer believe that ethics is founded

in religion, nor do we want a legal system to intervene in our moral, personal, private life. Recent liberation movements suffer from the fact that they cannot find any principle on which to base the elaboration of a new ethics. They need an ethics, but cannot find any other ethics than an ethics founded on so-called scientific knowledge of what the self is, what desire is, what the unconscious is, and so on.[32]

The Greek art of existence interested Foucault because it offered a "strong structure of existence without any relation to the juridical per se, [yet] with an authoritarian system, [and] . . . a disciplinary structure."[33] Greek ethics offered a more autonomous, more pluralistic, less pernicious mode of limiting freedom and forming the self than "modern morals." To be sure, these practices of self-creation were only relatively autonomous. The possibilities for self-constitution are not created ex nihilo. They are instead "patterns that [the individual] finds in his culture and which are proposed, suggested and imposed on him by his culture, his society, and his social group."[34] Niko Kolodny captures the essence of Foucault's position when he writes:

[T]his does not make ethical self-constitution a tragic resignation to determination by culture or history. Such resignation would follow only if Foucault conceptualized freedom in the form of absolute self-determination: if he held that the only freedom worth the name were freedom from every conceivable social constraint. . . . [T]he freedom Foucault has in mind is instead the relative freedom—marked by the fluidity, reversibility and mutability of relations of power—that individuals in one society enjoy relative to another.[35]

Of course, Foucault realized that a simple return to Greek ethics was neither possible nor desirable. He recognized that ancient "practices of freedom" were exercised in the context of sexual domination and slavery, that they were embedded in a cult of aristocratic virility. Nonetheless, he believed it was possible to retrieve the Greek notion of the self's work on itself in the present, to retrieve an art of existence to supplant the moralism and normalization operating in pernicious modern technologies of the self.

Foucault also admired the Greek's recognition of the social importance of art, of its applicability to life itself. "Why should the lamp or the house be an art object, but not our life?" he asks.[36] In a similar vein, Alasdair MacIntyre has suggested:

> [T]he cultural place of narrative has been diminished and the modes of interpretation of narrative have been transformed until it has become possible for modern theorists . . . to understand the form of narrative, nor as that which connects story-telling with the form of human life, but precisely as that which segregates narrative from life, which confines it to what is taken to be a separate and distinctive realm of art. . . . [T]he relegation of art by modernity to the status of an essentially minority activity and interest further helps protect us from any narrative understanding of ourselves.[37]

Like MacIntyre's, Foucault's aestheticism need not be read as either elitist or escapist. Indeed, it is echoed in Haraway's call for a cyborg politics, a politics that partly involves attention to forms of self-constitution and narrativization of marginal subjects that resist the normalizing tendencies of hegemonic medico-scientific discourses.

I have argued that feminists who have developed Foucault's radical insights are not obviously left without useful tools for struggle. Indeed, as I have suggested, Foucault's principal objective was not to provide an alternative emancipatory theory at all, but rather to provide tools that subjugated individuals might enlist in a particular set of struggles; namely, "struggles which question the status of the individual . . . struggles against the 'government of individualization.' "[38] If the practices of freedom that he identifies appear excessively individualistic, this is not because he is an individualist, but rather because this is the level of struggle on which he focused. To be sure, as we have seen, he recognized other forms of oppression as well. As Michael Kelly has pointed out, Foucault addresses "normative questions about resistance as practical not theoretical issues . . . [as] justified in the context of a practice. . . . The demands of critique arise from and are met by practice."[39] Criticisms of Foucault that fail to recognize the rather limited and specific nature of his project miss the point.

At the same time, Foucault's rhetoric is masculine, his perspective, androcentric, and his vision rather pessimistic. Nonetheless, his methods and cautionary tales have been useful and productive for feminist intellectuals struggling to combat dangerous trends within feminist theory and practice—feminist intellectuals who share neither his androcentrism nor his exclusive focus on subjection. Finally, Foucault asks us to reconsider the value of the emancipatory practices and theories that have been handed down to us through Western capitalist patriarchal traditions. Thus, his work fuels self-critical impulses within feminism that are indispensable.

Notes

1. Parts of this essay appeared in "Foucault, Feminism and Questions of Identity," in *The Cambridge Companion to Foucault*, ed. Gary Gutting (Cambridge: Cambridge University Press, 1994), 286–313. I thank Cambridge University Press for granting permission to include portions of that essay here.

2. Irene Diamond and Lee Quinby, eds., introduction to *Feminism and Foucault: Reflections on Resistance* (Boston: Northeastern University Press, 1988), x.

3. Deborah Cook has written a compelling defense of the importance of Foucault's interviews for understanding the political dimensions of his work in *The Subject Finds a Voice: Foucault's Turn Toward Subjectivity* (New York: Peter Lang, 1993), 97–107.

4. Nancy Fraser, *Unruly Practices: Power, Discourse, and Gender in Contemporary Social Theory* (Minneapolis: University of Minnesota Press, 1989), 49.

5. See chaps. 7 and 8 of *Unruly Practices* and her "A Genealogy of Dependency: Tracing a Keyword of the U.S. Welfare State," *Signs* (Winter 1994): 303–36.

6. Nancy Hartsock, "Foucault on Power: A Theory for Women?" in *Feminism/Postmodernism*, ed. Linda Nicholson (New York: Routledge, 1990), 168.

7. Hartsock, in "Foucault on Power," asks, "Why is it that just at the moment when so many of us who have been silenced begin to demand the right to name ourselves, to act as subjects rather than as objects of history, that just then the concept of subjecthood becomes problematic? Just when we are forming our own theories about the world, uncertainty emerges about whether the world can be theorized. Just when we are talking about the changes we want, ideas of progress and the possibility of systematically and rationally organizing human society becomes dubious and suspect. Why is it only now that critiques are made of the will to power inherent in the effort to create theory?" (163–64). See also Barbara Christian, "The Race for Theory," *Cultural Critique* 6 (Spring 1987): 51–63.

8. Hartsock, "Foucault on Power," 164.

9. Joan Cocks, *The Oppositional Imagination: Feminism, Critique, and Political Theory* (New York: Routledge, 1989), 74. See also Ann Ferguson, *Blood at the Root: Motherhood, Sexuality, and Male Domination* (London: Pandora, 1989) for a similar criticism.

10. Hartsock, "Foucault on Power," 171–72.

11. For examples of this nonfeminist criticism, see the articles by Taylor, Walzer, and Habermas in *Foucault: A Critical Reader*, ed. David Couzens Hoy (New York: Basil Blackwell, 1986).

12. Sandra Bartky, introduction to *Femininity and Domination: Studies in the Phenomenology of Oppression* (New York: Routledge, 1990), 7.

13. Jürgen Habermas, "Modernity—An Incomplete Project," trans. Seyla Benhabib, in *The Anti-Aesthetic*, ed. Hal Foster (Port Townsend, Wash.: Bay Press, 1983), 13. Quoted in Deborah Cook, *The Subject Finds a Voice*, 109.

14. Cook, *The Subject Finds a Voice*, 110.

15. Ibid., 116.

16. John Rajchman, *Truth and Eros: Foucault, Lacan, and the Question of Ethics* (New York: Routledge, 1991), 11.

17. Judith Butler, *Gender Trouble: Feminism and the Subversion of Identity* (New York: Routledge, 1990), 142.

18. Donna Haraway, "A Cyborg Manifesto: Science, Technology, and Socialist Feminism in the Late Twentieth Century," in *Simians, Cyborgs, and Women: The Reinvention of Nature* (New York: Routledge, 1991), 157.

19. Cf. Diana Fuss, *Essentially Speaking: Feminism, Nature, and Difference* (New York: Routledge, 1989), 101.

20. Haraway, "A Cyborg Manifesto," 176.

21. See Fuss, *Essentially Speaking*, 115, for Said quote.

22. Ideas developed in this section are largely indebted to my work with an honors student at Williams College, Niko Kolodny, whose outstanding thesis "The Late Foucault" has significantly influenced my reading of Foucault's work.

23. Michel Foucault, "The Subject and Power," afterword to *Michel Foucault: Beyond Structuralism and Hermeneutics*, by Hubert Dreyfus and Paul Rabinow (Chicago: University of Chicago Press, 1983), 232.

24. In his *Politics, Philosophy, Culture: Interviews and Other Writings, 1977–1984*, ed. Lawrence D. Kritzman (New York: Routledge, 1988), 294.

25. Foucault, "The Subject and Power," 213.

26. Michel Foucault, "Space, Knowledge, and Power," interview by Paul Rabinow in *The Foucault Reader*, ed. Paul Rabinow (New York: Pantheon, 1984), 246.

27. Michel Foucault, "What is Enlightenment?" in *The Foucault Reader*, ed. Paul Rabinow (New York: Pantheon, 1984), 43.

28. Ibid., 44.

29. Michel Foucault, "Truth, Power, Self: An Interview with Michel Foucault," in *Technologies of the Self*, ed. Luther H. Martin, Huck Gutman, and Patrick H. Hutton (Amherst: University of Massachusetts Press, 1988), 15.

30. Niko Kolodny, "The Late Foucault," 43.

31. Foucault, "The Subject and Power," 208.

32. Michel Foucault, "On the Genealogy of Ethics: An Overview of Work in Progress," in *The Foucault Reader*, ed. Paul Rabinow (New York: Pantheon, 1984), 343.

33. Ibid., 348.

34. Michel Foucault, "The Ethic of Care for the Self as a Practice of Freedom," in *The Final Foucault*, ed. James Bernauer and David Rasmussen (Cambridge: MIT Press, 1987), 11.

35. Kolodny, "The Late Foucault," 52.

36. Foucault, "On the Genealogy of Ethics," 350.

37. Alasdair MacIntyre, *After Virtue* (Notre Dame: University of Notre Dame Press, 1981), 210–11. This passage was quoted in Kolodny's "The Late Foucault."

38. Foucault, "The Subject and Power," 211–12.

39. Michael Kelly, "Foucault, Habermas, and the Self-referentiality of Critique," in *Critique and Power: Recasting the Foucault/Habermas Debate*, ed. Michael Kelly (Cambridge: MIT Press, 1994), 382.

8

Foucault's Mother

Jon Simons

Although subjectification, or *assujettissement*, is the focus of Foucault's work,* his gender blindness and androcentrism lead him, and perhaps his readers, to overlook its most significant manifestation.[1] In none of his analyses of that "form of power which makes individuals subjects" did Foucault pay any attention to women's enormous role, especially as mothers, in the process of subjectification.[2] His focus on disciplines that produce masculine rather than feminine bodies is implicitly a denial that we are all "of woman born" and mostly by women raised.[3] This same

---

*I thank Susan Hekman, Sarit Helman, Iddo Landau, and Niza Yanai for their comments on a previous draft of this essay. I also acknowledge my debt for my existence and nurturing to my mother, and for my ability to read and write to my other mothers (that is, primary school teachers), especially Lilian Ellman and Leila Abrahams.

denial surfaces in Foucault's affirmative project to suggest how current modes of subjection might be resisted and "new forms of subjectivity" be promoted through "arts of the self."[4] Here his focus on Greek and Hellenist models of self-constitution reaffirms typical masculinist conceptions of self-making, which implicitly denigrate the already existing "mother-made" self. Foucault thus robs himself of an important resource for his affirmative thought: a model of subjectification in which power is exercised over others in a nonsubjecting manner. Foucault overlooks the significant subjectifying power of women as caretakers which, as feminist theorists have pointed out, offers the most concrete model of power as empowerment, constituting initially helpless infants as autonomous adults.[5]

However, attention needs also to be paid to a less celebratory feminist attitude toward mothering: that much if not most of current mothering and caretaking is carried out on terms defined by men in order to serve patriarchal purposes.[6] Such claims can usefully be supplemented by an implicit argument in Foucault's work, according to which the caring labor of women, which should be included in what Foucault refers to as pastoralism, is integrated into humanist political rationality with its opposite, reason of state.[7] In the context of pastoralism, the role of mother has been instituted as a powerful subject position in itself, authorizing women through their articulation with what Foucault calls "bio-power." The individualizing care of pastoralism, however, is always subordinated to the demands of state whose military destructive capacities are enhanced along with the development of individual care.[8] Foucault is once again gender-blind as he disregards the gendered nature of this central antinomy of political reason, failing to note the cultural association of caring with women and war with men, along with the subordination of the former to the latter.

The above analysis poses a difficult strategic choice for feminism: Should women exploit their powerful subject positions, celebrating their subjectifying power while attempting to liberate it from patriarchal constraints? Or should women renounce mothering because it confines them to limited subject positions and is complicit with both patriarchy and bio-power? Foucauldian feminism suggests an alternative. Butler's feminist appropriation of Foucault raises the possibility that women's complicity with and subordinate position within bio-power can be a resource for resistance.[9] Then the question becomes how to use the empowerment or authorization of the subject position of the mother in order to subvert the patriarchal confines of mothering. How can the task of mothering be performed subversively in ways that simultaneously break the confinement of women to mothering and caring subject positions while retaining the empowerment authorized by such positions? Butler proposes a subversive strategy of parodic performance in order to disrupt the coherence of gendered identities in what she calls the heterosexual matrix. I appropriate her approach by suggesting that what is needed is a subversive performance of motherhood that disrupts the coherence of what I call the maternal matrix.

Women's Subjectifying Power

Foucault's earlier treatments of the constitution of subjects, or subjectification, relate to oppressive forms of subjectivity, the forms of subjectivity against which people resist.[10] As feminist critics have pointed out,[11] the processes of subjection described by Foucault are most appropriate for the production of men as "docile and productive" bodies in carceral institutions such as armies, factories, schools, and prisons through techniques of surveillance in the nineteenth century.[12] Not only does Foucault overlook the differential effects of modern modes of subjection on women; more significant, he offers no analysis of the specific disciplines to and by which women are subjected. In short, feminist critique has already established that Foucault is gender-blind with respect to subjection.

In order to widen the scope of feminist interpretations of Foucault, however, situations in which women are not only active agents in their own subjection, but also the primary agents in the subjectification of others, must also be addressed. Several feminists have turned to mothering in order to recover a crucial site of women's social agency. Rather than constantly harping on women's passivity and subordination in the face of male power, such theorists illustrate the power and responsibility in women's hands. For example, Ruddick objects to suggestions that women are victims by virtue of being mothers, because many women experience a sense of competence as mothers.[13] Mothers exercise control over their children, even though they may not feel powerful because of the external constraints on their power as mothers. Rich suggests that even male myths that express fear of female power may be resources for women as they are based on a real memory of maternal power.[14] From another perspective, in Chodorow's feminist object-relations theory, basic gendered personality is formed in relation to the woman, usually the biological mother, who provides primary care to the infant.[15] The degree and quality of care that she gives affects both the ability of boys to grow into men who will slot themselves into appropriate social roles and of girls to become mothers. In other words, women are actively central to social reproduction in modern society. Of course, mainstream accounts of socialization and social reproduction also focus on women's role, but feminist accounts seek to revalorize this domestic activity that is generally subordinated to public action. Although many feminist theorists are far from unequivocal about the power placed in their hands, the point here is that women do exercise such subjectifying power, and that Foucault ignores it.

In the absence of any acknowledgment of women's agency in the constitution of human subjects, Foucault appears to be a classic case of masculine denial that men, too, are of woman born. Feminists have remarked on ways in which men deny their debt to their mothers and women in general for their lives and their nurturance. For example, O'Brien discusses how men establish human nature as a second nature because they are alienated from the natural, reproductive process through which women are integrally linked to species continuity. Boys "come of age" as men after initiation ceremonies into the male, political world, which denigrates the natural, biological, and private world of the family and women. Men replace female procreativity with male creativity: for example, in the way that Greeks ensured their immortality not through the progeny of their wives but by achieving fame.[16] In the masculinist conception, human value derives from man's second nature, which is dependent on the denigration of the "mother-made" self. My suggestion, then, is that Foucault is typically masculinist in his denial of his debt to his "mother."[17]

Foucault's disregard for women's agency as mothers is not only highly problematic in feminist terms but even on his own terms. In his later work, Foucault embarks on an affirmative project in which he conceives of enabling processes of self-subjectification as "aesthetics of existence."[18] Crucial to this project is a model of subjectifying power that is not simultaneously subjecting and oppressive. A common critique of Foucault's early work in particular is that he regards all subjectifying power as oppressive. Wartenberg holds that for Foucault subjects are always the victims of the power, which is positive in that it makes them, but negative and dominative as it nonetheless alienates them.[19]

Foucault himself sensed the problem of portraying subjectification as always oppressive. In *The History of Sexuality*, Foucault reached an apparent impasse in which every attempt at liberation reinforced repression. Partly in order to break this deadlock, he shifted his attention from power/knowledge to what he called ethics, meaning "the kind of relationship you ought to have with yourself . . . which determines how the individual is supposed to constitute himself as a moral subject of his own actions." Foucault was not primarily interested in any mode of self-constitution, but in aesthetic modes in which one creates oneself as a work of art, rather than by conforming to universal moral codes or scientific truth about one's nature.[20] However, he does not mean by this that the self should be unconstrained, but should be formed through a disciplined "ascetic elaboration of the self," as in the case of the dandy Baudelaire.[21] Such arts of the self are stylizations of conduct,[22] entailing the application of technologies of the self, or exercises of power over oneself, in order to attain a state of happiness, or wisdom.[23] By looking back to the Greeks and Hellenists, Foucault found the practice of arts of the self that made "life into an oeuvre that carries certain aesthetic values."[24] My point here is that Foucault conceives of desirable forms of subjectivity attained through the exercise of subjectifying power. In this light, every form of subjectivity entails limits, but for desirable forms of subjectivity these limits will be more enabling than constraining. Foucault was neither interested in proving that all human existence is oppression nor in escaping from subjectivity into untrammeled freedom.[25] Rather, he was striving to end modern humanist oppressive modes of subjectification and "to promote new forms of subjectivity."[26]

It is, however, immediately obvious that even in this affirmative mood Foucault adopts a masculinist position of self-making that denigrates women's contribution to the fashioning of a beautiful existence. The first grounds for such suspicion is the context of the Greek and Hellenist ethical relation to the self that Foucault chooses to analyze in detail in two books. Sure enough, Foucault also details that particularly in the classical Greek period, arts of the self-constituted mastery of the self, of one's desires. Domination of oneself was a precondition for political domination of others, particularly women and slaves, and techniques for the government of the self were isomorphous with techniques for the government of households and cities.[27] Foucault explicitly objects to this linkage between care of the self and domination of others, finding nothing exemplary in elitist and masculinist Greek ethics.[28] He finds the virility and dissymmetry of Greek society "quite disgusting."[29]

Although Foucault does not see Greek ethics as a model to be imitated, he is nonetheless clearly fascinated by them. What is significant here is that Foucault does not conceive of a positive, enabling mode of subjectification other than in modes of *self*-formation. His whole focus is on self-fashioning, on creating oneself as a work of art. Grimshaw argues that Foucault's aesthetic ethic is masculinist and solipsistic, ignoring the need to sustain autonomy within frameworks of mutuality.[30] The aesthetics of existence that he envisages as alternatives to current forms of subjection do not include care by others, only care of oneself. In contrast, Balbus claims that Foucault should welcome mothering practices with infants as technologies of the self that enhance subjectivity.[31] Foucault is, then, typically masculinist because he overlooks the possibility of positive constitution at the hands of others, treating it instead as a loss of autonomy. At no point does he suggest that were they less virile, less concerned with self-mastery and the maintenance of personal autonomy, that arts of the self might include being made by (m)others too.

Several feminist theorists have discussed a masculine propensity not only to deny their debt to mothers for making them what they are, but also to regard mothering, or intimate care by others, as a threat to their autonomy and subjectivity. According to Chodorow because boys' Oedipal attachments are sharply curtailed, their ego boundaries are rigidly defined in terms of denial of relation and connection, especially to femininity. As adults, males sustain their gendered identity and cover their lack of real autonomy from social authority by continuing to deny dependence and attachment to women, whom they both fear and resent. Recognition and memory of dependence on women is experienced by men as regressive and nonautonomous.[32] Rich holds that "the male mind has always been haunted by the force of the idea of dependence on a woman for life itself." Men retain an ambivalent, anxious relation to women, because their mothers fulfill so many roles for them: seductress, castrator, restricter of personal growth, but also bringer of tenderness and security. Men continue to need women as mothers: only to women can men reveal their suffering (which fathers hold in contempt), but men also resent women for knowledge of their weakness.[33] Ambivalence toward women is a major theme presented by Dinnerstein, rooted in utter infantile dependence on the mother's body, which the infant at first takes to be the whole world. Mother brings both pain and pleasure, is both lovingly present and alarmingly absent. Consciousness and fear of maternal power is repressed, but is expressed through women's desire to have their power controlled by men and men's efforts to control the power of women.[34] In all three accounts, masculine identity is sustained by fear of women's subjectifying power, the power of mothers and primary caretakers that constitutes subjects in their early years.

Foucault represses the possibility that women and mothers exercise enabling subjectifying power, and that others as well as oneself can participate in the constitution of desirable forms of subjectivity. This is all the more regrettable because some feminist theories have developed a notion of power that could supplement and refine the notion of empowering subjectification that is needed for Foucault's affirmative project. Along with the recovery of agency in the institution of mothering is also feminist identification and celebration of a particular form of women's power. Wartenberg defines this as transformative power, which in contrast to power as domination, is exercised over others in order to empower those others and enhance their autonomy. The basis of such power is women's positions in nearly all human societies as primary caretakers. While the primary application of transformative power is that exercised by mothers over their children, Wartenberg extends it to cover other caretaking roles and nurturing practices such as teaching, therapy, and political organizing. Nurturing roles place many women in positions in which they exercise both "power to" transform other persons and "power over" those they transform. Unlike conventional forms of "power over," transformative power does not constitute domination, even though at times, such as toilet training, caretakers issue commands and prevent those in their care from doing as they wish.[35]

Significantly, two of the feminist theorists whom Wartenberg cites account for this alternative concept of power on the basis of women's standpoint. Whereas Foucauldian and standpoint feminism are usually posed in opposition to each other, I am arguing that they are compatible, at least in the resemblance between the notions of positive power they contain. "One can almost argue that there is a separate and distinct women's tradition of theorizing power," and this is because "women's lives make available a particular and privileged vantage point not only on the power relations between women and men but on power relations more generally." Hartsock reviews the theories of power put forward by

Arendt, Emmet, and Pitkin, arguing that they all conceive of power in terms of "energy, capacity and potential," rather than masculine domination, and suggesting that this is explainable from a feminist standpoint. The feminist standpoint is derived from women's different material experience, a consequence of the sexual division of labor, which "define[s] women's activity as contributors to subsistence and as mothers." Hartsock relates women's "production" of other human beings, mothering, to a different experience of power, one involving "[h]elping another to develop, the gradual relinquishing of control . . . understand[ing] the importance of avoiding excessive control in order to help others grow." Relying on Chodorow's object-relations theory, Hartsock explains that girls develop interpersonal and relational capacities based on empathetic ties to others. This occurs in the context of the nuclear family in which primary caretaking is performed almost exclusively by women, usually biological mothers, in relation to whom infants define ego-boundaries. Hartsock reads Chodorow's account of gendered personality formation as one of the material conditions that shape women's and men's consciousness. It can also be read as an account of how women are both constituted as subjects endowed with relational and nurturing capacities needed for mothering, and also have subjective wishes to locate themselves in positions in which they can employ those capacities. As Hartsock notes, many women's salaried work as nurses, social workers, and even secretaries entails using their relational and nurturing skills.[36] As has often been noted, women's salaried work is an extension of their unpaid work in the home.

Hartsock refers to Ruddick, who in a later work in which she in turn draws on Hartsock, explains women's consciousness ("maternal thinking") in terms of standpoint. Thinking "arises from and is shaped by the practices in which people engage," woman's practice being "the work of mothering." This work enacts a commitment to meet the needs of children for preservation, growth, and social acceptance through respective practices of preservative love, nurturance, and training. While providing protection for vulnerable infants, mothers learn to think about control in ways that accept their limited ability to make the world entirely safe for children whose will they cannot entirely control. Thus, although preservative love entails a scrutinizing attitude we might wish to compare with Foucault's notion of surveillance, good mothers in effect exercise their power with a degree of humility that precludes a drive to domination. In general, what characterizes the sort of power inherent in maternal practice is that it "is organized in terms of people's needs and pleasures" and aims to "give birth to and tend self-generating, autonomously willing lives." Thus, although mothers may sometimes coerce children, violence in particular threatens and compromises the ends of maternal work: preservation and growth.[37] In brief, feminist theories focused on mothering and caring practices include a concept of empowering subjectification of which Foucault could have made good use.

Foucault's oversight is particularly disturbing because on at least one occasion he approaches the feminist notion of empowering transformative power exercised by others. Observing the power relation between teacher and pupil in a school, Foucault states that there is no "evil . . . in the practice of someone who . . . knowing more than another, tells him what he must do, teaches him, transmits knowledge to him, communicates skills to him." There is, of course, a constant danger that in the context of a pedagogical institution children will be subject to "useless authority," but "power [itself] is not an evil."[38] The point, rather, is always to minimize the degree of domination in any power relation. Wartenberg also notes the difference between feminists who aspire to a world without power in the sense of domination, and those who recognize the necessity of power as empowerment. Yet, however beneficial nurturing power may be, it is also open to abuse, especially by narcissistic parents. In addition, teaching is one of those caring roles that Wartenberg includes in modes of transformative power,[39] so it is easy to see the link between Foucault's example and the subjectifying power of women and their authorization to use it within given contexts. Women as caretakers, like teachers, occupy subject positions in which they exercise the power available to them over others for the benefit of those others, empowering them and enhancing their subjective capacities. Were Foucault's thought less masculinist, he might have saved himself his journey back to classical Greece, and instead found models for positive subjectification in mothering and caretaking.

One of Foucault's own chosen arts of the self, writing, does not entail mastery of the self and others, but underlines the emphasis on self-making at the expense of "mother-making." He describes his works as fragments of an autobiography, not in the sense that each book simply tells the story of a stage of his life, but in the sense that Foucault works on his life, making and remaking himself through his books.[40] He forces himself to change his mind, to think differently, to treat his search for truth as a series of transforming ordeals.[41] However admirable this may be as a philosophical ethos, it makes it quite clear that his mother is not part of Foucault's autobiography, because she has no part in his self-formation.

Mothering in the Context of Bio-Politics

Thus far I have berated Foucault for denying the debt owed to women for the constitution of subjects. I have also presented the subjectifying power of women, in particular as mothers, in a predominantly positive light. There are, however, good feminist reasons for treating transformative or maternal power in less than celebratory terms, some of which tie in nicely with Foucault's implicit analysis of women's subject positions in the context of wider power networks. I shall first review some of the relevant feminist analyses and then suggest that a Foucauldian genealogy of mothering would be a useful addition.

The feminist reasons for regarding women's agency as mothers and caretakers with caution are implicit in the very project of recovering that agency from the constraints and impositions of the male-dominated contexts of mothering. Ruddick argues that maternal work is currently carried out in the shadow of an "idealogy of motherhood [which] is oppressive to women. It defines maternal work as a consuming identity requiring sacrifices of health, pleasure, and ambitions unnecessary for the well-being of children." She goes on to explain that the third maternal practice, which she calls training and which is equivalent to socialization, is the practice most vulnerable to inauthentic and unnecessary social demands on mothers. Definitions of social acceptability are determined by the Law of the Father, which circumscribes the power of mothers, who often transmit their own submission to authority to their children. Reflective mothers will become aware of the contradictions between their educative power and social demands, yet may still feel that it is best for their children to submit. Many women are devoting much of their energy to male-defined goals, working to make their children acceptable to the current social norms. Mothers are not so powerful as infants and male myths believe: "The hand that rocks the cradle has certainly not ruled the world."[42]

Rich is even more adamant about the degree of patriarchal control over motherhood. Male control of motherhood has turned women's reproductive power from a potentially fulfilling experience into a patriarchal institution, a form of "penal servitude" that confines women to their bodily functions, to the private family sphere, and denies their manifold potentialities. This institution has attained particularly restrictive forms in the industrialized West, where the home has ceased to be a productive economic unit, where many (especially middle-class) women have been pushed out of paid labor and confined to and isolated in the home, and where motherhood has become a "sacred calling," an exclusive and specialized activity for which only biological mothers are fully fit.[43]

The key element of male control of mothering, or primary care of children, is that it has been made an almost exclusively female occupation. Clearly, the confinement of so many women to mothering and caring roles has a significant impact on women's opportunities and status in general, constituting a primary factor in women's inequality, exploitation, and subordination. In addition, feminists detail the negative consequences of such mothering not only for women but also for the children they raise. Ruddick argues that children trained to obey by women who feel timid in the face of male authority will not develop the capacity for reflective judgment, thus failing to achieve the autonomy that is supposed to be the aim of transformative power.[44] Chodorow argues on similar lines that although boys detach themselves starkly from their mothers, they lack inner autonomy and either become rule-followers or internalize the values of organizations. Moreover, they often lead stunted, narcissistic emotional lives, denying their own needs for love. Such men are unable to fulfill the emotional needs of women, who then attempt to re-create primary emotional attachments through relations with other women and/or by assuming the role of mother themselves. It is not then only their economic dependence on men that presses women into heterosexual family relations, but also their gendered personality and associated emotional predilection. Because of the emotional stakes involved, mothers might often overinvest in their children, with further negative consequences. The cycle is repeated from generation to generation because "[a]s a result of having been parented by a woman, women are more likely than men to seek to be mothers." Expectations of women's concern for mothering provides grounds for an ideology that limits them to the domestic sphere, so that women "contribute to the perpetuation of their own social roles and position in the hierarchy of gender."[45] Given the negative consequences of mothering in the context of male domination, it is inappropriate simply to celebrate women's subjectifying power. To paraphrase Marx, women make children into adults, but they do not make them into adults in any way that they want.

In Foucauldian terms, the above feminist concerns indicate the significant constraints on women's subject positions as caretakers and mothers. In *The Archaeology of Knowledge* Foucault develops the concept of subjectivity as subject position.[46] The basic idea is that people occupy particular positions in which they can be enunciating subjects, or subjects who make statements. These positions are vacant places: different people can make the same statements from them, and different people can be located in them. Indeed, in order to be a subject an individual must occupy such a position. However, each individual is not free to occupy whichever position she wants or to say what she wants. For example, only a doctor who has been educated according to legally recognized procedures can make medical statements, while what she may say as a doctor is constrained by the parameters of medical discourse, the institutional site from which she speaks (such as her private consulting room or on a government commission), or whether she is in a situation in which she is to record observations, listen to her patient, or prescribe treatment. Foucault's analysis here in the context of statements and discourse is pertinent to all wider networks of power that ascribe positions to subjects in which they are variously authorized to speak and act. In other words, in order to grasp who is authorized to do what to whom, one must know the subject position of each within the local grammar of power relations.

Foucault's notion of subject positions can be used to show that many women, as mothers and caretakers, are located in subject positions that authorize a significant range of actions to subjectify others. Women attain particular forms of empowered subjectivity within motherhood, which should be seen, as Rich claims, as a social institution. Motherhood is an institution that authorizes women to act caringly and nurturingly with respect to children who are ascribed subordinate positions to those of women. It is mostly women who discipline children, especially infants, teaching them basic motor skills, imposing on them the fundamentals of social order in their relations with each other, and inducting them into the human world of language.

What is needed here is a more historical analysis than that which is offered by most feminist accounts of mothering, an analysis that enables us to deal with current structures of gender hierarchy and the intensified form of mothering that Rich sees as having emerged in the nineteenth century. Rich notes in passing that at the end of the eighteenth century there arose a new concern to keep alive illegitimate children instead of simply reacting punitively to women who committed infanticide on such offspring.[47] In Foucault's terms, such changes were part of the emergence of bio-politics, which is concerned with the enhancement of life forces. Bio-politics deals with social hygiene, rates of fertility and mortality, and birth control. Although Foucault does not mention them explicitly, pronatal policies are a common feature of bio-politics, which troubles itself with the health and size of populations, as well as the health of individuals. In the context of bio-politics in general and pronatal politics in particular, it is easy to grasp why there was a positive reassessment of women's reproductive capacities and at the same time a closer regulation of women in order to maximize those capacities. Women's reproductive capacities were at the heart of " 'biological responsibility' with regard to the species," which required greater consideration for women's health and hygiene, and thus a general improvement of their conditions.[48] Such thinking is evidence in a U.S. Supreme Court ruling of 1908, which held that because "healthy mothers are essential to vigorous offspring . . . the physical well-being of woman becomes an object of public interest and care in order to preserve the strength and vigor of the race."[49] If the greater consideration for women's conditions encouraged some feminist identification with bio-politics, in the hope that women could also gain more social salience, the increased regulation provoked some feminist rejections of mothering, either altogether, or in its current form.

Bio-politics itself should be regarded as a feature of modern power in general, which is pastoral by nature. Modern pastoral power is also concerned with enhancement of life, promoting secular forms of salvation in the form of health, well-being, and security.[50] This kindly, devoted form of power entails individual care and intimate knowledge of each member of the flock.[51] Its reemergence outside its ecclesiastical domain can be traced back to the sixteenth century, when the very idea of government became problematic and had to be rethought against the backdrop of state formation and Reformation and Counter-Reformation. There was a gradual shift away from the Machiavellian problem of retaining juridical sovereignty over territory and the subjects residing in it, toward the art of governing a state, meaning "to set up an economy involving the entire state that is to exercise towards the citizens, the wealth and behavior of each and everyone, a form of surveillance, of control which as watchful as that of the head of family over his households and goods." Government since then has involved the pursuit of positive goals, such as the growth of wealth and the health and welfare of populations. Moreover, the full development of government involves the displacement of the family in favor of population, the former becoming a segment of the latter, a bearer of traits and variables of importance to population. It is at this point that economy becomes political, rather than referring to the running of a household.[52]

The development of political economy as an art of government belongs to the general phenomenon of government as police, in the Continental tradition.[53] "Police" in this sense entails rational government intervention in all that pertains to population, to people's relations with one another, their economic relations, their health. While police is also regulation of society, it is regulation not for the sake of state control, but oriented toward increasing people's happiness, enhancing their lives and capacities. Police, then, might best be understood as a general term referring to the political technology by means of which pastoral power is exercised. Foucault traces the historical development of a positive, empowering form of power, a form of power that bears a close resemblance to a feminist notion of transformative power. Pastoral policing has as its aim the development of fuller, richer, healthier individuals, individuals of whom it takes care. It is no coincidence that some feminists associate themselves with this caring power that enhances individual lives, because the subject positions of many women as mothers and caretakers situate them precisely in the standpoint of those who exercise such power.

Donzelot's more detailed account of the policing of modern families casts more light on women's subject positions as mothers, housewives, and by extension, caretakers and social workers in the welfare system. He argues in so many words that the role of mother has been instituted as a powerful subject position in itself, authorizing women through their articulation with medicine, social philanthropy, education, and welfare in general.[54] Motherhood as we know it today, as caretaking and nurturing in addition to childbearing, comes into being along with government through the family.[55] In this light we can see mothering as the paradigm caring role, and locate it within contemporary networks of pastoral power of which the welfare state and caring professions are key manifestations. To a large extent, then, the subjectifying power that women have in these positions is defined and constrained by the overall "policing of families." Although there was some displacement of paternal authority in the family and a provision of maternal powers, women's new competences were tied to a set of responsibilities.[56] A male-dominated power structure controls the transformative power of mothering.

Foucault adds further reasons for impugning modern, pastoral police power, not so much in itself but because of the wider framework in which it is located. Pastoralism, "happened to combine with its opposite, the state," via police, which thus contains a fundamental paradox: it aims "to develop those elements constitutive of individuals' lives in such a way that their development also fosters that of the strength of the state."[57] The state is governed according to its own rationality, *raison d'Etat*, which aims at the enhancement of state power in the modern European context of a multiplicity of competing states. In other words, the state is interested in individuals insofar as each addition to their strength adds to its strength. Modern political rationality thus deploys around a central antinomy, which is that the "integration of the individuals in a community or a totality results from a constant correlation between an increasing individualization and the reinforcement of this totality."[58] Pastorship provides the individualizing effect of modern power, and reason of state through police produces the totalizing effect. Every advance in individual autonomy corresponds to an increase in capacities of the totality.

Another feature of this central antinomy is "[t]he coexistence in political structures o[f] large destructive mechanisms and institutions oriented toward the care of individual life."[59] The contemporaneity of the butchery of World War II and the benevolence of the Beveridge Program make sense only within this perverse rationality. "If genocide is indeed the dream of modern powers . . . it is because power is situated and exercised at the level of life, the species, the race," operating as "a power that exerts a positive influence on life."[60] Foucault positions himself in opposition to this political rationality and against its corresponding form of subjecting power.[61] The point, then, is not to reject all forms of individualizing power, "but to liberate us both from the state and the type of individualization which is linked to the state."[62] At present, caring, individualizing power subjects as it subjectifies, constituting both abject and subordinate subjects (which includes most women), and tying people to those subjectivities. So, in Foucault's view the good intentions of the caring professions—doctors, psychologists, educators, social workers—do not prevent them being mechanisms of normalizing subjection.[63]

Foucault's objections to nurturing, transformative power are not related to women's use of such power, but to the overall context in which such individualizing power is exercised. This context renders women's transformative, subjectifying power into modes of subjection. However, he is blind to the gendered consequences of the central political antinomy of modernity.[64] Foucault notes that the welfare state is one of the contemporary ways in which pastoral and state power are mediated.[65] He does not note that generally speaking, the welfare side of the antinomy is associated with women and the warfare side with men. Women's presence in modern political rationality is largely confined to pastoralism, in the caring professions that have sprung up along with the welfare state, and as bearers of its associated interests, such as health, childcare, education, social problems in general. Given that, ultimately, pastoralism and individualizing power are subordinated to reason of state and totalization,[66] we can see that women's political presence is also subordinated to that of men in modern political rationality. The social welfare issues with which women have been identified remain subordinated to the "bigger" political issues of war and peace. Typically, then, pronatal policies that increase the social status of mothers and justify social provision for the needs of women with children are implemented in countries, such as interwar France, where there is a felt need for a larger population in order to compete with enemies.

Foucault's account converges with feminist analyses of confinement of women to mothering and the domination of current modes of mothering by male interests. Trebilcot sees two feminist strategies at this juncture: either a rejection of mothering because it sustains patriarchy; or a reconception of mothering along women-defined lines.[67] Each of these approaches is extremely problematic, and thus it is fortunate that Foucauldian feminism generates an alternative strategy.

It does not make sense to reject mothering because it offered many women their most powerful subject position in the past and may still do so at present. Women were able to exploit their feminine identity of moral superiority: first, to justify their public action as campaigners against moral wrongs such as slavery and social problems such as drunkenness and prostitution, as well as work in the settlement houses; and then to justify their demand for political rights as lobbyists for these moral concerns. Indeed, women won the vote in the United States and United Kingdom after World War I not on the strength of liberal individualist arguments about their rights as human beings, but in an atmosphere in which it was hoped that women could make a special contribution to politics by introducing their maternal virtues and in which "maternal" welfare provisions appeared to be necessary to ward off social unrest and the Bolshevik threat.[68]

As Sawicki points out, women may well have to rely more on the capacities for resistance they have been endowed with as constrained subjects than do white males such as Foucault, and there is still much to be done to improve the situations of women as mothers and caretakers.[69] To forgo the agency and authority afforded by caring subject positions could be disastrously disabling for women and feminism. Indeed, Foucault himself suggests that at certain stages of struggle it is necessary to fight for the rights of an oppressed group, such as homosexuals, even though they must fight on the basis of an identity to which they have been subjected.[70] In the case of the women's movement, Foucault credits feminism for refusing to be tied to their sex and thus the identities to which they have been subjected.[71] His political judgment on this point is poor, given that most women still have many immediate needs and aims as women who remain tied to their gendered identities, such as the right to control one's own body.[72] As Friedan realized, women who choose to renounce motherhood, particularly those who pursue careers in male-dominated settings, often pay a heavy price because they are denied one of the main channels available for women's personal fulfillment and empowerment.[73] Obviously, a situation in which remaining childfree is an available social option is one to be worked for in the long term.[74] However, simply refusing the subject position of motherhood, thereby refusing to collaborate with bio-power, is a problematic strategy.

Rich and Ruddick (among others) pursue the second strategy of reconceiving mothering. Rich aims to recover a feminist experience of motherhood that had been repressed by patriarchy by reconnecting women to their bodily powers, thinking through the body to attain a new consciousness.[75] Ruddick focuses less on birthing and more on nurturing, specifically on turning socialization into a work of conscience that answers only the authentic needs of children and not male-defined social norms.[76] Both of these accounts are ahistorical, assuming that there potentially is or was a good, pure form of mothering that male oppression distorts. They thus fail to see that the very ideal norms of nurturing motherhood they take to be woman-defined or feminist are precisely the pastoral, caring norms defined by the policing of families. For example, Ruddick identifies with mothering as a commitment to meet the needs of children, such that child care becomes a regular and substantial part of one's life.[77] In doing so, she concurs with the functionalist confinement of women to their "natural role," which is expressed in patriarchal theories such as Erikson's, who asserted that women have "a biological, psychological, and ethical commitment to take care of human infancy."[78] The point is that women are committed by bio-power to that caring position. It is not that a norm of nurturing an infant toward autonomy and mutuality is in itself bad, but that pursuit of such norms without attention to their context will leave women in their current subordinated positions as mothers and caretakers.

In any case, the feminist choice is not between renouncing the subject position of mothering or remaining tied to it while trying to liberate it from male oppression. In general, the Foucauldian option for those who struggle against their subjection is to use the capacities and resources available to them in their particular subject position. It is perhaps significant that feminists have seen more clearly than other interpreters of Foucault the paradox inherent in his notion of subjectification: the constraining limitations that subject one (as a woman) are also the enabling limits that empower one with capacities of a resisting subject.[79] In Foucault's terms, all resisting subjects are caught in this paradox of refusing to be what they are.

The current subject positions of many women as mothers in particular and caretakers in general should thus be seen as authoritative positions to be exploited. However, simply to continue speaking and acting authoritatively as caretakers will leave women tied not only to networks of pastoral power but also to current identities and subjectivities that are subordinated to the needs of male-dominated society. How, then, can the authority of women's subject positions as mothers and caretakers be used in ways that subvert the rules?

Subversive Mothering as Feminist Strategy

The goal of the strategy I conceive as subversive mothering is to break simultaneously the confinement of women to mothering and caring subject positions while retaining the empowerment authorized by such positions. The presupposition is that release from such confinement would be a major step toward ending women's oppression in its modern form. On the assumption that this goal is morally valid, I seek the most effective strategies for its realization. First, though, a theoretical answer must be found for the question posed immediately above: How can maternal authorization be used subversively?

Butler's reworking of Foucault's notion of subjectification facilitates perception of subjection in a subject position as simultaneously a position of resistance that transforms rather than sustains that subjection. She explains that subjectification is not a causal process, resulting in a fixed identity as its effect. Rather, subjectification is, like power, a practice. It is a performative practice, requiring repeated and constant performance by the subject in order to continue to tie the subject to her identity. Gendered identity (and there is no ungendered identity) is repeated stylization of the body, reiteration of a code, or the regularized and constrained repetition of norms. In order to have a gendered identity one must actively identify with a position in this code.[80] One of the notions that Butler displaces is that there is some metaphysical subject called "power" or "culture" or even "patriarchy" that constitutes humans as objects, a misunderstanding that can be drawn from some of Foucault's formulations such as: "power . . . makes individuals subjects."[81]

One of the frequent feminist criticisms of Foucault is that he absolves men of responsibility for their oppression of women by referring to power anonymously, as if subjects exercising power are mere relays and that everyone, including the oppressed, also exercises power. In doing so, he loses sight of systematic power relations (such as domination) that typify gender relations, thus failing to note that men generally are in more powerful positions than women.[82] The question thus arises: Who subjects women? Does Butler lead us to blame the victim, as Hartsock suspects of Foucault?

Butler further clarifies the notion of subjectification, in a way that forestalls the need to blame victim or oppressor,[83] by referring to Nietzsche: "there is no being behind the doing: the 'doer' has simply been added to the deed by the imagination—the doing is everything."[84] It is our linguistic habits, our faith in grammar, that induces us to think of an essential agent as the cause of every deed. In this light, constitution as a gendered subject is doing rather than the result of a deed carried out by some agent. It is the constant repetition of gendered acts and gestures through which identity is incorporated. We are not, then, placed in particular subject positions by some invisible hand called "power" or "culture" or "patriarchy"; we ourselves must identify with subject positions. So, one does not put on one's makeup every day in order to express one's femininity, but putting on one's makeup every day is one of the many acts one must repeat everyday in order to be feminine. One's femininity is the apparent effect of those reiterated acts that conform to heterosexual norms.

Gendered subjectification is citation of an ideal of coherence between biological sex, social or cultural gender, and sexual desire or orientation, which is encoded in what Butler calls the heterosexual matrix.[85] This matrix both authorizes people to repeat those acts that constitute oneself, and constrains them to repeat only those permitted acts. We can see in this light that subjection, being tied to one's identity, is also in some sense empowering. Butler's account, however, shifts our understanding away from the notion of subjects occupying positions in which they are endowed with capacities for resistance, to one of subjects whose continued subjection depends on their continued action, or their continued complicity in their own subjectification. Thus, in Butler's view, the potential for action that subverts the heterosexual matrix and its coherent identities is significant. Such action is possible because it is not always easy to maintain the coherence of the matrix: desire often takes its own course; personality sits uneasily with anatomy. From the existence of such "abnormalities" we can learn both that the heterosexual matrix is not an unassailably solid structure of power, and that subjectivity need not conform to its constraints. We can see that heterosexual identities are not simply natural, or that people are not straight men and women unless they *do* straightness. We do not have identities unless we identify with them.

This line of thinking leads Butler to the idea that all gendered sexual identity is impersonation of a copy or approximation for which there is no original. This is another way of saying that there is no being behind the doing. There is no essential woman who exists independently of each woman's repeated performance of femininity. So, the performativity of gender identity always has something of the nature of drag in it, which highlights the contingency of supposedly natural identity. Butler has therefore proposed a subversive strategy based on parodic performance of gender identity. By accentuating the ideal of masculinity or femininity, but in an inappropriate context (such as the butch partner in a lesbian relationship), such parodic performance teaches that one can only approximate the norm or ideal that one is performing.

Butler's highly suggestive model must be adapted in order to be appropriate for the context of mothering. First, I shall introduce the concept of a "maternal matrix" in place of her heterosexual matrix.[86] Second, I suggest that parody is inappropriate in this context, though subversive performance remains the key to the strategy. The subject position and identity of mothering depends on a series of coherences among: (1) female anatomy; (2) desire to bear children; (3) preference for reproduction in secure heterosexual setting; (4) propensity and ability to rear children; (5) caring orientation to others; (6) predilection for domestic issues; (7) prioritization of children. Coherence between these tendencies constitutes the maternal matrix. Something along the lines of the maternal matrix has been recognized in feminism since the 1970s, at least. Gimenez refers to it as "pronatalism," which she defines as "the existence of structural and ideological pressures resulting in socially prescribed parenthood as a precondition for all adult roles." Gimenez stresses the robustness of what I call the maternal matrix, pointing out that women have few opportunities under current conditions of meaningful, rewarding lives other than motherhood.[87] In her review of feminist literature, she discusses Mitchell, who argues that women's oppression can be explained by the conjuncture of four structures: production, reproduction of children, sexuality, and the socialization of children.[88] The last three belong to the maternal matrix, and together they define and naturalize women's modern roles in the family. Childbearing is considered women's natural vocation, while (in the absence of contraception), (hetero)sexual activity is inherently linked to childbirth. Mitchell also argues that in modern times childrearing has become a much more intensive activity and thus the caring role of mothers has been stressed, although "there is no inherent reason why the biological and the social mother should coincide."[89] The disruption of the coherence of the maternal matrix has, in effect, been a mainstay of feminist strategy for years, focusing on the detachment of childbearing from childrearing.[90]

Chodorow probably offers the best model to explain how the coherence of the matrix is normally maintained, but also indicates some fragile connections in the matrix. For example, she argues that girls do not completely transfer primary love from a female to a male object, and thus the securing of heterosexuality is always problematic. As Chodorow notes, psychoanalysis in general assumes that the sexual destiny decreed by anatomy is uncertain,[91] and I am suggesting here that many more problematic coherences are required in order to sustain the maternal matrix and mothering identities.

Friedan's early insight was based precisely on conscious recognition of the failed coherence of white, middle-class American womanhood and motherhood. The feminine mystique is the ideal of femininity, including "nurturing maternal love," which many women were unable to live up to. Friedan describes the enormous efforts to persuade women to conform to the ideal of the happy housewife, through popularization of Freud and the magazine industry.[92] Although her account is certainly open to the notion of a "real" women's identity suppressed by male domination, it is also a demonstration of the intensive work needed to sustain a particular mothering identity. In this light, the problem without a name, or the dissatisfaction with women's identity as mother and housewife, is recognition of the unnaturalness of the maternal matrix. If ever there was an identity difficult to fulfill, it is that of the ideal mother. Rich describes the impossibility of giving the "unconditional" love and attention dictated by "the visual and literary images of motherhood as a single-minded identity," and her intense feelings of guilt when she could not give that love. "If I knew parts of myself existed that would never cohere to those images, weren't those parts then abnormal, monstrous?"[93] They were indeed monstrous, if the norm was that defined by the maternal matrix. Feminist recognition that women can only approximate their identities occurs through consciousness-raising, which is also expressed by the critical reflection on the fragile coherence of the maternal matrix in Friedan's and Rich's books. Ruddick explicitly discusses the need for critical reflection by mothers in order for them to grasp the gaps between the nonviolent ideals immanent in their practices and what they actually do.[94]

Butler treats parodic performance as her favored strategy for consciousness-raising, or in her terms, the denaturalization of identities. Parody exposes the fragile coherences of the matrix and thus contributes to its subversion. However, parody is not necessarily appropriate in the context of motherhood. As Butler herself argues, all parodic repetition contains elements of both subversion and appropriation of norms, while some imitations simply celebrate the norm (such as the affirmation of heterosexuality by Dustin Hoffman's character at the end of Tootsie).[95] Also pertinent is Tyler's point that parodic intentions are often overwhelmed by normalizing forces.[96] "Jewish mothers" have been parodying mothering for a while now, but they do not seem to have subverted it yet. Another major problem in applying parody to motherhood, in the form of hyperbolic imitation, is that children might pay the physical and psychological consequences for deliberate overinvestment. Moreover, as

Minson argues, "the child-oriented social norm," meaning the notion that each child should be reared in a stable domestic environment in which his or her development is optimized, is deeply embedded and would thus be difficult to displace by head-on assault.[97] The scope for playfulness is not so great as in the realm of gender impersonation.

What seems most relevant in Butler's strategy, if not parody as such, is the notion of subversive performativity, or the repetition of norms in "inappropriate" contexts, in ways that disrupt the maternal matrix. This is preferable to a simple refusal to mother, even though that detaches anatomy from both childbearing and childrearing, and possibly child-bearing from childrearing (for biological mothers who do not raise their own children). As discussed above, this strategy disempowers many women, and is also vulnerable to counterattack by the maternal matrix, which stigmatizes such women as failures, or as incomplete women. The renunciation of motherhood that was prevalent in earlier feminism probably had the perverse effect of reinforcing the matrix, not only because of the conservative, pro-family backlash but also because it posed the choice too starkly between being a mother and being a feminist. As do all direct negations, this approach validated the maternal norm by embodying the abnormal.

At this stage I wish to do little more than suggest some of the features of the subversive performance of mothering that would contribute most to an effective strategy. Subversive motherhood should aim, as far as possible, to focus on actions in which children are not directly involved. Rather, maternal practices should be performed in inappropriate political settings. One of the aims is to disrupt not only the coherence of the maternal matrix itself, but also the articulation of its pastoralism with the military state. In addition, the key coherence of the matrix—that is, the link among women, nurturing, and childcare—must be targeted by performing mothering care between adults as an aspect of friendship. It is to be hoped that this would have the additional effect of undermin-ing the current patterns of welfare care for adults that is integral to the correspondence of individualization and totalization. I shall now elabo-rate a little on each of these points.

If subversive performance of mothering is to remain constrained by social norms of child development, it makes more sense to focus on actions in which children are not directly involved. Ruddick is suggestive here, when she talks of ways in which mothers pursue the nonviolent principles of maternal thinking beyond the appropriate contexts. The

mothers of the Plaza de Mayo were being good mothers by caring about
the safety of their children, but they were not supposed to do that in
a public square. As Ruddick states, "these women fulfill traditional
expectations of femininity and at the same time violate them." They
subvert the maternal matrix by performing motherhood beyond its proper
domestic or "social" bounds, confronting the government on issues of
state security. What Ruddick calls a "women's politics of resistance"
does not simply affirm women's roles but also resists government policy.[98]

The protest of the Argentinian mothers also reminds us that mothering is done in a wider context, a context in which mothers' transformative power is circumscribed by oppressive totalities of power that take as
well as give life. The maternal matrix, then, is not an independent
network of life enhancement and individualization, but one that is
enmeshed in totalization, in the augmentation of subjecting power. As I
argued above, women's own subjectifying power as mothers and caretakers is on the whole confined to the pastoral side of modernity's key
political antinomy. The mothers of the Plaza de Mayo are not supposed
to cross the line into affairs of state. Their example suggests that
subversive mothering consists partly in its performance in the inappropriate sites of *raison d'Etat*.

The feminist peace politics that Ruddick discusses is certainly relevant
here, as it is the conscious performance of the nonviolent, antimilitarist
aspects of maternal practice in the public (and not merely social) sphere.
Although Ruddick, who on the whole celebrates mothering, does not
stress the point, such politics would also affect mothering itself, by
exposing the lack of coherence between the ideals of mothering and
much maternal practice, conducted in the shadow of the state.[99] Ruddick
is not in fact proposing "feminine" passive resistance, but a feminist
strategy that refigures mothering as a political subject position and pits its
pastoral, caring, nurturing practices and rationale against the militarist
practices and rationale of the state. Such subversive performance of
mothering articulates easily with other women's peace politics, not
necessarily undertaken as mothers. The Israeli peace group, Women in
Black, which protested against the Israeli Occupation, transgressed the
boundaries of "acceptable" women's public activity by holding a weekly
vigil in which they challeneged the government on issues of peace and
security, without relying on women's "legitimate" voices as mothers and
wives of soldiers.[100]

The comparison between Women in Black and the Mothers of the

Plaza de Mayo is informative as it shows the limitations of political performance of mothering that remains too closely tied to the maternal matrix. Ruddick is aware that the latter protest was limited as feminist politics, certainly as antimilitarist feminism, a limitation she ascribes to the absence of conscious pursuit of *feminist* politics. She gives feminist consciousness the task of distinguishing for mothers between "maternal militarism" and "the peacefulness latent in maternal practice," by subjecting "all womanly roles to critical reflection." The Mothers used patriotic rhetoric during the Malvinas-Falklands war, thereby failing to resist the destructive, totalizing powers of the state. Indeed, very often when women organize politically in time of war or national conflict they do so as loyal defenders of home and hearth, as "maternal militarists." In Ruddick's view, if mothers really thought through the significance of their practices, they would extend their maternalism universally instead of applying it particularly.[101]

However, I would suggest that there is an inherent limitation to the subversive potential of mothering that is performed while clinging closely to identities as mothers in addition to mothering practices. It is not simply a problem of sufficient maternal consciousness. When mothers act in the political arena, they cannot operate according to the familial relations of caring and intimacy. Even though they might enter politics in order to defend their interests as mothers and to champion the principles and values of pastoralism in the face of militarism, they cannot behave as mothers but must adopt the role of citizens.[102] In order to achieve maternal goals, mothers must behave more politically than maternally. There has always been a dilemma for women who wish to perform "maternal virtues" in the male-dominated public sphere without having those virtues corrupted. The root of the dilemma lies in the terms of the articulation between pastoralism and the state. If women acting politically as mothers remain tied to the identities to which they are subjected in the maternal matrix, they will not be able to subvert the matrix or disrupt the correspondence of individualization with totalization.

As discussed above, feminist politics is always conducted from an ambivalent and problematic position in which women must fight for their rights without ever ultimately identifying with their subordinated identity. Subversive performance of mothering is thus equally problematic. As I argued in the case of the Mothers of the Plaza de Mayo, too close an identification with domesticity and subjectivities sanctioned by the maternal matrix places limitations on subversive performance, although some sort of identification is necessary. I now discuss another approach, which possibly errs in the opposite direction by treating mothering analogously through the performance of mothering care and subjectifying power not between adults and children, but between more or less equal adults. Friendship can be conceived to include mutual care of adults in order to unsettle the habit of limiting empowering, "mothering" practices to relations between (mostly female) adults and children. Along these lines, Foucault conceives of a gay lifestyle that promotes an ethic of friendship, proliferating new forms of intimate and caring relations beyond those that are currently sanctioned in marriage and the family.[103] Butler remarks on the subversive "cultural reelaboration of the family" enacted by drag performers who live in houses in which they "mother" each other.[104]

On the one hand, the aim of this strategy is to disrupt the key coherence of the maternal matrix, the link among women, nurturing, and childcare. Yet, there is a wider political significance to adults "mothering" other adults: the potential to upset the correspondence of individualization and totalization. At present our child-centered notions of care and nurturance are too focused on the development of autonomy in an unequal relationship, rather than on relations between autonomized people who will nonetheless need continued nurturance in order to sustain their autonomy. One of the reasons why the "mothering" of adults is widely experienced by many as a loss of autonomy is that such mothering or care is given by the welfare state. Habermas points out that welfare policies were supposed to enhance the autonomy of those suffering from the effects of wage labor production and market forces. However, empowerment through welfare was matched by increased regulation and the development of legal-bureaucratic organizations.[105] If, as I have suggested, welfare is a social extension of mothering, a great deal of the care adults receive is given in disempowering contexts of enormous dissymmetry between welfare agencies and individual clients. In contrast to Dietz's ideal model of democratic politics as relations between autonomous equals,[106] it seems that too much of modern politics—that is, pastoral, welfare politics, which deals with social issues—is already "maternal" (in that citizens are subordinated to the state as children are to mothers) rather than political in an Aristotelian sense.

An alternative model is inherent in care given in friendship, which is exchanged between people who constantly reverse roles over the course of time. Adults also need nursing when they are sick, require their egos to be soothed every now and again, and should be told when they are behaving badly. In particular men, who are more prone than women to regard such mothering as a threat to their autonomy, might learn more easily how to give and take care together with their friends whom they consider as equals than in the context of co-parenting. However, it is women rather than men who are already authorized by caring subject positions to perform mothering subversively between adults, as indeed they already do in small homogeneous groups and in women's subcultures. Whereas feminist conceptions of such relations have tended to cling to familiar terms of sisterhood or mother-daughter bonds, it would be more appropriate to see them as what they are: caring adult relations of friendship. I am suggesting that one of the most significant strategies of subversive mothering is not political in any direct sense, but is a question of lifestyle. However, lifestyles that incorporate caring friendship might have far-reaching political implications. Friends who perform mothering subversively can constantly individualize each other without a totality of power developing. They thus also disturb the solidity of the current correspondence between the two poles of modernity's political antinomy.

In this essay I have read Foucault's political thought and analysis along with feminist thought about the transformative power of mothering. In doing so, I exposed Foucault's androcentrism and gender blindness in relation to women's subjectifying power as primary caretakers, which could have served him as a good model for positive modes of subjectification. Although I qualified the more celebratory features of feminist recuperation of mothering in light of a Foucauldian genealogy of mothering that supplements critical feminist analyses, I also argued that on the whole Foucauldian politics has much to gain from collaboration with feminism. Foucault has a posthumous debt not only to feminists who have reworked his ideas, but also to "essentialist" and "standpoint" feminists with whom his work is usually contrasted, but who have done the important work of recuperating the agency of mothering. Until now it has normally been asked whether Foucault and feminism are compatible, or whether a Foucauldian feminist politics is viable. Now it is pertinent to ask whether there can be a Foucauldian politics that is *not* feminist. If the disruption of the correspondence between individualization and totalization is a prerequisite for liberation, and if a feminist strategy of subversive mothering is integral to such disruption, then it is even more that women's liberation is at stake.

Notes

1. *Assujetissement* is often translated as subjectivation. I prefer the term subjectification as it conveys more of the sense of making subjects, and is thus closer to the notion of the constitution of subjects, which is both more common in feminist literature and also one of Foucault's alternative terms. See, for example, Michel Foucault, "Truth and Power," trans. Colin Gordon, in *Power/Knowledge: Selected Interviews and Other Writings, 1972–1977*, ed. Colin Gordon (New York: Pantheon, 1980), 117.

2. Michel Foucault, "The Subject and Power," afterword to *Michel Foucault: Beyond Structuralism and Hermeneutics*, by Hubert L. Dreyfus and Paul Rabinow (Chicago: University of Chicago Press, 1982), 212.

3. Sandra Lee Bartky, "Foucault, Femininity, and the Modernization of Patriarchal Power," in *Feminism and Foucault*, ed. Irene Diamond and Lee Quinby (Boston: Northeastern University Press, 1988), 63–64.

4. Foucault, "Subject and Power," 216.

5. Thomas E. Wartenberg, "The Concept of Power in Feminist Theory," *Praxis International* 8, no. 3 (1988): 304–9.

6. See, for example, Adrienne Rich, *Of Woman Born: Motherhood as Experience and Institution* (New York: Norton, 1976), 14. I use the term *patriarchy* loosely, to refer to plural and heterogeneous yet systematized structures of male domination and female subordination. I do not refer to a universal structure of male domination that exists in the same form across time and cultures.

7. Michel Foucault, "Omnes et Singulatim," in *The Tanner Lectures on Human Values II*, ed. Sterling McCurrin (Salt Lake City: University of Utah Press, 1981), 227.

8. Michel Foucault, *The History of Sexuality*, vol. 1, *An Introduction*, trans. Robert Hurley (New York: Pantheon, 1978), 136–37; Michel Foucault, "The Political Technology of Individuals," in *Technologies of the Self: A Seminar with Michel Foucault*, ed. Luther H. Martin, Huck Gutman, and Patrick H. Hutton (London: Tavistock, 1988), 147, 162.

9. Judith Butler, *Gender Trouble: Feminism and the Subversion of Identity* (New York: Routledge, 1990).

10. Foucault, "Subject and Power," 213.

11. Bartky, "Foucault, Femininity," 63–64.

12. See Michel Foucault, *Discipline and Punish: The Birth of the Prison*, trans. Alan Sheridan (New York: Vintage, 1979).

13. Sara Ruddick, *Maternal Thinking: Toward a Politics of Peace* (New York: Ballantine, 1989), 29–30.

14. Rich, *Of Woman Born*, 73.

15. Nancy Chodorow, *The Reproduction of Mothering: Psychoanalysis and the Sociology of Gender* (Berkeley and Los Angeles: University of California Press, 1978).

16. Mary O'Brien, *The Politics of Reproduction* (London: Routledge and Kegan Paul, 1983).

17. I am not arguing that Foucault himself ignored his actual mother. In fact, the biographical information available indicates that whereas his antipathy to his father never waned, he was always close to his mother. See Didier Eribon, *Michel Foucault*, trans. Betsy Wing (Cambridge: Harvard University Press, 1991), 14.

18. Michel Foucault, "On the Genealogy of Ethics: An Overview of Work in Progress," in *The Foucault Reader*, ed. Paul Rabinow (New York: Pantheon, 1984); Michel Foucault, *The History of Sexuality*, vol. 2, *The Use of Pleasure*, trans. Robert Hurley (Harmondsworth: Penguin, 1987); and Michel Foucault *The History of Sexuality*, vol. 3, *The Care of the Self*, trans. Robert Hurley (New York: Vintage, 1988).

19. Wartenberg, "Concept of Power," 310–11.

20. Foucault, "Genealogy of Ethics," 349–52.

21. Michel Foucault, "What is Enlightenment?" trans. Catherine Porter, in *The Foucault Reader*, ed. Paul Rabinow (New York: Pantheon, 1984), 41–42.

22. Foucault, *Use of Pleasure*, 92–93.

23. Michel Foucault, "Technologies of the Self," in *Technologies of the Self: A Seminar with Michel Foucault*, ed. Luther H. Martin, Huck Gutman, and Patrick H. Hutton (London: Tavistock, 1988), 18.

24. Foucault, *Use of Pleasure*, 10–11.

25. Foucault's work might best be interpreted as operating in a field of tension between these two poles of total oppression and absolute freedom, as I argue in Jon Simons, *Foucault and the Political* (London: Routledge, 1995), 3–5.

26. Foucault, "Subject and Power," 216.

27. Foucault, *Use of Pleasure*, 65–72, 76, 83.

28. Foucault, "Political Technology," 19; Michel Foucault, "The Return of Morality," trans. Alan Sheridan et al. in *Michel Foucault: Politics, Philosophy, Culture: Interviews and Other Writings, 1977–1984*, ed. Lawrence D. Kritzman (New York: Routledge, 1988), 244.

29. Foucault, "Genealogy of Ethics," 346.

30. Jean Grimshaw, "Practices of Freedom," in *Up Against Foucault*, ed. Caroline Ramazanoglu (London: Routledge, 1993), 68–70.

31. Isaac D. Balbus, "Disciplining Women: Michel Foucault and the Power of Feminist Discourse," *Praxis International* 5 (January 1986): 446–83.

32. Chodorow, *Reproduction*, 169, 190.

33. Rich, *Of Woman Born*, 11, 209–10.

34. Dorothy Dinnerstein, *The Mermaid and the Minotaur* (New York: HarperCollins, 1976).

35. Wartenberg, "Concept of Power."

36. Nancy Hartsock, *Money, Sex, and Power* (Boston: Northeastern University Press, 1983), 151–52, 210, 231, 236–39.

37. Ruddick, *Maternal Thinking*, 129, 9, 17, 71–73, 79, 130–31, 148, 168–171.

38. Michel Foucault, "The Ethic of Care for the Self as a Practice of Freedom," trans. J. D. Gauthier, in *The Final Foucault*, ed. James Bernauer and David Rasmussen (Cambridge: MIT Press, 1988), 18.

39. Wartenberg, "Concept of Power," 304, 313–14.

40. Michel Foucault, "Practicing Criticism," trans. Alan Sheridan et al. in *Michel Foucault: Politics, Philosophy, Culture: Interviews and Other Writings, 1977–1984*, ed. Lawrence D. Kritzman (New York: Routledge, 1988), 156.

41. Michel Foucault, "The Minimalist Self," trans. Alan Sheridan et al. in *Michel Foucault: Politics, Philosophy, Culture: Interviews and Other Writings, 1977–1984*, ed. Lawrence D. Kritzman (New York: Routledge, 1988), 14; Michel Foucault, "The Concern for Truth," trans. Alan Sheridan et al. in idem., 263–64.

42. Ruddick, *Maternal Thinking*, 29, 109–16, 36.

43. Rich, *Of Woman Born*, 11–12, 41–55.

44. Ruddick, *Maternal Thinking*, 117–18.

45. Chodorow, *Reproduction*, 190, 199, 206, 209.

46. Michel Foucault, *The Archaeology of Knowledge*, trans. Alan Sheridan (New York: Pantheon, 1972), 50–55, 71–76, 92–96.

47. Rich, *Of Woman Born*, 260.

48. Foucault, *History of Sexuality*, 1:139, 25, 118.

49. Cited in Susan Moller Okin, *Women in Western Political Thought* (Princeton: Princeton University Press, 1979), 257.

50. Foucault, "Subject and Power," 213, 215.

51. Foucault, "Omnes et Singulatim," 230, 237–38.

52. Michel Foucault, "Governmentality," trans. Rosi Braidotti, *Ideology and Consciousness* 6 (Autumn 1979): 5, 10, 13, 16–19.

53. Foucault, "Omnes et Singulatim," 246–53.

54. Jacques Donzelot, *The Policing of Families* (New York: Pantheon, 1979).

55. Jeff Minson, *Genealogies of Morals: Nietzsche, Foucault, Donzelot and the Eccentricity of Morals* (London: Macmillan, 1985), 208.

56. Parveen Adams and Jeff Minson, "The 'Subject' of Feminism," in *The Woman in Question*, ed. Parveen Adams and Elizabeth Cowie (Cambridge: MIT Press, 1990), 93.

57. Foucault, "Omnes et Singulatim," 227, 252.

58. Foucault, "Political Technology," 150–52, 162.

59. Ibid., 146.

60. Foucault, *History of Sexuality*, 137.

61. Foucault, "Political Technology," 161; Foucault, "Subject and Power," 212.

62. Foucault, "Subject and Power," 216.

63. Foucault, *Discipline and Punish*, 306.

64. Foucault's discussion of this political antinomy does not include economics, even though government and police must concern themselves with the material welfare of the population while also thereby augmenting national resources. Foucault's analysis might be extended by focusing on the process of capital accumulation, which always tends to the advantage of capital itself, however much it may enrich different socioeconomic classes. In other words, the same combination of totalization and individualization operates in capitalist economies. However, considerations of economics raise more complex questions about the gendered division between the two poles of the antinomy, which would require further exploration.

65. Foucault, "Omnes et Singulatim," 235.

66. Foucault, "Political Technology," 162.

67. Joyce Trebilcot, ed., *Mothering: Essays in Feminist Theory* (Savage, Md.: Rowman and Littlefield, 1983), 1.

68. Richard Evans, *The Feminists* (London: Croom Helm, 1977), 37–38, 232–37.

69. Jana Sawicki, *Disciplining Foucault: Feminism, Power, and the Body* (New York: Routledge, 1991), 105–6.

70. Michel Foucault, "Power and Sex: An Interview with Michel Foucault," trans. David J. Parent, *Telos* 32 (Summer 1977): 155.

71. Michel Foucault, "The Confession of the Flesh," in *Power/Knowledge: Selected Interviews and Other Writings, 1972–1977*, ed. Colin Gordon (New York: Pantheon, 1980), 219–20.

72. Irene Diamond and Lee Quinby, "American Feminism and the Language of Control," in *Feminism and Foucault*, ed. Irene Diamond and Lee Quinby (Boston: Northeastern University Press, 1988), 194–97.

73. Betty Friedan, *The Second Stage* (New York: Summit, 1986).

74. Martha Gimenez, "Feminism, Pronatalism, and Motherhood," *International Journal of Women's Studies* 3 (1980): 226–28.

75. Rich, *Of Woman Born*.

76. Ruddick, *Maternal Thinking*, 116–23.

77. Ibid., 17.

78. Cited in Okin, *Women in Western Political Thought*, 240.

79. Sawicki, *Disciplining Foucault*, 55–56.

80. Butler, *Gender Trouble*; and Judith Butler, *Bodies That Matter* (New York: Routledge, 1993). I have chosen to regard Butler's two books as essays in a continuing project rather than to identify the shifts between the first and second volume.

81. Foucault, "Subject and Power," 212.

82. Nancy Hartsock, "Foucault on Power: A Theory for Women?" in *Feminism/Postmodernism*, ed. Linda J. Nicholson (New York: Routledge, 1990), 168–70. Foucault does make specific reference to domination as a particularly congealed or systematized set of power relations. See Foucault, "Subject and Power," 226; Foucault, "Ethic of Care," 18–19. There is no reason why Foucauldian analysis of gender relations, with its local, capilliary approach that works from bottom up should not conclude, as do Foucault's own analyses of disciplinary and bio-power, with some account of consolidated domination, which in this case would be male domination. Butler's version is even more problematic than Foucault's, as she goes further than he in suggesting both that women exercise power in oppressed subject positions and in not attributing responsibility to men for women's subjection.

83. Butler, *Gender Trouble*, 25; Butler, *Bodies*, 7–9.

84. Friedrich Nietzsche, *The Birth of Tragedy and The Genealogy of Morals*, trans. Francis Golffing (New York: Doubleday Anchor, 1956), 178–79.

85. Butler, *Gender Trouble*, 17.

86. The pun on the meaning of the Greek word matrix (womb), which, as Butler explains, is related to the Latin "mater," is intended. See Butler, *Bodies*, 31–32.

87. Gimenez, "Feminism, Pronatalism," 218, 229–30.

88. Juliet Mitchell, *Women's Estate* (Harmondsworth: Penguin, 1971), 99–122.

89. Ibid., 119.

90. Okin, *Women in Western Political Thought*, 297.

91. Chodorow, *Reproduction*, 200, 154.

92. Betty Friedan, *The Feminine Mystique* (New York: Dell, 1964), 37.

93. Rich, *Of Woman Born*, 22–24.

94. Ruddick, *Maternal Thinking*, 136–37.

95. Butler, *Bodies*, 137.

96. Carole-Anne Tyler, "Boys Will Be Girls: The Politics of Gay Drag," in *Inside/Out: Lesbian Theories, Gay Theories*, ed. Diana Fuss (New York: Routledge, 1991).

97. Minson, *Genealogies of Morals*, 216.

98. Ruddick, *Maternal Thinking*, 229, 222-23.

99. Ruddick, *Maternal Thinking*, 219–51.

100. Sarit Helman and Tamar Rapoport, "Surviving through Ritual: The Puzzle of the Endurance of a Women's Peace Movement: 'Women in Black' " (Paper presented at the ISA Conference, Bielefeld, 1994).

101. Ruddick, *Maternal Thinking*, 233–42.

102. Mary Dietz, "Citizenship with a Feminist Face: The Problem with Maternal Thinking," *Political Theory* 13 (1985): 32–33. I do not wish to go further than this in my use of Dietz's argument, as she contrasts the relations of subordination between mother and child with a liberal ideal of equality between mutually respecting citizens, thus overlooking the deep inequalities existing between citizens who have differing degrees of power according to class, ethnicity, gender, and so forth.

103. Michel Foucault, "Friendship as a Way of Life," in *Foucault Live*, ed. Sylvère Lotringer (New York: Semiotext(e), 1989).

104. Butler, *Bodies*, 137.

105. Jürgen Habermas, *The Philosophical Discourse of Modernity*, trans. Frederick Lawrence (Cambridge: Polity Press, 1987), 289.

106. Dietz, "Citizenship," 31–32.

9

Feminism and Empowerment: A Critical Reading of Foucault

Monique Deveaux

Few thinkers have influenced contemporary feminist scholarship on the themes of power, sexuality, and the subject to the extent that Michel Foucault has.* Indeed, even scholars who dispute this thinker's claims are compelled to acknowledge the contribution his work represents in these areas. The years since Foucault's death have been marked by

*An earlier version of this paper was given at the annual conference of the Canadian Society for Women in Philosophy, 20–22 September, 1991 at the University of Winnipeg. I am grateful to James Tully and Peta Bowden for invaluable help with an earlier draft as well as for providing a stimulating seminar series on the feminist implications of Foucault's thought during the spring of 1990 in the Department of Political Science, McGill University, for which this essay was originally written. I am also indebted to David Kahane for helping me to clarify and sharpen my arguments by suggesting numerous improvements to subsequent versions.

intense interest in his writings, feminist and otherwise. Today, more than a decade after his death, it seems appropriate to reflect critically upon the central exchanges between feminist thought and Foucauldian theory.

This chapter looks at three "waves" of Foucauldian literature by feminist political theorists and philosophers. Although neither chronologically separate nor thematically discrete, these waves refer to bodies of work by feminist scholars in which different aspects of Foucault's work—all related primarily to the problematic of power—are used for distinctly feminist purposes. First-wave Foucauldian feminists, examined in the first section, appropriate Foucault's analysis of the effects of power on bodies and his notion of "bio-power." In the second section I take up feminist discussions of Foucault's account of the omnipresence of power—his view that "where there is power, there is resistance"—which he later formulates as a highly agonistic conception of power.[1] In the subsequent section, I examine a third wave of feminist literature that, while not ignoring these other features of power, focuses on his analysis of the effects of power on sex, and the production of subjectifying discourses on sex and sexual identity. Postmodern feminists in particular have been keen to utilize Foucault's assertion that prevailing categories of sex identity, far from "natural," are the result of a proliferation of discourses on sex signaled by the transition to a modern paradigm of power.

In reviewing these three waves of Foucauldian feminist literature, I argue that both the paradigms of power and the treatment of the subject[2] that emerge from Foucault's work are inadequate for feminist projects that take the delineation of women's oppression and the concrete transformation of society as central aims. As such, my position stands in contrast to recent, influential feminist Foucauldian arguments, such as those of Susan Hekman and Judith Butler.[3] Although Foucault's writings on power have a certain heuristic value for feminists, I suggest that two major pitfalls recommend against uncritical appropriations of his thought: the tendency of a Foucauldian conceptualization of the subject to erase women's specific experiences of power; and the inability of the agonistic model of power to account for, much less articulate, processes of empowerment. Finally, as an antidote to these problems, the fourth section of the article points to an emerging body of literature by feminist writers on the issue of empowerment that, I argue, serves as a more viable resource for feminist work on the themes of freedom, power, and empowerment.

The First Wave: Surveillance and Bio-Power

Just So Many Docile Bodies? Feminism and Panopticonism. The transition from sovereign, or monarchical, power to modern regulatory power comprised of disciplinary regimes, systems of surveillance, and normalizing tactics provides the backdrop to Foucault's early, "docile bodies" thesis. Modern power requires "minimum expenditure for the maximum return," and its central organizing principle is that of discipline.[4] Aspects of sovereign power are carried over into the modern period but function as ruses, disguising and legitimating the emerging discourse of disciplinary power. This new regime of control is minimalist in its approach (in the sense of lesser expenditures of force and finance) but more far-reaching and localized in its effect on bodies.

For Foucault, sex is the pivotal factor in the proliferation of mechanisms of discipline and normalization; it is also at the center of a system of "dividing practices" that separate off the insane, the delinquent, the hysteric, and the homosexual. As the sovereign's rights over the life and death of subjects began to shift in the seventeenth century, two axes or poles emblematic of the modern power paradigm evolved. They were the "anatomo-politics of the human body," which emphasizes a disciplined, useful body (hence, "docile bodies"); and the model Foucault calls the "bio-politics of the population," in which the state's attention turns to the reproductive capacities of bodies, and to health, birth, and mortality.[5] The prime focus of the first axis of power is thus "the body and its forces, their utility and their docility, their distribution and their submission."[6] The body becomes a "political field," inscribed and constituted by power relations.

Although the docile bodies thesis is later amended by Foucault in favor of a less reductionist, agonistic conception of the subject and power—and later still, by an emphasis on the "technologies of the self"[7]—his earlier paradigm has been used by feminists of this first wave of Foucauldian feminist literature to describe contemporary practices of femininity. Two specific aspects of Foucault's work are utilized in this project: the discussion of disciplinary measures in *Discipline and Punish*, encompassing the subthemes of docile bodies, surveillance, and the normalizing gaze; and, in the same text, the thesis on panopticonism, referring to Bentham's design for a prison that would leave prisoners perpetually exposed to view and therefore likely to police themselves.[8]

In feminist literature that appropriates the docile bodies paradigm, the transition from sovereign authority to modern, disciplinary forms of power is seen to parallel the shift from more overt manifestations of the oppression of women to more insidious forms of control. This new method is disciplinary in nature and more subtle in its exercise; it involves women in the enterprise of surveillance. The following description of modern power by Foucault provides the basis for an analysis, by scholars of this first wave, of what they call the "techniques of femininity":

> There is no need for arms, physical violence, material constraints. Just a gaze. An inspecting gaze, a gaze which each individual under its weight will end by interiorising to the point that he is his own overseer, each individual thus exercising this surveillance over, and against, himself. A superb formula: power exercised continuously and for what turns out to be at minimal cost.[9]

Feminist scholars who take up this conceptualization of power treat the account of self-surveillance suggested by the model of the Panopticon as a compelling explanatory paradigm for women's acquiescence to, and collusion with, patriarchal standards of femininity. However, it is an explanation that must be modified to fit feminist purposes. Sandra Bartky applauds Foucault's work on disciplinary practices in modernity and on the construction of docile bodies, but she cautions that his analysis "treats the body . . . as if bodily experiences of men and women did not differ and as if men and women bore the same relationship to the characteristic institutions of modern life." Thus, Bartky asks: "Where is the account of the disciplinary practices that engender the 'docile bodies' of women, bodies more docile than the bodies of men? . . . [Foucault] is blind to those disciplines that produce a modality of embodiment that is peculiarly feminine."[10]

Bartky's two theses are, first, that femininity (unlike femaleness) is socially constructed, with this feminine mold taking hold most powerfully through the female body; and, second, that the disciplinary practices that produce the feminine subject must be viewed as peculiarly modern in character, symptoms of the "modernization of patriarchal domination." Bartky describes three kinds of practices that contribute to the construction of femininity: exercise and diet regimes aimed at attaining an "ideal" body size and configuration; an attention to comportment and a range of "gestures, postures and movements"; and techniques that display the feminine body as an "ornamental surface," such as the use of cosmetics. These three areas combine to "produce a body which in gesture and appearance is recognizably feminine" and reinforce a "disciplinary project of bodily perfection."[11]

But just *who*, Bartky asks, is the disciplinarian in all this? Her response is that we need to look at the dual nature of feminine bodily discipline, encompassing its socially "imposed" and "voluntary" (or self-disciplining) characteristics. The imposed aspects of feminine bodily discipline are not restricted to messages from the beauty industry and society that women should look a certain way but also include negative repercussions in terms of personal relationships and job opportunities. Bartky accounts for the voluntary, self-disciplining dimension of these techniques of femininity in two ways. Women internalize the feminine ideal so profoundly that they lack the critical distance necessary to contest it and are even fearful of the consequences of "noncompliance"; and ideals of femininity are so powerful that to reject their supporting practices is to reject one's own identity.[12]

Bartky's use of the docile bodies and Panopticon theses is problematic for at least two reasons. First, it is not clear why Bartky argues that more subtle and insidious forms of domination characterize the modern era or what she calls the "modernization of patriarchal power." In fact, current examples abound of overt control of women's choices and bodies, like lack of accessible abortions and frighteningly high rates of rape and assault. This is not to suggest that glaring barriers to women's freedom should preclude reflection on less tangible obstacles but, rather, to point out the danger of taking up the latter in isolation from a broader discussion of women's social, economic, and political subordination.

Furthermore, the way Bartky conceives of women's interaction with their bodies seems needlessly reductionist. Women's choices and differences are lost altogether in Bartky's description of the feminine body and its attendant practices:

> To subject oneself to the new disciplinary power is to be up-to-date . . . it represents a saving in the economy of enforcement: since it is women themselves who practice this discipline on and against their own bodies, men get off scot-free. . . . The woman who checks her makeup half a dozen times a day to see if her

foundation has caked or her mascara has run, who worries that the wind or the rain may spoil her hairdo, who looks frequently to see if her stockings have bagged at the ankle or who, feeling fat, monitors everything she eats, has become, just as surely as the inmate of the Panopticon, a self-policing subject, a self committed to a relentless self-surveillance.[13]

This description may draw attention to the pernicious effects of cultural standards of attractiveness, but it blocks meaningful discussion of how women feel about their bodies, their appearance, and social norms. It obscures the complex ways in which gender is constructed, and the fact that differences among women—age, race, culture, class—translate into myriad variations in responses to ideals of femininity and their practices. Bartky's use of the docile bodies thesis has the effect of diminishing and delimiting women's subjectivity, at times treating women as cultural sponges rather than as active agents who are both constituted by, and reflective of, their social and cultural contexts.

Susan Bordo, in "The Body and the Reproduction of Femininity," also takes up Foucault's docile bodies thesis to show the ways in which women's bodies serve as a locus for the social construction of femininity. Bordo argues that anorexia nervosa and bulimia are located on a continuum with feminine normalizing phenomena such as the use of makeup, fashion, and dieting, all of which contribute to the construction of docile, feminine bodies. Thus, "anorexia begins, emerges out of . . . conventional feminine practice";[14] the docile feminine body becomes, in the case of the anorexic, the ultimate expression of the self-disciplining female caught up in an insane culture.

There are similarities between Bordo's and Bartky's appropriation of Foucault's model of disciplining power, but the two treatments are disanalogous in significant ways. Bordo's thesis that cultural practices are inscribed onto bodies is not so extreme as Bartky's "woman-as-Panopticon" picture. In contrast to the thesis that women's bodies and psyches are molded by a patriarchal culture, Bordo focuses on anorexics' and bulimics' relationships to their society and the ways in which these mediate the demands of a contradictory culture. For instance, she describes a teenage girl's growing awareness of social expectations and values and her impulse both to suppress feminine bodily development and resist the influence of her family by restricting her eating.[15] This does not indicate that it is appropriate to borrow the docile bodies thesis from Foucault unamended; instead, it seems that Bordo is able to steer clear of the totalizing picture of the self-disciplining Panopticon by modifying the paradigm to include accounts of women's understanding of their experiences.

The modification is insufficient, however; Bordo, like Bartky, loosely employs such concepts as "disciplinary techniques" and "normalization" to explain the forms and effects of feminine cultural practices. This unhelpful account of subjectivity derives from problems inherent in the docile bodies paradigm. Foucault's extreme reluctance to attribute explicit agency to subjects in his early account of power results in a portrayal of individuals as passive bodies, constituted by power and immobilized in a society of discipline. Significantly, this analysis gives way, in Foucault's later works, to a more complex understanding of power as a field of relationships between "free" subjects. Yet feminists have clearly found this first power paradigm's emphasis on the body a useful analytic tool with which to examine women's subjectification. Nevertheless, the limitations of Foucault's account of the modernization of power give us reason to take a critical distance from this aspect of his work. The appropriations discussed above indicate that there is a danger in employing the notion of self-policing, disciplined subjects in an ahistorical, *metaphorical* sense. Bartky—and to a lesser extent, Bordo—uses the docile body and the Panopticon as if these describe a wide range of subjectivities and practices, and this leads her to conflate women's myriad experiences of femininity. Lost are the historical context of Foucault's account of the modernization of power and the subtleties of his usage of "normalization" and bodily discipline by institutions and discourses.[16] Moreover, by treating the metaphor of docile bodies as a paradigm for women's experiences of femininity, Bartky and Bordo foreclose on the integration of Foucault's later work, including his admission that resistance is inherent to the strategic model of disciplined bodies. Indeed, given Foucault's subsequent revision and his preference for a more constitutive understanding of power in his later writings, we should ask whether any version of the "docile bodies" paradigm is useful for feminists.

Feminism and the Rise of Bio-Power.   The second axis of modern power is what Foucault calls the "bio-politics of the population," or simply "bio-power." The account of the rise of bio-power in the West in the modern period, signaling a whole new politics of population control and management, is used by some Foucauldian feminists of this first wave to cast light on those "discourses"—such as fetal protection laws and new reproductive and genetic technologies (NRGTs)—that directly affect women's control of their bodies and reproductive choices.[17]

Foucault uses the term "bio-power" to denote a transformation in the nature of the sovereign's power over its subjects, in which the state's focus on prohibition and juridical authority is replaced by new interests in the birth rate, education, discipline, health, and longevity of its population. Thus, what Foucault calls a "normalizing society" replaces the juridical authority of the sovereign. There is a concurrent shift from struggles for political rights to "life rights"; that is, a right to one's body, health, and the fulfillment of basic needs. As with the "docile bodies" aspect of modern power, sexuality is key to the exercise of bio-power: both axes of power—the body, and bio-power—revolve around sexuality, which in turn becomes "a crucial target of a power organized around the management of life rather than the menace of death." This focus is manifested in the sciences of the "new technology of sex" starting from the end of the eighteenth century: namely, pedagogy, medicine, and demography.[18] Of particular interest to feminists who employ the bio-power analysis are the accounts of discourses and innovations that facilitate increased state control of reproduction, or what Foucault calls the "socialization of procreation." These developments are used by feminists to theorize about current reproductive practices, ranging from birth control and abortion to new reproductive and genetic technologies.

Jennifer Terry uses Foucault's account of modern power to examine such issues as "prenatal surveillance," fetal rights discourse, and surrogacy. These practices stem from increased state concern for issues of population—birth, longevity, eugenics, health—and the focus for intervention is, not surprisingly, the domain of reproduction and prenatal care. Terry situates fetal rights discourses and "natal Panopticonism" against the backdrop of regulatory prenatal technologies, including "amniocentesis, sonograms, electronic fetal monitoring . . . sonar-produced video images," and "life-style monitoring" of pregnant women, which can include regular Breathalizer tests for women suspected of alcohol abuse.[19] She also points to legislative proposals in the United States that advocate mandatory HIV antibody testing for any woman who becomes pregnant and wishes to have a child and notes that there are several states that require HIV testing in order to obtain a marriage license. This ominous form of medical interference holds particularly serious implications for childbearing women, because it implies that the state should be permitted to override their choices on the grounds that they are potential transmitters of disease.

Similarly, Terry views fetal rights discourse as a new, legitimating ideology whose deeper aspiration is the control of reproduction and the lives of pregnant women. The new prenatal screening technologies are instrumental in allowing both state and medical authorities to view the fetus as separate from the mother, who is then subject to a range of suspicions concerning her behavior during pregnancy. For instance, the articulation of distinct fetal rights has been the outcome of a series of civil court cases throughout the 1980s in which mothers were sued for allegedly damaging their fetuses through irresponsible behavior.[20] Terry relates these developments to Foucault's bio-power paradigm in order to situate them within the overall context of increased state interest in population regulation.

Although part of Terry's argument falls back on the docile bodies thesis, the bio-power paradigm nevertheless seems appropriate to describe the dramatic character of medical and state intervention. Yet like the docile bodies thesis, Foucault's bio-power model deemphasizes agents' capacities to resist regulatory and disciplinary technologies. Terry is able to avoid the worst excesses of the paradigm by inserting descriptions of various resistances, both individual and collective, into her account. She points, for instance, to the Women's AIDS Network, an international group of women in law, health, and education who are concerned with HIV and AIDS and advocate women's rights to freedom from medical surveillance. Without such correctives, readers would be left with a profound sense of disempowerment in the face of ubiquitous state and medical surveillance of our reproductive lives. More important, failing to point out women's responses to this intervention would give a false picture of feminist politics. To give one example: women's health issues have been a consistent focus for feminist activism, more so today than ever, as evidenced by the renewed pro-choice movement, groups demanding increased funding for breast cancer research and treatment, grassroots initiatives to establish women's community health clinics, and so forth; by focusing solely on the effects of medical and state control of women's health and lives, we neglect to see these examples of resistance.

Foucault's bio-power analysis helps reveal the implications of mechanisms for the control and regulation of our bodies. However, taken unamended, the paradigm obscures both individual women's and collective struggles against coercive medical and social practices. As Terry's work shows, feminist appropriation of Foucault's bio-power framework must include discussions of strategies employed by women to mediate and resist encroachments on their bodies and lives.

The Second Wave: "Where there is power, there is resistance." A second wave of feminist literature has taken up Foucault's work on power in a different way, stressing the possibilities of resistance over the fact of domination. Here the focus is on Foucault's later development of an agonistic model of power—the notion that "where there is power, there is resistance"—as well as the assertion that individuals contest fixed identities and relations in subtle ways. This power paradigm has proved particularly helpful for feminists who want to show the diverse sources of women's subordination as well as to demonstrate that we engage in resistance in our everyday lives. Drawing upon the treatment of power and resistance in his *Power/Knowledge*, volume 1 of *The History of Sexuality*, and "The Subject and Power," this literature illustrates how Foucault challenges the assumption that power is located exclusively or even primarily in state apparatuses or in the practice of prohibition. By demanding that we look to the productive character of power and to the existence of multiple power relations—rather than to dualistic, top-down force—Foucault helps us move from a "state of subordination" explanation of gender relations, which emphasizes domination and victimization, to a more textured understanding of the role of power in women's lives. Viewing power as *constitutive* has helped many of us to grasp the interweaving nature of our social, political, and personal relationships.

Jana Sawicki points out that Foucault both reminds us of the importance of looking to subjugated knowledges and makes us circumspect about theories or movements that claim to offer a transcendence of power, or a power-free context. Foucault's account of power complements feminist concerns in that he "proposes we think of power outside the confines of State, law or class. . . . Thus, Foucault frees power from the political domain in much the same way as radical feminists did."[21] Similarly, Susan Hekman argues that feminists have much to learn from Foucault's antitotalizing conception of power, because it cautions us against invoking universalisms and quick-fix solutions for complex social and political relations. Moreover, she asserts that a Foucauldian view of power necessarily implies active resistance to discourses and practices that subordinate women, a conclusion she reaches by highlighting—and, I would argue, embellishing—accounts of resistance and political action in Foucault's work.[22]

A more critical body of work by feminist scholars takes issue with precisely those aspects of the agonistic model of power that this second wave finds so useful—the notion that power circulates and is *exercised* rather than possessed. Much of this criticism stems from wrongly reading Foucault as a postmodernist thinker, reflected in the allegations that he is a relativist (because antihumanist) and so guilty of overlooking the political aspects of power and resistance. Foucault's antimodernist rejection of truth is invoked to corroborate this analysis, as is his reluctance in his middle and later works to speak of social systems of domination. This position is best represented by Nancy Fraser, who contends that Foucault's agonistic notion of power posits that "power is productive, ineliminable, and therefore normatively neutral." By contrast, Fraser asserts that feminism needs to be able to distinguish between social practices that are "good" (less coercive) and "bad" (very coercive) and expresses nostalgia for Weberian distinctions among violence, domination, and authority.[23] Integral to this charge is Fraser's reading of Foucault as an antihumanist thinker who refuses to engage in normative discussions. Nancy Hartsock concurs with the conclusion that feminists cannot find normative grounding in Foucault's work and goes so far as to suggest that his theory undermines attempts at social change by obscuring the systematic nature of gender oppression. Echoing Fraser's criticism, she states that for Foucault, "power is everywhere and ultimately nowhere" and that "domination, viewed from above, is more likely to appear as equality." As an antidote to this distortion, Hartsock suggests that feminists need to "develop an account of the world which treats our perspectives not as subjugated or disruptive knowledges, but as primary and constitutive of a different world."[24]

Hartsock's claim that Foucault's model of power does not allow for an understanding of systematic injustic seems, at first glance, credible. Indeed, his account of power renders murky and less tangible numerous social relations, relations that feminists have argued constitute concrete oppression. Yet it is misleading to suggest that Foucault denies that such a situation exists: to the contrary, domination is by his account a frequent and at times inescapable reality.[25] Nor does it seem fair to impute to Foucault, as both Fraser and Hartsock do, a normatively neutral worldview, because his work reflects what are manifestly—if not always polemically—political concerns.

Staking out a middle ground between the criticisms of Fraser and Hartsock and the generosity of Sawicki and Hekman, I argue that Foucault's agonistic model of power is double-edged. It is useful for feminists to the extent that it disengages us from simplistic, dualistic accounts of power; at the same time, however, it obscures many important experiences of power specific to women and fails to provide a sustainable notion of agency. This is not an easily negotiated tension for feminists; as one critic comments, Foucault's "lack of a rounded theory of subjectivity or agency conflicts with a fundamental aim of the feminist project to rediscover and reevaluate the experiences of women."[26] Moreover, feminists in particular should be wary of Foucault's assertion that *all* social interactions are defined and thoroughly permeated by the exercise of power, as expressed in his view that "in human relations, whatever they are—whether it be a question of communicating verbally . . . or a question of a love relationship, an institutional or economic relationship—power is always present: I mean the relationship in which one wishes to direct the behavior of another."[27] If we agree with Hartsock's suggestion that feminists need to envisage a nondominated world, we should not slip into fatalistic views about the omnipresence of power. This means rejecting Foucault's view that absolutely *no* social or personal relations escape permeation by power.[28]

Agonistic Power. To illustrate the importance of rejecting, or at least amending, aspects of Foucault's approach, it is useful to consider some specific ways in which this model tends to obscure women's experiences of power. Let us consider Foucault's treatment of the subject, first with respect to freedom, then as concerns the issue of violence. In his later work, Foucault emphasizes that in order for a power relationship to exist, the subject on whom that "conduct" or governance is exercised must be a *free* subject. This appears at times as an essentialist freedom and at other times as a qualified liberty where "individual or collective subjects . . . are faced with a field of possibilities in which several ways of behaving, several reactions and diverse comportments may be realized." Here, power is separated off from force, violence, and domination, which do not involve any freedom on the part of the subject: "A relationship of violence acts upon a body or upon things; it forces, it bends, it breaks on the wheel, it destroys, or it closes the door on all possibilities. Its opposite pole can only be passivity, and if it comes up against any resistance it has no other option but to try to minimize it." In order for a relationship of power to exist, by Foucault's (later) account, a subject must be capable of action or resistance and be recognized as a person on whom force or "conduct" is exercised: thus, agonistic power is "a set of actions upon other actions."[29] This does not mean that domination is altogether antithetical to power. Rather, domination is the result of trajectories of force and power relations, culminating in a greater or lesser state of subordination, and correspondingly, with fewer or greater possibilities for resistance by subjects.[30] Yet power and domination remain different phenomena for Foucault.

From the perspective of feminist philosophy, it is important to ask whether this treatment of the subject enables us to recognize women's experiences of freedom and unfreedom. It would be difficult to argue that Foucault's account of the subject's capacity to resist power is simply untrue. Indeed, much feminist literature now stresses the importance of seeing women not as passive victims uniformly dominated but as active agents mediating their experiences. Nor does it seem accurate to claim that Foucault's reworking of the subject somehow compromises the political claim that women are indeed subordinated; domination is a state that Foucault is quick to acknowledge.[31] Yet what feminist theory does, and what Foucault does *not* do, is look closely and critically at the issue of freedom where it concerns women's responses to structural inequality and male violence.

To understand the workings of power and the responses that power elicits, it is necessary to ask how women experience freedom and barriers to freedom. This might involve, for instance, looking at what Virginia Held has referred to as internal impediments to women's freedom or empowerment.[32] Held points to Sandra Bartky's work on shame: "The heightened self-consciousness that comes with emotions of self-assessment may become, in the shame of the oppressed, a stagnant self-obsession. Or shame may generate a rage whose expression is unconstructive, even self-destructive. In all these ways, shame is profoundly disempowering."[33] Unlike her earlier "woman-as-Panopticon" analysis, Bartky's theorizing on shame posits women as active subjects capable of a range of responses to social power. Bartky also discusses sources of disempowerment for women often omitted from accounts of power and powerlessness: unreciprocated emotional labor, nurturing, and caregiving. This kind of disempowerment, because it "is more subtle and oblique, one that is rooted in the subjective and deeply interiorized effects upon women ourselves both of the emotional care we give and of the care we fail to get in return,"[34] is easily obscured by Foucault's agonistic model of power, because it reflects neither outright domination nor the intersubjective play of power between two free agents.

Feminists need to look at the *inner* processes that condition women's sense of freedom or choice, and to examine the external manifestations of power and dominance, without relying upon idealized notions of human agents as existentially free. Foucault's understanding of power is decidedly inadequate to this task. Women's "freedom" does not simply refer to subjects' objective possibilities for maneuvering or resisting within a power dynamic but concerns whether a woman *feels* empowered in her specific context. Because Foucault's account of the freedom of the subject determines the presence of power or "conduct"—as well as its opposite pole, violence or domination—based on the existence of objective points of resistance, it obscures the subjective aspects of power. As Lois McNay points out, in Foucault's theory, "power relations are only examined from the perspective of how they are installed in institutions and not from the point of view of those subject to power."[35] A feminist response to this failing might borrow from Virginia Held's objection to classical liberals' and contemporary libertarians' view of freedom as largely determined by the absence of "external impediments": feminists must emphasize, against this account, that "the self-development of women involves changing the affective tastes, the emotional coloration, with which we experience the world, not only the outer obstacles in that experience." Addressing women's freedom requires that we look at internal impediments to exercising choice as well as the tangible obstacles to its realization—and this means considering practices and conventions that may have disempowering effects not easily discernible to theorists who focus exclusively on political power. Finally, it involves recognizing certain experiences as ongoing expressions of resistance to power: "The power to give voice to one's aspiration to be heard is not so much the removal of an external impediment as the beginning of an internal empowerment."[36]

Foucault's agonistic model of power, skewed as it is toward a dynamic of *acting upon*, thus cannot provide feminists with the conceptual tools needed to understand empowerment and disempowerment, freedom and nonfreedom. To illustrate the inability of this framework to comprehend women's experiences of power, let us next consider the issue of male violence. First, recall Foucault's claim that violence and power are inherently different and separable, the former presupposing a situation of physical determination and the latter connoting a relation of "conduct," a dichotomy expressed in his claim that "where the determining factors saturate the whole there is no relationship of power; slavery is not a power relationship when a man is in chains."[37] Foucault's metaphoric slave in chains has no possibility of movement or resistance and is therefore situated in a context of violence and domination, not power.

What might agonistic power mean for feminists grappling with the question of women's experiences of rape, battery, and psychological abuse? To define male power as an inherently separable phenomenon from male force and domination, as Foucault would have us do, is to disregard the ways in which this power is frequently transformed into violence. A woman living in an abusive relationship feels the continuum of her partner's anger and force, sees that the day-to-day exercise of power is the stuff out of which explosions of abuse and violence are made. Foucault's distinctions between power and violence, freedom and domination, do not allow us to ask whether this woman feels complicit or victimized, powerless or empowered to leave the situation of abuse.

The issue of women's relation to violence and power is raised in a response by Monique Plaza to Foucault's position on rape. Foucault's view, expressed during a roundtable discussion, is that "when rape is punished, it is exclusively the physical violence that should be punished," and that one should consider rape "nothing but an assault." Foucault concludes that to punish rape as a sexual act is to shore up the apparatus of repression, infusing sex with repressive power; thus, he comments that sexuality should not "under any circumstances be the object of punishment."[38]

Plaza's response to Foucault is that he is setting up a false dichotomy between violence and sex. Rape, which is violent, forced sex, represents an imbroglio for Foucault, leading him to assert that the sexual part of rape should be exempted from punishment, leaving only force as deserving of sanction—a preposterous distinction. Women's unfreedom (as victims of rape) is thus superseded by the need to maintain men's freedom; that is, their freedom not to be punished for sex or to have their sex repressed. As Plaza writes, "what do they say except that *they want to defend the freedom that men have at the present time to repress us by rape? What do they say except that what they call (their) freedom is the repression of our bodies?*"[39]

I have brought up the issues of male violence and rape not to show that Foucault had invidious opinions or is a poor philosopher, but rather to illustrate that feminist theorists should approach his notions of the free subject and agonistic power with greater caution. To summarize, this caveat is necessary for four reasons: (1) because Foucault falsely posits "free agents" as a necessary feature of power; (2) because his analysis does not consider women's internal barriers to agency and choice, as with the example of shame; (3) because it sets up a false dichotomy between power and violence, as illustrated by the continuum of anger and physical abuse experienced by a battered woman; and (4) because it does not question the fact that in many societies, men's freedom (privilege, and so forth) is contingent upon women's unfreedom, as in the case of rape, rather than on the presence of a freely maneuvering antagonist. This does not mean feminists must jettison Foucault's framework of power relations altogether, but suggests that if we *do* wish to employ this part of the tool kit,[40] we must amend the thesis drastically to include inquiry into subjective aspects of power and, in particular, to reconceptualize the relationship between social and personal power and privilege, on the one hand, and violence, on the other. Despite the links between these, however, certain distinctions between power and force are warranted and crucial for feminists: there are real differences, for instance, between not being considered for a promotion on sexually discriminatory grounds, and being raped. It does not help feminists to insist on the existence of one single, global form of oppression that admits only of degree.[41]

Finally, as the discussion of lesbian and gay identity politics in the next section will show, the omission of an account of empowerment from Foucault's analysis of power should alert us to the limitations of his theory for feminist theory and praxis.

The Third Wave: Sexual Identity and Regimes of Truth/Power.   Following the intense interest in recent years in the themes of identity and difference, numerous scholars have used Foucault's work to suggest new ways of thinking about gender and sexual orientation. I shall use the example of lesbian and gay politics to show that, despite their initial appeal, Foucault's accounts of the subject and power contradict the aspirations of those who would mobilize around common, if contingent, identities.

Judith Butler is at the center of the third wave of Foucauldian feminist theory. In *Gender Trouble: Feminism and the Subversion of Identity*, Butler builds on Foucault's account of the proliferation of discourses on sex in the modern era. What we see today, she argues, is the constant reproduction of sexual identities via "an exclusionary apparatus of production" in which the meanings of these practices are curtailed, restricted, and reinforced. Whereas Foucault is most interested in the way regimes of power produce discourses on sexual perversion, pathology, delinquency, and criminality, and new subjects emerging from these categories, Butler is equally interested in the construction of gender and sexual minority identities. For feminists, her most controversial move is to use Foucault's thesis on modern power to deconstruct the very notion of woman. Butler proposes that we view gender as discursively and materially constructed through repetitive "performances" of "words, acts, gestures and desire." Foucault's influence on Butler's formulation is clear in her claim: "If the inner truth of gender is a fabrication and if a true gender is a fantasy instituted and inscribed on the surface of bodies then it seems that genders can be neither true nor false, but are only produced as the truth effects of a discourse of primary and stable identity." Rather than clinging to fixed notions of femaleness as necessary for feminist praxis, Butler suggests that we reconceptualize identity as "an effect" in order to destabilize gender and open up new, unforeseen possibilities for agency.[42]

A full discussion of Butler's work is not possible here, but I would like to address those aspects of Foucault's analysis of modern power that she invokes in arguing for a notion of sexuality as a site of contestation and subversion, and to consider the implications of such a strategy for lesbian and gay politics. Like Foucault, Butler suggests that sexual identities are constituted by regulatory practices and draws our attention to the instability of sexual categories. The backdrop to this thesis is found in Foucault's discussion of the rise of pastoral power in the West in the modern period; this power is salvation-oriented, individualizing (and at the same time totaling), and "linked with the production of truth—the truth of the individual himself."[43] This combination of tactics culminates in dividing practices and "true discourses" that confine the individual to a narrow, constructed identity, producing the modern category of the "homosexual" as well as other subject categories.

It is because minority sexual identities are so deeply couched in the dividing practices that first gave them meaning—established "through the isolation, intensification, and consolidation of peripheral sexualities"[44]—that Foucault discourages us from embracing these self-understandings in an uncritical way or as part of a political strategy. Not surprisingly, Foucault is dismissive of struggles that make sex the "rallying point" for resistance to the deployment of sexuality;[45] he contrasts "the homosexual liberation movements" with "the creative and interesting elements in the women's movements" and praises the latter for attempting to overcome their particular form of individualization, promoting "a displacement effected in reaction to the sexual centering of the problem, formulating the demand for new forms of culture, discourse, language . . . which are no longer part of that rigid assignation and pinning down to their sex which they had initially . . . been politically obliged to accept in order to make themselves heard." Gay men have not yet tried to desexualize their political platform as much as the feminist movement and instead have unwittingly made too much of their sexual orientation.[46] Just as he argues that rape should be desexualized, Foucault believes there is a need to "desex" political struggles, by which he means that the focus of a project of "liberation"—a concept he views with much suspicion—should take as its central task a more radical questioning of discourses that have made possible the categorization and persecution of individuals.

> It is the *agency* of sex that we must break away from, if we aim—through a tactical reversal of the various mechanisms of sexuality—to counter the grips of power with the claims of bodies, pleasures, and knowledges, in their multiplicity and their possibility of resistance. The rallying point for the counterattack against the deployment of sexuality ought not to be sex-desire, but bodies and pleasures.[47]

Butler concurs with Foucault's view that a politics placed squarely on fixed categories of gender and sexual orientation effectively reifies those identities. As an antidote to the production and reinforcement of fixed notions of sexual identity, Butler argues that homosexuality and heterosexuality—like gender—exist as enactments of cultural and aesthetic performances; even as these identities are performed and repeated, they are (in true Foucauldian form) being contested and unraveled. In an analysis that also borrows from Jacques Derrida, Butler claims that emancipatory discourses on sexuality unwittingly set up heterosexuality as *origin*, in the sense that homosexuality is viewed as a "copy" of the "original," or authentic, sexual identity.[48] To counteract this reification, Butler proposes to disrupt the logic that makes possible this dualistic formulation by underlining the contingency of the "sign" of sexual identity.

It is considerably less clear how a strategy of displacement translates into effective political action. Butler endorses Foucault's strategy and argues for a concept of politics as a constant undoing of the categories and gender norms that derive from, and are perpetuated by, sexual "performances." Crucially, however, she avoids the topic of how we go about employing for political purposes those same provisional identities. Indeed, it is not at all clear that Butler thinks this can be done successfully—that is, without reifying those subjectivities. Butler's ambivalence points to the sheer difficulty of such a project, as evidenced by her comment: "There is a political necessity to use some sign now, and we do, but how to use it in such a way that its futural significations are not foreclosed? How to use the sign and avow its temporal contingency at once?"[49] Similarly, Jana Sawicki incorporates Foucauldian premises in her assertions that we need to discover new ways of understanding ourselves and new ways of resisting how we have been socially defined and constructed. Unfortunately, as with Butler, Sawicki leaves us with little sense of how feminist politics can proceed if gender is to be displaced.[50]

The political ambivalence of a position that stresses the contingency of common self-understandings—or for Butler, the illusory nature of gender and sexual identities—is echoed in Foucault's own work. Foucault's view, as we have seen, is that subjects must displace the particular forms of subjectification that have oppressed them by expanding and critically reflecting upon both their definitions of shared identity and their domain of activism. This is as close as Foucault comes to suggesting what political resistance to oppression might look like, and the vagueness of his vision is reproduced by third-wave Foucauldian feminists. If, by the suggestion: "Maybe the target nowadays is not to discover what we are, but to refuse what we are," Foucault is advising that one take up a critical stance toward identities that have been constructed and reinforced by coercive discourses, the point is well taken.[51] This circumspection is also helpful as a caution against the sometimes homogenizing effect of identity politics—the tendency for a particular self-understanding to supersede others by setting up forms for what it means to be, and to live as, a lesbian or gay man. Yet several troubling questions remain. For example, *are* sexual identities strictly "constructed" via dividing practices that set homosexual off from heterosexual? Aren't a range of issues regarding sexual choice and the conscious appropriation of an identity simply being overlooked? Isn't it necessary, both for reasons of personal affirmation and political efficacy—in order to make rights-based claims, for instance—to assert the existence of the "categories" of women, lesbians, and gay men? And how does a group or an individual simultaneously resist an identity and mobilize around it for the purposes of empowerment and political action? These are questions that the arguments of third-wave Foucauldian feminists, like those of Foucault himself, necessarily raise. The fact that the questions go unaddressed speaks to the difficulties inherent in Foucauldian conceptions of identity and power.

Despite the initial usefulness of a deconstruction of sexual identity, then, Foucault's position leaves feminist theorists in something of a quandary. In particular, there are three concrete political problems raised by this approach that require attention. The first, perhaps most obvious, problem is that Foucault's treatment of sexual self-understanding gives insufficient attention to struggles by particular social movements and to the ways in which their participants perceive and creatively inhabit their own identities. Most lesbian and gay activists today place sexual orientation at the center of their struggles, which range from retrieving historical accounts of their communities to resisting homophobic violence and discrimination as concerns employment, health, and pension benefits, and so forth. For Foucault, such activities constitutes a dubious if not illogical strategy, because it casts these sexual identities as essential or biological rather than socially constructed. The end result is, as one critic notes of unmitigated social-constructionist theories in general, a tendency to treat lesbians and gay men who understand themselves in identity-bound terms as "victims of 'false consciousness,' unaware of the constructedness of their identities."[52]

Foucault's analysis also negates the importance of personal and group definition and affirmation, resources not easily replaced by the vague notion of identity contestation. Shane Phelan, for instance, has looked at the ways in which the construction of a positive lesbian identity and a community to support it, while rife with difficulties, has provided a base of emotional and political support for many lesbians. She cautions against the pitfalls of fixing a static description of lesbianism—since "every new definition . . . shades another, and this is a choice with political consequences"—agreeing with Foucault insofar as she argues tht lesbian feminists fall into "the trap of counterreification" in taking back the task of defining themselves. Yet in the final instance, Phelan believes it is possible and desirable to forge a critical, strategic politics that keeps identity at the center of its project.

> Identity politics does mean building our public action on who we
> are and how that identity fits into and does not fit into our

society. This is and must be the basis for political action that addresses nonjuridical, nonstate-centered power. . . . Identity politics must be based, not only on identity, but on an apprecia-tion for politics as the art of living together. *Politics that ignores our identities, that makes them "private," is useless; but non-negotiable identities will enslave us whether they are imposed from within or without.*[53](my emphasis)

A second, related problem with a Foucauldian analysis of identity is that it needlessly dichotomizes the debate on strategies for sexual minority politics, offering two disparate alternatives: on the one hand, the decision to keep sexuality and sexual choice at the center of a movement, to reappropriate these experiences as a departure point for political activism; on the other, Foucault's preferred option, that of "desexualizing" struggles and exploring new forms of pleasure and dis-course that do not feed back into the "pinning down" to one's sex. This ignores the possibility, illustrated by lesbian and gay communities over the past several decades, that these two political methods may be complementary tools of empowerment and political activism, pursued simultaneously. In particular, the idea of strategic essentialism—reappropriating and subverting an identity while maintaining an under-standing of its historical contingency—is overlooked by Foucault and is regarded with suspicion by this third-wave feminist literature.[54]

A final criticism both of Foucault's position on sexual identity and of third-wave feminist appropriations of his thesis on identity is that they leave untouched the subject's understanding of her conditions of oppression, and by implication, tend to foreclose discussions of agency and empowerment. This omission is crucial to the criticisms of Foucault's agonistic model of power and of his position on sexual identities. Many forms of resistance may go unnoticed if we begin from Foucault's call to desexualize struggles and so shun the minority identities that have been constructed by discourses on sex. For instance, it is unlikely that this approach to sexual identities can comprehend lesbian feminist politics, Stonewall, ACT UP, or even the institution of Gay Pride Day. Moreover, Foucault's treatment of power obscures the personal experiences behind such activism: these *may* contain elements of power relations in which the "acting upon" dynamic is appropriate; as, for example, in the case of specific demands directed at decision makers. Yet struggles such as these are also about personal empowerment and acting collectively to set an agenda for change. In effect, Foucault's power analysis prevents us from seeing or conceptualizing relationships in which the object is *neither* to *act upon* another in a power relation or to *resist* the attempts of governing conduct or a local manifestation of power; it is a framework that seems inappropriate for describing cooperative efforts aimed both at political transformation and personal empowerment and consciousness-raising.[55]

Foucault's analysis allows little room for an account of the processes involved in developing personal and collective capacities for political activism; empowerment is not about actions upon agents in a relationship of power and so cannot be understood within the confines of this analysis. A richer resource of alternative approaches to theorizing power and agency are to be found in works by such writers as Audre Lorde, Patricia Hill Collins, and bell hooks.

Conclusion: Feminism, Power, and Empowerment

> Feminist ideology should not encourage (as sexism has done) women to believe they are powerless. It should clarify for women the powers they exercise daily and show them ways these powers can be used to resist sexist domination and exploitation.
>
> —bell hooks, *Feminist Theory: From Margin to Center*

If empowerment is much more than a relationship of power, or an attempt to direct the behavior of others, what is the most useful conceptualization of this phenomenon for feminists? Rather than offering a single definition, I wish to hint at an array of useful accounts in feminist literature.

Audre Lorde writes of the importance of erotic power in our lives and the connections between agency and self-understanding: "Our acts against oppression become integral with self, motivated and empowered from within."[56] The relationship between personal experiences of disempowerment and oppression, on the one hand, and broader political action, on the other, has numerous illustrations in contemporary North American feminist politics. For instance, the advent of the direct-action Women's Action Coalition (WAC) in the United States in early 1992 (and soon after, in Canada) was motivated by a surge of frustration and anger in the wake of such events as the Kennedy rape trial and the

Supreme Court's disbelief in the testimony of Anita Hill, both of which resonated with the experiences of untold numbers of women.[57] WAC was successful precisely because it galvanized this discontent and recognizes the importance of empowerment: the women involved do not expect immediate political changes but know that their dramatic, vocal protests register their anger and convey the message that specific injustices will not be tolerated.

On a similar note, Patricia Hill Collins writes about the empowerment of black American women as an outcome of changed consciousness, resulting from both internal transformations and the effects of these transformations on the broader community.

> [C]hange can also occur in the private, personal space of an individual woman's consciousness. Equally fundamental, this type of change is also empowering. If a Black woman is forced to remain "motionless on the outside," she can always develop the "inside" of a changed consciousness as a sphere of freedom. Becoming empowered through self-knowledge, even within conditions that severely limit one's ability to act, is essential.

Collins writes of the importance of an alternative vision of power. In her view, "Black women have not conceptualized our quest for empowerment as one of replacing elite white male authorities with ourselves as benevolent Black female ones. Instead, African-American women have overtly rejected theories of power based on domination in order to embrace an alternative vision of power based on a humanist vision of self-actualization, self-definition, and self-determination."[58] bell hooks also believes it is important to consider the possibilities for political transformation that arise from our daily lives. Her notion of a "politics of location" as a revisioning exercise to counter the effects of hegemonic practices, as well as her concept of the dual nature of marginality—as "site of deprivation" and "space of resistance"—are useful analytic tools with which to examine black American struggles as well as women's specific empowerment.[59]

These feminist writings on empowerment suggest the need to place the subject's interpretation and mediation of her experiences at the center of our inquiries into the hows and whys of power. Such an analysis might ask: What do relationships of power feel like from the inside, where are the possibilities for resistance, and what personal and collective processes will take us there? A feminist analysis of power would avoid the omissions and problems of Foucault's understanding of power in four key ways. First, by conceptualizing women's relationships to their bodies as both a reflection of social construction *and* of their own responses to (and mediation of) the cultural ideals of femininity, it would avoid the pitfalls of a static, "docile bodies" paradigm of subjectivity. Second, it would reject aspects of Foucault's agonistic model of power—including his assertion that *all* relations are permeated by power, and the simplistic, false dichotomy of power versus violence or domination—and instead attend to the myriad sources of disempowerment and oppression experienced by human agents, especially women. Third, it would take seriously the issue of women's empowerment, their capacities for self-determination and freedom, and the conditions that facilitate their growth. And fourth, a feminist analysis of power would dispute both Foucault's view that sexual identities should not form the basis for lesbian and gay struggles and third-wave Foucauldian feminists' assertion that the category of "women" should be displaced from the center of feminist politics. This last point need not prevent those engaged in feminist theory and queer theory—nor, indeed, social movements themselves—from appreciating the significance of Foucault's discussion of the historical construction of marginalized identities.

Although the overall tone of this essay conveys more criticisms of Foucault than suggestions for feminist uses of his thought, this is not necessarily bad news. I think that feminist theorists have learned, and can learn still more, from Foucault. Although it is disappointing that his work does not engage directly with feminism, this does not diminish the heuristic usefulness of certain of Foucault's insights on power, resistance, and sexuality. It is vital, however, to maintain a critical awareness when attempting to appropriate Foucauldian concepts for feminist ends. In the process, we may find that there are resources within feminist theory that are more suited to the task of developing an alternative vision of power and empowerment than are attempts to make Foucault fit feminist purposes.

Notes

1. Foucault's reference to power as agonic, or agonistic, denotes his assertion that power circulates, is never fixed, and is really a network of relationships of power among subjects who are at least in some minimal sense free to act and to resist. This is the concept of power

developed in *Power/Knowledge: Selected Interviews and Other Writings, 1972–1977*, ed. Colin Gordon, trans. Colin Gordon et al. (New York: Pantheon, 1980), and in "The Subject and Power," afterword to *Michel Foucault: Beyond Structuralism and Hermeneutics*, ed. Paul Rabinow and Hubert Dreyfus (Chicago: University of Chicago Press, 1983). Agonistic comes from the Greek, *agon*, or combat, and connotes both the exercise of power and struggle (see Foucault's account of the agonic metaphor in "The Subject and Power," 222).

2. I refer to the subject in the singular throughout the essay for simplicity's sake but do not mean to imply that Foucault asserts the existence of a homogenous subject or subjectivity. Indeed, in response to this suggestion, Foucault comments: "(The subject) is not a substance; it is a form and this form is not above all or always identical to itself. You do not have towards yourself the same kind of relationship when you constitute yourself as a political subject who goes and votes or speaks up in a meeting, and when you try to fulfill your desires in a sexual relationship. . . . In each case, we play, we establish with one's self some different form of relationship. And it is precisely the historical constitution of these different forms of subject relating to games of truth that interests me." See "The Ethic of Care for the Self as a Practice of Freedom: An Interview with Michel Foucault," interview by Raul Fornet-Betancourt et al., trans. Joseph D. Gauthier, in *The Final Foucault*, ed. James Bernauer and David Rasmussen (Cambridge: MIT Press, 1988), 10.

3. See Susan Hekman, *Gender and Knowledge: Elements of a Postmodern Feminism* (Boston: Northeastern University Press, 1990); and Judith Butler, *Gender Trouble: Feminism and the Subversion of Identity* (New York: Routledge, 1990).

4. Michel Foucault, "Two Lectures," in *Power/Knowledge: Selected Interviews and Other Writings, 1972–1977*, ed. Colin Gordon, trans. Colin Gordon et al. (New York: Pantheon, 1980), 105.

5. Michel Foucault, *History of Sexuality*, vol. 1, *An Introduction*, trans. Robert Hurley (New York: Vintage, 1980), 139.

6. Michel Foucault, *Discipline and Punish: The Birth of the Prison*, trans. Alan Sheridan (New York: Vintage, 1979), 25.

7. For example, Foucault, in his 1982 lecture "Technologies of the Self," stated: "Perhaps I've insisted too much on the technology of domination and power. I am more and more interested in the interaction between oneself and others and in the technologies of individual domination, the history of how an individual acts upon himself, the technology of the self." Also important here is his emphasis on "governmentality," which he calls the "contact between the technologies of domination of others and those of the self." See Luther H. Martin, Huck Gutman, and Patrick H. Hutton, eds., *Technologies of the Self: A Seminar with Michel Foucault* (Amherst: University of Massachusetts Press, 1988), 19.

8. See also Foucault, "The Eye of Power," in *Power/Knowledge: Selected Interviews and Other Writings, 1972–1977*, ed. Colin Gordon, trans. Colin Gordon et al. (New York: Pantheon, 1980).

9. Ibid., 155.

10. Sandra Bartky, "Foucault, Femininity, and the Modernization of Patriarchal Power," in *Feminism and Foucault: Reflections on Resistance*, ed. Irene Diamond and Lee Quinby (Boston: Northeastern University Press, 1988), 63, 63–64.

11. Ibid., 64 and 66. Unfortunately, "femininity" as a construct is at no point historicized or contextualized in Bartky's analysis.

12. Ibid., 77–78.

13. Ibid., 81.

14. Susan Bordo, "The Body and the Reproduction of Femininity," in *Gender, Body, Knowledge*, ed. Alison Jaggar and Susan Bordo (New Brunswick: Rutgers University Press, 1989), 23.

15. Ibid. See also Bordo's "Anorexia Nervosa: Psychopathology as Crystallization of Culture," in *Feminism and Foucault: Reflections on Resistance*, ed. Irene Diamond and Lee Quinby (Boston: Northeastern University Press, 1988).

16. Foucault, in *Discipline and Punish*, and "Two Lectures," traces the emergence of specific disciplinary mechanisms such as prisons, hospitals, and schools to account for the formation of a "disciplinary society" beginning in the late seventeenth century; he emphasizes that the transition from sovereign to disciplinary power is a historically specific phenomenon.

17. Although I have chosen to distinguish between Foucault's "docile bodies" and "bio-power" theses, they are frequently run together in the literature. I treat them separately in order to show that the "bio-power" analysis, if amended, is much more useful for feminists than is the docile bodies thesis.

18. *History of Sexuality*, 1: 142–43, 145, 147, 116.

19. Jennifer Terry, "The Body Invaded: Medical Surveillance of Women as Reproducers," *Socialist Review* 19 (July–September 1989): 13–43, 20.

20. Terry, "The Body Invaded," 23, points out that in 1984, it became possible in the United States to charge a vehicle driver, including a pregnant woman, with manslaughter causing the death of a fetus. Additionally, legal theorist Patricia Williams cites one case among many in which a pregnant woman who was a known drug user was ordered put in jail by a judge in order to protect the fetus (Women and the Law lecture series, Law Faculty, McGill University, Montreal, 4 April 1990).

21. Jana Sawicki, "Identity Politics and Sexual Freedom," in *Feminism and Foucault: Reflections on Resistance*, ed. Irene Diamond and Lee Quinby (Boston: Northeastern University Press, 1988), 185 and 189; and her "Foucault and Feminism: Toward a Politics of Difference," *Hypatia* 1 (Fall 1986): 32, 26.

22. Hekman, *Gender and Knowledge*, 182–86.

23. Nancy Fraser, "Foucault on Modern Power: Empirical Insights and Normative Confusions," in her *Unruly Practices: Power, Discourse, and Gender in Contemporary Social Theory* (Minneapolis: University of Minnesota Press, 1989), 31, 32.

24. Nancy Hartsock, "Foucault on Power: A Theory for Women?" in *Feminism/Postmodernism*, ed. Linda J. Nicholson (New York: Routledge, 1990), 170, 168, 171.

25. Foucault, "The Ethics of Care for the Self," 12.

26. Lois McNay, "The Foucauldian Body and the Exclusion of Experience," *Hypatia* 6 (Fall 1991): 125.

27. Foucault, "The Ethics of Care for the Self," 11.

28. Peta Bowden suggests that Foucault's conception of power precludes a range of emotions and interpersonal experiences, because it insists that all relations are characterized by adversarial, agonistic power (seminar paper, Department of Political Science, McGill University, Montreal, April 1990).

29. To "conduct" in this Foucauldian sense can mean to direct others or even to coerce; Foucault also uses "conduct" as a noun to denote a way of behaving in an "open field of possibilities." See Foucault, "The Subject and Power," 220–21.

30. Foucault, "Power and Strategies," in *Power/Knowledge: Selected Interviews and Other Writings, 1972–1977*, ed. Colin Gordon, trans. Colin Gordon et al. (New York: Pantheon, 1980), 42.

31. Ibid. Despite Foucault's references to domination, he is often taken to purport the absence of domination per se. For instance, Biddy Martin argues that "there is the danger that Foucault's challenges to traditional categories, if taken to a 'logical' conclusion . . . could make the question of women's oppression obsolete." See her "Feminism, Criticism, and Foucault," in *Feminism and Foucault: Reflections on Resistance*, ed. Irene Diamond and Lee Quinby (Boston: Northeastern University Press, 1988), 17.

32. Virginia Held, "Freedom and Feminism," paper presented to the conference "The Intellectual Legacy of C. B. Macpherson," University of Toronto, 4–6 October 1989. For a revised version, see her *Feminist Morality: Transforming Culture, Society, and Politics* (Chicago: University of Chicago Press, 1993), chap. 9.

33. Sandra Bartky, "Shame and Gender," in her *Feminism and Domination: Studies in the Phenomenology of Oppression* (New York: Routledge, 1991), 97. Held quotes an earlier version of this work in her "Freedom and Feminism," 8.

34. Sandra Bartky, "Feeding Egos and Tending Wounds: Deference and Disaffection in Women's Emotional Labor," in her *Feminism and Domination: Studies in the Phenomenology of Oppression* (New York: Routledge, 1991), 111.

35. McNay, "The Foucauldian Body," 134.

36. Held, "Freedom and Feminism," 8, 12.

37. Foucault, "The Subject and Power," 221.

38. Monique Plaza, "Our Damages and Their Compensation—Rape: The 'Will Not to Know' of Michel Foucault," *Feminist Issues* 1 (Summer 1981): 25–35. Plaza quotes Foucault from a roundtable discussion published in *La Folie Encerclée* (Paris: Seghers/Lafont, 1977), 99. See Plaza, "Our Damages," 27, 26. A position on rape similar to that of Foucault has recently been espoused by Germaine Greer in various interviews and commentaries in print and television media in the United Kingdom.

39. Plaza, "Our Damages," 31.

40. Foucault suggests using theory as a "tool-kit"—in the sense of instrument—rather than as a total "system," in "Power and Strategies," 145.

41. I am indebted to Virginia Held for pointing out to me that distinctions between power and violence are important for feminists. Held draws a number of useful distinctions among power, force, coercion, and violence (personal communication, 5 June 1993).

42. Butler, *Gender Trouble*, 31–32, 136, 147. Butler's clearest definition of gender is found early on (p. 33) in her text: "Gender is the repeated stylization of the body, a set of repeated acts within a highly regulatory frame that congeal over time to produce the appearance of substance, of a natural sort of being."

43. Foucault, "The Subject and Power," 214.

44. Foucault, *History of Sexuality*, 1:48.

45. Foucault, "Confessions of the Flesh," in *Power/Knowledge: Selected Interviews and Other Writings, 1972–1977*, ed. Colin Gordon, trans. Colin Gordon et al. (New York: Pantheon, 1980), 219–20. See also the interview "The End of the Monarchy of Sex," trans. John Johnson, in *Foucault Live: Interviews, 1966–1984*, ed Sylvère Lotringer (New York: Semiotext[e], 1989).

46. Foucault, "Confessions of the Flesh," 220. Foucault appears to be referring to gay men, and not to lesbians, when he speaks of "homosexual movements"; moreover he contrasts this movement with "women," a distinction that is both misleading and ill-informed.

47. Foucault, *History of Sexuality*, 1:157.

48. Judith Butler, "Imitation and Gender Insubordination," in *Inside/Out: Lesbian Theories, Gay Theories*, ed. Diana Fuss (New York: Routledge, 1992), 18, 19, 29.

49. Ibid., 19.

50. Sawicki, "Identity Politics and Sexual Freedom," 189.

51. Foucault, "The Subject and Power," 216.

52. Stephen Epstein, "Gay Politics, Ethnic Identity: The Limits of Social Constructionism," *Socialist Review* 7 (May–August 1987), 22.

53. Shane Phelan, *Identity Politics: Lesbian Feminism and the Limits of Community* (Philadelphia: Temple University Press, 1989), 79, 156, 170.

54. See, for instance, Butler, "Imitation and Gender Insubordination," in *Inside/Out: Lesbian Theories, Gay Theories*, ed. Diana Fuss (New York: Routledge, 1992), 19–20.

55. Of the three types of relationships identified by Foucault—those of "objective capacities," relationships of communication, and power relations—none come close to describing what we understand as empowerment. The first refers to the *effects* of power, and the others identify the ways in which individuals or groups are brought together in a play of power, acting upon one another. See Foucault, "The Subject and Power," 217–18. Foucault considers even personal communication and love to be constituted by a dynamic of "acting upon." See his "Ethic of Care for the Self," 11.

56. Audre Lorde, "Uses of the Erotic: The Erotic as Power," in her *Sister Outsider: Essays and Speeches* (New York: Spinsters Ink, 1982; Trumansburg, N.Y.: Crossing Press, 1984), 58.

57. See Karen Houppert, "WAC," *Village Voice* 37 (9 June 1992): 33–38.

58. Patricia Hill Collins, *Black Feminist Thought: Knowledge, Consciousness, and the Politics of Empowerment* (New York: Routledge, 1991), 111, 224.

59. bell hooks, "Choosing the Margin as a Space of Radical Openness," in her *Yearning: Race, Gender, and Cultural Politics* (Boston: South End, 1990), 145, 149.

Part Four

Power/Politics

10

A Feminist Mapping of Foucauldian Politics

Moya Lloyd

"To claim that politics requires a stable subject is to claim that there can be no *political* opposition to that claim. Indeed, that claim implies that a critique of the subject cannot be politically informed critique but, rather, an act which puts in jeopardy politics as such. To require the subject means to foreclose the domain of the political, and that foreclosure, installed analytically as an essential feature of the political, enforces the boundaries of the domain of the political in such a way that that enforcement is protected from political scrutiny."[1] What is the relationship between the subject and politics within feminism? At present the

*I thank Susan Hekman, Iain MacKenzie, and Andrew Thacker for their helpful comments on an earlier draft of this essay.

dominant, though not uncontested, view is that a feminist emancipatory politics requires a coherent subject for liberation. Philosophical positions that radically challenge the notion of a unified subject are presented as threatening the very viability of feminist politics, as condemning "women" to perpetual oppression. "[W]ithout the possibility of a coherent self," Tress observes, "liberation becomes impossible. There is no one who persists, who remembers, whose experience and suffering counts; there is no one to emancipate."[2] By now, the argument is surely familiar: feminist politics is grounded in, or legitimated by, its ability to articulate and to implement the desires and goals of a specific constituency, a constituency on whose behalf is speaks the truth (or should that be, the Truth?) of oppression: namely, women. Feminism is, therefore, categorized as a species of representational or identity politics. Yet, as we know all too well, attempts to delineate the characteristics uniting all women have usually failed. The voices and writings of women of color (among others) have amply demonstrated the exclusionary and occlusive nature of these enterprises and of the inappropriateness of the category Woman or, indeed women (in any universalist or essentialist sense), in the face of the subject-in-difference. Added to this, of course, have been the dissonant strains of postmodern/poststructuralist theory as it has challenged the very idea of a unitary or stable subject. Even given these criticisms, some feminists have been reluctant to rethink the relationship between the feminist subject and feminist politics, continuing to view the idea of a politically informed critique of the subject as itself destructive of the very possibility of (feminist) politics *per se*.[3]

However, if the debate within feminism over the question of identity is to move beyond the aporia within which it is confined at present (that is, one which views only emancipatory politics as real feminist politics) then we have to tackle two questions. First, we have to ask (however speculatively), What kind(s) of subjectivities can demand and support feminist politics?[4] Second, what kinds of feminist politics could these subjectivities demand? We have, therefore, to explore ways of opening up, of breaching, the boundaries of the political set at present by the demand for a unitary subject. Here I shall explore this problematic from a Foucauldian perspective. In so doing, I shall be concentrating primarily on the second of the two questions sketched above; that is, on the types of politics made possible for discursively constituted (and, as we shall see, self-constituted) subjects.

One of the hallmarks of Foucault's genealogical analyses is his exploration of the constitution of subjectivity. He engages, that is, with the question of the political processes at work in subjectification; how, that is, politics constitutes the subject through the medium of power and how, therefore, there are no innocent subjects free from power. I propose that in his later (ethical and aesthetic) writings, he begins to ask questions about the kinds of political activities in which these processed subjects could engage. Many of his critics have contended that neither political programs nor political strategies can be distilled from his work. Sometimes this criticism has taken the form of a charge of a performative contradiction;[5] with others, it is an accusation of a general insensitivity to politics.[6] I shall offer an alternative interpretation: that Foucault's consideration of ethics offers a way of rethinking the politics–subject relationship; a rethinking that tenders some creative possibilities for a feminism itself querying the connections between the feminist subject and feminist politics. Specifically, I shall show that Foucault's later works offer a doubled politics: politics as critique and politics as an ethics (or stylistics of existence) that together have the potential to initiate strategies of transgression. I shall then explore the validity and appropriateness of these twin politics for feminism.

We can detect the origins of the twin politics (identified above) in the essay "The Subject and Power." Here Foucault outlines his reasons for turning to the question of self-subjectification. The current economy of power relations, he writes: "applies itself to immediate everyday life which categorizes the individual, marks him by his own individuality, attaches himself to his identity, imposes a law of truth on him which he must recognize and which others have to recognize in him. It is a form of power which makes individuals subjects."[7] The "government of individualization" (outlined in *Discipline and Punish* and *The History of Sexuality: An Introduction*), operates, according to Foucault, by binding individuals to certain normativized, and thus regulatory, identities. Foucault's response to this ensnarement is to advocate a two-course strategy. His first tack is to suggest a politics of refusal: that we "refuse what we are," thus rejecting the "kind of individuality which has been imposed on us for several centuries." His second is to suggest the promotion of "new forms of subjectivity" (216). These twin courses of action are only vaguely suggested. They are fleshed out in more detail in his later interviews and essays.[8] I begin by considering his first strategy—politics as critique—and its precursor politics as refusal.

What might be implied by a politics of refusal? Three options suggest themselves. First, that the politics of refusal is a purely reactive politics: an uncritical (maybe unconscious) resistance to power, a spontaneous politics.[9] Second, that it signifies a form of anarchic individualism; a belligerent refusal to name or be named.[10] Third, that refusal is founded upon a self-conscious and critical disavowal of the parameters of discursive constitution. Versions of all three can certainly be found in Foucault's work, however, it is this last version—the self-reflexive—that dominates his later ethical writings, and that is given its fullest articulation in the essay "What is Enlightenment?" and in the interview "Practising Criticism."

Foucault's preoccupation in "What is Enlightenment?" is with the ways in which subjects are located in the historical present: the ways they have of understanding, and of acting upon, themselves. This task, at once theoretical and practical, he labels "an attitude"; the attitude of modernity (39). Thinking with attitude crucially involves thinking critically. It involves the construction of an "historical ontology of ourselves": a critique, that is, "of what we are saying, thinking, and doing" (45). This form of liminal analysis, contesting the boundaries of discursivity, is premised upon an excavation of those chance, contingent, and arbitrary events that "have led us [historically] to constitute ourselves and to recognize ourselves as subjects" (46). Its aim, as he notes elsewhere, is to make "facile gestures difficult," to render alien modes of thought and behavior that we accept as normal and everyday.[11] It is this process of denaturalization—or problematization[12]—that grounds the politics of refusal; it is thinking with attitude that generates the conditions of possibility necessary for subjects to cha(lle)nge their identities.

Foucault makes it clear in "Practising Criticism" that this is not critique for the sake of critique. Critical work serves an essentially political function: "deep transformation" can only be carried out in a "free atmosphere"; that is, "one constantly agitated by a permanent criticism."[13] Far from being a spontaneous, and/or unthinking, gesture of rejection, then, the politics of refusal is underpinned, even made possible, by a politics of critique. "[A]s soon as one can no longer think things as one formerly thought them, transformation becomes both very urgent, very difficult, and quite possible."[14] Exposure of the chance and contingency at the root of all things suggests that all things may be different: that there is nothing necessary or absolute in their constitution and, as such, that they are all open to review, to change. It is the existence of conditions of possibility for critique that, in his words, enables subjects to identify the means of "no longer being, doing, or thinking what we are, do, or think";[15] of becoming other.

Furthermore, it is this activity of critique (or problematization) that, for Foucault, also forms the arena for collective political action. Rejecting traditional ideas about identity as the foundation for consensual politics (the prior identification of a "we" to ground and validate political activity), Foucault conjectures that the very process of the contestation and questioning implicit in critique can itself lead to the (temporary) formation of a community of action. He declares: "it seems to me that the "we" must not be previous to the question; it can only be the result—and the necessarily temporary result—of the question as it is posed in the new terms in which one formulates it."[16] Instead of attempting to determine in advance the features that may unite people in political action—as in those feminisms posited upon a fixation of the category "Woman"—Foucault proposes a politics that grows out of the radical unfixing or de-determination of identity. As a consequence, his conception of the relationship between the subject and politics is radically different from that traditionally assumed. As Shane Phelan observes, for feminism this means that the differences between women "are not to be disposed of by simply finding the unity 'beneath' the difference; unity is a production, shifting and unstable."[17] In place of the coherent subject as political agent, Foucault positions the processed subject whose very identity and capacity for agency rests upon fragile and repeatedly destructible foundations. This, however, is only half of the story.

The account of critique outlined in "What is Enlightenment?" and "Practising Criticism" is also regarded by Foucault as furnishing the bases for "politics as an ethics."[18] While the first task of critique is to instigate a genealogical inquiry, the second (ethical) task is to put that inquiry "to the test of reality" in order to "grasp the points where change is possible and desirable, and to determine the precise form this change should take."[19] Ethical work is, thus, experimental work. Where critique is fundamentally deconstructive (in a non-Derridean sense), politics as ethics is essentially creative. As Foucault puts it in "The Ethic of Care as a Practice of Freedom," ethical work is an "ascetical practice"; an exercise of the self upon the self through which subjects attempt to transform themselves and their behavior in the light of certain goals.[20]

Any number of exercises may be used in this process of self-transformation from writing the self (autobiography, diary, memoirs),[21] through dietetics and household management, the interpretation of dreams, to the production of the self as a work of art (Baudelaire the dandy).[22] The point is that they all involve the subject in the active (though not necessarily always independent) production of themselves. Ethical activity is perhaps best categorized, therefore, in terms of "technologies of the self":[23] practices of self-(re)invention, stylistics (or aesthetics) of existence, new modes of self-subjectification.

Ethics in this respect is tied closely to freedom. Freedom, in the Foucauldian sense, means something both very specific, and very distinct, from conventional understandings of freedom (in respect of the subject). Self-transformation is not an act of liberation. Liberation usually connotes one of two things: the emancipation of a (pre-discursive) subject from the strictures of oppression, and/or the arrival of the individual at an end state, a telos—freedom.[24] While Foucault is prepared to concede that variations on liberation are possible (such as a colonial people's overthrowing their oppressors), for him freedom is primarily a *practice*, an *askesis*. It is an incessant process; the repeated subversion and transformation of power relations in the production of the self.[25] Second, self-transformation always occurs within certain parameters; it is not creative work ex nihilo. As he notes: free beings are those "faced with a field of possibilities in which several ways of behaving, several reactions and diverse comportments may be realised."[26] There is choice, but not unlimited choice; the field of possibility is always already partially constituted. While there is scope for active self-fashioning, the practices of the self that the subject adopts are always in some way imbricated within or modulated by contemporary practices or existing (though not necessarily dominant) patterns of behavior.[27] As Grimshaw notes: "the idea of inventing a completely new ethical scheme would . . . be foreign to Foucault's thought; we *can* only start from where we are."[28]

There is, in this formulation of the self's relation to itself, a certain ambiguity insofar as it appears that the self's own constitutive practices are also the raw material for aesthetic elaboration.[29] How can that be? The answer appears to lie in Foucault's notion of critique: the ability to question and contest the parameters of discursive constitution. Foucault makes a distinction between "technologies of the self" and "technologies of power."[30] The latter, he proclaims elsewhere, are constituted by the "correlation between fields of knowledge, types of normativity, and forms of subjectivity in a particular culture."[31] These are precisely the materials upon which critique works: the manifold events that produce us as subjects of the historical present. One feature of technologies (or hermeneutics) of the self is an attempt to "decipher, recognize, and acknowledge" the ways in which this self is produced. This is the work of historical ontology, of problematization. One significant effect of problematization is the possibility of generating alternative practices of the self, an aesthetics of existence.[32] What lends force to this creative dimension is the fact that subjects are always constituted across a range of discourses and practices; the self is the site of multiple practices (some working in harmony, others in tension). There are, therefore, always interstitial possibilities for self-production. This is what furnishes the conditions of possibility for aesthetic formation.

Politics as ethics is not a medium of revolutionary emancipation, however. It is more a tool of resignification and reinvention; an ongoing agonistic with the *potential* for radical change. This radical edge occurs only when the ethics are combined with the practice of critique. As Probyn attests, it is this conjunction that actuates the self as the "articulation of a way of life, a set of technologies, and a theoretical project,"[33] what Schmid calls "the Self as possibility."[34]

What does this all have to do with feminism? First, most feminist accounts of Foucault have tended to concentrate on the genealogies and on the analytic of power. On the basis of this, many critics have rejected the turn to Foucault on the grounds that his subjects are merely the passive ciphers of power, unable to escape the ineluctable flow of discipline and normalization and, thus, incapable of subversive political activity. Foucault's shift to practices of the self, hailing as it does the possibility of individual creativity in the production of one's identity and, thus presumably, also of transgression suggests that a reappraisal of Foucault might be timely. If Foucauldian subjects can indeed escape the strictures of power, then perhaps feminists may be able to glean some-thing of use after all. Indeed, it is this shift in Foucault's work that provides the backdrop to the most comprehensive feminist evaluation of that work yet produced: Lois McNay's *Foucault and Feminism*.[35] In this text, Foucault is recuperated as an advocate of an emancipatory politics in the tradition of the Enlightenment.[36] Given feminisms' own impulses toward emancipation this latest reinterpretation of Foucault only provides additional impetus for another conversation between feminism and Foucault.

A second, related, reason exists for reading Foucault's later work: the recent debate within feminism about the nature of the relationship between the feminist subject and the kinds of political activity in which she can engage.[37] One of the consequences of this debate has been to prompt some creative thinking about how to reconfigure this relationship in the light of trenchant criticism both of the exclusionary nature of the category woman, and of the kinds of political activity allowed as feminist. I argue that Foucault's later work (as outlined above) offers a possible model of just such a reconfigured relationship.

I begin by exploring the claim that Foucault's ethics offers a more active notion of the acquisition of gender than signaled in his earlier work.[38] If Foucault's own attention to gender is, at best, heavily biased toward the processes of masculinization and, at worst, wholly insensitive to the differential patterns of feminization and masculinization, his ethics, it is suggested, may nevertheless offer feminists some tools with which to understand the "active and never-completed process of engendering or enculturation," the activities involved in becoming woman.[39] The presumption underlying this claim, that gender is "an active style of living one's body in the world,"[40] allows for consideration of the ways in which women are complicit in the acquisition of hegemonic patterns of femininity; one of the ways in which gender is currently produced. In her article "Foucault, Femininity, and Patriarchal Power" (an application of the terms of *Discipline and Punish* to contemporary practices of feminization), Sandra Bartky highlights a problem with a purely disciplinary turn to Foucault: since the practices of femininity are extrainstitutional, it is difficult to explain women's investment in them. Where the prisoner of the Panopticon cannot physically escape his(/her?) visibility and thus his(/her?) surveillance, women are not only not compelled to discipline their bodies ("no one is marched off to electrolysis at gunpoint") but they are, oddly, active initiators and innovators of practices of femininity.[41] So, how can this acquiescence, this involvement, be explained? Bartky's solution is to extend the concept of discipline to cover both the types of authoritarian structures/ institutions that Foucault analyzes (schools, prisons, hospitals), and voluntary submission to certain sorts of (what might usefully be termed) ascetic practices like Zen Buddhism. It is to this latter category that the practices of femininity are allotted. I propose that an alternative reading is possible if we apply notions of Foucault's practices/technologies of the self to the question of gendering. His definition of a technology of the self, therefore, would be a useful starting point. These, he asserts, are practices that enable: "individuals to effect by their own means or with the help of others a certain number of operations on their own bodies and souls, thoughts, conduct, and a way of being, so as to transform themselves in order to attain a certain state of happiness, purity, wisdom, perfection, or immortality."[42] The reasons why women engage in a bewildering range of feminizing practices are likewise manifold: as a means of self-beautification, a sign of arrival at adulthood, the dictates of certain jobs, narcissism, the desire for a sexual or marital partner; in order, that is, "to attain a certain state." Similarly, the actual practices used to produce (or stylize) the self will vary to some degree depending on the goal in mind, on financial considerations, on questions of access to specific techniques. That many of these practices and goals (from a feminist perspective) perpetuate dominant gender norms may be explained when it is remembered that Foucault argued that practices of the self derive from "patterns that he [the subject] finds in his culture" and which are "proposed, suggested and imposed on him" by that culture, the society he inhabits and "his social group."[43] For Bartky, practices of femininity and the different ends they serve offer only the illusion of freedom; they remain ineluctably representative of the "imperative to be 'feminine,' " an imperative that "serves the interest of domination."[44]

Foucault's perception that the self is constituted interpretively and, thus, dynamically in relation to the social realm (and to the availability of a wide variety of practices within that realm), clearly does not then, in itself, symbolize a moment of liberation from (here) the strictures of female oppression. This has led to the criticism that Foucault's aesthetic glosses over the ways in which different practices of the self are prioritized: "by reducing the varying techniques of the self to the same effective level of self 'stylisation,' " McNay suggests that Foucault fails adequately to distinguish between "practices that are merely 'suggested' to the individual and practices that are more or less 'imposed' in so far as they are heavily laden with cultural sanctions and taboos."[45] Without the presence of criteria to assist us in differentiating between autonomous, innovative activity and those activities induced by self-surveillance that reproduce prevailing social inequities, it is contended, the idea of style is not a useful tool for analyzing gender formation. Not only is the distinction between disciplined and autonomous action purportedly lost in Foucault's shift to the self[46] but identification is precluded of those sociocultural determinants that reify certain cultural norms to such an extent that their evasion becomes impossible.

This argument centers on the claim that Foucault's ethics are a corrective to some of the deficiencies of his work on docile bodies—the passive bearers of the imprint of power. By shifting attention entirely to the ethics, what slips from view is that Foucault perceived his later work as a complement to the earlier work, that he saw technologies of the self acting alongside technologies of domination. In the case of the production of gender, therefore, individuals are subject to a range of practices, some of which are capable of inversion, subversion, perversion, while others operate more or less rigidly. My argument is that it is the activity of critique that makes possible the differentiation between them. This, I contend, is what offers a radical edge to the stylistics of existence. It is not the activity of self-fashioning in itself that is crucial. It is the way in which that self-fashioning, *when allied to critique,* can produce sites of contestation over the meanings and contours of identity, and over the ways in which certain practices are mobilized.

This latter point is important, because there is, within certain feminist literature, an assumption that anything which co-operates in the maintenance of dominant cultural norms is necessarily tainted. Thus, dieting, exercise, and cosmetic surgery, regarded as pillars in the preservation of male power and female subordination, are perceived in themselves as oppressive. However, as Susan Bordo notes, "prevailing norms themselves [and, I would add, the practices that reinforce them] have transformative potential."[47] Although anorexia can certainly be read as a product of contemporary cultural demands for women's slenderness (Szekely's "the relentless pursuit of thinness" or Chernin's "the tyranny of slenderness"), it is not unequivocally the case that its practitioners see themselves as victims. Bordo remarks that many of the women she studied understood their actions in terms of control and power (192), as attitudes of resistance, even when, according to Grimshaw, their "whole life may in fact be damagingly and fatally *out* of control."[48] Similarly, although a program of rigorous weight-training may be designed to cultivate a "currently stylish look," it may nevertheless also produce the self-perception that muscles are empowering, that they actually enable a woman "to assert herself more forcefully at work."[49] In this way, particular practices of femininity have the potential to operate transgressively. The dilemma is that it is not feasible to picture in advance whether such practices reflect the internalization of hegemonic norms of femininity, or whether they are stages in self-aestheticization.

There is another dimension to this argument over gendering and its relation to liberty. McNay, for the most part, hitches the notion of liberty (autonomous and innovative action in her terms) to the possibility of emancipation.[50] Foucault does not. Foucault's understanding of the practices of liberty are that they are always already contextualized. His argument is that we can (sometimes) choose among them to "attain a certain state" (happiness, wisdom, purity, perfection). If I decide to produce myself as a slender, well-toned body (the current epitome of womanhood), a style "suggested" to me by my culture,[51] am I acting freely? In McNay's reading I would assume not, as I am acting in conformity with patriarchal norms of idealized femininity. In Foucault's reading, the case is less clear-cut. At one level this is an act of freedom: I can choose among a range of practices of the self in order to aestheticize myself in this way: opt for cosmetic surgery over diet; liposuction over exercise. However, another alternative is possible. Foucault's purpose in exploring ancient practices of the self was to suggest that contemporary mechanisms of subjectification are culturally specific, that other methods have been used in the past, that alternative means of understanding the self and relating to the self have been possible, and that (in an extrapolative gesture) other ways of constituting ourselves in the future are also possible. In addition, the politics of refusal sketched above, reinforces the sense that Foucault was searching for a way of challenging hegemonic conceptions of the self in the present. What is pivotal is the practice of critique, the exercise upon ourselves of a historical ontology that, in turn, generates the conditions of possibility for transgressing the boundaries of discursivity. So, as a feminist reflecting upon patriarchal iconography (idealized images of femininity), I may well deduce that I should refuse this particular form of cultural embodiment since it positions me as an inferiorized body, and as a second-class subject. I believe that some of the difficulty with this debate arises from the polysemy of the word "liberty": McNay allies it with emancipatory (that is, progressive) social transformation whereas Foucault sees it as a practice, an incessant evasion (via subversion, refusal, resignification) of normalization.

An explanation for this divergence of views is suggested by McNay's reading of Foucault as a particular kind of Enlightenment thinker; one, that is, who "affirms autonomy as a worthwhile goal of emancipatory politics."[52] Unlike many commentators who view Foucault as writing in opposition to the project of the Enlightenment, McNay attempts to establish a continuity between Foucault's work and this project. Her central thesis is that Foucault, recognizing the limitations of his earlier analyses of the subject (too saturated by power to act independently), turns his attention to the problem of the self. This shift in emphasis has a very specific goal: to find a way out of the impasse created by the recognition that the dissolution of subjectivity necessarily entails the dissolution of agency. Foucault's route to the self and, thus, to a viable politics, begins with an "attempt to rework some of the Enlightenment's central categories":[53] the substitution (at the core of critique) of multiple, historically specific forms of rationality for a founding, universal form of rationality; the uncoupling of agency from the humanist (static) subject; the replacement of the idea of emancipation as the recovery of an authentic self with the notion of emancipation as the freedom to invent a self.[54] Although these moves release Foucault from some of the earlier constraints of his work, McNay argues (much in the way that Nancy Fraser does of the earlier work) that his project is still fatally flawed.[55] Foucault, it appears, is insufficiently true to the Enlightenment after all.

> Whilst Foucault appears to make use of some of the central concepts of the Enlightenment and humanist thought, he constantly retreats from making any definitive statement about the normative basis of his ethics. The use of the rhetoric of political engagement without grounding it in a coherent normative standpoint results in a series of contradictions that run through Foucault's work and make it problematic for feminists.[56]

While there is much that is persuasive about McNay's more general interpretation of Foucault, it is at this point that I part company with her. Her rejection of Foucault elides two very different conceptions of the Enlightenment: one that perceives it as a set of principles or concepts (progress, autonomy, emancipation, rationality) and the other (which, I shall demonstrate, is Foucault's preferred version), the Enlightenment as an attitude: a mode of asking questions about the constitution of the historical present. McNay criticizes Foucault for using some of the key themes of the Enlightenment but not all; for borrowing or "retaining" (though in highly moderated form, it must be said) the notions of autonomy, rationality, and an acting self without (and this is the crucial flaw) the idea of normative underpinnings.[57] In making this judgment, McNay aligns Foucault with the very Enlightenment tradition he explicitly rejects. She locates him, that is, within the doctrinal tradition: the tradition usually associated with the Kant of the transcendental subject, the Kant of universal judgment. Foucault is categoric, however, that the Kant he is drawing on is not the Kant of the three *Critiques*, espousing universal principles of moral and of political action, but the Kant of *Was ist Aufklärung?* advocating an interrogative relationship with contemporary reality; Kant with attitude. Foucault returns to the Enlightenment not to retrieve a set of concepts (palliatives for his earlier failed enterprise) but to revivify a critical posture. The "thread that may connect us with the Enlightenment," he asserts, "is not faithfulness to doctrinal elements, but rather the permanent reactivation of an attitude"; that is, the philosophical ethos he identifies as "a permanent critique of our historical era."[58] This is why, in "What is Enlightenment?" when he shifts his attention to the question of modernity, and asks how it is possible to disconnect the "growth of capabilities" from the "intensification of power relations," Foucault turns to Baudelaire (48). "Baudelairean modernity is an exercise in which extreme attention to what is real is confronted with the practice of a liberty that simultaneously respects this reality and violates it" (41). This process of respect and violation that characterizes the attitude of modernity combines two factors: a critical interrogation of the present ("the attitude that makes it possible to grasp the 'heroic' aspect of the present moment" [40]) and a mode of relating to oneself (an aesthetic). Baudelaire is important precisely because his understanding of the modern subject is of a subject who seeks not to " 'liberate man in his own being' "—to find himself—but of a subject who must "face the task of producing himself" (42). In echoing Baudelaire, Foucault effectively shifts the grounds of inquiry from a knowledge-ethics relationship to an ethics-aesthetics relationship.[59] The absence of normative underpinnings in Foucault's work stems, therefore, from the way in which he unhitches ethics from any form of truth-seeking, yoking it instead to practices of self-aestheticization. It is the significance of this move to the aesthetic that McNay underestimates.[60] But it is also this move that is crucial in explicating how ethico-aesthetic work may be transgressive politically.

As we have seen, Foucault's twin perceptions that the self is constituted intertextually across a range of discursive practices, and that the subject is active in the negotiation of those discursive practices, is not necessarily transgressive. But, I argue, it can be. One core feature of the ethics is that it offers up the chance of being other. In the context of this paper, this implies that alternative modes of engendering are possible. As feminists, we repeatedly assert that it is the codification and organization of the world into gendered hierarchies that constructs women's oppression under patriarchy; thus any chance to bend, disrupt, or undermine gender norms would seem to beckon seductively. This temptation to trouble gender (if I may paraphrase Judith Butler) has an altogether more transgressive potential when we bear in mind that feminism itself frequently operates with the binary dualism at the core of the gender edifice: the division of the world into female/feminine subjects/victims versus male/masculine subjects/perpetrators. So, I propose that one result for feminism of a turn to the doubled politics of critique and ethics is to allow us to think beyond this ontology of gender. In order to illustrate what such a *transgressive* politics might look like, I examine Butler's stylistics of existence; a stylistics that strongly echoes the call for respect and violation typified by Baudelairean modernity.[61]

Foucault contends that one motivation for technologizing the self is that it presents a means of subverting the regulatory impulses of governmentalizing power. Judith Butler, in *Gender Trouble*, proposes that the dominant economy of gender within feminism itself is just such an instance of governmentalization. Drawing on the work of various psychoanalytic schools within feminism, Butler argues that expressive categories of gender, far from describing reality, actually establish a normative matrix setting the "prescriptive requirements whereby sexed or gendered bodies come into cultural intelligibility" (148). They define, and thereby foreclose, what constitutes the female/feminine subject. Butler, in a typically Foucauldian move, wishes to refuse this categorization of identity. It is, she claims, inadequate to capture the variety of gender positions currently occupied by subjects. So what is its significance? It operates as a way of instituting and, thence, normalizing heterosexual relations; the male/masculine–female/feminine binary. All the gestures, acts, desires that are reputedly evidence of a masculine or feminine gender identity are exposed, by Butler, as the effects of discursive practices, the purpose of which is to publicly regulate (hetero)sexuality. In this argument, gender identity is actually an effect of "corporeal signification."[62] It is performative; that is, it relies upon a "*stylized repetition of acts.*"[63]

The assertion of the imitative nature of gender identity is used by Butler in two ways: first, to shatter the illusion of heterosexual coherence at the base of gender identification; and second, to suggest the possibility of a "perpetual displacement" of gender norms. It is on this second axis that I concentrate. Since gender is performative, Butler contends, it can be, and indeed already is, utilized in subversive ways by individuals—as a transgressive stylistics of existence to repeatedly disrupt hetero-logic. To parody gender is to engage in an "improvisational theatre"[64] where the bodily self is repeatedly remade and resignified, and where the dominant norms of gender are revealed as so many fabrications. The more selves work upon themselves in this way—the more, that is, that they technologize themselves—the more indeterminate and less regulatory gender becomes. Like Foucault's practices of freedom, parody is unceasing, multiply productive, repeatedly subversive; it is a process of problematization. By positively valorizing gender dissonance Butler is not only querying some of the ways in which feminists have thought about women's oppression, she is also suggesting that acceptance of the constitutiveness of subjectivity does not entail the demise of feminist politics. Rather, it announces a need for its reconfiguration; a reconfiguration that grows out of a limit-attitude and that defamiliarizes mundane and naturalized actions, making "facile gestures difficult."[65]

Parody is not immune from criticism. If its transformative potential relies upon a capacity to step outside of gender as a category then it would seem utopian, since human existence is always already (in some respects, at least) gendered existence. Butler acknowledges this. Like Foucault's notion of ethical practice, parodic acts of self-resignification occur in the interstices between the range of discourses and mechanisms that produce us as (gendered) subjects. As Butler observes: gender performativity was not meant to imply that "one woke up in the morning, perused the closet or some more open space for the gender of choice, donned that gender for the day, and then restored the garment to its place at night."[66] Rather, it revealed the ways in which gender practices both are and can be a site of contestation and critical agency, open to reformulation and slippage. The assertion that "sex," "gender," and "sexuality" are forms of entrenched cultural performance should not occlude the possibility of creating gender trouble.

Butler's account of gender performativity operates on parallel lines to Foucault's injunction in "The Subject and Power" to critically refuse dominant modes of subjectivity and to develop alternative forms of subjectification. It stands as one feminist example of the workings of a stylistics of existence predicated upon a critical analysis of the manner in which a strategy of normativity (here hetero-logic) functions in malestream and feminist discourse. *Gender Trouble* represents a feminist articulation of radical unfixing or de-determination of identity.

But how effective is it as a means of disputing dominant gender norms? Does it merely offer a superficial tinkering with the surface of gender identity while the social, political, and economic edifices of gender hierarchy remain in place? In other words, what kind of politics does the ethics entail? Taking Butler's stylistics as an example, the "ethics" presents a politics that works by contestation, de-determination, exposing the very politicization of subjectification. It posits the indeterminacy of gender (identity) as a resource for feminist politics. For a critic, such as McNay, however, the ethics seems only to offer an individualized (or individualistic), limited reformism. While acknowledging that Foucault's later work permits him to develop "a more active notion of how individuals assume their gender identity"[67] than found in his earlier texts, McNay argues that the concept of self-stylization is not an appropriate category with which to tackle the "deeply entrenched cultural norms in which our bodies are embedded."[68] In particular, self-stylization is unable to tackle the "involuntary and biological dimensions to sexuality";[69] questions of the emotional and affective. Her contention is that even though Foucault may persuade about the socially constructed nature of sexuality, and about the chances of reconceptualizing bodily impulses and desires, his theory is incapable of tackling all the issues involved in the constitution of individuals as sexual subjects.[70]

It is not clear to me that Foucault actually invested techniques of the self with the power that McNay wants to impute to them: that is, that self-stylization was capable of overcoming or, indeed, explaining all aspects of gendering. That aside, McNay's fundamental disagreement with Foucault's position concerns the nature of political activity. McNay observes that "the most serious drawback with Foucault's presentation of the self as *a solitary process, rather than as a socially integrated activity*, is that it is unclear how such an ethics translates into a politics of difference that could initiate deep-seated social change."[71] This judgment raises a number of important questions: Do acts of self-formation necessarily have to be conducted in isolation? If not, what kinds of socially integrated activity can they feed into?

I begin by questioning what is meant by the claim that ethical work is a solitary process. A number of interpretations are available. It may mean that we design individualized plans for self-constitution that draw not on the wealth of practices available to us in our communities, but upon the resources of our imaginations.[72] This seems to go against Foucault's assertion that practices of the self are "not something that the individual invents by himself."[73] Alternatively, it may mean that we choose among a range of currently available options in order to produce ourselves in certain ways. Self-stylization becomes a kind of nomadic bricolage. This is certainly closer to the spirit of Foucault's studies: practices of the self "are patterns that he [the subject] finds in his culture."[74] Going back to Judith Butler here may be helpful. The contention that "gender is a kind of persistent impersonation that passes as the real" is given one form of corporeal expression in the performance of the drag artist whose appropriation of the practices of femininity is utilized to stylize an alternative self.[75] He exploits patterns already coded in his own society and inverts them, recodes them, invests them with different cultural valences. While the activities of self-production may take place in isolation (that is, in private), the very fact that the drag artist performs for a public takes those activities out of the private realm into the social sphere. In the same way, the Greek men studied by Foucault wanted to produce themselves as responsible citizens, competent to direct their societies: that is, their private productions were to have cultural resonance. It is the nature of this cultural resonance, however, that cannot (always) be pre-scribed. Drag, as a parody of femininity, may function to expose the performative, unnatural dimension of all gender identity; or, it may work to demonstrate the permeability of the heterosexual matrix. Conversely, it may be understood as yet more evidence of the privileged position of the "male" agent who can don (at will) the artifices of femininity while retaining the cultural power of masculinity.[76]

The point is, though, that unless practices of the self remain entirely privatized, there is always the chance of public impact as self-stylized beings interact with others. This does not in any way guarantee that dominant social structures will crumble as a result. One person's refusal to conform to gender stereotypes does not ipso facto fissure the edifice of gender hierarchy. However, it is clear that the political impact of transgressive acts will be greatest where those acts impinge *critically* upon social consciousness. How? By utilizing existing practices in subversive ways so as to provoke a new manifestation or a new encoding of the symbolics of certain practices, gestures, modes of behavior. Here Butler's example of "die-ins" is useful. When performed by Act Up (the lesbian and gay activist group in the United States), they had a dramatic impact on public awareness. Why? First, because they were already legible insofar as they were "drawing on conventions" of previous protest cultures (particularly the anti-nuclear movement). Second, and conversely, because they were a "renovation," a "new adumbration of a certain kind of civil disobedience." People were compelled to stop and re-read what was happening. As political actions, they worked because they "posed a set of questions without giving you the tools to read off the answers."[77] They provoked confusion, out of which grew a problematization—a questioning, critical thought. As Foucault writes in *The Use of Pleasure*, it is a manner of analyzing "not behaviours or ideas, nor societies and their 'ideologies,' but the *problematizations* through which being offers itself to be, necessarily, thought—and the *practices* on the basis of which these problematizations are formed."[78] The most radical instantiations of practices of the self are those that have this impact; the ones that provoke a critical, querying reaction. For Foucault, transgressive politics is precisely dependent upon this critical work. This is the limit-attitude in operation. Politics, in this sense, depends upon freeing ourselves from the "sacrilization of the social as the only reality"; that is, in isolating the fault-lines in discourse and in refiguring modes of (self-)subjectification.[79]

The general context for this essay is a concern with the question of what happens to feminist politics if we accept that subjects are discursively constituted. One consequence of this acceptance is the rejection of the kind of emancipatory politics predicated upon a coherent subject possessing the necessary autonomy with which to transform the world. It is, therefore, vital that feminism must, at least, consider what other kinds of feminist politics could be demanded by processed subjects. I argued that Foucault's later work indicates a number of routes of inquiry: specifically, it suggests a doubled trajectory of critique and ethics whose goals were to motivate political activity out of this very problematization of subjectivity. Foucault's critical ontology and his account of self-aestheticization were responses to the regulation of identity present in an increasingly normalizing and governmentalizing society. Together, they appear to offer transgressive, even transformative, potential.

This shift in emphasis in Foucault's work resonates creatively with a number of feminist concerns. Given the priority of the category of gender within feminist theory, the fact that the ethics points to a more interactive process of gendering than his earlier works is clearly of use to feminists attempting to explain women's apparent complicity in "patriarchal" practices. In the process, it forces us to consider what exactly is meant by liberty or freedom of choice. The acknowledgment that the intertextual production of subjectivity is open to subversion from within (that is, by processed subjects themselves), in itself, signals some interesting directions for feminist politics. As my discussion of Butler demonstrated, if the binary dualism at the base of gender hierarchy operates politically within feminism to rigidify further the hold of heteronormativity, then Foucauldian-style refusals of identity breach that hierarchy at a representational level, at least. It is the critical, contestatory nature of these transgressions that is essential both as a means of revealing the fabricated nature of the gender division, and as a spur to the creation of new forms of subjectivity—ones outside the sway of the current economy of sex/gender.

The most radical implication of Foucault's later writings is that in forcing us to rethink the subject, it also compels us to rethink the political. First, the idea of discursively constituted subjectivity disallows the logic required by conventional notions of emancipation: that is, the liberation of men and women in their essential beings. Second, as the opening quotation from Butler intimates, the very notion of an essential (stable, coherent) subject can itself be construed as politically inscribed or encoded. Third, this latter fact also suggests that the coherent subject is just another ruse of power, disguising or camouflaging the ways in which the political (as an arena of action) is defined, constituted, and foreclosed in the process. Thus, the plausibility of emancipating this subject is exposed as a chimera. By refiguring subjectivity, thinkers such as Foucault instate an inquiry into alternative modes of political practice; they problematize the parameters of the political and (and this is the crucial point) they figure another "domain of the political," rather than the demise of the political. For feminism, this has a number of implications. Installing the discursively constituted subject at the heart of feminist inquiry creates the conditions of possibility for a feminist praxis sensitive to difference and aware of the normalizing tendencies within feminism's own discursive practices. Further, if we follow Foucault, we have the outlines of some other (nonemancipatory) political trajectories amenable to feminism. Political trajectories that eschew the route of the political program in favor of a set of mechanisms for tackling daily living; trajectories centered around critique and the possibility of producing new modes of subjectivity (as yet, not guessed at). It is precisely this lack of pre-scription (the adumbration in advance of the details of political struggle), however, that is also unsettling for feminism. As Jean Grimshaw comments, Foucault "implicitly suggests a politics which includes, at the least, a recognition of ambiguity, contradiction and complexity at its heart."[80] However, rather than regard such ambiguity, contradiction, and complexity as problematic, I would, on the basis of the argument developed in this essay, present these ambiguities, contradictions, and complexities as productive. While Foucault certainly does not have all the answers for contemporary feminism, his ethical work signals some of the political routes feminists might consider in an attempt to reconfigure the links between the subject and politics.

Notes

1. Judith Butler, "Contingent Foundations: Feminism and the Question of Postmodernism," in Feminists Theorize the Political, ed. Judith Butler and Joan W. Scott (London: Routledge, 1992), 4; emphasis in original.

2. Darryl McGowan Tress, "Comments on Flax's 'Postmodernism and Gender Relations in Feminist Theory,' " Signs: Journal of Women in Culture and Society 14, no. 1 (Autumn 1988): 197; emphasis in original.

3. See Butler, "Contingent Foundations."

4. Jane Flax, "The End of Innocence," in Feminists Theorize the Political, 446.

5. See, for instance, Jürgen Habermas, The Philosophical Discourse of Modernity: Twelve Lectures, trans. Frederick Lawrence (Cambridge: Polity Press, 1987); and Nancy Fraser, "Foucault on Modern Power: Empirical Insights and Normative Confusions," in her Unruly Practices: Power, Discourse and Gender in Contemporary Social Theory (Minneapolis: University of Minnesota Press, 1989), 17–34.

6. See, for instance, Michael Walzer, "The Politics of Michel Foucault," in Foucault: A Critical Reader, ed. David Couzens Hoy (Oxford: Basil Blackwell, 1986), 63, 65, 67; and Peter Dews, Logics of Disintegration: Post-Structuralist Thought and the Claims of Critical Theory (London: Verso, 1987), 161–65.

7. Michel Foucault, "The Subject and Power," afterword to Michel Foucault: Beyond Structuralism and Hermeneutics, 2d ed., ed. Paul Rabinow and Hubert Dreyfus, with an interview by Michel Foucault (Chicago: University of Chicago Press, 1983), 212.

8. See for example Michel Foucault, "What is Enlightenment?" and "Practising Criticism," in Michel Foucault: Politics, Philosophy, Culture: Interviews and Other Writings, 1977–1984, ed. Lawrence D. Kritzman, trans. Alan Sheridan et al. (London: Routledge, 1988), 152–56; and "The Ethic of Care as a Practice of Freedom," in The Final Foucault, ed. J. Bernauer and D. Rasmussen (Cambridge: MIT Press, 1988).

9. The History of Sexuality, vol. 1, An Introduction (Harmondsworth: Penguin, 1980), 96.

10. "Polemics, Politics and Problematizations," in *The Foucault Reader*, ed. Paul Rabinow (New York: Pantheon, 1984), 383–85; "The Masked Philosopher," in *Politics, Philosophy, Culture*, 323–30.

11. "Practising Criticism," 155; see also "Polemics, Politics and Problematizations," 381–90; *The Use of Pleasure* (Harmondsworth: Penguin, 1987), 14–24; "On Power," in *Politics, Philosophy, Culture*, 107–8; and "Power and Sex," in *Politics, Philosophy, Culture*, 124.

12. Problematization is a key term for Foucault. See, for instance, "Polemics, Politics and Problematizations," 384, and *Use of Pleasure*, 11.

13. "Practising Criticism," 154.

14. Ibid., 155.

15. "What is Enlightenment?" 46. The role of the thought is significant in Foucault's work; it is this which provides the possibility of critical reflection. The issue raised by this is whether thought is somehow able to transcend the constitutiveness of discourse, truth, rationality, and so on, all of which are read by Foucault as so many cultural artifacts, or whether our mode of critical thinking is in itself unavoidably contemporary. There appears to be support for both positions in Foucault's work. The former is given clearest expression in the context of a 1984 interview where he claims "thought is what allows one to step back from . . . [a] way of acting or reacting, to present it to oneself as an object of thought and question it as to its meaning, its conditions, and its goals." ("Polemics, Politics and Problematizations," 388). Thought, in this respect, is a work of freedom. The alternative view appears in the essay "What is Enlightenment?" where Foucault strongly suggests that our present modality of critique is imbricated in the attitude of the Enlightenment, and given voice by Kant.

16. "Polemics, Politics and Problematizations," 385.

17. Shane Phelan, "Foucault and Feminism," *American Journal of Political Science* 34, no. 2 (May 1990): 428.

18. Michel Foucault, "Politics and Ethics: An Interview," in *The Foucault Reader*, 375.

19. "What is Enlightenment?" 46.

20. "Ethic of Care," 2.

21. Elspeth Probyn provocatively suggests that here the memoirs of both Herculine Barbin and Pierre Rivière are noteworthy as examples of the ways in which "by putting themselves into discourse by writing their memoirs, they transformed themselves in print." To some extent, both can be seen as confessional productions of the self. It is in the opportunity for "fessing up a self" that Probyn locates a means of refiguring feminist notions of experience. Elspeth Probyn, *Sexing the Self: Gendered Positions in Cultural Studies* (London: Routledge, 1993), 120, 117. On the problems of the experiential within feminism, see Judith Grant, *Fundamental Feminism: Contesting the Core Concepts of Feminist Theory* (London: Routledge, 1993).

22. Michel Foucault, "What is Enlightenment?" 39–42; *The Use of Pleasure*; "The Aesthetics of Existence," in *Foucault Live: Interviews, 1966–1984*, ed. Sylvère Lotringer, trans. John Johnson (New York: Semiotext[e], 1989), 311; "The Return to Morality," in *Foucault Live*, 321–22; *The Care of the Self* (Harmondsworth: Penguin, 1990).

23. "Technologies of the Self," 18.

24. Arguably, Marxism stands as an example of the former, while Rousseau's depiction of liberty in *The Social Contract* could be seen as an example of the latter.

25. "Ethic of Care," 3–4.

26. "Subject and Power," 221.

27. *Use of Pleasure*; "Practising Criticism," 11; *Politics, Philosophy, Culture*, passim; *Care of the Self*.

28. Jean Grimshaw, "Practices of Freedom," in *Up Against Foucault: Explorations of Some Tensions between Feminism and Foucault*, ed. Caroline Ramazanoglu (London: Routledge, 1993), 59; emphasis in original.

29. Christopher Norris, " 'What is Enlightenment?': Kant and Foucault," in *The Cambridge Companion to Foucault*, ed. Gary Gutting (Cambridge: Cambridge University Press, 1994), 166.

30. "Technologies of the Self," 18.

31. *Use of Pleasure*, 4. Of course, Foucault continues to talk about subjectivity in "technologies of the self" but not from the perspective of objectivization, rather from the perspective of self-recognition and self-subjectification.

32. Ibid., 5, 11. In typical fashion, Foucault rejects a unilinear causality between problematization and practice. Just as problematization can prompt alternative practices, so too can alternative practices prompt further problematization.

33. Probyn, *Sexing the Self*, 123.

34. Schmid, cited in Probyn, *Sexing the Self*, 123. See Phelan, "Foucault and Feminism," 429.

35. Lois McNay, *Foucault and Feminism: Power, Gender and the Self* (Cambridge: Polity, 1992).

36. Sometimes McNay renders this Enlightenment "anti-humanist"; at other times she suggests that it is explicitly humanist. The interpretation of Foucault offered here rejects the latter reading: for Foucault the Enlightenment he avows is crucially antihumanist. See Foucault, "What is Enlightenment?" 43–45.

37. See, for example, the recent essays in *Feminists Theorize the Political*, ed. Butler and Scott.

38. McNay, *Foucault and Feminism*, 71; Grimshaw, "Practices of Freedom," 51–72. I should state here that I do not subscribe to the view that there is a radical disjuncture between Foucault's genealogical work and the later ethics. I do not, that is, support the opposition between docile bodies and self-forming subjects sketched by, for instance, Grimshaw and McNay. Although certainly underdeveloped, there are several moments in the genealogies where Foucault announces that selves are not simply the ciphers of power: the idea of resistance, the assertion of the "soul" as a processed self (in *Discipline and Punish: The Birth of the Prison* [Harmondsworth: Penguin, 1979], 16) and statements about the potentiality of critique in the collection *Power/Knowledge: Selected Interviews and Other Writings, 1972–1977*, ed. Colin Gordon (New York: Pantheon, 1980).

39. McNay, *Foucault and Feminism*, 71.

40. Judith Butler, "Variations on Sex and Gender: Beauvoir, Wittig and Foucault," in *Feminism as Critique: Essays on the Politics of Gender in Late Capitalist Societies*, ed. Seyla Benhabib and Drucilla Cornell (Cambridge: Polity, 1987), 131; McNay, *Foucault and Feminism*, 72.

41. Sandra Lee Bartky, "Foucault, Femininity and the Modernization of Patriarchal Power," in *Feminism and Foucault: Reflections on Resistance*, ed. Irene Diamond and Lee Quinby (Boston: Northeastern University Press, 1988), 75.

42. Foucault, "Technologies of the Self," 18.

43. "Ethic of Care," 11.

44. Bartky, "Foucault, Femininity and the Modernization of Patriarchal Power," 76.

45. McNay, *Foucault and Feminism*, 74; Grimshaw, "Practices of Freedom," 66.

46. Grimshaw, "Practices of Freedom," 66.

47. Susan Bordo, "Feminism, Foucault and the Politics of the Body," in *Up Against Foucault*, 192.

48. Grimshaw, "Practice of Freedom," 67; emphasis in original.

49. Bordo, "Feminism," 192–93.

50. McNay, *Foucault and Feminism*, 102, 104, 197.

51. I use the word "suggested" here deliberately since, as the discussion of Bartky's work

indicated, dieting, exercise, liposuction, and the wearing of makeup are not usually compulsory in our society. There may be strong reasons to conform, but the possibility of resistance is still present. The idea of practices "imposed" upon us seems to reduce the latitude for insolence. It should also be noted that not all feminists are opposed to the ideas of self-aestheticization even when in conformity with dominant stereotypes, on the grounds that it is an assertion of "taking one's life into one's own hands"; thus, an act of self-assertion. See K. Davis, "Remaking the She-Devil: A Critical Look at Feminist Approaches to Beauty," *Hypatia* 6, no. 2 (1991): 21–43.

52. Ibid., 197.

53. McNay, *Feminism and Foucault*, 5.

54. See Grimshaw, "Practices of Freedom," 55, 59.

55. See Nancy Fraser, "Foucault on Modern Power," 17–34. Fraser too ties Foucault to the conceptual ideals of the Enlightenment, stating that his deployment of terminology such as the "carceral society" is evidence of an incipient commitment to the principles of freedom, justice, and so forth typical of Enlightenment liberalism. McNay extends this style of analysis to his later works.

56. Ibid., 117; see also 8.

57. Grimshaw suggests conversely that, in fact, there is an explicit normative framework underpinning the ethics but one that, ultimately, remains harnessed to a masculinist conception of the self ("Practices of Freedom," 61, 70). I have dealt, in detail, with the question of Foucault on norms elsewhere. See Moya Lloyd, "The (F)utility of a Feminist Turn to Foucault," *Economy and Society* 22, no. 4 (November 1993): 437–60.

58. Foucault, "What is Enlightenment?" 42. Interestingly, McNay does explore Foucault's notion of the Enlightenment as attitude and explores some of the beneficial effects of such a stance for an anti-essentialist feminism. However, she continues to discuss him in terms of a set of concepts: "Although he may reject the Enlightenment belief in a universal rationality, what Foucault retains from the Enlightenment is the notion of autonomy which is regarded as essential to a state of positive liberty" (*Foucault and Feminism*, 90).

59. Norris, " 'What is Enlightenment?': Kant and Foucault," 172.

60. Moreover McNay is misguided in articulating Foucault to the humanist tradition. In the essay "What is Enlightenment?" Foucault is again clear that he rejects humanism with its dependence on a certain conception of man: the transcendental subject, the originary locus of knowledge and truth. Indeed, he regards humanism as standing in a state of tension with the attitude of the Enlightenment, which he wishes to reactivate. His ethical subject may have more room for autonomous action than his earlier disciplined subject appeared to have, but she is not a humanist subject; she is constituted by, and constitutive of, the practices and discourses that converge to process her identity ("What is Enlightenment?" 44).

61. Judith Butler, *Gender Trouble: Feminism and the Subversion of Identity* (London: Routledge, 1990), 139.

62. Judith Butler, "Gender Trouble, Feminist Theory and Psychoanalytic Discourse," in *Feminism/Postmodernism*, ed. Linda Nicholson (London: Routledge, 1990), 336.

63. Butler, *Gender Trouble*, 139. Butler uses the example of "drag" to illustrate the performativity of gender. Since I have dealt with this in some detail elsewhere, I shall not dwell on it here. See instead Moya Lloyd, "Foucault's 'Care of the Self': Some Implications for Feminist Politics," in *Foucault the Legacy: Conference Proceedings* (forthcoming).

64. Peter Osborne and Lynn Segal, "Gender as Performance: An Interview with Judith Butler," *Radical Philosophy* 67 (Summer 1994): 33.

65. Foucault, "Practising Criticism," 155.

66. Judith Butler, *Bodies That Matter: On the Discursive Limits of "Sex"* (New York: Routledge, 1993), x.

67. McNay, *Foucault and Feminism*, 71.

68. Ibid., 80.

69. Ibid., 80. Significantly, when McNay talks about gender she frequently slips into a discussion about sexuality as if the two terms are simply interchangeable. While sexuality is an important facet of gender identity, it is not its only feature.

70. Criticizing Foucault for failing to deal with psychic identity neglects the extent to which Foucault's own discussion and pursuit of an economy of bodily pleasures outside of the dominant modes of psychoanalytic discourse (Freud, Lacan, and so on) may in itself be a productive move. It may enable us to think pleasure (or libido) outside of the reductive categories typical of much feminist theory where sex(uality) is the privileged signifier, where sexuality is equated with genital sex (albeit the two lips of Irigaray's woman).

71. McNay, *Foucault and Feminism*, 177; my emphasis. See also Grimshaw, "Practices of Freedom," 68.

72. There is an obvious question here: To what extent can our imagination (imaginary) escape culture?

73. Foucault, "Ethic of Care," 11.

74. Ibid., 11.

75. Butler, *Gender Trouble*, x.

76. The example of the ambivalence of drag as a subversive practice is strengthened when we attempt to think of the opportunities for women to cross-dress; they appear limited, and moreover, loaded with connotations contrary to those attaching to male cross-dressing.

77. Osborne and Segal, "Gender as Performance," 38.

78. Foucault, *Use of Pleasure*, 11; emphasis in original. See Probyn, *Sexing the Self*, 127–28.

79. "Practising Criticism," 154–55.

80. Grimshaw, "Practices of Freedom," 58.

11

Foucault on Power: A Theory for Feminists

Amy Allen

The issue of whether or not the work of Michel Foucault is useful for feminist theory and practice has been the subject of lively debate.[*] On the one hand, some feminists, including Chris Weedon[1] and Jana Sawicki,[2] have argued that an appreciation and appropriation of Foucault's work is necessary for the continued flourishing of feminist political practice. On the other hand, others, like Nancy Hartsock,[3] have claimed that Foucault's work should not be appropriated by feminists. Many feminists are drawn to address this issue because of Foucault's provocative and highly original analysis of power. This is understandable insofar as

[*]Many thanks to Nancy Fraser, Evelyn Brister, Susan Hekman, Richard Lynch, Christopher Zurn, and Christopher Leazier for their helpful comments on earlier versions of this essay.

feminist theory and political practice have as a goal the critique and transformation of a set of relations of power—a set defined by the intersection of sexism, racism, class oppression, and heterosexism, to name only the most conspicuous axes. This goal requires a thorough feminist analysis of power, one that pays careful attention to several competing theories of power, including Foucault's.

In this essay, I contribute to this feminist analysis of power by considering the following question: Is Foucault's theory of power[4] useful for feminism? Many feminists have already asked this question, and they have answered it in quite different ways. These different responses seem to be, at least in part, the result of a lack of agreement on the criteria of how Foucault's theory of power is to be judged. In other words, feminists who have asked about the usefulness of Foucault's conception of power have failed to address fully the prior question: What do we, as feminists, need a theory of power to do? That is to say, for which phenomena should a feminist theory of power be able to account? This question carries with it a set of related questions, including the following: In what way(s) are sexism, racism, class oppression, and heterosexism power issues? At what levels does the power of the privileged operate? What does it mean to accuse someone of taking advantage of or perpetuating a system of domination? What amount of responsibility can be attributed to those who take advantage of and/or perpetuate systems of domination? And, finally, how are we to understand the complex intersection of all of the multifarious relations of power with which feminism should be concerned?

As I obviously cannot adequately address all of these questions in one chapter, I shall concentrate here on only two tasks. I begin by consider-ing what feminists need in a theory of power and sketching out the various levels of analysis that should be included in an adequate feminist account of power. Then, I turn to the question of how useful Foucault's conception of power is for feminism by examining how well it is able to account for the levels I have delineated. Finally, I conclude that Foucault's theory of power is extremely useful for feminism in that it enables us to work on many of the levels necessary for a satisfactory feminist theory of power. However, since there are some levels that a Foucauldian framework is incapable of illuminating, a complete feminist analysis must supplement this framework with other ways of thinking about power.

I should begin by noting that my analysis here is concerned more with a feminist theory of domination than with a feminist theory of power. The word "power" is a bit ambiguous in this context: saying that a person "has power" can either mean that she has the capacity to *do* something, or that she has power *over* another individual. Moreover, even if we narrow down our definition of power merely to mean "power over another individual," it is not clear that all relationships in which an individual has power over another are necessarily oppressive.[5] For purposes of clarity, then, let me note that in this paper, I am using "power" to mean *an oppressive power-over relation*. For this reason, I shall be using the terms "power" and "domination" interchangeably.[6] My understanding of what an oppressive power-over relation entails will become more apparent throughout the course of the chapter.

The two primary levels of analysis with which a feminist theory of power must be concerned are the *microlevel* and the *macrolevel*. The microlevel of analysis targets the foreground of particular oppressive power-over relations. That is to say, it examines a specific power relation between two individuals or groups of individuals. The macrolevel of analysis, on the other hand, focuses on the background to such particular power relations. In other words, it examines the cultural meanings, practices, and larger structures of domination that make up the context within which a particular power relation is able to emerge. It will be helpful to explicate these levels by referring them back to a particular feminist issue, thus, indicating the practical implications of the analysis. For this reason, as I discuss these levels, I shall take up the example of sexual harassment.

The Microlevel As I mentioned above, at the microlevel, the analysis focuses on the foreground of particular domination relations. Thus, at this level, the aim is to describe the domination relation that exists when one individual (or discrete group of individuals) exercises power over another individual (or discrete group). For example, in a case of sexual harassment, the microlevel of analysis will concentrate on what takes place in the particular interactions between those involved: professor and student, boss and employee, and so on. This is not to say that the harassment is not serious or important to the victim; "micro" simply means that the focus is on the relatively small number of social agents who are directly involved in the power relation, and not on the set of background relations that form the context for that power relation. It is important to remark here that an analysis of power relations that remained solely on the microlevel would be incomplete and inadequate. A power relation studied in isolation from its cultural and institutional context is easily perceived as an anomaly, and not as part of a larger system of domination like sexism, racism, and so on. Thus, though the microlevel is *analytically* distinct from the macrolevel, in reality, the latter must be discussed in order to fully illuminate the former.

The Macrolevel The macrolevel of analysis, which describes the background set of social relations that ground every microlevel domination relation, is considerably more complex. What I have called the macrolevel of analysis is similar to what Thomas Wartenberg has labeled the "situated conception of power." This notion of power, Wartenberg writes,

> conceptualizes the role of "peripheral social others." By calling this account of power "situated," I stress the fact that the power dyad is itself situated in the context of other social relations through which it is actually constituted as a power relationship.[7]

As Wartenberg points out, a specific power relation must be situated within a larger context in order to understand how it is "actually constituted as a power relationship." In other words, the macrolevel of analysis is designed to give an account of how relations between distinct individuals come to be, so to speak, power-ed.

The background on which the macrolevel of analysis concentrates can be further broken down into at least four distinct aspects, which I present in order of increasing complexity.

(a) *cultural meanings.* First, culturally encoded meanings and understandings are crucial to particular domination relations. A feminist analysis of power carried out on the macrolevel must examine the way that key concepts such as femininity, masculinity, and sexuality are understood in a given cultural context. Further, such an analysis must also be attentive to the fact that the meanings ascribed to "femininity," "masculinity," and "sexuality" vary widely along race, ethnicity, class, and sexual orientation lines. Thus, with regard to a given instance of sexual harassment, an analysis of cultural meanings must investigate the different constructions of these key terms, which may be exploited or manipulated by the harasser.

(b) *practices.* These multiple culturally encoded understandings are reflected in the second aspect of the macrolevel: the development of particular social practices. As a result, a feminist analysis of power that works on the macrolevel needs to study the ways in which such meanings are intertwined with relevant practices. With respect to sexual harassment, for example, how the practice of flirting is carried out within certain contexts is essential for understanding harassment and differentiating the former from the latter. That this is the case is evidenced by the fact that many men bemoan feminists' criticisms of sexual harassment, appealing, either implicitly or explicitly, to the claim that it is acceptable for men to flirt with their female co-workers or employees. Further, the practice of flirting also varies widely according to how sexuality, masculinity, and femininity are understood by the individuals involved. Thus, a feminist analysis of power that targets the background to particular domination relations must be attentive to both culturally encoded meanings and the practices of which they are a part.

It is important to note here that these meanings and practices are often internalized by those who are dominated, a phenomenon to which feminists must pay careful attention. Internalization involves the process, either conscious or unconscious, by which a dominated individual comes to accept meanings and adopt practices that reflect and reinforce the power of the dominant individual. Consider a secretary who is being sexually harassed by her boss, an executive. If his harassment is subtle enough, she may explain it away to herself and to others as harmless flirting, which she may consider an acceptable practice in which employers and employees engage. Or, she may accept a certain understanding of femininity according to which (some) women are supposed to act coy and demure, even in the face of difficult or uncomfortable situations. Thus, she would be likely to respond to her boss' comments or actions, which make her quite uncomfortable, by either smiling demurely or simply remaining silent. Ironically, though she might do so in the hopes of ending the harassment, the result is likely to be continued abuse. Feminists need to investigate this kind of internalization in order to understand fully how power works at the levels of cultural meanings and social practices.

(c) *surface structures of domination.* An analysis of the background to particular power relations needs to involve two different kinds of structural analysis. The first understands structure as an observed, de facto pattern of inequality. In this sense, an analysis of structures of domination involves what Nancy Fraser and Linda Nicholson have characterized as the "identification and critique of macrostructures of inequality and injustice which cut across the boundaries separating relatively discrete practices and institutions."[8] According to Fraser and Nicholson, such an analysis allows "for critique of pervasive axes of stratification, for critique of broad-based relations of dominance and subordination along lines like gender, race and class" (23). In other words, this aspect of the macrolevel of analysis is what enables us to say things like "people of color are oppressed by whites," and "women are oppressed by men," and "women of color are oppressed by white women," and so on. Further, it allows us to assert that these statements have meaning across stretches of time and within diverse cultures, even though the particular forms that oppression takes in various times and cultures will necessarily be quite different.

An analysis of this kind of structure of domination is integral to feminist theorizing about power. If we are unable to talk about "the oppression of women," then we are going to have a much more difficult time identifying a particular social interaction as an instance of male domination. Absent the context of an observed pattern of inequality, individual abuses of power are easily dismissed as anomalies or mere personality conflicts. Sexual harassment provides a good example of this point. Before a large pattern of harassment had been observed and documented, it was impossible for women who were harassed to name their experience as "sexual harassment." As a result, these women had a great deal of trouble proving that what happened to them was an abuse of male power and a violation of their right to equality.[9] Since this sense of the structural aspect of the macrolevel of analysis is concerned with the emergence of observed patterns of inequality, I shall call it an analysis of surface structures of domination.

(d) *deep structures of domination.* Such an analysis can be contrasted with an analysis of deep structures of domination, which relies on a second sense of structure. In this sense, a structural account involves searching for an explanatory framework that will illuminate or explicate the observed patterns of inequality that make up surface structures of domination. For example, with respect to sexual harassment, one might locate the gender division of labor as the deep structure that gives an account of how a pattern of sexual harassment is able to develop over time. If one isolated the gender division of labor as the relevant deep structure, than one could go on to explore how the fact that most women who work for wages end up in the so-called pink-collar ghetto— working as secretaries, nurses' aides, domestic workers, elementary school teachers, and so on—affects the frequency of instances of sexual harassment. Of course, one might argue for other phenomena as the relevant deep structure of domination; however, whatever structure one chooses to isolate, it should explicate the emergence of the particular surface structure under consideration.

In the previous section, I considered the question, On which levels of analysis ought a feminist theory of power be able to work? Having briefly sketched out an answer to that question, I turn now to a consideration of how the levels I have just discussed can be elucidated by a Foucauldian analysis of power. I should note that it is not my intention here to give a complete account and critique of Foucault's theory of power; rather, I explore the ways in which Foucault's analysis might be put to use in the construction of a feminist theory of domination. For whatever it is worth, I think that Foucault himself would have approved of this application of his work. As he said once about Nietzsche:

> For myself, I prefer to utilise the writers I like. The only valid tribute to thought such as Nietzsche's is precisely to use it, to deform it, to make it groan and protest. And if commentators say that I am being faithful or unfaithful to Nietzsche, that is of absolutely no interest.[10]

First, the microlevel. Unlike many theorists of power, Foucault emphasizes microlevel power relations. Rather than centering his analysis of power on a discussion of legitimate and illegitimate uses of power by the state, Foucault endeavors to offer what he calls a "micro-physics" of power,[11] an examination of specific power relations at the level of the everyday. As Foucault puts it, he is interested in "power at its extremities," as opposed to "regulated and legitimate forms of power in their central locations."[12] In Foucault's account, power operates locally, circulates in the capillaries of the social body, and emanates from every point in the social field.[13] In other words, Foucault's analysis of power is extremely concerned with the microlevel of analysis.

That Foucault discusses the operations of power on a local, minute, and everyday level makes his theory of power quite helpful for thinking about microlevel domination relations. Indeed, sexual harassment is an example of an exercise of power that does not necessarily take place in the center of the social body; that is, it is not a practice imposed by the state or official economy (which is not to say that sexual harassment does not go on in those sectors or that it is not sanctioned by them). Rather, sexual harassment takes place in the capillaries of the social body: it is a power relation that emanates from all of the extremities of the social field; it springs up in classrooms, offices, construction sites, military establishments, and so on. It is a local power relation in which individual men or groups of men exercise power over individual women or groups of women. As such, it seems to me that sexual harassment is just the sort of micropractice of power that Foucault's analysis was designed to illuminate.

By focusing his examination of power on local, minute force relations and the micropractices that arise out of those relations, Foucault gives feminists a constructive framework within which to think about micro-level abuses of power, like sexual harassment. However, as I argued above, the microlevel is only analytically distinct from the macrolevel; thus, the former can only be fully understood in conjunction with the latter.

Second, macrolevel abuses of power. Foucault does more than expose the various ways in which power operates at the microlevel; he also studies the circulation of power through cultural discourses, social practices, and institutional contexts. In this respect, his analysis of power provides feminists with some useful ways of thinking about power at the macrolevel, as well. However, Foucault's analysis of power is not by itself adequate for the task of establishing a feminist theory of power: in some instances, Foucault's work merely points us in interesting directions; in others, it falls short altogether.

Third, cultural meanings. In his discussions of power in *Discipline and Punish* and *The History of Sexuality*, Foucault investigates the ways in which discourses about criminality, sexuality, and deviance both produce and are produced by relations of power. In this way, Foucault offers an account of how we have come to understand what it means to be a criminal, to have a sex, and to be a deviant. For example, in *Discipline and Punish*, Foucault discusses the creation of the notion of "delin-quency": "The success of the prison, in the struggles around the law and illegalities, has been to specify a 'delinquency.' . . . [T]his process . . . constitutes delinquency as an object of knowledge."[14] In other words, the prison system did more than simply transform some of its inmates into recurring (if petty) offenders; according to Foucault, it also created the notion of the delinquent to describe that group of people. In so doing, it constructed the cultural meaning of delinquency.

Even in his investigations in sexuality, however, Foucault unfortunately neglects many of the cultural meanings most relevant to a feminist theory of power. A feminist analysis of cultural meanings should nevertheless draw on Foucault if it is going to interrogate cultural concepts such as masculinity, femininity, heterosexuality, and homosexuality. Such an analysis will need to lay out the ways in which these cultural meanings both reinforce and are reinforced by the oppressive power relations with which they are intertwined. With respect to sexual harassment, such an analysis will need to consider, for example, the cultural association of men—particularly men of color—with aggression and sexual prowess, or of white women with coy flirtatiousness, or of women of color with sexual promiscuity. Further, it will need to offer an account of the "accusation" of homosexuality often aimed at one who claims to have been harassed, and the exploitation of the cultural specter of the lesbian from which that accusation draws its force. Feminists who are going to engage in such investigations can learn a great deal from Foucault's own intricate accounts of the creation of cultural meanings.

Judith Butler has offered a feminist investigation into the meanings of sexuality, femininity, heterosexuality, and lesbianism that is, at least partially, inspired by Foucault.[15] Her analysis in *Bodies that Matter* addresses the following question: "To what extent is 'sex' a constrained production, a forcible effect, one which sets the limits to what will qualify as a body by regulating the terms by which bodies are and are not sustained?"[16] According to Butler, the production of "sex" as a cultural phenomenon requires the constitution of a cultural discourse about sexuality—a discourse containing highly specific definitions of masculinity, femininity, homosexuality, heterosexuality, and so on. Further, the production of "sex" as a cultural category entails the production of sexed bodies. Butler's discussion of the construction of "sex" and "the sexes" offers an illuminating analysis of the operation of power at the level of cultural meanings. In Butler's account, in a culture in which heterosexist discourse is hegemonic (such as our own), the meanings attached to concepts such as masculinity, femininity, and so on, will reflect that heterosexism. In this way, Butler conducts a feminist analysis of the operation of power at the level of cultural meanings that can be seen as a fruitful continuation of Foucault's account of power.

Fourth, practices. In addition to providing feminists with resources for examining the workings of power at the level of cultural meanings, Foucault offers insights into the instantiation of power relations through social practices. For example, in *Discipline and Punish*, Foucault discusses the practice of punishment as the focal point for a continually transforming set of power relations that cuts across divergent institutional contexts. The same disciplinary practices—practices that include minute regulations of movement, detailed time schedules, and perpetual surveillance—are put to use in the army, the school, the prison, and the factory. Indeed, since they share the same set of disciplinary social practices, it is hardly surprising to Foucault that "prisons resemble factories, schools, barracks, hospitals, which all resemble prisons."[17]

Though Foucault gives interesting accounts of certain kinds of practices, he once again ignores those aspects of power that differentially affect women. This had led Sandra Bartky to wonder:

> Where [in Foucault's work] is the account of the disciplinary practices that engender the "docile bodies" of women, bodies more docile than the bodies of men? Women, like men, are subject to many of the same disciplinary practices Foucault describes. But he is blind to those disciplines that produce a modality of embodiment that is peculiarly feminine.[18]

Since Foucault does not give an account of those social practices that affect women in particular, Bartky offers her own analysis of this phenomenon. She focuses on three social practices whose object is the disciplining of the female body: constant dieting aimed at keeping the body thin; constriction of gestures and limitation of mobility, which serve to keep the body from taking up too much space; and ornamentation, which makes the body a pleasant sight (66–71). Moreover, all of these practices have their basis in particular cultural definitions of femininity. Bartky's analysis of these practices and of the understanding of femininity they uphold is an explicit continuation and appropriation of Foucault's account of disciplinary practices.

In addition, Bartky brings out an important feature of these social practices and the cultural notion of femininity in which they are grounded. Drawing on Foucault's discussion of the Panopticon—which functions by convincing prisoners that they may at any time be under surveillance, thereby inducing them to monitor themselves constantly[19]—Bartky claims that these feminine practices likewise compel women to discipline ourselves. She writes,

> it is women who practice this discipline on and against their own bodies. . . . The woman who checks her make-up half a dozen times a day to see if her foundation has caked or her mascara run, who worries that the wind or rain may spoil her hairdo, who looks frequently to see if her stockings have bagged at the ankle, or who, feeling fat, monitors everything she eats, has become, just as surely as the inmate of the Panopticon, a self-policing subject, a self committed to a relentless self-surveillance. This self-surveillance is a form of obedience to patriarchy. (80)

In this way, Bartky describes the internalization by women of practices and understandings of femininity that reinforce the very power relations that oppress them. As I argued above, an account of this kind of internalization of mechanisms of domination by the dominated is extremely important for a feminist theory of power.[20]

Once again, it seems that feminists can learn valuable lessons from Foucault about how to investigate the workings of power. With respect to sexual harassment, for example, one might follow Foucault and explore the way that power functions in instances of harassment by considering relevant social practices and the notions of femininity with which they are intertwined. Further, following Foucault and Bartky, one would need to isolate the ways in which women have internalized practices and cultural understandings that affect their reactions to harassment. For example, one could examine the acceptance on the part of some women of the idea that a man's persistent unwanted sexual advances are a natural part of his masculinity. Similarly, one could explore the disciplinary practice by which women sometimes censor our own speech, deciding ahead of time that we will not be taken seriously or that we will be ostracized if we do speak—a practice that discourages women who are harassed from speaking out against their harassers. Such a feminist analysis of cultural meanings and social practices would be deeply indebted to Foucault's discussions of power.

Fifth, surface structures of domination. I have emphasized the importance of discussing the oppression of women in terms of what I have called surface structures of domination: observed, de facto patterns of inequality. Foucault agrees that it is necessary to theorize the ways in which local, unstable power relations at the extremities of the social body are integrated into larger networks of power. This is what he calls an "ascending analysis of power," an analysis that starts

> from its infinitesimal mechanisms, which each have their own history, their own trajectory, their own techniques and tactics, and then see[s] how these mechanisms of power have been—and continue to be—invested, colonised, utilised, involuted, transformed, displaced, extended, etc., by ever more general mechanisms.[21]

Similarly, Foucault claims that "manifold relationships of force that take shape and come into play in the machinery of production, in families, limited groups, and institutions, are the basis for wide-ranging effects of cleavage that run through the social body as a whole."[22] What Foucault calls "wide-ranging effects of cleavage," and "ever more general mechanisms," represent in his work the same level of analysis that I have characterized as the level of surface structures of domination. That is, they represent the level at which local, microlevel power relations have been integrated into patterns of power that cut across temporal, institutional and contextual barriers.[23]

Foucault's ascending analysis of power is somewhat different from what I am calling an analysis of surface structures of domination, however. Foucault explicitly resists the equation of power with domination; as a result, the general mechanisms of power I discussed above are not, in Foucault's eyes, necessarily oppressive. Power is not oppressive for Foucault because power relations—both at the local and at the most general levels—are always variable and unstable. I take this to mean that Foucault believes that power may be exercised by any of the parties in the relation at any time; in other words, in his view, being in a position to exercise power today does not mean that one will be in such a position tomorrow.

This easily mutable kind of power is distinguished from

> states of domination, in which the relations of power, instead of being variable and allowing different partners a strategy which alters them, find themselves firmly set and congealed. When an individual or a social group manages to block a field of relations of power, to render them impassive and invariable and to prevent

all reversibility of movement—by means of instruments which can be economic as well as political or military—we are facing what can be called a state of domination. [24]

According to Foucault, then, in a state of domination, the loose network of power relations in which power usually circulates freely is "congealed," so that power cannot circulate to some parts of the social body. Foucault does not see anything wrong with power so long as it is allowed to flow freely throughout the social network; it is only when this free flow of power ceases (that is, when a state of domination exists) that there is something to which one ought to object. It is for this reason that Foucault has claimed that we should not struggle for a society in which there is no power—this is, in his view, impossible—rather, we should struggle for a society in which there is no, or very little, domination. [25]

The problem with a feminist appropriation of Foucault's analysis on this point is that he seems to be offering us two completely different ways of understanding power, neither of which are, in themselves, adequate. On the one hand, there are general networks or patterns of power, in which unstable and variable force relations allow power to circulate freely. On the other hand, there are states of domination, in which power does not circulate freely, such that some individuals are left completely unable to exercise power. Each of these options, however, is inadequate for a feminist analysis of surface structures of domination. Though it is certainly true in some instances that the power relations within which women are situated prove to be reversible and unstable, sadly, this is not always the case. Similarly, though we would certainly want to call the oppression of women a "state of domination," it does not seem at all accurate to follow Foucault in saying that because women are dominated, the power relations in which we are caught are "impassive and invariable and . . . prevent all reversibility of movement." Rather, what is peculiar about the oppression that women face is that sometimes the power relations in which we find ourselves prove to be reversible, and sometimes they do not. In other words, it is not the case that the network of power relations in which women find ourselves is *congealed*, so that women are incapable of exercising power; instead, this network is *constricted*, so that women's range of options for the exercise of power is limited.

For example, when an executive sexually harasses his secretary, this abuse of power takes place against the background of a general, observed cleavage of power. If we adopt Foucault's first understanding of power, we have to say that the secretary is always able to occupy a position that allows her to turn the tables on her boss and exercise power over him (or over the situation). Clearly, although this may sometimes be the case, it will not always be. On the other hand, if we take up Foucault's account of states of domination, we have to claim that this secretary is always unable to exercise power in this context, that she is incapable of resisting. Obviously, this is also not always the case. It is my contention, however, that it is always the case that the secretary's options are constricted; she simply does not have the same range of options that the executive has. Indeed, this is part of what it means to say that there is a wide-ranging network of power that has been observed over a long period of time. Furthermore, how narrowly or loosely constricted her options are will be determined by a number of factors, including how much access she has to money, information, a language that will enable her to protest the harm, cultural support for her protest, institutions set up to prevent harassment, and so forth, all of which will depend in turn on other variables such as her race, ethnicity, class, and sexual orientation.

Though Foucault recognizes the need for an account of something like what I have called surface structures of domination, he nevertheless insists that we ought to be careful in constructing such an account. The danger is, as Foucault put it with reference to Marxism, that "anything can be deduced from the general phenomenon of the domination of the working class."[26] We might paraphrase Foucault, and say that "anything can be deduced from the general phenomenon of the domination of men over women." As a result, Foucault wisely cautions us not to find domination wherever we happen to go looking for it. However, his own account of this level of analysis relies on his distinction between power and domination, a distinction that makes no sense when applied to the power relations that are the object of feminist analysis. As a result, Foucault's discussion of this level of analysis is ultimately inadequate.

Sixth, deep structures of domination. I have argued that a feminist theory of power ought to be able to illuminate what I have called deep structures of domination, which serve as explanatory frameworks for observed patterns of inequality. Though Foucault's analysis of power has proved useful, at least to some degree, for a discussion of each of the other levels of analysis I have considered, it seems that Foucault is unable to be of any assistance at this point. As should be fairly clear by now, Foucault's main focus in his discussion of power is on individuals and the social practices and cultural definitions that affect their relations with one another. Though he indicates that he thinks that the local, minute power relations that occur at the individual level can and do become integrated into larger patterns of power (or of domination), he does not spend a great deal of time discussing how this happens. And he spends no time at all considering the kinds of deep structures of domination—such as the gender-division of labor—that might shed light on those surface structures.

Though Foucault does not seem to be very interested in discussing what I have called deep structures of domination, at the same time, his own account of power does not preclude such an analysis. This is an important point: if Foucault's own theory of power were to rule out the possibility of conducting deep structural analysis, then it would be impossible to argue, as I would like to, that we can supplement a Foucauldian theory of power with such an analysis in order to produce a complete feminist theory of power. A Foucauldian perspective would preclude this kind of structural analysis if it were construed as a foundationalist enterprise or a search for the mythical origins of oppression. However, an analysis of the logic behind observed patterns of inequality need not be—indeed, I would argue that it cannot be—conducted in such a manner.[27]

I have argued that there are two primary levels of analysis on which a feminist theory of power ought to be able to operate: the microlevel and the macrolevel. Further, I have discussed the various aspects of the macrolevel in order of increasing complexity. Finally, I have measured Foucault's discussions of power against these different levels of analysis, in order to determine the usefulness of his work for the development of a feminist theory of power. It should be clear by now that I believe that Foucault can be very helpful on certain levels of analysis for feminists who are trying to construct such a theory. His detailed discussions of microlevel power relations, of cultural meanings, and of social practices can provide—and have provided—feminists with many useful lines of thought to pursue.

Nevertheless, I agree with Linda Alcoff that there are "limits to a collaboration"[28] between feminists and Foucault. Foucault's theory of power is not by itself up to the task of building a feminist theory of power. His account of power is insufficiently structural to do justice to the power relations that affect and, to some extent, define the lives of women.[29] Though he seems to recognize the place in a theory of power for an account of wide-ranging, general mechanisms of power—what I have called surface structures—his work does not provide the necessary resources for this kind of investigation. Further, he does not give us any assistance in examining deep structures of domination. In my estimation, feminists can and should make use of Foucault's considerable contributions to the study of power as we attempt to construct a feminist theory of power. Since Foucault's account of power is insufficiently structural, however, we will have to look elsewhere for resources on which to draw in the examination of the structural aspect of the oppression of women.

Notes

1. Chris Weedon, *Feminist Practice and Poststructuralist Theory* (Oxford: Basil Blackwell, 1987).
2. Jana Sawicki, *Disciplining Foucault: Feminism, Power and the Body* (New York: Routledge, 1991).
3. Nancy Hartsock, "Foucault on Power: A Theory for Women?" in *Feminism/Postmodernism*, ed. Linda J. Nicholson (New York: Routledge, 1990).
4. I realize that Foucault would not have used the phrase "theory of power" to describe his work. However, this essay is not about Foucault's project per se; rather, it is about how power can be reconstructed from resources in Foucault's work and measured against the needs of a feminist theory of power.
5. For example, the pedagogical relationship is one in which teachers wield a certain amount of power over students; however, it is not obvious that this is necessarily an oppressive relationship. For an illuminating discussion of the differences between "power to," "power over," and "domination," see Thomas E. Wartenberg, *The Forms of Power: From Domination to Transformation* (Philadelphia: Temple University Press, 1990), especially chaps. 1 and 6.
6. Let me emphasize that it is *not* my contention that domination is the only or true meaning for the word "power." On the contrary, I think that it is very important for feminists to understand power in a positive sense, as the capacity to do something. I take it that this is more or less the sense of power that is captured in the term "empowerment." Though I believe this to be an extremely important area of feminist analysis, I do not have the time to do justice to its complexities in this essay.
7. Wartenberg, *Forms of Power*, 142.
8. Nancy Fraser and Linda J. Nicholson, "Social Criticism without Philosophy: An Encounter Between Feminism and Postmodernism," in *Feminism/Postmodernism*, ed. Linda J. Nicholson (New York: Routledge, 1990), 23.
9. On this point, see Catharine A. MacKinnon, *Sexual Harassment of Working Women* (New Haven: Yale University Press, 1979).
10. Michel Foucault, "Prison Talk," in *Power/Knowledge: Selected Interviews and Other Writings, 1972–1977*, ed. Colin Gordon (New York: Pantheon, 1980), 53–54.
11. Foucault, *Discipline and Punish: The Birth of the Prison*, trans. Alan Sheridan (New York: Vintage, 1979), 26.
12. Foucault, "Two Lectures," in *Power/Knowledge*, ed. Gordon, 96.

13. This does *not* mean, however, that domination is everywhere, or that all power relations are relations of domination, or that we have no hope of escaping domination. I shall discuss the way that Foucault draws the distinction between power and domination, a distinction he only makes in some late interviews, when I consider the macrolevel of analysis.

14. Foucault, *Discipline and Punish*, 277.

15. Butler remains critical of Foucault, however. See, for example, her *Bodies that Matter: On the Discursive Limits of "Sex"* (New York: Routledge, 1993), 22.

16. Butler, *Bodies that Matter*, 23. Butler's discussion of "sex" in *Bodies that Matter* entails a reworking of the account of gender performativity laid out in her earlier work; see her *Gender Trouble: Feminism and the Subversion of Identity* (New York: Routledge, 1990). That account was criticized for the paradoxical way in which it lent itself both to naively voluntaristic and to starkly deterministic views of the acquisition of gender identity. For Butler's own discussion of the inadequacies of her earlier analysis, see *Bodies that Matter*, x–xi.

17. Foucault, *Discipline and Punish*, 228.

18. Sandra Bartky, "Foucault, Femininity, and the Modernization of Patriarchal Power," in *Femininity and Domination: Studies in the Phenomenology of Oppression* (New York: Routledge, 1990), 65.

19. See Foucault, *Discipline and Punish*, 201ff.

20. For more examples of this kind of analysis that are also inspired by Foucault, see Susan Bordo, "Anorexia Nervosa: Psychopathology as the Crystallization of Culture," in *Feminism and Foucault: Reflections on Resistance*, ed. Irene Diamond and Lee Quinby (Boston: Northeastern University Press, 1988); reprinted in Bordo, *Unbearable Weight: Feminism, Western Culture, and the Body* (Berkeley and Los Angeles: University of California Press, 1993).

21. Foucault, "Two Lectures," in *Power/Knowledge*, ed. Gordon, 99.

22. Foucault, *The History of Sexuality*, vol. 1, *An Introduction*, trans. Robert Hurley (New York: Vintage, 1978), 94.

23. Unfortunately, Foucault did not leave us with many detailed accounts of how this process of integration of local power relations into large, general power mechanisms takes place. The best account he does give of this is probably his discussion of "bio-power"; see Foucault, *History of Sexuality*, 1:139–45. On this point, see also Nancy Fraser, "Foucault on Modern Power: Empirical Insights and Normative Confusions," in *Unruly Practices: Power, Discourse and Gender in Contemporary Critical Theory* (Minneapolis: University of Minnesota Press, 1989), 24–25.

24. Foucault, "The Ethic of Care for the Self as a Practice of Freedom," in *The Final Foucault*, ed. James Bernauer and David Rasmussen (Cambridge: MIT Press, 1988), 3.

25. Ibid., 18.

26. Foucault, "Two Lectures," in *Power/Knowledge*, ed. Gordon, 99–100.

27. For a discussion of the possibility of such an antifoundationalist account of structures of domination, see Fraser and Nicholson, "Social Criticism without Philosophy," and Fraser, "False Antitheses: A Response to Seyla Benhabib and Judith Butler," *Praxis International* 11, no. 2: 166–77.

28. I borrow this phrase from Linda Alcoff. See Alcoff, "Feminist Politics and Foucault: The Limits to a Collaboration," in *Crises in Continental Philosophy*, ed. Arlene Dallery and Charles Scott (Albany: State University of New York Press, 1990). The limits that Alcoff suggests are different from those that I would suggest, however.

29. On this point, see Hartsock, "Foucault on Power," 168–69.

12

The Philosopher's Prism: Foucault, Feminism, and Critique*

Terry K. Aladjem

Something changes when the work of a lifetime is viewed posthumously.* There is an almost desperate attempt to grasp the oeuvre, and the mortal person of the author becomes the measure of the whole to which hindsight lends a special unity. It is ironic, however, when that honor is bestowed on one whose every expression questioned the unity and coherence of modern subjectivity, including that of his own authorship.[1] So it may seem unjust that in death, Michel Foucault, or who he

*This essay develops my remarks at the Spring 1988 meeting of the Western Political Science Association in response to papers by Eloise Buker, Nancy Hartsock, and Susan Hekman and comments by Christine Di Stefano and Michael Shapiro. I am grateful to the panelists, and to Tedros Kiros, Tracy Strong, and an anonymous reviewer for their helpful comments.

was as a politically motivated individual, has become the measure of what he wrote. Understandably one wants to find what made him tick, to dissect the corpus and find the magic and make it work for the many worthy causes that he might have championed. We might wish to have Foucault the ghostly critic take us back to the "vantage point" and the "method" that made his analysis compelling—but this, of course, is precisely the sort of thing that he was unwilling to do.

Indeed, it was that tremendous uneasiness about going back and assuming the transcendent perspective of modern reason that character- ized Foucault's approach to history. Like the spirit guide who brings us near but will not let us touch the world of the dead, Foucault would only address the past in the most elliptical ways. A curious refusal to lead, to judge, or to tell the "truth" about that history made him unlike other critics. Always consistent with his own understanding of the pervasiveness of power, he would deny that he had escaped the effects of power or that the critical detachment of authorship should give him any special claim on its "truth." A profound humility before the complex enclosures of the historical past and the variety of human existence moves on every page of his writings, and it is from this that we may learn the most from him.

At first, that humility must seem frustrating to the critic who has struggled with oppression and won some special insight. It might seem disturbingly neutral, if not objective, and it is hard to see how it could be useful to criticism. The feminist might regard it as an affront or a dismissal of precisely what she has gained in resisting subjugation, and she would be right, at least, that it does not duplicate her particular awareness of the effects of power. But if Foucault is not a guide or simple ally, there may be other ways in which he complements her enterprise. If we are tempted to ask whether Foucault was a feminist, then, or whether his work shares the same ends, we may miss the more subtle instruction that his analysis affords.

I suggest that there is a certain congruence between Foucault's analysis of power and that of many feminists; that the two often articulate different aspects of the same critical space. At the very least, the feminist critique of the hierarchical divisions of Western reason finds a complement in Foucault's refusal to engage that reason—a seemingly passive posture that becomes a most powerful analytical device. I take that humility seriously and regard Foucault's work not as a completed system that issues forth in guidelines for our own political practice, but as a series of questions and a brace of cautions that may be useful to a feminist analysis of power and to critical concerns about liberalism and modernity.

Among others, Susan Hekman and Eloise Buker have pointed out the similarities between Foucault's unwillingness to adopt the categories of Enlightenment thinking and feminist challenges to the same divisive knowledge.[2] Feminist analysis tends to regard the Western antinomies of subject and object, mind and body, reason and emotion, culture and nature, sanity and hysteria, and public and private all in their gendered meaning and suspicious correspondence with the hierarchical division of Male and Female. That these are instrumentalities of power or that there is a "male ethic" running through them is axiomatic for Foucault as well,[3] but he does not allow himself the distance to comment and condemn, and he is unwilling to turn the tables by giving favor to the subordinate pole. To do so, for him, would be to indulge power from another direction, to attempt to raise what power has stunted as a principle of opposition to power. Instead, he represents those couplings as such, without taking sides, and here, what seems like positivist objectivity amounts to a refusal to indulge these divisions of knowledge from any angle. It is this intransigence that gives Foucault his critical edge. If not objectivity, an odd neutrality allows the work to act as a refracting stone on the very same emanations of knowledge and power, an obstinate prism that reveals something new and perishable about them.

Of course, that resistance to the categories of Enlightenment reason poses an extraordinary dilemma for all postmodern criticism. Not only were such "foundationalist" categories as "truth," "essence," "human nature," "rationality," or "consciousness" the instruments of modern power; they have also been the tools of criticism that hold the promise of "liberation."[4] Hence, there is reason to suspect that the liberation from modernity that is grounded in the assumptions of modernity may repeat the same mistakes. Says Foucault,

> I've always been a little distrustful of the general theme of liberation, to the extent, that, if one does not treat it with a certain number of safeguards and within certain limits, there is a danger that it will refer back to the idea that there does exist a nature or human foundation which as a result of a certain number of historical, social, or economic processes, found itself

concealed, alienated or imprisoned in and by some repressive mechanism. In that hypothesis it would suffice to unloosen these repressive locks so that man can be reconciled with himself.[5]

There is a warning here that the totalizing vision which accepts such a "human foundation" is always in danger of leading back to a totalizing practice—and even the critical dichotomy of "appearance and reality" falls on a similar fate.[6] So it is, for example, that the rigorous awareness of the antinomies of Western thought offered by Lukács did not prevent him from deploying his own divisive scheme of true and false consciousness, which in turn may have led to revolutionary excess and elitism.[7] Yet Foucault has avoided that legacy of Enlightenment even as it has been extended through Marx, and he does not permit himself to ascend the privileged perch of reason or true consciousness like the modern critic. He cannot step "outside" of power, because there is no outside of power, and no one, oppressed or otherwise, can have such unencumbered access to its truth.

So it is in making the suggestion that there is no outside of power that Foucault poses his most poignant warning to critical analysis. If criticism, that of feminism included, sets out to right the scales of power merely by taking sides in a world of those who "have" power and those who do not, of dominators and dominated, it may preserve the old dichotomies of power in spite of itself. Even a metaphysics of gender runs that risk, not because it has focused on gender but because it is a *metaphysics* of that Western variety that mirrors its own origins in domination. For feminism, then, as Judith Butler's work suggests, Foucault sharpens the warning that the analysis which privileges "gender," or woman as "other," may still speak from within the paradigm that made them both what they are; it may confirm that "diadic gender system" by making a metaphysical standard out of it.[8] At the least, this would seem to be a worthy, almost Marx-like caution for the critic who might stray from the historical context or make utopian leaps beyond it.

But it is here, too, that Foucault's resistance—even to the modestly transcendent categories of a critical humanism—seems to leave us in an utterly hopeless situation. He seems to foreclose every appeal beyond the radically distinct contexts that he displays. If there is no "outside" of power, no privileged perspective of the oppressed that reveals the whole truth, and not even a gendered "core of identity" outside of what power has defined it to be, then it seems that we can only capitulate to power—*unless* it is possible that from within the context that conceals no hidden message and admits of no one truth, a proliferation of different voices may be heard, each questioning power in different ways.[9]

It is possible, in other words, that by denying that his analysis can produce a unitary vision of truth outside of power and suggesting that power is itself a " 'regime' of truth," he creates an opening for a different sort of politics.[10] If arriving at "truth" is not possible, and the contentious construction of truth is what defines politics in the first place, then challenging " 'truth games' "[11] from a variety of angles *within* power is a worthy political enterprise. Now, he says, "the political question is not error, illusion, alienated consciousness or ideology; it is truth itself."[12] This is not politics as a means to truth, but as the activity of contesting truths; it is a struggle with and within power, rather than a struggle for power.

To question the political nature of truth is something that feminists and other critics have done for a long time. But with Foucault, the questioning itself is a political art and the refractory historical method emerges as political strategy. As John Rajchman and others have suggested, his is largely a labor of *questions* and not the sort of inquiry that yields *answers*.[13] The analysis of the "surfaces" of power, like his interrogation of the ways in which sexuality has been "problematized," always invites a further questioning and renewed interrogations of history. It does not play on timely sympathies; it does not wring timeless lessons out of history, and it does not settle things once and for all. The endless inquiry has no need of final answers to enduring moral questions. It has the humility to entertain all questions and questioners and to be satisfied with the open-ended debate. One might wonder whether the way of the question might ultimately offer a more useful opening for those who are relatively powerless than that of the answer.

With this in mind, we may make sense of the truly disturbing fact that in Foucault's last volume on the history of sexuality, there appears to be no "woman"—none, anyway, who speaks against the classical male ethic of the "care of the self" or who seems to comment on the Christian tradition of marriage.[14] Here, there does seem to be a danger of losing "her" comment on the impenetrable power in which she is supposedly enmeshed. Yet perhaps she really is there in Foucault's work posing a sort of question. In refusing to assert his own perspective he is unwilling to posit hers, and yet she stands in the same relation to the texts of his *History of Sexuality* as the mad individual, the deviant, the prisoner, or "mankind" in general stand in relation to the texts of his earlier work. Perhaps she is speaking by virtue of her absence, and by *not* attributing a voice to her that resonates with modern subjectivity, an expression of who she really was might be heard from within the vortex of the power that defines her. Foucault's attentive silence may make women less reified and not more, and much like the broader phenomenon of the "shrinking woman" that Christine Di Stefano has identified in postmodern thought, it may enjoin us to return and listen again for her distinctive expressions. Indeed, says Di Stefano, "the figure of the shrinking woman may perhaps be best appreciated and utilized as an aporia within contemporary theory: a recurring paradox, question, dead end or blind spot to which we must repeatedly return."[15]

By posing this absence of woman as an unarticulated question, Foucault the interrogative critic may have goaded us once again into a renewed inquiry: to return to what is very much her story. Now she does not appear as a transcendent gender or persistent consciousness, or as a vicarious expression of modern individualism, but as something defined in her particularity. Again, the *absence* of the subject—female or otherwise—categorically determined once and for all, invites the question: How has her subjectivity *variously* been constituted? What have been the spectra of her existence?

All of this may seem too wishful or apologetic. I do seem to have credited Foucault for what he has left out, just as I appear to have credited him for relinquishing certain responsibilities of authorship. After all, by the extraordinary omission of a "female perspective," Foucault has very nearly assumed the "androcentric" attitude with which Eloise Buker associates him.[16] But somehow he remains a critic—subversive and not proud of anything in that attitude. From the perspective that moves within the games of male power displaying its different guises, he has decentered and disrupted the very same "androcentrism." He has stepped within the context of power without adopting the point of view of the prevailing power, and with the relativistic eye of the visitor, he surveys everything evenly so that it is all oddly diminished. If he seems to dissolve the category of woman within power—which is dangerous—he has also begun to dissolve the very power that defines her *as such*.

Yet in the broader sense, it appears that this dissolving criticism has proceeded at the expense of those concepts of "domination" and "patriarchy" that were indispensable to criticism—*unless* Foucault has also shattered these into a specificity that refines the analysis of power, and unless he has restored the examination of particulars that had been lost to the "universalizing" gaze of criticism. If the absence of the "subject" poses the question of how subjects are constituted, this suspension of critical categories directs attention back to the radically distinct contexts in which they were. Just as the idiosyncratic individual surfaces from time to time in Foucault's work, so does the unique historical situation, and like a strangely inverted Marxism, contextually formed practices are the beginning and the end of the discussion, if not the universal categories that had once shed light on them. Now it is in meeting Foucault's recalcitrant eye that the elements of those contexts appear to be transformed.

Specifically, then, we may see how Foucault and feminism might complement one another in the analysis of marriage. Buker reminds us that it is the critical "perspective of the wife, and only this, that teaches us that the 'velvet chains' of modern marriage are still chains."[17] In this feminist analysis, the chains of marriage stretch across historical contexts like a timeless undifferentiated oppression, and the oppositional "perspective" that is bound by them would seem to persist intact, hidden, and waiting as well. But this transcendent critical perspective is a modern one. There have been many wives in many ages who may not have perceived the chains as chains and have not participated in the institution of matrimony in the same way. In Foucault's examination of marriage, that perspective has dissolved within the many contexts of marriage. It does not instruct us by finding common cause among all the forms of marriage, but our attention is drawn to the distinctive bonds of "marriage*s*" instead. With Foucault, the "velvet chains" of modern marriage appear to be very different from the constraints of marriage in the past century and still more different from the classical male ethic of self-mastery that extended its particular dominion over the household, the wife, and the slave.[18]

Really, the more subtle aspect of Buker's point as well, is not the sameness or immutability of marital chains but the discriminating comparison that makes the modern ones seem "soft." The feminist inclination to find transhistorical solidarity with all women is qualified and refined by the equally powerful draw of historical distinction, which, in turn, resists the distortions of comparison and assimilation. Accordingly, in the shattered image of power that Foucault represents to us, we are inclined to ask what the "chain" is and where the "velvet" is and precisely how they coalesce in a *distinctive* power. As feminists, we might also be inclined to wonder about the specific ways in which women are subjugated or constitute themselves in power or, like the prisoners of Panopticon, how they might be "caught up in a power situation of which they themselves are the bearers."[19] Paradoxically, a *suspension* of empathy with the oppressed may sometimes invite more subtle revelations about power, and we are reminded that the respect for the integrity of distinctive experiences is the only genuine basis for such communion, historically *or* in contemporary political struggle. It seems that Foucault's hard, unsympathetic analytic displays components of power much as a prism reveals something more elemental than a mirror about the same light.

Once again, in refusing to define the subject—of any type or gender—and in rejecting transcendent categories and perspectives, Foucault has refused leadership of the more (masculine) pedantic variety. He cannot tell feminists or anyone else what to do if he is to be consistent with his own analysis of power, and the more we look to him posthumously for guidance, the more he eludes us. But just as he returns us inexorably to the historical context and resists the impulse to transcend it, he seems to advocate an oddly restrained variety of "local" political resistance, a kind of practice that boasts of no more privileged consciousness than he allows himself in analysis. Susan Hekman has emphasized the theoretical importance of this idea, but practically, as she suggests, it will have to be filled out.[20] Practically, this would not seem to be the resistance of local community leaders anxious to restore a sense of normalcy and virtue but that which arises at sites where the normalizing constraints of power are felt. If power relations assume "multiple forms," resistance must at least be "multiple,"[21] and as feminists would likely agree, it must be localized and concentrated in regions once thought too intimate for political struggle.

Yet in detailing these challenges to power, Foucault remains deficient or deliberately incomplete, and there is much more that may now be said of the one context and the struggle from "within." Within power, it would seem that there must be smaller "regimes" that are not seamlessly woven in with the rest, and if these do not offer a vantage point that should be valorized in critical practice, indeed because they do not, they must still be the locus of such "multiple" resistances. There are those who stand in different relations to the power that moves within and defines them, those who think the unthinkable, and those whose "bodies and pleasures"[22] are more *tensely* restricted than others. Being differently formed in power, as idiosyncratic beings or members of a group, they deserve the same distinction and integrity that Foucault has accorded to historical epochs. Foucault's "missing persons" (to use Buker's phrase)—prisoners, the insane, the wealthy, the impoverished, or the colonized, women, and especially children with needs and bodies not yet wholly formed in power[23]—must each bear the marks of power differently within them*selves*. Although Foucault will not say how, there are those whose self-knowledge strains the greater "power/knowledge" that defines them, who form discourses that are not identical with the greater discourse, and for all of its normalizing effects, power does not fall evenly over all.

If Foucault's hardened refusal to amplify those voices of resistance within power reveals something more of its complexity, feminism reminds us that they are expressions of resistance nonetheless, and our understanding of power might benefit from both kinds of insight. Together they might reveal ways in which power constitutes identity and is occasionally transgressed by those who seek to generalize their own discontentment, even if they are not the vanguard or the embodiment of some transcendent idea of freedom. Here we might think of the "local" struggle of Las Madres de la Plaza de Mayo, the Argentine mothers of "disappeared" persons, whose efforts have been richly detailed in this country by Jean Elshtain. In resistance to political oppression, their self-constitutive discourse combines what Elshtain calls "the language of a mother's loss," with a rather more global "language of human rights."[24] Each of the two different kinds of expression has been self-consciously altered in the heroic effort by which these women have politicized their own particular locus in power—as mothers and something more.

It would seem that this complex movement combines resistance to the particular ways in which these women have been constituted in power with a sweeping redefinition of themselves and their motherhood that challenges the powers that be. What it means to be a mother in that Argentine context has now been posited differently, and the constituting power that Foucault might have depicted is confronted by self-constitutive practices. In the process, these women have made something *more* of a politicized motherhood that transports them and made something *less*—or rather, more parochial and manifest—out of the language of universal human rights as well. In this, it would seem that their special efforts do correspond with Foucault's general suggestion that "the critique of what we are is at one and the same time the historical analysis of the limits that are imposed on us and an experiment with the possibility of going beyond them."[25]

Still, it must seem that Foucault is deficient in explaining such things. How would that local action, a feminist or any other struggle against oppression, become possible for him? How can it be grounded if not in the universalizing discourse of rights and freedom that emerged with the Enlightenment? It can be grounded, one might reply, because that discourse did not arise only in an intellectual enlightenment but from particular, local experiences with power—not in a dialectical sweep of historical change or an awakening of a latent consciousness or freedom but in particular "transgressions."[26] It arose in "*practices* of liberty" and "*practices* of freedom" of the sort that Foucault identifies in the aftermath of "liberation" from a colonial situation.[27] Such *transgressive practices* might make liberty manifest without making grandiose claims for liberty, and in them, it is not just a principal of freedom that is at stake but continuous self-formative acts of freedom. In such practices, people might generate "rights" and articulate them as such, but that is different from relying on a catalogue of rights that makes them "individuals." They might fashion communities of people who are at one and the same time resistant to the dictates of community—be they habitual and traditional or abstract and liberal—and this, at least, is one direction in which Foucault's contextual understanding might lead political practice.

It appears that this much of Foucault ought to strike a sympathetic chord with the growing number of critics of liberal "rights-based" thinking.[28] Many feminists, postmodernists, and communitarians proclaim the impoverishment of that tradition, its lack of specificity, equity, or moral suasion. Yet Foucault does not set out to attack the liberal tradition so much as to reveal the ways in which its own constellation of freedom is *also* a construction of power. For him, such freedoms are suffused with disciplines and at once pose limits for the very thematic interests they would advance. If the individual obtains rights in that tradition, this would be another way in which identity has been "problematized" and certain liberties set up within constraints. Thus, and for all of his reluctance to discuss "the subject" or to canonize that "individual" who was the vital theoretical entity of liberalism, it should not really be surprising that Foucault's final work concerns the care and constitution of the "self."

Here, the later Foucault reveals himself as an ethicist of sorts, declaring that he would fight the "fascism in us all."[29] The almost flat, relativistic descriptions of power, knowledge, and discursive norms in different contexts reveals how individuals are constituted as normative beings and how they constitute themselves within, if not against, the normative currents of power. If there is no particular faith in human essences or in freedom's own valiant struggle against authority here, it is not capitulation to authority either, and something like a Nietzschean will may occasionally assert itself within a moral domain. At least, the march through many forms of ethical self-mastery suggests a profusion of possibilities. Because each is positively constructed for Foucault—and never simply forged in negation, prohibition, or repression—others might be generated in varying degrees of self-consciousness. And if such ethical schemes are constructed in recognition of the very human variety that some would suppress, that leaves open the possibility—although Foucault did not develop it—of an ethics of multiplicity that not only tolerates but values human differences.

Accordingly, when he is asked of his last work: "Should we actualize this notion of the care of the self in the classical sense against modern thought?" Foucault says, "Absolutely."[30] But does he want to reinstate the classical male ethic? Not at all. Rather, he wants to generalize its capacity for self-formation in an utterly new way; to allow a freer range of choices among the elements that Western thought had once already defined and restricted. Now the interrogative criticism that Rajchman identified in the work becomes an "endless questioning of constituted experiences,"[31] a certain "choosing" or "inventing" of oneself amid the constitutive elements of power, and not just in spite of them or by an imagined negation that risks duplicating them.

In a way, this ethical turn of Foucault's takes the feminist notion that the "personal is political" to a limit without disregarding the problematic of the "situated self." Once again, it acknowledges particular constructs of freedom *within* the context of power and recognizes their critical import without proclaiming them as universals. Yet in all of this there are recognizable tensions of freedom and constraint, and it might seem, as Nancy Fraser has suggested, that Foucault has "smuggled back in" certain priorities of a liberal humanism, relying on a reader's "familiarity with and commitment to modern ideals of autonomy, reciprocity, dignity, and human rights."[32] But to characterize him in this way may miss the subtle mechanism by which he tests the same ideals. Indeed, Foucault enjoins us to return to reexamine the conditions of confinement and discipline that shaped our conception of freedom in the first place, and by the repeated return to the periods that prefigure modernity, he has shaken the complacency with which we accept it now. Far from relying on such modern ideals, he is reviving the contexts of their origination in a way that tests them, which has the dual effect of challenging their abstraction and revealing their inspiration. Here, if there is not a secret liberalism, there is a certain fascination with a *thematics* of liberalism.

So it is that the language of "practices" and "uses" of freedoms and pleasures in Foucault's later work seems to promise a certain "liberty," not because it affirms a *principle* of liberty but because it displays the *thematic elements* of constraint and self-constitution in a strangely re-fracted light. He returns us to scenes of an earlier discipline, to constructions of power that precede the Enlightenment as if to say that ours are quite different, but without forgetting that the rhetoric of freedom poses new constraints that delimit our "freedom." Like a prism, the work breaks up and reveals the emanations of power and knowledge as they were arranged before and during the Enlightenment, as if to demand that we see a more complete spectrum of "uses" in each.

Displayed in their historical variety in this way, the elements of liberalism are stretched to the point of dissipation. We are invited to view them in the spectral form that recalls their origins, where the promise of unfolding liberties is still affixed to the most devilish confinements. Now the very definitions of illness, criminality, or sexuality are each regarded as categories of enlightened knowledge that *contain* knowledge and that represent limiting conditions for freedom. What once appeared as the mysterious contradictions of a liberal freedom that promised equality and relied on inequality can now be seen as the restrictive norms that inevitably attend and enable those "freedoms." It follows that where Marxists and many feminists would realize the promises of liberalism by reversing the social order of domination, Foucault's work invites a different set of trespasses on the constitutive elements of the diffuse power that is the fabric of that "freedom" itself. In this, he confronts us abruptly with the problematics of constraint and self-formation as they have found one peculiar expression in liberalism.

With Foucault, then, the receptive reader will find that the themes of liberalism have been shaken loose from a narrow, complacent meaning in a way that may inspire feminism and other criticism to construe them differently. There is *freedom*, not a universal juridical principal of freedom of the sort that liberalism had articulated, but freedoms posed in the shadows of constraint or imprisonment, and occasionally, the transgressive, self-generative acts that test those limits. There is *individuality* in the acts that might rearrange the elements of an inescapable power, or in the idiosyncrasy that defies its ability to define. A certain *equality* is advanced in the analysis as the same steady eye surveys everyone and no one principle or voice is privileged. This is not an abstract equality accompanied by the usual methodological objectivity, but an expression of the very sort of humility that "practices" of equality require, one that recognizes the integrity of human differences without leveling them. In this, there is something like the liberal *toleration* in which people reluctantly endure the presence of "others," only now the evenhanded relativism of the analysis of power positively values their "differences" and what they reveal about power. Finally, there is *truth*, no longer the one "truth" or facticity that has been the aim of so much Enlightenment reason—the qualification or secret hope for its tolerance—but the "truth telling" that was the subject of Foucault's last seminar.[33] To value that telling of truth would strain the Millian reverence for the unpopular opinion as a means to some greater truth, as it might ultimately encourage a discursive community of "discordant concordance" in which many different voices are valued for themselves and a more honest pluralism might emerge.[34]

There may not be the sort of politics that builds new systems here, but the humble interrogation of these liberal themes anticipates a reconstituted ethics with profound political implications. It is an ethics that has learned something from the classical virtues and from the liberal ethos without quite adopting either—one that might involve the "care of the female self," as Buker would call for it,[35] within a broader care of the self and others. Paradoxically, Foucault's humility before many realities and his obstinate refusal to judge them do serve that end. That resilience has the extraordinary effect of expanding meanings and exposing the limitations by which they are constituted—almost unwittingly, it introduces the possibility of a nonrestrictive, positive ethic that is political, at least, as the ethical care of the self once was. It foreshadows a politics that does not depend on ultimate truth to pursue freedom, which remains diverse, interrogative, localized, and trans-gressive.

In this, Foucault is a useful companion to the feminist critic of liberalism and modernity. Yet his oddly contextual thought is useful because it is irreducible, and we would do well not to enlist him or expect things from him in regions where he was reluctant to tread. In the end, if Foucault does not lead, his vision reveals the complexity of the practices of the past in a way that may help us to construct practices of freedom with a similar regard for the richness and diversity of the present.

Notes

1. See a related discussion in Michael Shapiro, *Language and Politics* (Oxford: Basil Blackwell, 1984), 132.

2. Such views are developed by Susan Hekman, "From Monism to Pluralism, The Feminization of Epistemology," *Women & Politics* (Fall 1987); and "Foucault and Political Action: A Feminist View," manuscript; and by Eloise A. Buker, "A Feminist Deconstruction of Foucault: Hidden Desires and Missing Persons," manuscript.

3. Michel Foucault, *The History of Sexuality*, vol. 2, *The Use of Pleasure*, trans. Robert Hurley (New York: Vintage, 1988), 22.

4. Susan Hekman, "From Monism to Pluralism," makes a similar point concerning Foucault's antifoundationalism.

5. Michel Foucault, "The Ethic of Care for the Self as a Practice of Freedom: An Interview with Michel Foucault on January 20, 1984," conducted by Raul Fornet-Betancourt, Helmut Becker, and Alfredo Gomez-Müller and trans. J. D. Gauthier, S. J., *Philosophy and Social Criticism* 12 (Summer 1987): 113.

6. See the discussion in William E. Connolly, *Appearance and Reality in Politics* (Cam-bridge: Cambridge University Press, 1987).

7. Georg Lukács, *History and Class Consciousness: Studies in Marxist Dialectics*, trans. Rodney Livingstone (Cambridge: MIT Press, 1972), 156. In this vein, Isaac Balbus warns against equating an "epistemology of totality" and a "politics of totalitariansim." Nevertheless, the presumptions of truth, of omniscient consciousness and "correct thinking" may have a certain unfortunate correspondence. See Isaac D. Balbus, "Disciplining Women: Michel Foucault and the Power of Feminist Discourse," in *Feminism as Critique: On the Politics of Gender*, ed. Seyla Benhabib and Drucilla Cornell (Minneapolis: University of Minnesota Press, 1987), 114.

8. Judith Butler, "Variations on Sex and Gender: Bouvoir, Wittig and Foucault," in *Feminism as Critique*, ed. Seyla Benhabib and Drucilla Cornell (Minneapolis: University of Minnesota Press, 1987), 136–40. See related comments in Nancy Hartsock, "Rethinking Modernism: Minority vs. Majority Theories," *Cultural Critique*, no. 7 (Fall 1987): 202–6.

9. Thomas Flynn, "Foucault as Parrhesiast: His Last Course at the College de France, 1984," *Philosophy and Social Criticism* 12 (Summer 1987): 223, aptly identifies Foucault's strategy of employing a "plurality of counterpositions, of points of resistance, of styles of

life—of 'truths.' " Similarly, Judith Butler suggests that Foucault's strategy of "proliferation" diffuses the binary opposition of gender, in "Variations on Sex and Gender," 138.

10. Michel Foucault, *Power/Knowledge: Selected Interviews and Other Writings, 1972–1977*, ed. Colin Gordon, trans. Colin Gordon et al. (New York: Pantheon, 1980), 133.

11. Michel Foucault, *Technologies of the Self: A Seminar with Michel Foucault*, ed. Luther H. Martin, Huck Gutman, and Patrick H. Hutton (Amherst: University of Massachusetts Press, 1988), 15, 18.

12. Foucault, *Power/Knowledge*, 133. Foucault goes on to suggest here, "detaching the power of truth from the forms of hegemony," not because truth deserves autonomy but because there is always a suspicious link between the privilege of power and the epistemological privilege of truth.

13. John Rajchman, *Michel Foucault: The Freedom of Philosophy* (New York: Columbia University Press, 1985); and "Ethics After Foucault," *Social Text*, nos. 13–14 (Winter–Spring 1986): 179. See Susan Hekman, "Foucault and Political Action," 11.

14. Eloise Buker, "A Feminist Deconstruction," 4, 8, characterizes this "absence" of women as "actors" in Foucault's work as a silence: "This silence displays the role of women as bodies for reproduction rather than as humans able to enter into community." And again: "his silence articulates women as objects, victims of domination, not as actors, subjects of domination." Yet Foucault's "silence" does not "display" or "articulate" an objectification of women as if to confirm it so much as it raises questions about how anyone becomes a subject or actor. The point here is that he initiates a different interrogation of the matter by not rushing to fill that silence.

15. Christine Di Stefano, "Dilemmas of Difference: Feminism, Modernity, and Postmodernism," *Women & Politics* 8, nos. 3–4 (1988): 20.

16. Eloise Buker, "A Feminist Deconstruction," 4, 8.

17. Commenting on modern marriage as Foucault has characterized it in *The Care of the Self* (New York: Pantheon, 1986), 172, Buker suggests that "from the perspective of the 'wife,' it only adds a bit of velvet to the chains, because it does not create a space for the wife to emerge as a 'self' or a 'citizen' even within the narrow context of marriage" ("A Feminist Deconstruction," 14). But perhaps the word "perspective" belongs in quotation here along with the rest precisely because it is a historical eventuality that that "narrow context" had made so difficult to obtain.

18. Michel Foucault, *The Use of Pleasure* (New York: Vintage, 1986); see, for example, 63–77, 143–51.

19. Michel Foucault, *Discipline and Punish: The Birth of the Prison*, trans. Alan Sheridan (New York: Vintage, 1979), 201.

20. Susan Hekman, "Foucault and Political Action," 17.

21. Foucault, *Power/Knowledge*, 142.

22. Nancy Fraser offers an insightful discussion of Foucault's preference for the use of this phrase in comments on the eighteenth century. He reserves the analytical conjunction "sex-desire" for more contemporary discussions. See Nancy Fraser, "Foucault's Body-Language: A Post-Humanist Political Rhetoric?" *Salmagundi*, no. 61 (Fall 1983): 61–63.

23. Gad Horowitz, "The Foucaultian Impasse: No Sex, No Self, No Revolution," *Political Theory* 15 (1987): 64–73, makes much of the missing child and childhood in Foucault's work and suggests, critically, that this corresponds to his resistance to a Freudian notion of psychological repression and to his radical redaing of the latter. I have raised a related question about the critical, contextual challenge posed by memories of childhood in "Memory, Culture and Critical Reflection," Ph.D. diss., University of Massachusetts, 1986.

24. Jean Bethke Elshtain, "Antigone's Daughters Reconsidered: Continuing Reflections on Women, Politics and Power," manuscript, 15.

25. Susan Hekman, "Foucault and Political Action," 17, comments on the import of this passage from *The Foucault Reader*, ed. Paul Rabinow (New York: Pantheon, 1984), 50.

26. Here, I am suggesting that Foucault's notion of "transgressive" rather than dialectical change may have a special implication for situated political acts. See, for example, *The Archaeology of Knowledge*, trans. Alan Sheridan (New York: Harper and Row, 1976), 4; and *Language, Counter-Memory, Practice*, ed. Donald F. Bouchard, trans. Donald F. Bouchard and Sherry Simon (Ithaca: Cornell University Press, 1980), 29–52.

27. Michel Foucault, "The Ethics of Care," 113–14.

28. Benhabib and Cornell quote Michael J. Sandel, *Liberalism and Its Critics* (New York: New York University Press, 1984), 5–6, in expressing the same conjunction of views. See their *Feminism as Critique*, 12.

29. Foucault, preface to *Anti-Oedipus: Capitalism and Schizophrenia*, by Gilles Deleuze and Felix Guattari, trans. Robert Hurley, Mark Seem, and Helen R. Lane (Minneapolis: University of Minnesota Press, 1983). See the discussion in Alexander E. Hooke, "The Order of Others: Is Foucault's Antihumanism Against Human Action?" *Political Theory* 15 (1987): 54.

30. Foucault, "The Ethic of Care," 125.

31. Rajchman, *Michel Foucault: The Freedom of Philosophy*, 7: "Ethics after Foucault," 167. See also the discussion in Hekman, "Foucault and Political Action," 11–12.

32. See Fraser, "Foucault's Body-Language," 59. Hartsock, "Rethinking Modernism," 203, cites this passage in support of her critique of Foucault, while Hekman, "Foucault and Political Action," 10, suggests that Fraser's is a rather "backward looking" reading of the same.

33. Flynn, "Foucault as Parrhesiast," 223.

34. See William E. Connolly, *Political Theory and Modernity* (Oxford: Basil Blackwell, 1988), 170. Although less "hostile" toward democracy than Nietzsche and less "ambivalent" about it than Foucault, Connolly applauds the appreciation for "discordance" in both and suggest that it may coexist democratically with "concordance" without subjecting human differences to normalizing disciplines or a "politics of insidious assimliation." See William E. Connolly, *Politics and Ambiguity* (Madison: University of Wisconsin Press, 1987), 13–14.

35. Buker, "A Feminist Deconstruction," 3–6.

Select Bibliography

Adams, Parveen, and Jeff Minson. "The 'Subject' of Feminism." In *The Woman in Question*, edited by Parveen and Elizabeth Cowie. Cambridge: MIT Press, 1990.

Aladjem, Terry K. "Memory, Culture and Critical Reflection." Ph.D. dissertation, University of Massachusetts, 1986.

Alcoff, Linda Martín. "Feminist Politics and Foucault: The Limits to a Collaboration." In *Crises in Continental Philosophy*, edited by Arlene Dallery and Charles Scott. Albany: State University of New York Press, 1990.

Althusser, Louis. *For Marx*. Translated by Ben Brewster. New York: Pantheon, 1970.

Anzaldúa, Gloria. *Borderlands: The New Mestiza = La Frontera*. San Francisco: Spinsters Ink/Aunt Lute, 1987.

Ayalah, Daphna, and Issac Weinstock. *Breasts: Women Speak About Their Breasts and Their Lives*. New York: Simon and Schuster, Summit Books, 1979.

Balbus, Isaac D. "Disciplining Women: Michel Foucault and the Power of Feminist Discourse." In *Feminism as Critique: On the Politics of Gender*, edited by Seyla Benhabib and Drucilla Cornell, 110–27. Minneapolis: University of Minnesota Press, 1987.

———. "Disciplining Women: Michel Foucault and the Power of Feminist Discourse." *Praxis International* 5, no. 4 (January 1986): 466–83.

Bartky, Sandra. "Feeding Egos and Tending Wounds: Deference and Disaffection in Women's Emotional Labor." In her *Feminism and Domination: Studies in the Phenomenology of Oppression*. New York: Routledge, 1991.

———. "Foucault, Femininity, and the Modernization of Patriarchal Power." In *Femininity and Foucault: Reflections on Resistance*, edited by Irene Diamond and Lee Quinby. Boston: Northeastern University Press, 1988.

———. Introduction to *Femininity and Domination: Studies in the Phenomenology of Oppression*. New York: Routledge, 1990.

———. "Shame and Gender." In her *Feminism and Domination: Studies in the Phenomenology of Oppression*. New York: Routledge, 1991.

Beauvoir, Simone de. *The Second Sex*. Translated by H. M. Parshley. New York: Bantam, 1961.

Berman, Marshall. *All That is Solid Melts into Air: The Experience of Modernity*. New York: Simon and Schuster, 1982.

Bordo, Susan. "Anorexia Nervosa: Psychopathology as the Crystallization of Culture."

In *Feminism and Foucault: Reflections on Resistance,* edited by Irene Diamond and
Lee Quinby. Boston: Northeastern University Press, 1988.
———. "The Body and the Reproduction of Femininity." In *Gender, Body, Knowledge,*
edited by Alison Jaggar and Susan Bordo. New Brunswick: Rutgers University
Press, 1989.
———. "Feminism, Postmodernism, and Gender-Skepticism." In *Feminism/Postmodern-
ism,* edited by Linda Nicholson. New York: Routledge, 1990.
———. *Unbearable Weight: Feminism, Western Culture, and the Body.* Berkeley and Los
Angeles: University of California Press, 1993.
Buker, Eloise. "A Feminist Deconstruction of Foucault: Hidden Desires and Missing
Persons." Unpublished manuscript.
Burke, Edmund. *A Philosophical Enquiry into the Origin of the Sublime and the Beautiful.*
Oxford: Oxford University Press, 1990.
Butler, Judith. *Bodies that Matter: On the Discursive Limits of "Sex."* New York:
Routledge, 1993.
———. "Contingent Foundations: Feminism and the Question of Postmodernism." In
Feminists Theorize the Political, edited by Judith Butler and Joan W. Scott. London:
Routledge, 1992.
———. *Gender Trouble: Feminism and the Subversion of Identity.* New York: Routledge,
1990.
———. "Gender Trouble, Feminist Theory and Psychoanalytic Discourse." In *Feminism/
Postmodernism,* edited by Linda Nicholson. London: Routledge, 1990.
———. "Imitation and Gender Insubordination." In *Inside/Out: Lesbian Theories, Gay
Theories,* edited by Diana Fuss. New York: Routledge, 1992.
———. *Subjects of Desire: Hegelian Reflections in Twentieth-Century France.* New York:
Columbia University Press, 1987.
———. "Variations on Sex and Gender: Beauvoir, Wittig and Foucault." In *Feminism
as Critique,* edited by Seyla Benhabib and Drucilla Cornell. Minneapolis: Univer-
sity of Minnesota Press, 1987.
Chodorow, Nancy. *The Reproduction of Mothering: Psychoanalysis and the Sociology of
Gender.* Berkeley and Los Angeles: University of California Press, 1978.
Christian, Barbara. "The Race for Theory." *Cultural Critique* 6 (Spring 1987): 51–63.
Cocks, Joan. *The Oppositional Imagination: Feminism, Critique and Political Theory.* New
York: Routledge, 1989.
Collins, Patricia Hill. *Black Feminist Thought: Knowledge, Consciousness, and the Politics
of Empowerment.* New York: Routledge, 1991.
———. "The Social Construction of Black Feminist Thought." *Signs* 14, no. 4 (Summer
1989): 745–73.
Connolly, William E. *Appearance and Reality in Politics.* Cambridge: Cambridge Univer-
sity Press, 1987.
———. *Political Theory and Modernity.* Oxford: Basil Blackwell, 1988.
———. *Politics and Ambiguity.* Madison: University of Wisconsin Press, 1987.
Cook, Deborah. *The Subject Finds a Voice: Foucault's Turn Toward Subjectivity.* New York:
Peter Lang, 1993.
Davis, K. "Remaking the She-Devil: A Critical Look at Feminist Approaches to Beauty."
Hypatia 6, no. 2 (1991): 21–43.
Deleuze, Gilles, and Felix Guattari. *Anti-Oedipus: Capitalism and Schizophrenia.* Trans-
lated by Robert Hurley, Mark Seem, and Helen R. Lane. With a Preface by
Michel Foucault. Minneapolis: University of Minnesota Press, 1983.
Derrida, Jacques. "Choreographies. Interview with Christie V. McDonald." *Diacritics* 12
(1982): 66–76.

Dews, Peter. *Logics of Disintegration: Post-Structuralist Thought and the Claims of Critical Theory*. London: Verso, 1987.

Di Stefano, Christine. "Dilemmas of Difference: Feminism, Modernity, and Postmodernism." *Women & Politics* 8, nos. 3–4 (1988): 1–24.

Diamond, Irene, and Lee Quinby. "American Feminism and the Language of Control." In *Feminism and Foucault*, edited by Irene Diamond and Lee Quinby. Boston: Northeastern University Press, 1988.

———. Introduction to *Feminism and Foucault: Reflections on Resistance*, edited by Irene Diamond and Lee Quinby. Boston: Northeastern University Press, 1988.

Dietz, Mary. "Citizenship with a Feminist Face: The Problem with Maternal Thinking." *Political Theory* 13, no. 1 (1985): 19–38.

Dinnerstein, Dorothy. *The Mermaid and the Minotaur*. New York: HarperCollins, 1976.

Donzelot, Jacques. *The Policing of Families*. New York: Pantheon, 1979.

Dreyfus, Hubert L., and Paul Rabinow. *Michel Foucault: Beyond Structuralism and Hermeneutics*. With an Afterword by Michel Foucault. Chicago: University of Chicago Press, 1982.

DuBois, W. E. B. *The Souls of Black Folk*. New York: Fawcett World Library, n.d.

Dworkin, Gerald. "The Nature and Value of Autonomy." Unpublished transcript, 1983.

Elshtain, Jean Bethke. "Antigone's Daughters Reconsidered: Continuing Reflections on Women, Politics and Power." Unpublished manuscript.

Epstein, Stephen. "Gay Politics, Ethnic Identity: The Limits of Social Constructionism." *Socialist Review* 7 (May–August, 1987): 9–54.

Eribon, Didier. *Michel Foucault*. Translated by Betsy Wing. Cambridge: Harvard University Press, 1991.

Evans, Richard. *The Feminists*. London: Croom Helm, 1977.

Ferguson, Ann. *Blood at the Root: Motherhood, Sexuality, and Male Domination*. London: Pandora, 1989.

Ferguson, Kathy. *The Man Question: Visions of Subjectivity in Feminist Theory*. Berkeley and Los Angeles: University of California Press, 1993.

Fornet-Betancourt, Raul, et al. "The Ethic of Care for the Self as a Practice of Freedom: An Interview with Michel Foucault." In *The Final Foucault*, edited by James Bernauer and David Rasmussen, translated by Joseph D. Gauthier. Cambridge: MIT Press, 1988.

Foucault, Michel. "An Aesthetics of Existence." In *Michel Foucault: Politics, Philosophy, Culture, Interviews and Other Writings, 1977–1984*, edited by Lawrence D. Kritzman, translated by Alan Sheridan et al. New York: Routledge, 1988.

———. *The Archaeology of Knowledge*. Translated by Alan Sheridan. New York: Pantheon, 1972.

———. "The Concern for Truth." In *Politics, Philosophy, Culture: Interviews and Other Writings, 1977–1984*, edited by Lawrence D. Kritzman, translated by Alan Sheridan et al. New York: Routledge, 1988.

———. *Discipline and Punish: The Birth of the Prison*. Translated by Alan Sheridan. New York: Vintage, 1979.

———. "The End of the Monarchy of Sex." In *Foucault Live: Interviews, 1966–1984*, edited by Sylvère Lotringer, translated by Dudley M. Marchi. New York: Semiotext(e), 1989.

———. "The Ethic of Care for the Self as a Practice of Freedom." Translated by J. D. Gauthier. In *The Final Foucault*, edited by James Bernauer and David Rasmussen. Cambridge: MIT Press, 1988.

———. "Friendship as a Way of Life." In *Foucault Live*, edited by Sylvère Lotringer. New York: Semiotext(e), 1989.

————. *The Foucault Effect.* Edited by Graham Burchell, Colin Gordon, and Peter Miller. Chicago: University of Chicago Press, 1991.

————. "Governmentality." Translated by Rosi Braidotti. *Ideology and Consciousness* 6 (Autumn 1979).

————. *Herculine Barbin: Being the Recently Discovered Memoirs of a Nineteenth-Century French Hermaphrodite.* Translated by Richard McDougall. New York: Pantheon, 1980.

————. *The History of Sexuality.* Vol. 1, *An Introduction.* Translated by Robert Hurley. New York: Pantheon, 1978.

————. *The History of Sexuality.* Vol. 2, *The Use of Pleasure.* Translated by Robert Hurley. New York: Pantheon, 1983; Harmondsworth: Penguin, 1987.

————. *The History of Sexuality.* Vol. 3, *The Care of the Self.* Translated by Robert Hurley. New York: Pantheon, 1986; Vintage, 1988.

————. *I, Pierre Rivière, Having Slaughtered My Mother, My Sister, and My Brother . . . : A Case of Parricide in the Nineteenth Century.* Translated by Frank Jellinek. New York: Pantheon, 1975.

————. "La Loi de la Pudeur." Interview. *Recherches* 37 (April 1979): 69–82.

————. *Language, Counter-Memory, Practice.* Edited by Donald F. Bouchard, translated by Donald F. Bouchard and Sherry Simon. Ithaca: Cornell University Press, 1977.

————. "The Minimalist Self." In *Michel Foucault: Politics, Philosophy, Culture: Interviews and Other Writings, 1977–1984,* edited by Lawrence D. Kritzman, translated by Alan Sheridan et al. New York: Routledge, 1988.

————. "Nietzsche, Genealogy, History." In *Language, Counter-Memory and Practice: Selected Essays and Interviews,* edited by Donald F. Bouchard, translated by Donald F. Bouchard and Sherry Simon. Ithaca: Cornell University Press, 1980.

————. "Omnes et Singulatim." In *The Tanner Lectures on Human Values II,* edited by Sterling McCurrin. Salt Lake City: University of Utah Press, 1981.

————. "On the Genealogy of Ethics: An Overview of Work in Progress." In *The Foucault Reader,* edited by Paul Rabinow. New York: Pantheon, 1984.

————. *The Order of Things: An Archaeology of the Human Sciences.* New York: Vintage, 1973.

————. "The Political Technology of Individual." In *Technologies of the Self: A Seminar with Michel Foucault,* edited by Luther H. Martin, Huck Gutman, and Patrick H. Hutton. London: Tavistock, 1988.

————. "Power and Sex: An Interview with Michel Foucault." Translated by David J. Parent. *Telos* 32 (Summer 1977): 152–61.

————. "Power and Strategies." In *Power/Knowledge: Selected Interviews and Other Writings, 1972–1977,* edited by Colin Gordon, translated by Colin Gordon et al. New York: Pantheon, 1980.

————. *Power/Knowledge: Selected Interviews and Other Writings, 1972–1977.* Edited by Colin Gordon. Translated by Colin Gordon et al. New York: Pantheon, 1980.

————. "Practicing Criticism." In *Michel Foucault: Politics, Philosophy, Culture: Interviews and Other Writings, 1977–1984,* edited by Lawrence D. Kritzman, translated by Alan Sheridan et al. New York: Routledge, 1988.

————. "The Return to Morality." In *Michel Foucault: Politics, Philosophy, Culture: Interviews and Other Writings, 1977–1984,* edited by Lawrence D. Kritzman, translated by Alan Sheridan et al. New York: Routledge, 1988.

————. "Sexual Morality and the Law." In *Michel Foucault: Politics, Philosophy, Culture: Interviews and Other Writings, 1977–1984,* edited by Lawrence D. Kritzman, translated by Alan Sheridan et al., 271–85. New York: Routledge, 1988.

———. "Space, Knowledge and Power." Interview by Paul Rabinow. In *The Foucault Reader*, edited by Paul Rabinow. New York: Pantheon, 1984.

———. "The Subject and Power." Afterword to *Michel Foucault: Beyond Structuralism and Hermeneutics*, 2d ed., edited by Paul Rabinow and Hubert Dreyfus, with an interview by Michel Foucault. Chicago: University of Chicago Press, 1983.

———. "Technologies of the Self." In *Technologies of the Self: A Seminar with Michel Foucault*, edited by Luther H. Martin, Huck Gutman, and Patrick H. Hutton. Amherst: University of Massachusetts Press, 1988.

———. *Technologies of the Self: A Seminar with Michel Foucault*. Edited by Luther H. Martin, Huck Gutman, and Patrick H. Hutton. Amherst: University of Massachusetts Press, 1988.

———. "Truth, Power, Self: An Interview with Michel Foucault." In *Technologies of the Self: A Seminar with Michel Foucault*, edited by Luther H. Martin, Huck Gutman, and Patrick H. Hutton. Amherst: University of Massachusetts Press, 1988.

———. "Truth and Subjectivity." Howison Lectures, University of California at Berkeley, October 20–21, 1980.

———. "Two Lectures." In *Power/Knowledge: Selected Interviews and Other Writings, 1972–1977*, edited by Colin Gordon, translated by Colin Gordon et al. New York: Pantheon, 1980.

———. "What is Enlightenment?" Translated by Catherine Porter. In *The Foucault Reader*, edited by Paul Rabinow. New York: Pantheon, 1984.

Flax, Jane. "The End of Innocence." In *Feminists Theorize the Political*, edited by Judith Butler and Joan W. Scott. London: Routledge, 1992.

Flynn, Thomas. "Foucault as Parrhesiast: His Last Course at the College de France, 1984." *Philosophy and Social Criticism* 12 (Summer 1987): 213–29.

Fraser, Nancy. "False Antitheses: A Response to Seyla Benhabib and Judith Butler." *Praxis International* 11, no. 2 (1991): 166–77.

———. "Foucault's Body-Language: A Post-Humanist Political Rhetoric?" *Salmagundi* 61 (Fall 1983): 61–63.

———. "Foucault on Modern Power: Empirical Insights and Normative Confusions." In her *Unruly Practices: Power, Discourse and Gender in Contemporary Social Theory*. Minneapolis: University of Minnesota Press, 1989.

———. "A Genealogy of *Dependency*: Tracing a Keyword of the U.S. Welfare State." *Signs* (Winter 1994): 303–36.

———. *Unruly Practices: Power, Discourse and Gender in Contemporary Social Theory*. Minneapolis: University of Minnesota Press, 1989.

———, and Linda J. Nicholson. "Social Criticism Without Philosophy: An Encounter Between Feminism and Postmodernism." In *Feminism/Postmodernism*, edited by Linda J. Nicholson. New York: Routledge, 1990.

Friedan, Betty. *The Feminine Mystique*. New York: Dell, 1964.

———. *The Second Stage*. New York: Summit, 1986.

Fuss, Diana. *Essentially Speaking: Feminism, Nature, and Difference*. New York: Routledge, 1989.

Galeano, Eduardo. *Century of the Wind*. New York: Pantheon, 1988.

———. "In Defense of the Word: Leaving Buenos Aires, June, 1976." In *The Graywolf Annual Five: Multi-Cultural Literacy*, edited by Rick Simonson and Scott Walker. Saint Paul, Minn.: Grayworld, 1988.

García Márquez, Gabriel. *The Fragrance of Guava*. Translated by Ann Wright. London: Verso, 1982.

Gilligan, Carol. *In a Different Voice: Psychological Theory and Women's Development*. Cambridge: Harvard University Press, 1982.

Gimenez, Martha. "Feminism, Pronatalism, and Motherhood." *International Journal of Women's Studies* 3, no. 3 (1980): 215–40.

Gough, Jamie. "Childhood Sexuality and Pedophilia." In *The Age Taboo: Gay Male Sexuality, Power and Consent*, edited by Daniel Tsang. London and Boston: Gay Men's Press and Alyson Publications, 1981.

Gould, Carol C. "Private Rights and Public Virtues: Women, the Family, and Democracy." In *Beyond Domination: New Perspectives on Women and Philosophy*, edited by Carol Gould. Totowa, N.J.: Rowman and Allenheld, 1983.

Grant, Judith. *Fundamental Feminism: Contesting the Core Concepts of Feminist Theory*. London: Routledge, 1993.

Grimshaw, Jean. "Practices of Freedom." In *Up Against Foucault: Explorations of Some Tensions between Feminism and Foucault*, edited by Caroline Ramazanoglu. London: Routledge, 1993.

Habermas, Jürgen. "The Entwinement of Myth and Enlightenment: Rereading *Dialectic of Enlightenment*." *New German Critique* 26 (Spring–Summer 1982): 13–30.

———. *Legitimation Crisis*. Translated by Thomas McCarthy. Boston: Beacon, 1975.

———. "Modernity—An Incomplete Project." In *The Anti-Aesthetic*, edited by Hal Foster, translated by Seyla Benhabib. Port Townsend, Wash.: Bay Press, 1983.

———. "Modernity versus Postmodernity." *New German Critique* 22 (Winter 1981): 3–14.

———. *The Philosophical Discourse of Modernity: Twelve Lectures*. Translated by Frederick Lawrence. Cambridge: Polity Press, 1987.

Haraway, Donna. "A Cyborg Manifesto: Science, Technology, and Socialist Feminism in the Late Twentieth Century." In *Simians, Cyborgs, and Women: The Reinvention of Nature*. New York: Routledge, 1991.

———. "Situated Knowledges: The Science Question in Feminism and the Privilege of Partial Perspective." *Feminist Studies* 14, no. 3 (Fall 1988): 575–99.

Harding, Sandra. *The Science Question in Feminism*. Ithaca: Cornell University Press, 1986.

Hartsock, Nancy. "Foucault on Power: A Theory for Women?" In *Feminism/Postmodernism*, edited by Linda J. Nicholson. New York: Routledge, 1990.

———. *Money, Sex, and Power: Toward a Feminist Historical Materialism*. Boston: Northeastern University Press, 1984.

———. "Rethinking Modernism: Minority vs. Majority Theories." *Cultural Critique* 7 (Fall 1987): 202–6.

Heidegger, Martin. "The Age of the World Picture." In *"The Question concerning Technology" and Other Essays*, translated by William Lovitt, 115–24. New York: Garland, 1977.

———. "The Letter on Humanism." Translated by Frank A. Capuzzi. In *Basic Writings*, edited by David Farrell Krell, 189–242. New York: Harper and Row, 1977.

———. "Overcoming Metaphysics." In *The End of Philosophy*, translated by Joan Stambaugh, 84–110. New York: Harper and Row, 1973.

———. "The Question Concerning Technology." In *"The Question Concerning Technology" and Other Essays*, translated by William Lovitt, 3–35. New York: Garland, 1977.

Hekman, Susan. "Foucault and Political Action: A Feminist View." Unpublished manuscript.

———. "From Monism to Pluralism, The Feminization of Epistemology." *Women & Politics* (Fall 1987): 65–84.

———. *Gender and Knowledge: Elements of a Postmodern Feminism*. Boston: Northeastern University Press, 1990.

Held, Virginia. *Feminist Morality: Transforming Culture, Society, and Politics.* Chicago: University of Chicago Press, 1993.
————. "Freedom and Feminism." Paper presented at the Intellectual Legacy of C. B. Macpherson Conference, University of Toronto, October 4–6, 1989.
Helman, Sarit, and Tamar Rapoport. "Surviving through Ritual: The Puzzle of the Endurance of a Women's Peace Movement: 'Women in Black.'" Paper presented at the ISA Conference, Bielefeld, 1993.
Hooke, Alexander E. "The Order of Others: Is Foucault's Antihumanism Against Human Action?" *Political Theory* 15 (1987): 38–60.
hooks, bell. "Choosing the Margin as a Space of Radical Openness." *Yearning: Race, Gender, and Cultural Politics.* Boston: South End, 1990.
Horowitz, Gad. "The Foucaultian Impasse: No Sex, No Self, No Revolution." *Political Theory* 15 (1987): 64–73.
Houppert, Karen. "WAC." *Village Voice* 37 (9 June 1992): 33–38.
Hoy, David Couzens, ed. *Foucault: A Critical Reader.* New York: Basil Blackwell, 1986.
————. "Power, Repression, Progress: Foucault, Lukes, and the Frankfurt School." *Triquarterly* 52 (Fall 1981): 43–63.
————. "The Unthought and How to Think It." American Philosophical Association, Western Division, 1982.
Hurtado, Aida. "Relating to Privilege: Seduction and Rejection in the Subordination of White Women and Women of Color." *Signs* 14, no. 4 (Summer 1989): 833–55.
Irigaray, Luce. *This Sex Which is Not One.* Translated by Catherine Porter with Carolyn Burke. Ithaca: Cornell University Press, 1985.
Jaggar, Alison M. *Feminist Politics and Human Nature.* Totowa, N.J.: Rowman and Allenheld, 1983.
Jameson, Fredric. "History and Class Consciousness as an 'Unfinished Project.'" *Rethinking Marxism* 1, no. 1 (Spring 1988).
Kelly, Michael. "Foucault, Habermas and the Self-Referentiality of Critique." *Critique and Power: Recasting the Foucault/Habermas Debate,* edited by Michael Kelly. Cambridge: MIT Press, 1994.
King, Deborah. "Multiple Jeopardy, Multiple Consciousness: The Context of a Black Feminist Ideology." *Signs* 14, no. 1 (Fall 1988): 42–72.
Kolodny, Niko. "The Late Foucault." Unpublished thesis.
de Lauretis, Teresa. "The Technology of Gender." In her *Technologies of Gender: Essays on Theory, Film, and Fiction,* 1–30. Bloomington: Indiana University Press, 1987.
Lemert, Charles, and Garth Gillan. *Michel Foucault: Social Theory and Trangression.* New York: Columbia University Press, 1982.
Lloyd, Moya. "Foucault's 'Care of the Self': Some Implications for Feminist Politics." *Foucault the Legacy: Conference Proceedings.* Forthcoming.
————. "The (F)utility of a Feminist Turn to Foucault." *Economy and Society* 22, no. 4 (November 1993): 437–60.
Lorde, Audre. *The Cancer Journals.* Spinsters/Aunt Lute, 1980.
————. *Sister Outsider: Essays and Speeches.* New York: Spinsters Ink, 1982.
————. "Uses of the Erotic: The Erotic as Power." In *Sister Outsider: Essays and Speeches.* Trumansburg, N.Y.: Crossing Press, 1984.
Lukács, Georg. *History and Class Consciousness: Studies in Marxist Dialectics.* Translated by Rodney Livingstone. Cambridge: MIT Press, 1972.
MacIntyre, Alasdair. *After Virtue: A Study in Moral Theory.* Notre Dame: University of Notre Dame Press, 1981; 2d ed. 1984.
MacKinnon, Catharine A. *Sexual Harassment of Working Women.* New Haven: Yale University Press, 1979.

Major-Poetz, Pamela. *Michel Foucault's Archaeology of Western Culture*. Chapel Hill: University of North Carolina Press, 1983.

McNay, Lois. "The Foucauldian Body and the Exclusion of Experience." *Hypatia* 6 (Fall 1991): 125–39.

———. *Foucault and Feminism: Power, Gender and the Self*. Cambridge: Polity, 1992; Northeastern University Press, 1993.

Megill, Alan. *Prophets of Extremity*. Berkeley and Los Angeles: University of California Press, 1985.

Memmi, Albert. *The Colonizer and the Colonized*. Boston: Beacon, 1967.

Minson, Jeff. *Genealogies of Morals: Nietzsche, Foucault, Donzelot and the Eccentricity of Morals*. London: Macmillan, 1985.

Mitchell, Juliet. *Women's Estate*. Harmondsworth: Penguin, 1971.

Mohanty, Chandra Talpade. "Under Western Eyes." *Boundary 2* 12, no. 3 and 13, no. 1 (Spring–Fall 1984): 333–58.

Mouffe, Chantel. "Radical Democracy: Modern or Postmodern." Translated by Paul Holdenraber. In *Universal Abandon: The Politics of Postmodernism*, edited by Andrew Ross. Minneapolis: University of Minnesota Press, 1988.

Nietzsche, Friedrich. *The Birth of Tragedy and The Genealogy of Morals*. Translated by Francis Golffing. New York: Doubleday Anchor, 1956.

———. *The Gay Science*. Translated by Walter Kaufmann. New York: Vintage, 1974.

———. *The Will to Power*. New York: Random House, 1968.

Norris, Christopher. " 'What is Enlightenment?': Kant and Foucault." In *The Cambridge Companion to Foucault*, edited by Gary Gutting. Cambridge: Cambridge University Press, 1994.

O'Brien, Mary. *The Politics of Reproduction*. London: Routledge and Kegan Paul, 1983.

Osborne, Peter, and Lynn Segal. "Gender as Performance: An Interview with Judith Butler." *Radical Philosophy* 67 (Summer 1994): 32–39.

Okin, Susan Moller. *Women in Western Political Thought*. Princeton: Princeton University Press, 1979.

Phelan, Shane. "Foucault and Feminism." *American Journal of Political Science* 34, no. 2 (May 1990): 421–40.

———. *Identity Politics: Lesbian Feminism and the Limits of Community*. Philadelphia: Temple University Press, 1989.

Plaza, Monique. "Our Damages and Their Compensation—Rape: The 'Will Not to Know' of Michel Foucault." *Feminist Issues* 1 (Summer 1981): 25–35.

Poster, Mark. *Foucault, Marxism and History*. Oxford: Basil Blackwell, 1984.

Presland, Eric. "Whose Power? Whose Consent?" In *The Age Taboo: Gay Male Sexuality, Power and Consent*, edited by Daniel Tsang. London and Boston: Gay Men's Press and Alyson Publishers, 1981.

Probyn, Elspeth. *Sexing the Self: Gendered Positions in Cultural Studies*. London: Routledge, 1993.

Rabinow, Paul, ed. *The Foucault Reader*. New York: Pantheon, 1984.

Rajchman, John. "Ethics After Foucault." *Social Text* 13–14 (Winter–Spring 1986): 165–83.

———. *Michel Foucault: The Freedom of Philosophy*. New York: Columbia University Press, 1985.

———. *Truth and Eros: Foucault, Lacan, and the Question of Ethics*. New York: Routledge, 1991.

Rawls, John. "Kantian Constructivism in Moral Theory." *Journal of Philosophy* 77, no. 9 (September 1980): 505–72.

———. A *Theory of Justice*. Cambridge: Belknap Press of Harvard University Press, 1971.

Reeves, Tom. "Loving Boys." In *The Age Taboo: Gay Male Sexuality, Power and Consent*, edited by Daniel Tsang. London and Boston: Gay Men's Press and Alyson Publishers, 1981.

Rich, Adrienne. *Of Woman Born: Motherhood as Experience and Institution*. New York: Norton, 1976.

Rorty, Richard. *Contingency, Irony, and Solidarity*. Cambridge: Cambridge University Press, 1989.

———. "Postmodern Bourgeois Liberalism." *Journal of Philosophy* 80 (October 1983): 583–89.

———. "Solidarity or Objectivity?" In *Post-Analytic Philosophy*, edited by John Rajchman and Cornel West, 3–19. New York: Columbia University Press, 1985.

Rubin, Gayle. "Thinking Sex: Notes for a Radical Theory of the Politics of Sexuality." In *Pleasure and Danger*, edited by Carole S. Vance. Boston: Routledge and Kegan Paul, 1984.

Ruddick, Sara. *Maternal Thinking: Toward a Politics of Peace*. New York: Ballantine, 1989.

Said, Edward W. *Orientalism*. New York: Vintage, 1978.

Sandel, Michael J. *Liberalism and Its Critics*. New York: New York University Press, 1984.

Sangari, Kum Kum. "The Politics of the Possible." *Cultural Critique*, no. 7 (Fall 1987).

Sawicki, Jana. *Disciplining Foucault: Feminism, Power and the Body*. New York: Routledge, 1991.

———. "Foucault and Feminism: Toward a Politics of Difference." *Hypatia* 1 (Fall 1986): 23–36.

———. "Foucault, Feminism, and Questions of Identity." In *The Cambridge Companion to Foucault*, edited by Gary Gutting, 286–313. Cambridge: Cambridge University Press, 1994.

Schor, Naomi. "Dreaming Dissymmetry: Barthes, Foucault, and Sexual Difference." In *Coming to Terms: Feminism, Theory, Politics*, edited by Elizabeth Weed, 47–58. New York: Routledge, 1989.

———, and Elizabeth Weed, eds. "Another Look at Essentialism." *difference: A Journal of Feminist Cultural Studies* 1, no. 2 (1989).

Seidman, Steven. *Embattled Eros: Sexual Politics and Ethics in Contemporary America*. New York: Routledge, 1992.

Shapiro, Michael. *Language and Politics*. Oxford: Basil Blackwell, 1984.

Simons, Jon. *Foucault and the Political*. London: Routledge, 1995.

Singer, Linda. "Bodies—Powers—Pleasures." *differences* 1 (1989): 45–66.

———. *Erotic Welfare: Sexual Theory and Politics in the Age of Epidemic*. New York: Routledge, 1990.

Taylor, Charles. "Foucault on Freedom and Truth." *Political Theory* 12, no. 2 (1984): 152–83.

Terry, Jennifer. "The Body Invaded: Medical Surveillance of Women as Reproducers." *Socialist Review* 19 (July–September 1989): 13–43, 20.

Trebilcot, Joyce, ed. *Mothering: Essays in Feminist Theory*. Savage, Md.: Rowman and Littlefield, 1983.

Tress, Darryl McGowan. "Comments on Flax's 'Postmodernism and Gender Relations in Feminist Theory.' " *Signs: Journal of Women in Culture and Society* 14, no. 1 (Autumn 1988): 196–200.

Tyler, Carole-Anne. "Boys Will Be Girls: The Politics of Gay Drag." In *Inside/out: Lesbian Theories, Gay Theories*, edited by Diana Fuss. New York: Routledge, 1991.

Walzer, Michael. "The Politics of Michel Foucault." In *Foucault: A Critical Reader*, edited by David Couzens Hoy. Oxford: Basil Blackwell, 1986.

————. *Spheres of Justice: A Defense of Pluralism and Equality.* New York: Basic Books, 1983.

Wartenberg, Thomas E. "The Concept of Power in Feminist Theory." *Praxis International* 8, no. 3 (1988): 304–9.

————. *The Forms of Power: From Domination to Transformation.* Philadelphia: Temple University Press, 1990.

Weedon, Chris. *Feminist Practice and Poststructuralist Theory.* Oxford: Basil Blackwell, 1987.

Weeks, Jeffrey. *Sexuality and Its Discontents: Meanings, Myths, and Modern Sexualities.* New York: Routledge, 1985.

Wynter, Sylvia. "On Disenchanting Discourse: 'Minority' Literary Criticism and Beyond." *Cultural Critique,* no. 7 (Fall 1987): 235–37.

Young, Iris Marion. "Breasted Experience." In her *Throwing Like a Girl and Other Essays in Feminist Philosophy and Social Theory.* Bloomington: Indiana University Press, 1990.

————. "Humanism, Gynocentrism, and Feminist Politics." *Hypatia: A Journal of Feminist Philosophy* 3, special issue of *Women's Studies International Forum* 8, no. 3 (1985): 173–85.

————. "Throwing Like a Girl." In her *Throwing Like a Girl and Other Essays in Feminist Philosophy and Social Theory.* Bloomington: Indiana University Press, 1990.

Contributors

TERRY K. ALADJEM is a lecturer on Social Studies and associate director of the Derek Bok Center for Teaching and Learning at Harvard University. He is completing a book manuscript titled *Vengeance and Democratic Justice* and an article on "Argument and the Anxiety over Difference in Democratic Theory."

LINDA MARTÍN ALCOFF is associate professor of philosophy and women's studies at Syracuse University. She is the co-editor of *Feminist Epistemologies* (Routledge, 1993), author of *Real Knowing* (Cornell University Press, 1996), and now working on a book entitled *Visible Identities: Essays on Race, Gender, and Subjectivity.*

AMY ALLEN is completing her doctoral dissertation on feminist theory and power at Northwestern University, where she teaches philosophy and women's studies.

JUDITH BUTLER is professor of rhetoric and comparative literature at the University of California at Berkeley. She is author of *Subjects of Desire: Hegelian Reflections in Twentieth-Century France* (1987), *Gender Trouble: Feminism and the Subversion of Identity* (1990), and *Bodies That Matter: On the Discursive Limits of Sex* (1993). She is currently at work on a manuscript on speech acts and injurious language.

MONIQUE DEVEAUX is a doctoral student in the Faculty of Social and Political Science, University of Cambridge (Newnham College). Her dissertation addresses challenges to liberal and neo-Kantian conceptions of culture, community, and identity posed by feminists, proponents of multiculturalism and others. She has written recently on feminist moral theory for *Hypatia* and the *European Journal of Philosophy*.

NANCY FRASER is professor of political science on the Graduate Faculty of the New School for Social Research. Her new book, *Justice Interruptus: Rethinking Key Concepts of a "Postsocialist" Age*, will be published by Routledge in 1996. She is the author of *Unruly Practices: Power, Discourse, and Gender in Contemporary Social Theory* (University of Minnesota Press and Polity Press, 1989) and the co-editor of *Revaluing French Feminism: Critical Essays on Difference, Agency, and Culture* (Indiana University Press, 1992).

HONI FERN HABER was assistant professor of philosophy at the University of Colorado at Denver. She published *Beyond Postmodern Politics: Lyotard, Rorty, Foucault* (Routledge, 1994).

NANCY C. M. HARTSOCK teaches in the political science department at the University of Washington. She is the author of *Money, Sex, and Power: Toward a Feminist Historical Materialism*. She is working on a critique of postmodernist theories' effects on feminist theory, to be titled *Postmodernism and Political Change*.

MOYA LLOYD is a lecturer in political theory in the Department of Politics at Queen's University of Belfast. She has published articles on contemporary feminist theory and the relationship between Foucault and feminism. She is writing *A Feminist Politics of Difference* (Sage) and co-editing (with Andrew Thacker) *The Impact of Michel Foucault on the Humanities and Social Sciences* (Macmillan).

E. L. MCCALLUM is a Ph.D. candidate in the Modern Studies Program at the University of Wisconsin–Milwaukee. She is completing a dissertation on fetishism, entitled "Object Lessons: Fetishism, Subjective Knowledge, and Objective Desire."

JANA SAWICKI is professor of philosophy and women's studies at Williams College and chair of Women's Studies. She is the author of *Disciplining Foucault: Feminism, Power and the Body* (Routledge, 1991). Her current research is on confessional narrative and feminist politics.

JON SIMONS is a lecturer in the Postgraduate School of Critical Theory at the University of Nottingham, England. He is the author of

Foucault and the Political (1995) as well as several articles in his field of oppositional postmodern political thought. He is currently working on essays toward a fictive approach to an effective political theory of resistance.

Index

friendship, motherhood and, 204–6
Fuss, Diana, 78

Galeano, Eduardo, 47
Gay Science, 144
gender: childhood sexuality and, 92–93; essentialist debate concerning, 77–78; freedom and, 251–52; function of, in Foucault's work, 77–97; linguistics of, 83–84; mothering and, 180–81, 190–91, 205–6; parody and, 254–56; sexuality and, 6–7, 77–97; subversive mothering and, 197–206, 209n.82; truth/power and sexual identity and, 226–32, 237n.42; women's subjectifying power and, 181–88
Gender Trouble: Feminism and the Subversion of Identity, 6, 226–32, 254–56
genealogical critique, feminist theory and, 162–70, 242–60
"Gestell" of sexuality, 84–85, 96–97
Gilligan, Carol, 35
Gimenez, Martha, 199
"god-trick" concept, Enlightenment and, 41, 43–44, 54n.11
Gough, Jamie, 123, 134n.16
Gould, Carol, 35
governmentality, 235n.7
Greek ethics: Foucault on, 170, 174–77; Foucault's subjectification and, 179–80, 182–88
Greer, Germaine, 237n.38
Grimshaw, Jean, 184, 246, 250, 262n.38, 263n.57
Grubman-Black, Stephen D., 124

Haber, Honi Fern, 7, 137–54
Habermas, Jürgen: emancipatory force, 23, 165; Foucauldian feminism and, 2, 5; Foucauldian humanism and, 28, 32–36, 170, 172; on Foucault as "Young Conservative," 15; Kantian ethics and, 24, 28–29; modernity vs. postmodernity, 15–16; on welfare policies, 204
Haraway, Donna, 18, 54n.11, 55n.33, 168–69, 176
Hartsock, Nancy, 2, 4–5, 8; on Foucault and feminist theory, 221–22, 265; on motherhood, 185–87; on postmodernism and political change, 39–53; on power and freedom, 162–64, 167, 169–71, 177n.7
Hegel, G. F. W., 23–24; lord/bondsman mythology and, 110

hegemonic discourse, childhood sexuality and, 103
Heidegger, Martin, 15–16, 19–20, 23, 33; on essence of technology, 84–85
Hekman, Susan, 212, 221, 285, 290
Held, Virginia, 223–24, 237n.41
Henahan, Donal, 75n.10
Herculine Barbin, 22, 74n.5
heterosexual matrix, 198–200, 209n.86
heterosexuality: cultural meanings of power and, 272–73; identity and, 60–74, 75n.7, 228–32; official sanctioning of, 103; politics of pedophilia and, 117–33; Rubin's radical sexual politics and, 114–16; sexual difference and, 82–83
Hill, Anita, 233
historiography, Cartesianism and, 19
History of Sexuality, The, 6, 22–23, 30–31, 59, 61, 69; cultural meanings of power and, 272–73; death and politics in, 72–73; disciplinary power in, 161–70; feminist theory and, 160; gender and, 79–81, 83, 85–86; resistance and power in, 220–22; subjectification in, 183; truth and sexuality in, 86–91
Hocquenghem, Guy, 102–12, 114, 120
homophobia, law and, 103
homosexuality: Butler's discussion of, 6; cultural meanings of power and, 272–73; death and, 71–74, 75n.10; Foucault's philosophy and, 61–74; identity in AIDS epidemic and, 68–74; legal repression of, 102–3; pathologizatin of, 70–71; pedophilia and, 7, 103, 117–33; Rubin's radical sexual politics and, 114–16; truth/power and sexual identity and, 228–32, 237n.46
Horkheimer, 165
Horowitz, Gad, 297n.23
Hoy, David, 18–19, 23, 25
humanism: concept of Man and, 20–22; Foucault's late work on, 170–77; Foucault's rejection of, 5, 19–36; interdisciplinary feminist interpretation, 35–36; modernity and, 17–20; normalizing-disciplinary power and, 27–28; normative grounds for rejection f, 30–31
Hume, David, 141
Hurtado, Aida, 51

identity: AIDS epidemic and, 68–70; Foucault on politics of, 8; gender and, 91–97, 97n.13; homosexuality and, 68–70; political agency